American Foreign Service Authors:

A Bibliography

by

Richard Fyfe Boyce

and

Katherine Randall Boyce

The Scarecrow Press, Inc.
Metuchen, N. J.   1973

Library of Congress Cataloging in Publication Data

Boyce, Richard Fyfe.
    American foreign service authors.

    1. Authors, American--Bibliography. 2. United
States--Diplomatic and consular service--Biography--
Dictionaries.   I. Boyce, Katherine Randall, joint
author. II. Title.
Z1224.B68   016.081   73-9780
ISBN 0-8108-0639-8

Dedicated to

The Department of State

and

All Who Serve It Abroad

"A papyrus from Thebes dating from shortly after
the reign of Amunhotep III praises learning for its
own sake. 'Be a scribe,' it says, 'that thy name
may live. Better is a book than a tomb in the
West ... better than a stele in a temple.' It tells
of great men of the past whose mortuary rites have
been long neglected, whose tombs have crumbled
into dust, the very sites forgotten, 'but their
names are still pronounced because of the books
they made' and will last 'to the limits of eternity'."

[from the book Thebes: In the Time of Amunhotep
III, by Elizabeth Riefstahl. Norman: University
of Oklahoma Press, 1964; page 85.]

FOREWORD

This bibliography includes the published works of
American foreign service authors, beginning with Benjamin
Franklin, and including wives. The arrangement is simply
alphabetical by author.

It includes only those who have served abroad under
the aegis of the State Department. The subject matter, and the
time of writing or of publication of the item are irrelevant.
The rank of the writer, from ambassador to clerk, is likewise irrelevant.

The bibliography is limited to the authors of books.
With few exceptions it does not list the authors of magazine
articles, speeches, eulogies, lectures, orations, reviews,
essays, separate chapters of books, reports, letters and
other short works unless such items are (a) collected and
published in book form, (b) are over 50 pages in length,
(c) have special historic importance, or (d) are poems,
plays or musical productions.

An exception to the above is the case of Joseph
Emil Wiedenmayer, Jr., whose pamphlet "Listen Please"
and whose efforts on behalf of deaf people all over the
world during and since his 22 years in the foreign service
have earned him a "People-to-People Program" citation for
his "outstanding contribution to international good will."

There are approximately 760 authors listed herein.
Though the authors of this bibliography have worked dili-
gently for over four years they do not claim it to be complete, either as to authors or their works. Notices appeared
in the DACOR Bulletin and the American Foreign Service
Journal to induce foreign service authors to inform us of
their published books, but the response is not believed to
be complete.

The Department of State does not have a complete
alphabetical file of all the foreign service personnel who

v

served abroad. In the 1957 Biographic Register of the State Department there is a list of all American diplomatic agents prior to 1789 and all chiefs of mission from 1789 to 1957. All these names have been run through the card catalogue of the Library of Congress. However, the files of the Library of Congress are not complete. Also, there are gaps in the early official published lists of foreign service personnel overseas. In none of the published official records do the names of the clerical staff appear, though the published lists of officers do include, besides chiefs of mission, the names of all other ranks of diplomatic and consular officers at each post whose commissions were signed by the President or by the Secretary of State.

Finally, it should be pointed out that there was no career foreign service prior to 1906. All appointments of diplomatic and consular officers were political and subject to change with each change of administration. No officers could expect to survive a change of administration though there were exceptions. Nevertheless, the Department of State, in spite of constantly changing personnel from the Secretary of State on down, was a permanent, constitutional agency of the government and issued regulations and directives to the separate diplomatic and consular "services," such as they were. Its personnel abroad was, however fluid, a "foreign service."

ACKNOWLEDGMENTS AND CREDITS

The authors have received valuable assistance from many persons, including the following:

Mrs. Shirley R. Newhall, Editor of the American Foreign Service Journal, for publicity which elicited responses from numerous authors.

Mrs. Helen Lehman, formerly of the Library of Congress, whose assistance in verifying the works of a large portion of the authors was invaluable.

Samuel Sokobin, of Atherton, California, a retired Foreign Service Officer with many years in the Far East, an expert in the Chinese language and history, who supplied information on many former officers in China, especially prior to 1900.

Lewis M. Bright, Librarian of the State Department, who was very helpful in supplying biographic material on foreign service officers before 1900.

William C. Affeld, Jr., Executive Director of Diplomatic and Consular Officers, Retired, Inc. (DACOR) and members of the DACOR Library Committee.

John H. Stutesman, Jr., Dean of the School for Professional Studies, Foreign Service Institute, Department of State, who proffered a helpful list of foreign service authors.

Mrs. C. E. H. Druitt, of Washington, who generously spent many hours in the Library of Congress checking names, titles, dates.

Dr. Milton O. Gustafson, of the National Archives, Washington, who located the official records of the service in the Embassy in Paris in 1918 of James Thurber and Stephen Vincent Benét when all other sources failed.

Mr. Monroe Causley, of Florida Atlantic University, Boca Raton, Florida, who verified the background of many authors.

Our daughter-in-law, Helen Boyce, who translated from the German numerous titles of the books written in that language.

Rev. George X. Gallas, Pastor of the Greek Orthodox Church of the Annunciation of Miami, Florida, who translated from the Greek the titles of the books written in that language by Rev. Jonas King, American consular officer in Greece, 1851-68.

SOURCES FOR THIS BOOK

1. American Consular Bulletin (1919-1924), published by the American Consular Association, Washington.

2. American Foreign Service Journal (1924 to date), published by the American Foreign Service Association, Washington.

3. DACOR Bulletin (1951 to date), published by DACOR, Inc. (Diplomatic and Consular Officers, Retired, Inc.) Washington.

4. Department of State Newsletter of the Department of State. Washington: Superintendent of Documents, U. S. Government Printing Office.

5. The Biographic Register of the Department of State, published intermittently from the mid-nineteenth century to 1900 and annually since then. Washington: Superintendent of Documents, U. S. Government Printing Office.

6. Foreign Service List of the Department of State, published three or four times a year for over 50 years. Superintendent of Documents, U. S. Government Printing Office.

7. Dictionary of American Biography (1927 to date), compiled by the American Council of Learned Societies. New York: Scribners.

8. National Cyclopaedia of American Biography (1892-1965), New York: White.

9. Who's Who In America (1898 to date), Chicago: Marquis.

10. Who Was Who, Chicago: Marquis.

11. Encyclopaedia Britannica, Chicago: Encyclopaedia Britannica, Inc.

12. Library of Congress, Washington, D. C. Catalogue file of authors and titles. The Library of Congress is a selective depository of less than half the works published each year in the United States.

    Works printed in America before 1801 are available in the Library of Congress in the Readex Microfilm Edition of Early American Imprints, published by the American Antiquarian Society.

13. Department of State Library, Washington. A selective depository of works on foreign affairs.

14. Historical Office of the State Department, Washington.

15. Personnel Office of the Department of State, Washington.

16. National Archives, Washington.

17. Bibliography on United States Diplomacy by Elmer Plischke. Philadelphia: American Academy of Political and Social Science, 1972. Monograph No. 13. pp 290-342.

18. American Diplomacy. A Bibliography of Bibliographies, Autobiographies, and Commentaries. College Park, Md.: Bureau of Governmental Research, University of Maryland, 1957. 26 p.

THE BIBLIOGRAPHY

ABRAMOWITZ, Morton I., 1933- . Foreign Service
Officer 1958- . Chinese language officer. Served
in Taipei, Hong Kong, Washington, London (Institute
for Strategic Studies).
Remaking China Policy. U. S.-China Relations and
Governmental Decision-making. With Richard Moor-
steen. Foreword by John K. Fairbank and Nicholas
B. Katzenbach. Cambridge: Harvard University
Press, 1971. 128 p.

ADAMS, Abigail (Smith), 1744-1818.
Letters of Mrs. Adams, Wife of John Adams. 2d ed.
Boston: C. C. Little and J. Brown, 1840. 447 p.
A 4th ed. with an introductory memoir by her grand-
son, Charles Francis Adams, revised and enlarged
with an appendix containing letters addressed by John
Q. Adams to his son on the study of the Bible.
Boston: Wilkins, Carter & Co., 1848. 472 p.
New Letters of Abigail Adams, 1788-1801. Ed. by
Stewart Mitchell. Boston: Houghton Mifflin, 1947.
281 p.

ADAMS, Charles Francis, 1807-1886. Son of John Quincy
Adams, grandson of John Adams. Accompanied his
father to Russia while the latter was American Minis-
ter to that country and learned French as a child,
1809-1817. Active in business.
The Works of John Adams. Second President of the
United States: With a Life of the Author, Notes and
Illustrations, by his Grandson, Charles Francis Adams.
Boston: Little, Brown & Co., 1850-1856. 10 vols.
Freeport, N. Y.: Books for Libraries Press, 1969.
10 vols.
The Life of John Adams, Begun by John Quincy Adams
and Completed by Charles Francis Adams. Boston:
Little, Brown & Co., 1850-1856. New York: Haskell
House, 1968. 2 vols.
(Edited) Letters of Mrs. Adams... [See: Abigail
Adams.]

1

(Edited) Memoirs of John Quincy Adams... [See: John
  Quincy Adams.]
(Edited) Familiar Letters of John Adams and His Wife...
  [See: John Adams.]
An Appeal from the New to the Old Whigs, by a Whig of
  the Old School. Boston: Russell, Odearne & Co.,
  1835. 52 p.
Texas and the Massachusetts Resolutions. Boston: East-
  burn's Press, 1844. 54 p.
What Makes Slavery a Question of National Concern.
  Boston: Little, Brown & Co., 46 p.
Struggle for Neutrality in America. New York: C.
  Scribner's & Co. 1871. 52 p.
Diary. Aida Di Pace Donald and David Donald, ed.
  Cambridge, Mass.: Belknap Press of the Harvard
  University Press, 1964. 4 vols.
Railroads, Their Origin and Problems. Rev. ed. with
  appendix. New York: Harper & Row, 1969. 230 p.

ADAMS, Henry Brooks, 1838-1918. Son of Charles Francis
  Adams, great-grandson of John Adams. Served as
  private secretary to his father while the latter was
  Minister to Great Britain, 1861-68. Professor of
  history at Harvard. Editor of the North American
  Review.
Mont-Saint-Michel and Chartres. Privately printed 1904.
  Published by Institute of Architects, Boston: Houghton
  Mifflin & Co., 1913. 401 p.
The Education of Henry Adams. [an autobiography,
  written in 1905, privately printed 1906] Published
  Boston: Houghton Mifflin, The Riverside Press
  (Cambridge), 1918. 519 p.
History of the United States from 1801 to 1817. [First
  privately printed] Published New York: C. Scribner's
  Sons, 1889-91. 9 vols.
The Life of Albert Gallatin; The Writings of Albert Gal-
  latin. Philadelphia: J.B. Lippincott & Co., 1879.
  3 vols. 697 p.
John Randolph. Boston: Houghton Mifflin & Co., 1882.
  313 p.
Historical Essays. New York: C. Scribner's Sons, 1891.
  422 p.
Chapters of Erie and Other Essays, with Charles Francis
  Adams, Jr. Boston: J.R. Osgood Co., 1871. 429 p.
Letter to American Teachers of History. Washington:
  Press of J.H. Furst Co., 1910. 214 p.

The Degradation of the Democratic Dogma. Introduction
by Brooks Adams. New York: Macmillan Co., 1919.
317 p.
Letters to a Niece and Prayer to the Virgin of Chartres,
with "A Niece's Memories" by Mabel La Farge. Boston: Houghton Mifflin & Co., 1920. 133 p.
Democracy, [a novel]. Published anonymously according
to Henry Holt. New York: Henry Holt & Co., 1880.
374 p.
Esther, [a novel]. by Frances Snow Compton (pseud).
New York: Henry Holt & Co., 1884. 302 p.
(Edited) Documents Relating to New England Federalism
1800-1815. Boston: Little, Brown & Co., 1877.
437 p.
Memoirs of Marau Taaroa, Last Queen of Tahiti. Printed
in Paris (no pub.) 1901. 196 p.
The Life of George Cabot Lodge. Boston: Houghton
Mifflin Co., 1911. 206 p.
A Cycle of Adams Letters, edit. by W. C. Ford. Boston:
Houghton Mifflin Co., 1920. 2 vols.
(Edited) The Writings of Albert Gallatin 1761-1849.
Philadelphia: J. B. Lippincott & Co., 1879. 3 vols.
Tahiti, Memoirs of Arii Taimai E Marama of Eimeo,
Teriirere of Tooarai, Terrinui of Tahiti. New York:
Scholars' Facsimiles and Reprints, 1947. 196 p.
The Great Secession Winter of 1860-61, and Other Essays.
New York: Sagamore Press, 1958. 428 p.
Henry Adams and His Friends: A Collection of his Un-
published Letters. Boston: Houghton Mifflin Co.,
1947. 797 p.
A Henry Adams Reader, ed. with an introduction by
Elizabeth Stevenson. Garden City, N. Y.: Doubleday,
1958. 392 p.
Letters of Henry Adams (1858-1891), ed. by Worthington
Chauncey Ford. Boston: Houghton Mifflin Co., 1930.
552 p.
The War of 1812. Washington: The Infantry Journal
(n. d.) 377 p.

ADAMS, John, 1735-1826. Joint Commissioner to the
Court of France, to replace Silas Deane, on the Commission with Benjamin Franklin and Arthur Lee--
April 1778; Minister to negotiate a treaty of peace and
commerce with Great Britain, 1780; Joint Commissioner
with Benjamin Franklin, John Jay and Henry Laurens
to negotiate a treaty of peace with Great Britain;
signed definitive treaty in 1783 in Paris; Minister to

negotiate treaty of amity and commerce with the Netherlands, signed preliminary treaty 1782, mission termi-
nated 1788. Joint Minister with Benjamin Franklin and
Thomas Jefferson to negotiate treaties of amity and
commerce with European countries and the Barbary
States 1784; signed treaty with Prussia 1785, Morocco
1787. Minister to Great Britain 1785-88. Adams
served simultaneously under his commissions to Great
Britain, the Netherlands, other European countries and
the Barbary States. Second President of the United
States 1797-1801.

John Adams, 1735-1826; Chronology, Documents and Bibliographical Aids. edit. by Howard F. Bremer. New
York: Dobbs Ferry. Oceana Publications, 1967.
88 p.

Microfilms of the Adams papers. Owned by the Adams
Manuscript Trust and deposited in the Massachusetts
Historical Society. Boston: 1954.

The Works of John Adams, Second President of the United
States: With a Life of the Author, Notes and Illustrations, by His Grandson Charles Francis Adams. Boston: Little, Brown & Co., etc. 1850-56. 10 vols.

A Collection of State-Papers, Relative to the First Ac-
knowledgement of the Sovereignty of the United States
of America, and the Reception of Their Minister Plenipotentiary, by Their Mightinesses the States General
of the United Netherlands. To Which is Prefixed, the
Political Character of John Adams, Ambassador Plenipotentiary ... By an American. Likewise, An Essay
on Canon and Feudal Law, by John Adams, Esq.
London: Printed for J. Fielding, etc., 1782. 100 p.

The Adams-Jefferson Letters; the Complete Correspondence
Between Thomas Jefferson and Abigail and John Adams.
Edit. by Lester J. Cappon. Chapel Hill: Published
for the Institute of Early American History and Culture
at Williamsburg, Va., by the University of North Carolina Press, 1959. 2 vols.

John Adams, Knox, and Washington. Worcester, Mass.:
American Antiquarian Society. Proceedings 1947.
56 p.

Correspondence Between the Hon. John Adams ... and
the late Wm. Cunningham, Esq., beginning in 1803 and
ending in 1812. Boston: E. M. Cunningham, 1823.
219 p.

The Correspondence of John Adams, Esquire, Late President of the United States of America; Concerning the
British Doctrine of Impressment; and Many Interesting

Things Which Occurred During His Administration:
Originally Published by the Boston Patriot. Baltimore:
Published at the office of the Evening Post, by H.
Niles--Sept. 15, 1809. G. Dobb and Murphy, print-
ers. 72 p.
Correspondence of John Adams and Thomas Jefferson
(1812-1826) Selected with Comment by Paul Wilstach.
Indianapolis: The Bobbs-Merrill Co., c1925. 196 p.
Correspondence of the Late President Adams. Originally
published in the Boston Patriot. In a series of let-
ters... Boston: Everett and Munroe, 1809-10.
572 p.
Deeds and Other Documents Relating to the Several Pieces
of Land, and to the Library Presented to the Town of
Quincy, by President Adams, together with a Catalogue
of the Books. Cambridge: Printed by Hilliard and
Metcalf, 1823. 67 p.
A Defence of the Constitutions of Government of the United
States of America, Against the Attack of M. Turgot in
His Letter to Dr. Price, dated the twenty-second day
of March, 1778. By John Adams. New ed. London:
Printed for J. Stackdale, 1794. 3 vols.
Diary and Autobiography. L. H. Butterfield, editor,
Leonard C. Faber and Wendell D. Garrett, assistant
editors. Cambridge: Belknap Press of Harvard Uni-
versity Press, 1961. 4 vols.
Discourses on Davila. A series of papers, on political
history. Written in the year 1790, and then published
in the Gazette of the United States. By an American
Citizen... Boston: Printed by Russell and Cutler,
1805. 248 p.
The John Adams Papers. Selected, edited, and inter-
preted by Frank Donovan. New York: Dodd, Mead,
1965. 335 p.
Legal Papers of John Adams. L. Kinvin Wroth and Hiller
B. Zobel, editors. Cambridge, Mass.: Belknap Press
of Harvard University Press, 1965. 3 vols.
Letters of John Adams Addressed to His Wife. Edit. by
his grandson, Charles Francis Adams. Boston: C. C.
Little and J. Brown, 1841. 2 vols.
Familiar Letters of John Adams and His Wife, Abigail
Adams During the Revolution. With a Memoir of Mrs.
Adams. Edit. by Charles Francis Adams. Freeport,
N.Y.: Books for Libraries Press, 1970. 424 p.
Novanglus and Massachusettensis; or, Political Essays
Published in the years 1774 and 1775, on the Principal
Points of Controversy Between Great Britain and Her

Colonies. The former by John Adams ... the Latter
by Jonathan Sewall ... To Which Are Added a Number
of Letters, Lately Written by President Adams to the
Honourable William Tudor; Some of Which Were Never
Before Published. Boston: Printed and published by
Hews & Goss, 1819. 312 p.

The Selected Writings of John and John Quincy Adams.
Edit. and with an introd. by Adrienne Koch and William
Peden. New York: A. A. Knopf, 1946. 413 p.

The Spur of Fame: Dialogues of John Adams and Benjamin Rush, 1805-1813. Edit. by John A. Schutz and
Douglass Adair. San Marino, Calif.: Huntington Library, 1966. 301 p.

Statesman and Friend: Correspondence of John Adams
with Benjamin Waterhouse, 1784-1822. Edit. by
Worthington Chauncey Ford. Boston: Little, Brown
and Co., 1927. 178 p.

Twenty-six Letters, Upon Interesting Subjects, Respecting
the Revolution of America. Written in Holland, in the
year 1780. By His Excellency John Adams, While He
Was Sole Minister Plenipotentiary from the United
States of America, for Negotiating a Peace, and a
Treaty of Commerce with Great Britain. London:
Printed for the subscribers, 1786. 89 p.

Papers, 1775-1819. 70 items in New York Historical
Society collections.

Adams Family Papers, 1639-1889. 175 ft. In Massachusetts Historical Society Library.

ADAMS, John Quincy, 1767-1848. Served briefly as private
secretary to American Minister to Russia in 1781; was
secretary to his father, John Adams, during the peace
negotiations with Great Britain, 1782-1783; Minister
Resident to the Netherlands, 1794-1797; Minister to
Prussia, 1797-1801; Minister to Russia, 1809-1814;
head of Commission that negotiated Treaty of Ghent
with Great Britain, 1814; Minister to Great Britain,
1815-1817. Secretary of State, 1817-1825. President
of the United States, 1825-1829.

Writings of John Quincy Adams, ed. by Worthington
Chauncey Ford. New York: Macmillan Co., 1913-1917.
7 vols.

The Diary of John Quincy Adams, 1794-1845: American
Diplomacy, and Political, Social, and Intellectual Life
from Washington to Polk, ed. by Allen Nevins. New
York: F. Ungar, 1928, 586 p.

Memoirs of John Quincy Adams, Comprising Portions of

his Diary 1795 to 1848, ed. by Charles Francis Adams.
Philadelphia: J. B. Lippincott & Co., 1874-1877. 12
vols. (2 reels)

Adams Family. Microfilms of Adams papers, owned by
the Adams Manuscript Trust, deposited in the Massachusetts Historical Society. Boston, 1954.

Selected Writings of John and John Quincy Adams, ed.
with an introduction by Adrienn Koch & William Peden.
New York: Alfred A. Knopf, Inc. 1946. 413 p.

Life in a New England Town. (a diary as a law student, 1787-
88) Ed. by Charles Francis Adams, Jr. Boston: Little,
Brown & Co., 1903. 204 p.

Documents Relating to New England Federalism, 1800-
1815, ed. by Henry Adams. New York: B. Franklin.
1969. 437 p.

Letters on Silesia. London: J. Budd, 1804. 387 p.
Paris: (trans. by) J. Dupuy, 1807.

Lectures on Rhetoric and Oratory. Cambridge, Mass.:
Printed by Hilliard & Metcalf. 1810. 2 vols.

Duplicate Letters, The Fisheries and the Mississippi.
Washington: Davis and Force. 1822. 256 p.

Correspondence between John Quincy Adams and Several
Citizens of Massachusetts, concerning the Charge of a
Design to Dissolve the Union. Boston: Press of the
Boston Daily Advertiser, 1829. 80 p.

Dermot Macmorrogh, or the Conquest of Ireland. Boston:
I. N. Whiting, 1832. 108 p.

Speech upon Right of Petition, June-July 1838. Washington: Printed by Gales and Seaton, 1838. 131 p.

Jubilee of the Constitution. New York: S. Colman, 1839.
136 p.

Letters on the Masonic Institution. Boston: Press of
T. R. Marvin, 1847. 284 p.

Poems of Religion and Society. New York: Miller, Orton & Mulligan, 1848. 116 p.

John Quincy Adams and American Continental Empire;
Letters, Papers and Speeches. Chicago: Quadrangle
Books, 1965. 157 p.

ADAMS, Marian (Hooper), 1843-1885.
The Letters of Mrs. Henry Adams, 1865-1883. Ed. by
Ward Thoron. Boston: Little, Brown & Co., 1936.
587 p.

ADEE, Alvey Augustus, 1842-1924. Secretary of Legation
at Madrid and Chargé d'Affaires, 1870-1877; Chief
Diplomatic Bureau State Department, 1878; 3rd

Assistant Secretary of State, 1882; Assistant Secretary
of State, 1886-1924.
William Shakespeare, 1564-1616. The Bankside Shakespeare, ed. by Appleton Morgan. New York: The
Shakespeare Society of New York, 1888-1906. 22 vols.
(500 copies.)

AGETON, Arthur Ainsley, 1900-71. U. S. Navy 1923-47,
retired as Rear Admiral. Author. M. A. Johns
Hopkins Univ. 1953. Taught creative writing at George
Washington Univ. Involved in producing training films
for Naval Academy. Ambassador to Paraguay 1954-57.
Dead Reckoning Altitude and Azimuth. Washington: Gov-
ernment Printing Office for Hydrographic Office, 1932.
49 p. (3 editions)
The Jungle Seas. New York: Random House, 1954.
339 p.
Manual of Celestial Navigation. New York: D. Van No-
strand & Co., 1961. 104 p.
The Marine Officer's Guide. with Gerald C. Thomas,
Robert D. Heinl, Jr. Annapolis: U. S. Naval Aca-
demy, 1967. 625 p.
Mary Jo and Little Lui. New York: Whittelsey House,
1945. 52 p.
Naval Leadership and the American Bluejacket. New
York: Whittelsey House. New York: McGraw-Hill
1944. 91 p.
Naval Officer's Guide. New York: Whittelsey House,
1943.
Hit The Beach. (pub. not known) 1961.
Admiral Ambassador to Russia. with Admiral H. Stand-
ley. (Admiral Standley's story as Ambassador to Rus-
sia) Chicago: H. Regnery Co., 1955. 533 p.

ALDEN, William Livingston, 1837-1908. Journalist and
novelist. Consul General in Rome during President
Cleveland's 1st administration, 1886-1890.
Domestic Explosives and Other Sixth Column Fancies.
New York: Lovell, Adam, Wesson & Co., 1877.
334 p.
Shooting Stars as Observed from the "Sixth Column" of
the Times. New York: G. P. Putnam's Sons, 1878.
224 p.
The Cruise of the Canoe Club. New York: Harper &
Bros, 1883. 166 p. (Edit.) Trying to Find Europe.
New York: Harper Bros. 1905. 1889. 167 p.
Among the Freaks. London: Longmans Green, 1896.

195 p.   55 illus. by J. P. Sullivan and Florence K.
  Upton.
Cat Tales.   (pub. not known) 1905
(Edit.) The Adventures of Jimmy Brown written by him-
  self. New York: Harper Bros., 1885.   236 p.
The Canoa and the Flying Proa: or, Cheap Cruising and
  Safe Sailing. New York: Harper Bros., 1878.   98 p.
Christopher Columbus (1440-1506).   The First American
  Citizen. New York: Holt & Co., 1881.   287 p.
The Comic Liar: a Book Not Commonly Found in Sunday
  Schools. by the Funnyman of the New York Daily
  Times. New York: G. W. Carleton & Co., 1883.
  334 p.
The Cruise of the "Ghost." New York: Harper Bros.,
  1882.   210 p.
Drewitt's Dream: A Story. New York: Appleton Co.,
  1902.   321 p.
The Moral Pirates. New York: Harper Bros., 1888.
  147 p.
A New Robinson Crusoe. New York: Harper Bros.,
  1888.   147 p.
Told by the Colonel.   illus. by Richard Jack and Hal
  Hurst. New York: J. S. Tait & Sons, 1893.   176 p.

ALISON, Charlotte (Smith).   Wife of Eugene Frederick
  Quinn, 1935- . Foreign Service Officer 1958- .
  United States Information Agency.   Served in Washing-
  ton, Rabat, Port-au-Prince, Ouagadougou, Saigon,
  Yaounde.
Mandingo Kingdom of the Senegambia.   Evanston, Ill.:
  Northwestern University Press, 1972.

ALLEN, Horace Newton, 1858-1932.   Medical Missionary
  and physician to the Korean Court, Secretary of Legation, Seoul, 1890; Minister Resident and Consul General, Seoul 1897; Minister at Seoul 1901-05.
A Chronological Index: Some of the Chief Events in the
  Foreign Intercourse of Korea from the Beginning of the
  Christian Era to the Twentieth Century.   Seoul: Press
  of the Methodist Publishing House, 1901.   69 p.
Korean Tales. New York: G. P. Putnam's Sons, 1889.
  193 p.
Korea: Fact and Fancy. A republication, combining the
  two books above. Seoul: Press of the Methodist Publishing House, 1904.   285 p. Again, in the Korean
  language, 1966.
Things Korean: A collection of Sketches and Anecdotes,

Missionary and Diplomatic. New York: Fleming H.
Revell Co., 1908. 256 p.

ALLEN, Katherine (Martin). (Mrs. George Venable Allen)
(Wife of Ambassador George Venable Allen (1903-1970)
Foreign Service Officer 1930-1966. Served in Kingston (B. W. I.), Shanghai, Patras, Cairo, State Department, Ambassador to Iran 1946-48, to Yugoslavia 1949,
to India and Nepal 1953, Ass't Sec. State 1955, Ambassador to Greece 1956, Dir. U. S. Information Agency
1957, Dir. Foreign Service Institute 1966. Career
Ambassador.)
Foreign Service Diary. Washington: Potomac Books,
1967. 285 p.

ANDERSON, Isabel Weld (Perkins), 1876-1948. Wife of
Ambassador Larz Anderson [q. v.] See Bibliography of
the Works of Isabel Anderson. by Eleanor Wilbur
Pomeroy. Medford, Mass.: C. A. A. Parker, 1935.
18 p.

Travel and Fiction

The Spell of Japan. Boston: The Page Co., 1914.
396 p. Maps, plates.
The Spell of the Hawaiian Islands and the Philippines.
Boston: The Page Co., 1916. 373 p. maps, plates.
The Spell of Belgium. Boston: The Page Co., 1917.
442 p. maps, plates.
Odd Corners. New York: Dodd, Mead & Co., 1917.
368 p.
Zigzagging. Boston: Houghton Mifflin Co., 1918. 269 p.
Zigzagging the South Seas. Boston: B. Humphries, 1937.
262 p.
Presidents and Pies; Life in Washington 1897-1919. Bos-
ton: Houghton Mifflin Co., 290 p.
Polly and the Pagan; Her Lost Letters. Foreword by
Basil King. Boston: The Page Co., 1922. 239 p.
The Kiss and the Queue. Boston: The Four Seas Co.,
1925. 324 p.
The Wall Paper Code, and Other Stories. Boston: The
Four Seas Co., 1926. 198 p.
Under the Black Horse Flag: Annals of the Weld Family
and Some of Its Branches. Boston: Houghton Mifflin
Co., 1926. 291 p.
From Corsair to Riffian. Boston: Houghton Mifflin Co.,
1927. 209 p.
Circling Africa. Boston: Marshall Jones Co., 1929.
270 p.

Circling South America. Boston: Marshall Jones Co.,
1929. 214 p.
A Yacht in the Mediterranean Seas. Boston: Marshall
Jones Co., 1930. 428 p.
In Eastern Seas, With a Visit to Insulinde and the Golden
Cheronese. Boston: Bruce Humphries, Inc., 1934.
351 p.
Books and Plays For Children
The Great Sea Horse, and Other Stories. Boston: Little,
Brown Co., 1909. 251 p.
Captain Ginger Aboard the Gee Whiz. Illus. by H. Boyl-
ston Dummer. Boston: C. M. Clarke Publishing Co.,
1911. 56 p.
Captain Ginger's Fairy. Illus. by H. Boylston Dummer.
Boston: C. M. Clarke Publishing Co., 1911. 56 p.
Captain Ginger Goes Travelling. Boston: C. M. Clarke
Publishing Co., 1911.
Captain Ginger's Playmates. Boston: C. M. Clarke
Publishing Co., 1911.
Captain Ginger's Eater of Dreams. Boston: C. M.
Clarke Publishing Co., 1911.
Captain Ginger's Sun Boy. Boston: C. M. Clarke Pub-
lishing Co., 1911.
Topsy Turvy and the Gold Star. Boston: Little Brown
Co., 1920. 40 p.
Everyboy and Other Plays for Children... Illus. by
Junius Cravens. New York: Shakespeare Press, 1914.
155 p.
Little Madcap's Journey, a Fairy Extravaganza. music
by Julia Ward Howe. Boston: Walter Baker Co.,
1931.
The Magic Bough. Boston: Walter H. Baker Co., 1937.
88 p.
Sir Frog Goes A-Travelling. Boston: Walter H. Baker
Co., 1935. (Dramatization of a Japanese legend.)
The Green Turban and Under the Bo Tree. 2 one-act
plays. Boston: The Christopher Publishing House,
1937. 46 p.
Freedom. (Civil War drama) Medford, Mass.: C. A. A.
Parker, 1933.
Other Productions
The Witch in the Woods. Music by Edith Dalton. Pro-
duced at Weld Garden, Brookline. 1925.
Merry Jerry. Produced by the Junior League at Peabody
House, Boston: 1928.
Justice Whisker's Trial. Produced at Norwalk, Conn.:
1929.

Marina. Music by Grace Warner Gulesian. First pro-
duced by Children's Theatre, Boston: 1930.
Dick Whittington. Music by Grace Warner Gulesian.
First produced by Children's Theatre, Boston: 1931.
The Rescue of Santa Claus. Music by Arthur Weld.
First produced by Children's Theatre, Boston: 1931.
The Gee Whiz. Produced by the Cheerio Choristers in
Boston, 1933 and 1934.
King Foxy. Music by Pierre de Reeder. Produced by
Charlotte Lund Opera Co. New York City: 1933.
Robinson Crusoe. Produced at Repertory Theatre. Bos-
ton: 1934.
Wing. Produced by Children's Theatre. Boston: 1934.
The Whole World Over: War Verses. Boston: B.
Humphries Inc., 1926. 291 p.
I Hear a Call. (poetry) Cambridge, Mass.: Riverside
Press, 1938.
Near and Far. Boston: publishers unknown, 1949. 70 p.
(Edited) Larz Anderson: Letters and Journals of a Dip-
lomat. Foreword by Charles Francis Adams. New
York: Fleming H. Revell Co., 1940. 672 p.
(Edited) Anderson, Nicholas Longworth, 1838-1892. The
Letters and Journals of Nicholas Longworth Anderson:
Harvard, Civil War, Washington, 1854-1892. New
York: Fleming H. Revell Co., 1942. 320 p.

ANDERSON, Larz, 1866-1937. Diplomatic Service 1891-97.
Served in London and Rome before becoming Ambas-
sador to Belgium in 1911 and to Japan 1912-13.
Larz Anderson: Letters..., ed. by Isabel Anderson [his
widow] with a foreword by Charles Francis Adams.
New York: Fleming H. Revell Co., 1940. 672 p.

ANDERSON, Richard Clough, Jr., 1788-1826. First United
States diplomatic representative to Colombia, 1821-26.
Died at his post of yellow fever. His name is on the
Foreign Service Roll of Honor plaque in the Department
of State.
The Diary and Journal of Richard Clough Anderson, Jr.
1814-1826. ed. by Alfred Tischendorf and E. Taylor
Parke. Durham, N.C.: Duke University Press, 1964.

ANDREWS, Christopher Columbus, 1829-1922. Editor of St.
Cloud (Minnesota) News. Minister to Sweden and Nor-
way 1867-77. Consul General to Brazil 1882-85.
Pioneer in forestry conservation in the United States.
Brazil: Its Condition and Prospects. New York:

Appleton Press, 1887. 352 p.
Minnesota and Dakotah. In letters descriptive of a tour
  through the northwest in the autumn of 1856. Washing-
  ton: 2nd. ed. R. Farnham, 1857. 215 p.
Digest of the Opinions of the Attorney General of the
  United States, From 1791-1856. Washington: W. M.
  Morrison Co., 1857.
A Practical Treatise on the Revenue Laws of the United
  States. Boston: Little, Brown & Co., 1858. 408 p.
Hints to Company Officers on the Military Duties. Writ-
  ten while in Confederate prisons. New York: D. Van
  Nostrand Co. Inc. 1863. 68 p.
My Experience in Rebel Prisons. Minnesota Commandery
  of the Military Order of the Loyal Legion of the United
  States. 4th series, 1898. pp. 24-40.
History of the Campaign of Mobile. New York: D. Van
  Nostrand Co. Inc., 1867. 276 p.
Spring Wheat Culture in the Northwest. Washington:
  Government Printing Office, 1882. 99 p.
(Edited) History of St. Paul, Minnesota. with illus. and
  biographical sketches. Syracuse, N.Y.: Mason &
  Co., 1890. 224 p.
Recollections 1829-1922. Ed. by his daughter, Alice E.
  Andrews, with an introd. by William Watts Folwell.
  Cleveland: Arthur Clark Co., 1928. 327 p.
Report on Pauperism and Poor-Laws in Sweden and Nor-
  way. London: J. S. Levey, 1877.
Life and Manners in Sweden and Norway. privately pub-
  lished.

ANDRUS, James Russell, 1902- . Teacher 1925-42. State
  Department and foreign aid 1945-66. Served in Ran-
  goon, Karachi, Baghdad, Seoul, Vientiane, Washington.
Basic Problems of Relief, Rehabilitation and Reconstruc-
  tion in Southeast Asia. New York: International Sec-
  retariat, Institute of Pacific Relations, 1945. 74 p.
  London: Oxford University Press. 1946.
Burmese Economic Life. Foreword by J. S. Furnivall.
  Stanford, Calif.: Stanford University Press, 1948.
  362 p. maps.
Economy of Pakistan. with A. F. Mohammed. Stanford,
  Calif.: Stanford University Press, 1958. 517 p.
Rural Reconstruction in Burma. Foreword by Hon. Dr.
  Ba Maw. Bombay: Oxford University Press, 1936.
  145 p.
Trade, Finance and Development in Pakistan. with
  Azizali Mohammed. Stanford, Calif.: Stanford

University Press, 1966. 289 p. Also London: Oxford University Press.

ANGELL, James Burril, 1829-1916. Journalist, educator. President University of Michigan 1871-1909. Minister to China 1880-81, to Turkey 1897-98.
From Vermont to Michigan: Correspondence of James Burrill Angell: 1869-1871. Foreword by his son, James Rowland Angell. Ann Arbor, Mich.: University of Michigan Press, 1936. 301 p.
Reminiscences of James Burrill Angell. New York: Longmans, Green, 1912. 258 p.
Selected Addresses by James Burrill Angell. New York: Longmans, Green, 1912. 258 p.

ANSLINGER, Harry Jacob, 1892- . Foreign Service Officer 1918-26. Served in The Hague, Hamburg, La Guaira, Nassau. From 1930--Commissioner of Narcotics, Treasury Department. Retired in 1962.
The Murderers: The Story of the Narcotics Gang. with Will Cursler. New York: Farrar, Straus & Cudahy, 1961. 307 p.
The Protectors: The Heroic Story of the Narcotics Agents, Citizens and Officials. with J. Dennis Gregory. New York: Farrar, Straus & Cudahy, 1964.
The Traffic in Narcotics. with William Tompkins. New York: Funk & Wagnalls, 1953. 354 p. Illus. and maps.

ARMSTRONG, Hamilton Fish, 1893- . Artist, author, editor, correspondent. Military Attaché in Serbia 1918. State Department 1942-44. Special Assistant to Ambassador in London with personal rank of Minister 1944-45.
(Edited) The Foreign Affairs Reader. New York: Council of Foreign Relations, 1947. 429 p.
(Edited) Foreign Affairs Bibliography. with R. G. Woolbert and William Leonard Langer. New York: Harper & Bros. for the Council on Foreign Relations, 1933. 551 p.
The Calculated Risk. New York: The Macmillan Co., 1947. 68 p.
Chronology of Failure: The Last Days of the French Republic. New York: The Macmillan Co., 1940. 202 p. maps.
Europe Between Wars? New York: The Macmillan Co., 1934. 115 p.

When There Is No Peace. New York: The Macmillan
Co., 1939. 236 p.
Hitler's Reich. The First Phase. New York: The Mac-
millan Co., 1933. 73 p.
The New Balkans. Introd. by Archibald Cary Coolidge.
New York: Harper & Bros., 1926. 179 p.
Those Days. (autobiography) New York: Harper & Row,
1963. 151 p.
Tito and Goliath. New York: The Macmillan Co., 1951.
312 p.
We or They: Two Worlds in Conflict. New York: The
Macmillan Co., 1936. 106 p.
Where the East Begins. New York: Harper & Bros.,
1939.
Can America Stay Neutral? with Allen Dulles. New
York: Harper & Bros., 1939. 277 p.
Can We Be Neutral? with Allen Dulles. New York:
Harper & Bros. for the Council on Foreign Relations,
1936. 191 p.
(Edited) The Book of New York Verse. New York: G.
P. Putnam's Sons, 1917. 450 p.
Peace and Counterpeace: From Wilson to Hitler. Mem-
oirs of Hamilton Fish Armstrong. New York: Harper
& Row, 1971. 585 p.

ARMSTRONG, John, 1758-1843. Minister to France 1804-
1810.
Notices of the War of 1812. Narrative of the Affair of
Queenstown; in the War of 1812. New York: Leavitt,
Lord & Co. Boston: Crocker & Brewster, 1836. 2
vols.
A Treatise on Agriculture. New York: Harper & Bros.,
1839. 282 p.

ARMSTRONG, William H., 1932- . Clergyman. Foreign
Service Reserve Officer, Peace Corps. 1966- .
Served in Addis Ababa, Director in Mbabane, Swazi-
land.
Organs for America: The Life and Work of David Tan-
nenberg. Foreword by E. Power Biggs. Philadelphia:
University of Pennsylvania Press, 1967. 154 p.

ARNESON, R. Gordon, 1916- . Government official. Foreign Affairs Officer 1948-56. Foreign Service Officer
1956-62. Served in State Department, London, Oslo.
Industrial Concentration and Tariffs. with Clifford Lester
James and Edward C. Welsh. Washington: Government

Printing Office, 1940. 326 p.
(Edited) Washington '66. Directory of Washington. Potto-
mac Books.

ARNOLD, Julean H., 1876- . Chinese language officer and
consular officer 1902-14, again 1939-40. Department
of Commerce foreign service 1914-39. Served in Peking, Dalny, Shanghai, Foochow, Tansui, Amoy, Chefoo, Hankow, Shanghai.
China: A Commercial and Industrial Handbook. with
Consular officers in China. Washington: Government
Printing Office, 1926. 818 p. tables, maps, dia-
grams. Also in Chinese.
China Through the American Window. Compiled by Arnold. Shanghai: American Chamber of Commerce,
1932. 85 p. maps, diagrams. Also in Chinese.
Education in Formosa. Washington: Government Printing
Office. United States Bureau of Education Bulletin No.
5. 1908. 70 p.
Far Eastern Markets for American Hardware. with oth-
ers. Washington: Government Printing Office, for
Commerce Department. 1917. 145 p.
Commercial Handbook of China. Washington: Government
Printing Office for the Department of Commerce. Vol.
1, with various consular officers. Vol. 2, with Chinese and American contributors. Plates. maps, ta-
bles, charts. 1919-20.

ASHABRANNER, Brent K., 1921- . Engineer. Ethiopian
U.S. Cooperation Education Program 1955-57. Foreign
Service Reserve Officer 1957- . With Peace Corps
1962- . Served in Addis Ababa, Tripoli, Lagos, New
Delhi, Washington.
A Moment in History. New York: Doubleday & Co. Inc.,
1971. 392 p.

ASTOR, William Waldorf, 1848-1919. Minister to Italy
1882-85. Moved to England 1899. Became a British
subject and anti-American. Created Baron of Astor of
Hever Castle 1916.
Valentino: An Historical Romance of the Sixteenth Century in Italy. New York: Charles Scribner's Sons,
1885. 325 p.
Sforza. A Story of Milan. New York: Charles Scribner's Sons. 1889. 282 p.

ATTWOOD, William, 1919- . Newspaper correspondent,

editor. Ambassador to Guinea 1961, to United Nations
1963, to Kenya 1964-66.
The Decline of the American Male. with George B.
  Leonard, Jr., and J. Robert Moskin. New York:
  Random House, Inc. 1958. 66 p.
Still the Most Exciting Country. Alfred A. Knopf, Inc.,
  1955. 117 p.
The Man Who Could Grow Hair; or, Inside Andorra.
  drawings by Roger Duvoisin. New York: Alfred A.
  Knopf, Inc., 1949. 240 p.
The Reds and the Blacks: A Personal Adventure. New
  York: Harper & Row, 1967. 341 p.
The Fairly Scary Adventure Book. Drawings by Bob
  Bugg. New York: Harper & Row, 1969. 96 p.

AVERY, Benjamin Parke, 1828-1875. Journalist. Editor
  of several newspapers in California. Minister to
  China 1874-75. Died at post. His body embalmed by
  the surgeon of the Russian Legation, and shipped home.
California Pictures in Prose and Verse. Cambridge,
  Mass.: Riverside Press, 1878. 344 p.

AYERS, Thomas William, 1922- . Born in China. News-
  paper reporter and correspondent in China. United
  Nations Relief and Rehabilitation Administration in
  China in 1946. State Department 1947. Office of
  Military Government of United States in Germany 1947.
  United States Information Agency 1961- . Served in
  China, Hong Kong, Saigon, Germany, Washington.
Chang Chi-Tung and Educational Reform in China. Cam-
  bridge, Mass.: Harvard University Press (Harvard
  East Asian Series, 54), 1971. 304 p.

BACON, Robert, 1860-1919. Banker, soldier. Assistant
  Secretary of State 1905-09, Secretary of State 1909,
  Ambassador to France 1909-12.
For Better Relations with our Latin American Neighbors.
  Washington: Carnegie Endowment for International
  Peace, 1915. 186 p.
Robert Bacon: Life and Letters. by James Brown Scott.
  Introd. by Elihu Root. Foreword by Earl Haig. Gar-
  den City, N.Y.: Doubleday, Page & Co., 1923.
  459 p.
(Edited with James Brown Scott) Addresses on Government
  and Citizenship. by Elihu Root. Cambridge: Harvard
  University Press, 1916. 552 p.
(Edited with James Brown Scott) Addresses on

International Subjects. by Elihu Root. Cambridge:
Harvard University Press, 1916. 663 p.
(Edited with James Brown Scott) Addresses on Latin
America and the United States. by Elihu Root. Cam-
bridge: Harvard University Press, 1917. 302 p.
(Edited with James Brown Scott) Men and Policies. by
Elihu Root. Cambridge: Harvard University Press,
1925. 511 p.
(Edited with James Brown Scott) The Military and Colonial
Policy of the United States. Addresses and reports by
Elihu Root. Cambridge: Harvard University Press,
1916. 502 p.
(Edited with James Brown Scott) Miscellaneous Addresses.
by Elihu Root. Port Washington, N.Y.: Kennikat
Press, 1916. 313 p.
(Edited with James Brown Scott) North Atlantic Coast
Fisheries Arbitration at the Hague: Argument on Be-
half of the United States. by Elihu Root. Cambridge:
Harvard University Press. London: H. Mitford, 1917.
445 p.
(Edited with James Brown Scott) The United States and the
War. Mission to Russia. Political Addresses. by
Elihu Root. Cambridge: Harvard University Press,
1918. 362 p.

BADEAU, Adam, 1831-1895. Secretary of Legation at Lon-
don, then Consul General 1870-81. Consul General at
Havana 1882-84.
Military History of Ulysses S. Grant. New York: D.
Appleton & Co., 1868-1881. 3 vols.
Grant in Peace. Hartford: S. S. Scranton & Co., 1887.
501 p.
The Vagabond. New York: Rudd & Carlton, 1859.
368 p.
Conspiracy: A Cuban Romance. New York: R. Worth-
ington, 1885. 324 p.
Aristocracy in England. New York: Harper & Bros.,
1886. 306 p.

BAKER, Henry Dunstan, 1873-1939. Newspaper reporter
and editor. Consular and Foreign Service Officer
1907-1926. Served in Hobart (Tasmania), Sydney, New
Zealand, Nassau, India, Bombay, Petrograd, Trinidad.
Russian Market for American Hardware. Under direction
of Baker, then Commercial Attaché at Petrograd.
Washington: Government Printing Office, 1916.
111 p.

BAKER, Ray Stannard, 1870-1946. Author, editor. Special
Commissioner to Great Britain, France and Italy 1918;
Director of Press Bureau of American Commission to
Negotiate Peace, Paris, 1919.
Adventures in Contentment. by David Grayson (pseud.)
   illus. by Thomas Fogarty. New York: Doubleday,
   Page & Co., 1907. 249 p.
Adventures in Friendship. by David Grayson (pseud.)
   illus. by Thomas Fogarty. Garden City, N.Y.: Dou-
   bleday, Page & Co., 1910. 232 p.
Adventures in Understanding. by David Grayson (pseud.)
   illus. by Thomas Fogarty. Garden City, N.Y.: Dou-
   bleday, Page & Co., 1925. 273 p.
Adventures of David Grayson. (pseud.) illus. by Thomas
   Fogarty. Garden City, N.Y.: Doubleday, Page &
   Co., 1925. 249 p.
American Chronicle. the Autobiography of Ray Stannard
   Baker. (David Grayson) New York: Charles Scrib-
   ner's Sons, 1945. 531 p.
The Countryman's Year. by David Grayson (pseud.) illus.
   by Thomas Fogarty. Garden City, N.Y.: The Sun
   Dial Press, 1943. 270 p.
Following the Color Line: American Negro Citizenship in
   the Progressive Era. Introd. and notes to the Torch-
   book Ed. by Dewey W. Grantham, Jr. New York:
   Harper & Row, 1964. 311 p.
The Friendly Road: New Adventures in Contentment. by
   David Grayson. (pseud.) illus. by Thomas Fogarty.
   Garden City, N.Y.: Doubleday, Page & Co., 1913.
   342 p.
Great Possessions. a New Series of Adventures. by David
   Grayson (pseud.). illus. by Thomas Fogarty. Garden
   City, N.Y.: Doubleday, Page & Co., 1917. 208 p.
Under My Elm. Country Discoveries and Reflections. il-
   lus. by David Hendrickson. Garden City, N.Y.: Dou-
   bleday, Doran & Co., Inc., 1942. 278 p.
Woodrow Wilson and World Settlement. Written from his
   unpublished and personal material. Gloucester, Mass.:
   P. Smith, 1960. c1922. 3 vols. In Russian, Vol. I.
   1923. 451 p.
Woodrow Wilson: Life and Letters. Garden City, N.Y.:
   Doubleday, Page & Co., 1927-39. 8 vols.
Papers. 1836-1946. 61 ft. (ca. 30,000 items) Manuscript
   Division of the Library of Congress.
The Versailles Treaty and After: An Interpretation of
   Woodrow Wilson's Work at Paris. New York: Doran,
   1924.

What Wilson Did at Paris. Garden City, N.Y.: Doubleday, Page & Co., 1919.

BALDRIDGE, Letitia. Private secretary to the wife of Ambassador David K. E. Bruce in Paris 1949-52. Secretary to Ambassador Clare Boothe Luce in Rome 1953-56. Social secretary to President Kennedy's wife in the White House 1961-63.
Roman Candle. [Biography of Ambassador Clare Boothe Luce] Cambridge: Riverside Press. Boston: Houghton, Mifflin Co., 1961. 308 p.
Of Diamonds and Diplomats. [Autobiography] Boston: Houghton, Mifflin Co., 1968. 337 p.

BALLANTINE, Joseph William, 1888- . Born in India of American Missionary parents. Foreign Service Officer 1909-47. Began as Japanese language officer. Served in Tokyo, Kobe, Yokohama, Dairen, State Department, London, Canton, Mukden, Ottawa, Director of Office of Far Eastern Affairs.
Formosa - A Problem for the United States. Washington: Brookings Institution, 1952. 218 p. Intro. by Richard Fyfe Boyce.
Japanese As It Is Spoken. A Beginner's Grammar. Stanford, Calif.: Stanford University Press, 1945. 255 p.
A Foreign Policy for the United States. (edited by Quincy Wright) with others. Chicago: University of Chicago Press, 1947. 404 p.
Japan. a symposium ed. by Hugh Borton, co-authored by Ballantine and others. Ithaca, N.Y.: Cornell University Press, 1958.
(Co-author) The Strenuous Decade: China's Nation-Building Efforts, 1927-1937. New York: St. John's University Press, 1970. 400 p.

BALLANTINE, Leslie (Frost). Wife of Joseph W. Ballantine [Q.V.] Daughter of Robert Frost, American poet.
Murder at Large. New York: Coward-McCann Inc., 1930.
Not Really. [children's stories]. New York: Coward-McCann Inc., 1929.
Come Christmas. anthology of Christmas poems and prose. New York: Coward-McCann Inc., 1929.
The Korea Story. with John Caldwell. Chicago: Henry Regnery Co., 1952. 180 p.
Really Not Really. [children's stories.] New York: Devin-Adair Co., 1966. 63 p.

Digging Down to China. [children's stories.] New York:
  Devin-Adair Co., 1968. 86 p.
New Hampshire's Child. facsimile reproduction of journal
  kept by Leslie Frost when she was 5-9 years old.
  Albany, N.Y.: State University of New York Press,
  1969.

BANCROFT, Edgar Addison, 1857-1925. Lawyer, orator.
  Ambassador to Japan 1924-25. Died there. Given an
  impressive funeral and his body returned to the United
  States on a Japanese warship.
The Chicago Strike of 1894. (privately printed) Chicago:
  Gunthorp Warren, 1895. 73 p.
The Mission of America, and Other Speeches of Edgar
  Addison Bancroft. ed. by Fredrick Bancroft. Intro.
  by John H. Finley. Washington: 1927. 166 p.

BANCROFT, George, 1800-1891. Historian, teacher. Min-
  ister to Great Britain 1846-49; to Germany 1867-74.
Memorial Address on the Life and Character of Abraham
  Lincoln. before both Houses of Congress, 12 October
  1866. Washington: 1866. 80 p. (100 copies) Gov-
  ernment Printing Office.
The George Bancroft Papers at Cornell University, 1811-
  1901. ed. by Herbert Finch. Ithaca, N.Y.: Cornell
  University Press, 1965. (microfilm, 7 reels. 1965)
A History of the United States From the Discovery of the
  American Continent. Boston: Little, Brown & Co.,
  1834-1875. 10 vols. Many editions and translations.
  Last revision 1883-1905. New York: D. Appleton Co.
  6 vols.
History of the American Revolution. Boston: Little,
  Brown & Co., 1852-75. 7 vols.
History of the Battle of Lake Erie, and Miscellaneous
  Papers. by George Bancroft and Life and Writings of
  George Bancroft. by Oliver Dyer. New York: R.
  Bonners Sons, 1891. 128 p.
History of the Colonization of the United States. Boston:
  Little, Brown & Co., 1838-57. 3 vols. plates, maps.
History of the Formation of the Constitution of the United
  States of America. New York: D. Appleton Co.,
  1882. 2 vols.
Literary and Historical Miscellanies. New York: Harper
  & Bros., 1855. 517 p.
Martin Van Buren to the End of his Public Career. New
  York: Harper & Bros., 1889. 239 p.
The American Revolution. Boston: Little, Brown & Co.,

1860-75. 4 vols. (In French, 3 vols.)
The Life and Letters of George Bancroft. Edit. by M. A.
DeWolfe Howe, 1908. 2 vols.

BARBER, Willard Foster, 1909- . Foreign Service Officer
1938-62. Served in Washington, Lima, Bogota, Warsaw, Foreign Service Institute, Assistant Secretary of
State for Inter-American Affairs.
Internal Security and Military Power. Counter-Insurgency
and Civic Action in Latin America. With Dr. C.
Neale Ronning. Columbus, Ohio: Ohio State University Press, 1966. 340 p.

BARGHOORN, Frederick Charles, 1911- . History teacher,
State Department and Foreign Service Reserve Officer
1941-45. Served in Moscow and Kuibyshev.
Politics in the U.S.S.R. Boston: Little, Brown & Co.,
1966. 418 p. map.
The Soviet Cultural Offensive and the Role of Cultural
Diplomacy. Princeton, N.J.: Princeton University
Press, 1960. 358 p.
The Soviet Image of the United States: A Study in Dis-
tortion. New York: Harcourt, Brace & World Inc.,
1950. 297 p.
Soviet Russian Nationalism. New York: Oxford Univer-
sity Press, 1956. 330 p.
Modern Political Parties: Approaches to Comparative
Politics. With others. Ed. by Sigmund Newmann.
Chicago: University of Chicago Press, 1952. 400 p.

BARLOW, Joel, 1754-1812. One of the "Hartford Wits."
Author, poet and liberal thinker. He arranged for the
publication of Thomas Paine's "The Age of Reason"
while the latter was in prison. One of Barlow's publications was suppressed in England and he was for-
bidden entry into England for a while. He lived in
Europe from 1788 to 1805. Consul at Algiers 1795-
1805. Arranged treaties with Tunis, Algiers and Tri-
poli. Minister to France 1811-12. Died tragically in
Cracow, Poland, in an unsuccessful attempt to get
Napoleon Bonaparte to sign a trade agreement with the
United States.
Advice to the Privileged Orders in the Several States of
Europe Resulting from the Necessity and Propriety of
a General Revolution in the Principle of Government.
New York: Childs & Swaine, 1792-94. 2 vols. In
French, Paris: Barois 1794.

The Columbiad, a Poem. Philadelphia: Fry & Kammerer
for C. & A. Conrad & Co., 1807. 454 p. [Paid for
by Robert Fulton.]
Letters from Paris to the Citizens of the United States of
America. London: for J. Ridgeway by A. Wilson,
1800. 116 p. (Duane pamphlets.)
Joel Barlow to his Fellow Citizens of the United States of
America on Certain Political Measures Proposed to
their Consideration. Philadelphia: W. Duane, 1801.
70 p.
A Letter, Addressed to the People of Piedmont, on the
Advantages of the French Revolution, and the Necessity
of Adopting its Principles in Italy. Translated from
the French by the author. London: D. I. Eaton, 1795.
48 p.
A Letter to the National Convention of France on the De-
fects in the Constitution of 1791, Etc. New York:
Thomas Greenleaf, 1792. 70 p.
Prospectus of a National Institution to be Established in
the United States. Washington: S. H. Smith, 1806.
44 p.
The Vision of Columbus - a Poem in Nine Books. [This
formed the basis for the "Columbiad."] Hartford,
Conn.: Hudson & Goodwin, 1787. 258 p.
The Life and Letters of Joel Barlow. by Charles Burr
Todd. New York: G. P. Putnam's Sons, 1886.
306 p.

BARNARD, Daniel Dewey, 1796-1861. Minister to Prussia
1850-53.
Discourse on Life, Services and Character of Stephen
Van Rensselaer. Albany: Hoffman White, 1839. 70 p.
Discourse on Life, Character and Public Services of Am-
brose Spencer, Late Chief Justice of the Supreme
Court. Albany: W. C. Little & Co., 1849. 104 p.
Speeches in the Assembly of New York. Albany: Oliver
Steele, 1838. 228 p.

BARNARD, John Lawrence, 1912- . Writer. State Depart-
ment and Foreign Service Officer 1946-66. Served in
Antwerp, Nice, Aruba, Nassau.
Land of Promise. Garden City, N.Y.: Doubleday, Doran
Co., 1942. 268 p.
Revelry by Night. Garden City, N.Y.: Doubleday, Doran
Co., 1941. 273 p.

BARNES, William, 1914-1967. Foreign Service Officer

1937-62. Served in Amsterdam, Buenos Aires, Monte-
video, Hamilton, Lisbon, Helsinki, Washington, Foreign
Service Institute.
The Foreign Service of the United States: Origins, De-
velopment, and Functions. with John Heath Morgan.
Washington: Historical Office, Department of State,
1961. 430 p. Illus. portraits. Department of State
Publication No. 7050.

BARRETT, John, 1866-1938. Minister to Siam 1894-98; Advisor to Adm. Dewey in Philippines 1898-99; Commercial Commissioner to China, Japan, Philippines Islands,
Korea, Siberia, India, Australia and Europe 1899; U. S.
Delegate to 2nd Pan American Conference in Mexico
City 1901-02; Commissioner General to Asia, Australia
and Europe for the St. Louis Exposition 1902-03; Min-
ister to Argentina 1903-04; to Panama 1904-05; to
Colombia 1905-06. Negotiated first Protocol for set-
tlement of dispute over Panama Canal. Director Gen-
eral of the Pan American Union 1907-20.
Admiral George Dewey. New York: Harper Bros., 1893.
279 p.
Pan American Union - Peace, Friendship Commerce.
Washington: Pan American Union, 1911. 253 p.
Panama Canal - What It Is, What It Means. Washington:
Pan American Union, 1913. 120 p.
Latin America, Land of Opportunity. [reprint of reports
and articles.] Washington: Government Printing Of-
fice, 1909. 104 p.
Pan American Commerce, Past Present and Future.
Washington: Pan American Union, 1919. 473 p.

BARTON, Donald Richmond, 1913- . Editor, reporter.
Foreign Service Auxiliary and Reserve Officer 1944-
52. Served in Ankara, Istanbul, Teheran, Athens.
Before Your Eyes: The Way of Life in a Museum.
Evanston, Ill.: Row, Peterson & Co., 1941. 64 p.
Iran. with cooperation of American Geographical Society.
Garden City, N. Y.: Doubleday & Co., Inc., 1958.
64 p.
Iron and Steel. with cooperation of American Geographi-
cal Society. Garden City, N. Y.: Doubleday & Co.,
Inc., 1959. 64 p. maps.
Once in Aleppo. New York: Charles Scribner's Sons,
1955. 424 p. [fiction]

BARTON, Robert, 1920- . United States Information

Service 1948- . Served in Washington, Columbia
   University, Montevideo, Madrid, Santo Domingo, La
   Paz, Guadalajara.
A Short History of Bolivia. Cochabamba, Bolivia: Los
   Amigos del Libro. New York: Stechert-Hafner Inc.,
   1968. 344 p. Illus. by Hemenway. photos, maps,
   append. bibliog.
The International Activities of Columbia University. New
   York: Columbia University Press, 1961.

BARTON, Thomas Pennant, 1803-1869. Secretary of Legation, Paris 1833, Chargé d'Affaires 1835-36.
Catalogue of Barton Collection. Boston Public Library,
   1888. 2 vols., in one. (12,000 volumes of Shakespeare and Shakespeariana, and miscellaneous)

BAX, Emily, 1882-1943. Secretary in Embassy, London.
Miss Bax of the Embassy. Boston: Houghton Mifflin
   Co., 1939. 310 p.

BAXTER, Craig, 1929- . History teacher. Foreign Ser-
   vice Officer 1956- . Served in Bombay, Washington,
   New Delhi, University of Pennsylvania, Lahore.
The Jana Sangh, A Biography of an Indian Political Party.
   Philadelphia: University of Pennsylvania Press, 1969.
   352 p.
District Voting Trends in India. New York: Columbia
   University Press, 1969. 378 p.

BAYARD, Richard Henry, 1796-1868. Lawyer, senator.
   Chargé d'Affaires Belgium 1850-53.
Bayard Papers. Washington: American Historical Asso-
   ciation Reports, 1913. II.

BEAULAC, Willard L., 1899- . Foreign Service Officer
   1921-62. Served in Puerto Castillo, Arica, Port-au-
   Prince, Managua, San Salvador, Washington, Guate-
   mala, Habana, Madrid, Ambassador to Paraguay, to
   Colombia, to Cuba, to Chile, to Argentina. Dep.
   Commandant National War College. Career Minister.
Career Ambassador. New York: The Macmillan Co.,
   1951. 262 p.
Career Diplomat. New York: The Macmillan Co., 1964.
   199 p.
Red Cross. U.S. National Red Cross. Managua Earth-
   quake Official Report, 1931. 43 p.
A Diplomat Looks at Aid to Latin America. Carbondale,

Ill. : Southern Illinois University Press, 1970. 148 p.

BELMONT, August, 1816-1890. Banker, patron of the arts,
sportsman. Born in Germany. Came to United States
1837, naturalized 1844. Austrian Consul General in
the United States 1850. United States Minister to the
Netherlands 1853-57.
A Few Letters and Speeches of the Late Civil War. New
York: privately printed, 1870. 126 p.
Letters, Speeches and Addresses of August Belmont.
New York: privately printed, 1890. 236 p.

BENET, Rosemary (Carr). Wife of Stephen Vincent Benét.
[Q. V.]
Sing a Song of Americans: Fifteen Songs from a Book of
Americans. by Rosemary and Stephen Vincent Benét.
Music by Arnold Shaw. Illus. by Mollie Shuger. New
York: Musette Publishers, Inc., 1941. 79 p.

BENET, Stephen Vincent, 1898-1943. Poet, novelist, short
story writer. Clerk in Embassy Paris 1918. Benét
received the Pulitzer award for poetry in 1929.
America. New York: Farrar & Rinehart, Inc., 1944.
122 p. Published in several editions 1944-46, includ-
ing translations in Arabic, German, French, Polish
and Italian.
John Brown's Body. written 1928, edit. and annotated by
Mabel A. Bessey. New York: Farrar & Rinehart,
Inc., c1941. 432 p.
The Devil and Daniel Webster. Illus. by Harold Denison.
New York: Farrar & Rinehart, Inc., 1937. 61 p.
[The story was the basis for a play, an opera and a
motion picture.]
Jean Huguenot. New York: H. Holt & Co., 1923. 292 p.
The Heart of Peggy O'Neill. [Play in seven scenes, with
John Farrar, based in part on a novel by Alfred Henry
Lewis entitled "Peggy O'Neill. "] [Q. V. Margaret
O'Neale]
The Last Circle, Stories and Poems. New York: Farrar,
Straus & Co., 1946. 309 p.
Poesías Escogidas. (traducciones y comentario por
Susannah B. de Vaillant) Lima, Peru: Historia, 1944.
71 p.
Selected Works of Stephen Vincent Benét. New York:
Farrar & Rinehart Inc., 1942. 2 vols. Vol. 1 poetry.
Vol. 2. prose.
Selected Letters. Edit. by Charles A. Fenton. New

Haven: Yale University Press, 1960. 436 p.
Sing a Song of Americans: Fifteen Songs from A Book of
 Americans. by Rosemary and Stephen Vincent Benét.
 Music by Arnold Shaw. Illus. by Mollie Shuger. New
 York: Musette Publishers, Inc., 1941. 79 p.
The Stephen Vincent Benét Pocket Book. Edit. and with
 an Introd. by Robert Van Gelder. New York: Pocket
 Books, Inc., 1946. 414 p.
Stephen Vincent Benét on Writing. A Great Writer's Let-
 ters of Advice to a Young Beginner. Edit. and with
 comment by George Abbe. Brattleboro, Vt.: S.
 Greene Press, 1964. 111 p.
Tales Before Midnight. New York: Farrar & Rinehart,
 Inc., c1919. 274 p.
They Burned the Books. New York: Farrar & Rinehart,
 Inc., 1942. 25 p. "The first performance was given
 under the auspices of the Council on Books in War-
 time and the Writers War Board, on Monday evening,
 May 11, 1942, over WEAF and the National Broadcast-
 ing Company network."
Twenty Five Short Stories. Garden City, N.Y.: The
 Sun Dial Press, 1943. 305 p.
La Valle delle Sabine. Traduzione di Margherita Santi
 Farina. Milan: Longanesi, 1948. 287 p.
We Stand United, and Other Radio Scripts. Fore. by
 Ernest Stock. New York: Farrar & Rinehart, Inc.,
 1945. 210 p.
Western Star. New York: Farrar & Rinehart, Inc.,
 1943. 181 p.

BENJAMIN, Samuel Greene Wheeler, 1837-1914. Author,
 painter. Born in Greece of missionary parents. Lived
 in Greece till 18 years old. Linguist. Successful
 marine painter in Boston. Forty-five crossings of the
 Atlantic, mostly in sailing ships, and never sea-sick,
 which he claimed was due to his whiskey and tobacco.
 Rarely drank water. He was the first Minister to
 Persia, 1883-85. He liked mariners and Turks and
 distrusted missionaries.
Constantinople, the Isle of Pearls and Other Poems.
 Boston: N.J. Bertlett, 1860. 96 p.
Art in America. New York: Harper Bros., 1880. 214 p.
Contemporary Art in Europe. New York: Harper Bros.,
 1877. 163 p.
Multitudinous Seas. New York: D. Appleton Co., 1879.
 132 p.
The Choice of Paris: A Romance of the Troad. New

York: Hurd & Houghton, 1870. 342 p.
The Atlantic Islands as Resorts of Health and Pleasure.
New York: Harper Bros., 1878. 274 p.
The Cruise of the Alice May in the Gulf of St. Lawrence
and Adjacent Waters. Reproduced from Century Maga-
zine. New York: D. Appleton Co., 1885. 129 p.
A Group of Etchers. New York: Dodd, Mead & Co.,
Inc., 1882. 42 p.
Our American Artists. Boston: D. Lothrop, 1879. 62 p.
Seaspray: or Facts and Fancies of a Yachtsman. New
York: Benjamin & Bell, 1887. 298 p.
Tom Roper: A Story of Travel and Adventure. Philadel-
phia: Daughaday & Becker, 1868. 245 p.
Troy: Its Legend, History and Literature. with a sketch
of the topography of the Troad in the light of recent
investigation. New York: C. Scribner's Sons, 1880.
179 p.
The Turk and the Greek: or, Creeds, Races, Society and
Scenery in Turkey, Greece and the Isles of Greece.
New York: Hurd & Houghton, 1867. 268 p.
The World's Paradises: or Sketches of Life, Scenery and
Climate in Noted Sanitaria. New York: D. Appleton
Co., 1880. 238 p.
The Life and Adventures of a Free Lance: Being the Ob-
servations of Samuel Green Wheeler Benjamin. [auto-
biography, posthumously published] Burlington, Vt.:
Free Press, 1914. 430 p.
Persia and the Persians. Boston: Ticknor Co., 1887.
507 p.
The Story of Persia. New York: G. P. Putnam's Sons,
1887. 304 p.
What is Art? or Art Theories and Methods Concisely
Stated. Boston: Lockwood, Crooks Co., 1877. 57 p.

BENTON, William, 1900- . Government official, publish-
er, advertising, senator. Assistant Secretary of State.
Ambassador to UNESCO, London, 1945.
This is the Challenge: The Benton Reports of 1956-58 on
the Nature of the Soviet Threat. Ed. by Edw. W.
Barrell. New York: Associated College Presses,
1958. 254 p.
The Voice of Latin America. New York: Harper & Row,
1961. 202 p.
The Voice of Latin America. with Kalman Silvert. New
York: Harper & Row, 1965. 202 p.
The Teachers and the Taught in the USSR: a Personal
Report. New York: Atheneum Publishers, 1966. 174 p.

BERDING, Andrew Henry, 1902- . Writer, journalist.
Director of Information for Marshall Plan in Rome and
in Washington 1946-48. Deputy Director United States
Information Agency, Washington 1953-1957; Assistant
Secretary of State for Public Affairs 1957-61. Distin-
guished Service Award for work in developing the United
States Information Agency.
The Making of Foreign Policy. Washington: Potomac
  Books, 1966. 95 p.
Dulles on Diplomacy. Princeton, N.J.: D. Van Nostrand
  Co. Inc., 1965. 184 p.
Foreign Affairs and You: How American Foreign Policy
  Is Made and What It Means to You. Garden City,
  N.Y.: Doubleday & Co., Inc., 1962. 264 p.

BERGH, Henry, 1811-1888. Pioneer in humane treatment
  of animals. Founder of the first Society for the Prevention of Cruelty to Animals. Secretary of Legation,
  St. Petersburg 1863-64. Wrote plays, sketches and
  poetry.
Married Off - A Satirical Poem. London: Ward & Lock,
  75 p. New York: Carleton, 1862. 75 p.

BERLE, Adolph Augustus, Jr., 1895-1971. Lawyer. As-
  sistant Secretary of State 1938-44. Ambassador to
  Brazil 1945-46.
The American Economic Republic. New York: Harcourt,
  Brace & World, Inc., 1963. 247 p.
The Bank that Banks Built - Savings Bank & Trust Co.,
  1933-58. New York: Harper & Bros., 1959. 100 p.
Cases and Materials in the Law of Corporate Finance.
  St. Paul, Minn.: West Publishing Co., 1930. 911 p.
Cases and Materials in the Law of Business Organizations.
  with William C. Warren. Brooklyn: Brooklyn Founda-
  tion Press, 1948. 1344 p.
Cases and Materials in the Law of Corporate Finance.
  with Roswell Magill. St. Paul, Minn.: West Publish-
  ing Co., 1942. 912 p.
L'Homme et la Propriété, Resolution du Systeme de la
  Proprieté Libre. Paris: Hermann & Cie., 1939.
  58 p.
Latin America: Diplomacy and Reality. New York:
  Harper & Row, for the Council on Foreign Relations,
  1960. 144 p.
Liquid Claims and Natural Wealth. with Victoria J. Ped-
  erson. New York: The Macmillan Co., 1934. 248 p.
The Modern Corporation and Private Property. with

Gardner Means. New York: Commerce Clearing
House, Inc., 1933. 396 p.
New Directions in the World. New York: Harper Bros.,
1940. 141 p. Essays on U.S. Foreign Policy by One
of the Makers.
Power Without Property: A New Development in Ameri-
can Economy. New York: Harcourt, Brace & World,
Inc., 1959. 184 p.
Studies in the Law of Corporate Finance. Chicago: Gal-
laghan & Co., 1928. 199 p.
Tides of Crisis: A Primer of Foreign Relations. New
York: Reynal & Co., Inc., 1957. 328 p.
Three Faces of Power. New York: Harcourt, Brace &
World, Inc., 1967. 83 p.
Twentieth Century Capitalist Revolution. New York:
Harcourt, Brace & World, Inc., 1954. 192 p.
America's Recovery Program. with John Dickinson, A.
Heath Onthank and others. New York: Oxford Univer-
sity Press, 1934. 253 p.
Inventions and Their Management. Scranton, Penna.:
International Textbook Co., 1937. 733 p. with L.
Sprague de Camp.
Power. New York: Harcourt, Brace & World, Inc.,
1969. 603 p.
Natural Selection of Political Forces. Lawrence: Univer-
sity of Kansas Press, 1950. 103 p.

BETHEL, Paul Duane, 1918- . Writer and librarian 1945-
49. Foreign Service Staff and United States Information Agency officer 1949-61. Served in Hamburg,
Nuremberg, Bremen, Yokohama, United States Information Administration Nagoya, Tokyo, Havana.
The Losers. The Definitive Report, by an Eyewitness,
of the Communist Conquest of Cuba, and the Soviet
Penetration of Latin America. New Rochelle, N.Y.:
Arlington House, 1969. 615 p.

BIDDLE, Nicholas, 1786-1844. Scholar, orator, financier,
Secretary to Minister John Armstrong, Paris 1804.
Secretary of Legation London 1806-07. President of
the first Bank of the United States.
The Correspondence of Nicholas Biddle, Dealing with Na-
tional Affairs, 1807-1844. Ed. by Reginald C. Mc-
Grane. Boston: Houghton Mifflin Co., 1919. 366 p.
Eulogium on Thomas Jefferson, Delivered before the
American Philosophical Society, on the Eleventh Day
of April, 1827. Philadelphia: R. H. Small, 1927. 55 p.

Reply to the Report of a Committee of the Bank of the
  United States, of Pennsylvania.   Paris: Printed by E.
  Briare, 1841.   67 p.
(Edited) The Journals of the Expedition under the Com-
  mand of Capts. Lewis and Clark, to the Sources of the
  Missouri, Thence Across the Rocky Mountains and
  Down the River Columbia to the Pacific Ocean, Per-
  formed during the years 1804-5-6 by Order of the Gov-
  ernment of the United States. Introd. by John Lake-
  less, and illustrated with water colors and drawings by
  Carl Bodmer and other contemporary artists.   New
  York: Heritage Press, 1962.   2 vols.

BIGELOW, John, 1817-1911.   Editor and author.   Editor of
  New York Post 1848-61.   Consul General at Paris
  1861-64.   Minister to France 1864-66.
The Bible that Was Lost and Is Found.   New York: New
  Church Board of Publication, 1912.   120 p.
Les Etats-Unis d'Amerique: Leur Histoire Politique,
  Leur Resources Mineralogique, Agricoles, Industrielles,
  et Commerciales, et la Part Pour Laquelle Ils Ont
  Contribue a la Richesse et a la Civilization du Monde
  Entier.   Paris: L. Hachette & Cie., 1863.   551 p.
France and the Confederate Navy, 1862-1868.   An Inter-
  national Episode.   New York: Bergman Publishers,
  1968.   (reprint of 1888 edition, New York: Harper &
  Bros., 247 p.)
Gli Stati Uniti d'America Nel 1863.   Milan: Corona e
  Caimi, 1863.   470 p.
France and Hereditary Monarchy.   London: S. Low, Son
  & Marston.   New York: Charles Scribner's Sons,
  1871.   80 p.
Jamaica in 1850: or, the Effects of Sixteen Years of
  Freedom on a Slave Colony.   New York: G. P. Put-
  nam's Sons, 1851.   214 p.
Lest We Forget: Gladstone, Morley and the Confederate
  Loan of 1863: A Rectification.   New York: DeVinne
  Press, 1905.   65 p.
The Life of Samuel J. Tilden.   New York: Harper &
  Bros., 1895.   2 vols.
Memoir of the Life and Public Service of John Charles
  Fremont.   New York: Derby & Jackson, 1856.   480 p.
Molinos the Quietest.   New York: Charles Scribner's
  Sons, 1882.   127 p.
The Mystery of Sleep.   New York: Harper & Bros.,
  1897.   139 p.
Retrospections of an Active Life.   New York: Baker &

Taylor Co., 1909-1913. 5 vols. (vols. 4 and 5 by
his son)
Toleration and Other Essays and Studies: Posthumous.
Introd. by Glenn Frank. New York: New Church
Press, 1927. 162 p. Reprinted as Toleration and
Other Essays. Freeport, N.Y.: Books for Libraries
Press, 1969. 162 p.
William Cullen Bryant. Boston: Houghton Mifflin Co.,
1890. 355 p.
The Wit and Wisdom of the Haytians. New York: Scrib-
ner & Armstrong, 1877. 112 p.
Bigelow Papers. 28 ft. in Library of Congress MSS Div.
(Edited and compiled) Ben Franklin's Works, Letters,
Scientific Correspondence, Etc. New York: G. P.
Putnam's Sons, 1887-1888. 10 vols.
(Edited) Ben Franklin's Autobiography. Philadelphia: J.
B. Lippincott Co., 1869. 409 p.

BINGHAM, Jonathan Brewster, 1914- . Lawyer. Alien
Enemy Control. Deputy Administrator Technical Co-
operation 1951-53. Served in the Near East 1951-53.
Shirt-Sleeve Diplomacy: Point 4 in Action. New York:
John Day Co., 1953. 303 p.

BIRD, Eugene Hall, 1925- . Foreign Service Officer 1952- .
Served in Jerusalem, Foreign Service Institute, Beirut,
Cairo, Bombay, Superior Honor Award, New Delhi,
Merit honor Award, Jidda.
The Generation Gap. [poetry, with his son Peter Kai
Bird] New Delhi: Vanity Publishers, Caxton Press,
1972. 72 p.

BLACK, Cyril Edwin, 1915- . Educator. History instructor at Princeton 1939-43. Foreign Service Auxiliary
Officer 1943-45. Served in State Department, Naples,
Sofia. Political Advisor to Supreme Allied Command-
er, Mediterranean theater.
Dynamics of Modernization: a Study in Comparative His-
tory. New York: Harper & Row, 1966. 207 p.
The Eastern World Since 1945. Boston: Ginn & Co.,
1967. 96 p.
The Establishment of Constitutional Government in Bul-
garia. Princeton: Princeton University Press, 1943.
344 p.
One World History. Boston: Ginn & Co., 1960. 709 p.
The People's Democracies of Eastern Europe. New
York: Alfred A. Knopf, Inc., 1953. 265 p.

Readings on Contemporary Eastern Europe. New York:
  National Committee for a Free Europe, 1953. 346 p.
Re-Writing Russian History: Soviet Interpretations of
  Russia's Past. New York: Research Program on
  USSR. Frederick A. Praeger, Inc., 1956. 413 p.
Twentieth Century Europe, A History. with E. C. Helm-
  reich. New York: Alfred A. Knopf, Inc., 1950.
Neutralization and World Politics. with others. Prince-
  ton, N. J.: Princeton University Press, 1968. 195 p.
(Edited) American Teaching About Russia. with John M.
  Thompson. Bloomington: Indiana University Press,
  1959-60. 189 p.
(Edited) Challenge in Eastern Europe: 12 Essays. Fore-
  word by Joseph C. Grew. New Brunswick, N. J.:
  Rutgers University Press, 1954. 276 p.
(Edited) Communism and Revolution: the Strategic Issues
  of Political Violence. with Thomas P. Thornton.
  Princeton, N. J.: Princeton University Press, 1964.
  467 p.
(Edited) Joint Committee on Slavic Studies - Transforma-
  tion of Russian Society Etc. Since 1861. Cambridge,
  Mass.: Harvard University Press, 1960. 695 p.

BLANCKE, Wilton Wendell, 1908-1971. Free lance journal-
  ism, advertising. Foreign Service Officer 1942-67.
  Served in Berlin, Havana, Hanoi, Burma, Vientiane,
  Frankfort, Congo (Brazzaville). Ambassador to Braz-
  zaville 1960, also to Chad, to Gabon, to Central Afri-
  can Republic 1961-64. Foreign Service Inspector,
  Consul General Monterrey 1964-67.
The Foreign Service of the United States. New York:
  Frederick A. Praeger, Inc., 1969. 286 p.
Juarez of Mexico. New York: Frederick A. Praeger,
  Inc., 1971. 152 p. map, illus., bibliog.

BLATTY, William Peter, 1928- . U. S. Air Force 1951-
  54. United States Information Agency 1955-57. Served
  in Beirut.
The Exorcist. New York: Harper & Row, 1971. 340 p.
I, Billy Shakespeare. Drawings by Victoria Chess.
  Garden City, New York: Doubleday & Co. Inc., 1965.
  89 p.
John Goldfarb, Please Come Home! Garden City, N. Y.:
  Doubleday & Co., Inc., 1963. 158 p.
Twinkle, Twinkle, "Killer" Kane. Garden City, N. Y.:
  Doubleday & Co. Inc., 1966. 184 p.
Ulysses and the Cyclops: a Tale from Homer's Odyssey.

An Interpretation by James J. Cullen with William
Peter Blatty. Illus. by Kay Vallejo. Los Angeles:
Microclassics Press, 1956. unpaged.
Which Way to Mecca, Jack? Illus. by Gil Miret. New
York: B. Geis Associates, distributed by Random
House, 1960. 256 p.

BLISS, Foster Cornelius, 1838-1885. Private secretary to
Minister J. W. Webb in Rio, 1861; private secretary
to Minister Charles A. Washburn in Asuncion 1866.
Translator in State Department, Secretary of Legation
in Mexico 1870-74. Contributed 1500 biographies to
Johnson's New Universal Encyclopaedia 1874.
The Conquest of Turkey. with L. P. Brockett. Phila-
delphia: Hubbard Press, 1878. 768 p.

BOERNSTEIN, Henry, 1805-1892. His name at birth was
George Christian Heinrich Boernstein. Born in Hamburg, Germany. Came to United States in 1848.
Journalist, playright, editor. Consul at Bremen 1861-
66. (Great-grandfather of Foreign Service Officer
Ralph Augustus Boernstein, 1893-1969). [Boernstein
published other books and plays. His records have
been lost.]
Seventy Five Years in the Old and New World. [in Ger-
man] Leipzig: Otto Wigand, 1884. 2 vols. [Also
published serially in the "Illinois Staatszeitung" in
Chicago.]

BOHAN, Merwin Lee, 1899- . Consular officer 1919-20;
Trade Commissioner, Department of Commerce 1927-
41; Foreign Service Officer 1941-49. Served in Mexi-
co City, Havana, Guatemala, San Salvador, Honduras,
Peru, Ecuador, Chile, Colombia, Bolivia, Buenos
Aires, Department of State. Ambassador to the Inter-
American Economic and Social Council 1951-55. United
States Commissioner to Joint Brazil-United States Eco-
nomic Development Commission 1952-53. United States
member of the GATT Conference at Torquay, 1950-51.
Investment in Cuba. Washington: Government Printing
Office for the Department of Commerce, 1956. 200 p.
Investment in Chile. with Morton Pomeranz. Washing-
ton: Government Printing Office for the Department
of Commerce, 1960. 282 p.

BOHLEN, Charles Eustis, 1904- . Foreign Service Officer
1929-1969. Served in Prague, Paris, Moscow, State

Department, Tokyo, Chief of Division of Eastern European Affairs, Assistant Secretary of State, Career
Minister, Counselor to Department of State, Ambassador to Russia 1953, to the Philippines 1957, Special
Assistant to the Secretary of State 1959, Career Ambassador 1960, Ambassador to France 1962-68. Deputy
Under Secretary of State 1968-69.
Witness to History--1929-1969. New York: W. W. Norton & Co., Inc., 1973.

BOKER, George Henry, 1823-1890. Playwright, poet.
Minister to Turkey 1871-75; to Russia 1875-78.
The Book of the Dead. Philadelphia: J. B. Lippincott
Co., 1882. 214 p. [a defense of his father.]
Galaynos. [play in blank verse.] Printed from the act-
ing copy as performed at the Theatre Royal. London:
G. H. Davison, 1849. 68 p. Philadelphia: E. G.
Butler, 1848. 218 p. (full text)
Lydia: A Tragic Play. 1885; rewritten Glaucus 1886.
Edited by Edw. Sculley Bradley, Philadelphia: Univer-
sity of Pennsylvania Press, 1929. 102 p. Again by
Edw. Sculley Bradley as Glaucus & Other Plays.
Princeton, N.J.: Princeton University Press, 1940.
228 p.
Konigsmark, The Legend of the Hounds and Other Poems.
Philadelphia: J. B. Lippincott Co., 1869. 244 p.
1929 edition with Introd. by Owen Culbertson, New
York: W. E. Rudge. Includes 200 deluxe copies with
hand-colored illus. by Gordon Ross.
The Lessons of Life and Other Poems. Philadelphia:
G. S. Appleton, 1848. 190 p.
Plays and Poems. a collection of plays published in 1856.
[Boker wrote 314 plays and sonnets.] 2nd edition.
Boston: Ticknor & Fields, 1856. 2 vols.
Poems of the War. Boston: Ticknor & Fields, 1864.
202 p.
Sonnets: A Sequence on Profane Love. Edit. by Edward
Sculley Bradley. Philadelphia: University of Penn-
sylvania Press, 1929. 173 p.
The Podesta's Daughter, and Other Miscellaneous Poems.
Philadelphia: A. Hart, 1852. 156 p.

BOND, Niles Woodbridge, 1916- . Foreign Service Officer
1940-69. Served Havana, Yokohama, Madrid, Bern,
State Department, Air War College, Tokyo, Pusan,
Seoul, Rome, Rio, Harvard, Sao Paulo--Consul General
with personal rank of Minister.

Arcanum. [poetry] Sao Paulo, Brazil: Livraria Martins
Editora. In English and Portuguese. Portuguese
translation by Guilherme de Almeida. Illus. by Guilherme de Faria, 1966. 71 p.
Elegos. [poetry] Sao Paulo, Brazil: Livraria Martins
Editora. In English and Portuguese. Portuguese
translation by Pamela Bird. Illus. by Marguerita.
1967. 109 p.

BONNER, Paul Hyde, 1893- . Business executive, writer,
Foreign Service Reserve Officer 1947-50. Served in
Rome.
Aged in the Wood: Stories and Sketches of Fishing and
Shooting. New York: Charles Scribner's Sons, 1958.
157 p.
Amanda. New York: Charles Scribner's Sons, 1957.
314 p.
Ambassador Extraordinary. [fiction] New York: Charles
Scribner's Sons, 1962. 306 p.
The Art of Llewellyn Jones. New York: Charles Scrib-
ner's Sons, 1959. 372 p.
Collection of Paul Hyde Bonner of New York. New York:
American Art Association. Anderson Galleries, 1934.
67 p.
Excelsior. New York: Charles Scribner's Sons, 1955.
279 p.
The Glorious Mornings: Stories of Shooting and Fishing.
New York: Charles Scribner's Sons, 1954. 228 p.
Hotel Talleyrand. [fiction] New York: Charles Scribner's
Sons, 1953. 300 p.
SPQR. [fiction] New York: Charles Scribner's Sons,
1952. 325 p.
Sale Catalogue of Private Library of Paul Hyde Bonner
as Offered by Dutton's Inc. New York: 1931. 138 p.
With Both Eyes Open. New York: Charles Scribner's
Sons, 1956. 117 p.

BONSAL, Philip Wilson, 1903- . Telephone executive in
Cuba, Spain, and Chile 1926-35. Foreign Service Officer 1938-64. Served in Havana, State Department,
Madrid, The Hague, Paris, Ambassador to Colombia
1955, to Bolivia 1957, to Cuba 1959, to Morocco 1961-
63. Foreign Service Inspector 1963-64.
Cuba, Castro and the United States. Pittsburgh: University of Pittsburgh Press, 1971. 330 p.

BONSAL, Stephen, 1865-1951. Newspaper correspondent,

writer.   Covered Bulgarian-Servian war, Macedonian
uprising, Sino-Japanese war, Cuban insurrection,
Spanish-American war, China Relief Expedition, Matos
revolution in Nevezuela, Russo-Japanese war, Madero
revolution in Mexico, etc.   Secretary of Legation and
Chargé d'Affaires in Madrid, Peking, Tokyo and Korea
1893-97.
The American Mediterranean.   New York: Moffat, Yard
   Co., 1912.   488 p.
Edward Fitzgerald Beale: A Pioneer in the Path of Em-
   pire, 1822-1903.   New York: G. P. Putnam's Sons,
   1912.   312 p.
The Fight for Santiago: The Story of the Soldiers in the
   Cuban Campaign.   From Tampa to the Surrender.
   New York: Doubleday & McClure, 1899.   543 p.
The Golden Horseshoe: Extracts from Letters of Captain
   H. L. Herndon - On Duty in the Philippine Islands.
   New York: Macmillan Co., 1900.   316 p.
Heyday in a Vanished World.   New York: W. W. Norton
   Co., 1937.   455 p.
Morocco As It Is, With an Account of Sir Charles Evan
   Smith's Recent Mission to Fez.   London: W. H. Allen
   Co., 1894.   349 p.
The Real Condition of Cuba Today.   New York: Harper
   & Bros., 1897.   156 p.
Suitors and Suppliants: The Little Nations at Versailles.
   Introd. by Arthur Krock.   Port Washington, N.Y.:
   Kennikat Press, 1946.   301 p.
Unfinished Business.   Paris-Versailles 1919.   Introd. by
   Hugh Gibson.   Garden City, N.Y.:   Doubleday, Doran
   Co., 1944.   313 p.   [Excerpts from author's diary
   while President Wilson's confidential interpreter at the
   Paris Peace Conference in 1919.]   Pulitzer Prize.
When the French Were Here.   From unpublished reports
   and letters in archives of France and the Library of
   Congress.   Port Washington, N.Y.:   Kennikat Press,
   1945.   263 p.
The Cause of Liberty.   London: M. Joseph Ltd., 1947.
   240 p.   Originally When the French Were Here.

BOOTHE, Clare   (See Clare Boothe Luce)

BOWDOIN, James, 1752-1811.   Merchant.   Minister to Spain
   1804-14.   Conducted negotiations for cession of Florida
   from England and France.   Spain was then under Napoleon.
Opinions Respecting the Commercial Intercourse Between

The United States of America, and the Dominions of
Great Britain, Including Observations upon the neces-
sity of an American Navigation Act. Boston: Printed
and sold by Samuel Hall, No. 53 Cornhill, 1797. 61 p.
(Translated) Instruction Pour Les Bergers et Pour Les
Propietaires de Troupeaus. by Louis Daubenton.
Paris: Mme. Huzard, 1810. 480 p.

BOWEN, Herbert Wolcott, 1856-1927. Writer, Consul and
Consul General at Barcelona 1890-1899. Minister
Resident and Consul General to Persia 1899-1901.
Minister to Venezuela 1901-15.
Before the International Tribunal at The Hague: Great
Britain, Germany, and Italy Against Venezuela et al.
Preliminary Examination on Behalf of the United States.
Supplementary to the Preliminary Examination Already
Submitted to the Tribunal on Behalf of Venezuela.
Herbert W. Bowen, William L. Penfield, Counsel.
Washington? 1905? 49 p.
In Divers Tones. Boston: J. G. Cupples, 1890. 123 p.
International Law: A Simple Statement of Its Principles.
New York: G. P. Putnam's Sons, 1896. 165 p.
Losing Ground: A Series of Sonnets. Boston: J. G.
Cupples & Co., 1892. 76 p.
Recollections, Diplomatic and Undiplomatic. New York:
F. H. Hitchcock, 1926. 320 p.
Verses. Boston: Cupples, Upham Co., 1884. 129 p.

BOWERS, Claude Gernade, 1879-1958. Journalist, historian,
writer, editor, columnist, politician. Ambassador to
Spain 1933-39; to Chile 1939-53.
Beveridge and the Progressive Era. Boston: Houghton
Mifflin Co., for New York Literary Guild, 1932.
610 p.
Chile Through Embassy Windows. New York: Simon &
Schuster, 1958. 375 p.
Indianapolis in the "Gay Nineties": High School Diaries
of Claude G. Bowers. Indianapolis: Indiana Historical
Society, 1964. 241 p.
The Irish Orators: A History of Ireland's Fight for Free-
dom. Indianapolis: The Bobbs-Merrill Co., Inc.,
1916. 528 p.
Jefferson and Hamilton: The Struggle for Democracy in
America. Boston: Houghton Mifflin Co., 1925. 531 p.
Jefferson in Power, The Death Struggles of the Federal-
ists. Boston: Houghton Mifflin Co., 1936. 538 p.
The Life of John Worth Kern. Indianapolis: Hollenbeck

Press, 1918.   475 p.
Making Democracy a Reality: Jefferson, Jackson, Polk.
   Memphis: Memphis State College Press, 1954.   170 p.
My Life: The Memoirs of Claude Bowers.   New York:
   Simon & Schuster, Inc., 1962.   346 p.   Pub. post-
humously by his daughter, Patricia.
My Mission to Spain: Watching the Rehearsal of World
   War II.   New York: Simon & Schuster, Inc., 1954.
   437 p.
The Party Battles of the Jackson Period.   Boston: Hough-
   ton Mifflin Co., 1922.   506 p.
Pierre Vergniaud, Voice of the French Revolution.   New
   York: The Macmillan Co., 1950.   535 p.
The Spanish Adventures of Washington Irving.   Boston:
   Houghton Mifflin Co., 1940.   306 p.
The Tragic Era: The Revolution After Lincoln.   Cam-
   bridge, Mass.: Houghton Mifflin Co., 1920.   567 p.
The Young Jefferson - 1743-1789.   Boston: Houghton
   Mifflin Co., 1945.   544 p.

BOWLES, Chester, 1901- . Advertising, Congressman,
   Governor of Connecticut, politician, author.   Ambas-
   sador to India 1951-53.   Under-Secretary of State and
   Ambassador-at-Large 1961-63.   Ambassador to India
   1963-68.
Ambassador's Report.   New York: Harper Bros., 1954.
   415 p.
American Politics in a Revolutionary World.   Cambridge:
   Harvard University Press, 1956.   131 p.
The Coming Political Breakthrough.   New York: Harper
   Bros., 1959.   209 p.
The Conscience of a Liberal.   New York: Harper & Row,
   Publishers, 1962.   351 p.
The Makings of a Just Society: What the Past War Years
   Have Taught Us About National Development.   New
   Delhi: Delhi University Press, 1963.   120 p.
New Dimensions of Peace.   New York: Harper & Bros.,
   1955.   391 p.
Tomorrow Without Fear.   New York: Simon & Schuster,
   Inc., 1946.   88 p.
Africa's Challenge to America.   Berkeley, Calif.: Uni-
   versity of California Press, 1956.   134 p.
Ideas, People and Peace.   New York: Harper & Bros.,
   1958.   151 p.
A View From New Delhi: Selected Speeches and Writings.
   New Haven: Yale University Press, 1969.   268 p.
Promises to Keep: My Years in Public Life, 1941-1969.

New York: Harper & Row, 1971. 657 p.

BOWLES, Cynthia. Wife of Ambassador Chester Bowles.
At Home in India. New York: Harcourt, Brace Co.,
1956. 180 p. Illus. with photos.

BOWMAN, Heath, 1910- . Author, editor. Foreign Service
Officer 1946-69. Served in Santiago, Washington,
Rome, Paris, Belgrade.
Mexican Odyssey. with Sterling Dickinson. New York:
Willett, Clark & Co., 1935. 292 p.
Westward From Rio. with Sterling Dickinson. New
York: Willett, Clark & Co., 1936. 351 p.
Death is Incidental: A Tale of the Mexican Revolution.
with Sterling Dickinson. Chicago: Willett, Clark Co.,
1937. 111 p.
Crusoe's Island: In the Caribbean. New York: Bobbs-
Merrill Inc., 1939. 339 p.
All Your Born Days. New York: Bobbs-Merrill Inc.,
1939. 348 p.
Hoosier. New York: Bobbs-Merrill Inc., 1941. 360 p.

BOYCE, Katherine Randall, 1898- . Wife of Foreign Ser-
vice Officer Richard Fyfe Boyce. [Q. V.]
Bibliography of American Foreign Service Authors. with
Richard Fyfe Boyce. Metuchen, N. J.: The Scarecrow
Press, 1973.

BOYCE, Richard Fyfe, 1896- . Foreign Service Officer
1920-48. Served in Kingston (Jamaica), Nassau, Ham-
ilton (Ontario), Nuevo Laredo, Barcelona, Yokohama,
Lima, Havana, Melbourne.
The Diplomat's Wife. Fore. by Joseph C. Grew. New
York: Harper Bros., 1956. 230 p.
A History of Dacor. (Diplomatic and Consular Officers,
Retired.) with a chapter on "The Family" by George
Venable Allen. Washington: DACOR, Inc., 1969.
168 p.
Bibliography of American Foreign Service Authors. with
Katherine Randall Boyce. Metuchen, N. J.: The
Scarecrow Press, 1973.

BRADEN, Spruille, 1894- . Mining engineer, manufacturer,
businessman, Special Ambassador and Chairman of the
American Delegation at the Chaco Peace Conference at
Montevideo 1935-37. Ambassador to Colombia 1939-
42, to Cuba 1942-45, to Argentina 1945. Assistant

Secretary of State for Inter-American Affairs 1945-47.
Como Me Agradaria Que Fuesen Algunos Aspectos de la
  Politica Exterior de los Estados Unidos: Tres Conferencias. Lima: Ediciones C. E. U. C., 1960. 63 p.
The Chaco Peace Conference: Report of the Delegation
  of the United States of America of the Peace Conference Held at Buenos Aires, July 1, 1935 - January
  23, 1939. Washington: Government Printing Office,
  1940. 198 p.
Diplomats and Demagogues: the Memoirs of Spruille
  Braden. New Rochelle, N. Y.: Arlington House, 1971.
  496 p.

BRADFORD, Saxton Edward, 1907-1966. Newspaper editor.
  Foreign Service Auxiliary, Foreign Service Reserve,
  Public Affairs Officer 1941-66. Served in Buenos
  Aires, State Department, National War College, Tokyo,
  Madrid, Mexico City. United States Information Agen-
  cy.
The Battle for Buenos Aires. New York: Harcourt,
  Brace, Inc., 1943. 307 p.
Spain In The World. Princeton, N. J.: Van Nostrand
  Co., Inc., 1962. 121 p.

BRETT, Homer, 1877-1965. United States Postal Service
  1898-1911. Foreign Service Officer 1911-41. Served
  in Maskat (Muskat Oman), Tenerife, La Guaira, Caracas, Tacna-Arica, Iquique, Bahia, Nottingham, Bristol, Milan, Rotterdam, Callao-Lima.
Blueprint for Victory. New York: Appleton-Century,
  1942. 215 p.

BRIGGS, Ellis Ormsbee, 1899- . Writer. Foreign Service
  Officer 1925-62. Served in Callao-Lima, Washington,
  Liberia, London, Geneva, Havana, Santiago, Chungking. Chief Division of Latin-American Affairs, Director of Office of American Republics Affairs, Ambassador to Dominican Republic 1944-45, to Uruguay
  1947, to Czechoslovakia 1949, to Korea 1952, to Peru
  1955, to Brazil 1956, to Greece 1959. Career Ambassador.
Shots Heard Round the World. An Ambassador's Hunting
  Adventures on Four Continents. Illus. by Rudolph
  Freund. New York: The Viking Press, Inc., 1957.
  149 p.
Farewell to Foggy Bottom. The Recollections of a Career
  Diplomat. New York: David McKay Inc., 1964.
  306 p.

Anatomy of Diplomacy: The Origin and Execution of
American Foreign Policy. New York: David McKay
Inc., 1968. 248 p.

BRIGGS, Lawrence Palmer, 1880- . Teacher. Foreign
Service Officer 1914-35. Served in Rangoon, Riviere
du Loup, Nuevitas, Bahia, Quebec.
Ancient Khmer Empire. Philadelphia: The American
Philosophical Society, 1951. 295 p.
A Pilgrimage to Angkor, Ancient Khmer Capital. Oak-
land, Calif.: Holmes Book Co., 1943. 95 p.

BROKAW, Clare (Boothe) (See Clare Boothe Luce)
Stuffed Shirts. Illus. by Shermund. New York: H.
Liveright, 1931. 326 p.

BROWN, James, 1766-1835. Minister to France 1823-29.
A Digest of the Civil Law Now in Force in the Territory
of Orleans With Alterations and Amendments to the
Present System of Government. with Moreau Liset.
By Authority. New Orleans: Printed by Bradford &
Anderson, Printers to the Territory, 1808. 491 p.
Letters of James Brown to Henry Clay, 1804-1835. Edit.
by James A. Padgett. New Orleans? 1941? "Re-
printed from the Louisiana Historical Quarterly, Vol.
24, No. 4. October 1941. "

BROWN, John Lackey, 1914- . University professor.
European editor of Houghton Mifflin Co., correspondent
of New York Times and other periodicals. Foreign
Service Reserve Officer, United States Information Ad-
ministration 1949. Foreign Service Officer 1957-68.
Served in Paris, Brussels, Rome, Mexico City.
The Methodus of Jean Bodin. Washington: Catholic Uni-
versity of America Press, 1939. 212 p.
Panorama de la Litterature Contemporaine aux Etats-Unis.
Paris: Gallimard, 1954. Vol. I. Received the Grand
Prix de la Critique. 653 p. Vol. II. Paris: Galli-
mard, 1971. 702 p.
Hemingway. in the collection La Bibliothéque Idéale.
Paris: Gallimard, 1961. 304 p.
Discovering Belgium. Amsterdam-Brussels: Elsevir-
Lumiére, 1957.
Il Gigantesco Teatro: Saggi Europei e Americani. Rome:
Opera Nuove, 1963. 361 p.
Diálogos Trasatlanticos. Mexico: Limusa-Wiley, 1966.
426 p.

Signs. [verse] Paris: Henneuse, 1956. 54 p.
Weights and Measures. [verse] Paris: Henneuse, 1958.
63 p.
Another Language. [verse] Milan: Il Pesce d'Oro, 1961.
56 p.
Numina. [verse] Paris: Henneuse, 1969. 73 p.
Report on France. with Jerome S. Bruner. New York:
Rockefeller Foundation, 1946. (mimeographed form)
(Edited) So You're Going to Paris. Boston: Houghton
Mifflin Co., 1947.

BROWN, John Porter, 1814-1872. Diplomat. Orientalist.
Served in Turkey 1832-72. Assistant Dragoman 1832,
Consul 1835, Dragoman 1836. Consul General 1857.
Secretary 1858. Chargé d'Affaires several times.
The Dervishes; or, Oriental Spiritualism. Edit. with in-
trod. and notes by H. A. Rose, with 23 illustrations.
London: Oxford University Press, 1927. 496 p.
First edition published in 1868.
(Translation) Turkish Evening Entertainments. The Won-
ders of Remarkable Incidents and the Rareties of Anec-
dotes, by Ahmed ibn Hemden the ketkhoda, called the
"Sohailee." New York: G. P. Putnam, 1850. 378 p.
First published in Turkish in 1840.
(Translation) On the Tesavof, or Spiritual Life of the
Saffees. by Muhammed Misri. Journal of the Ameri-
can Oriental Society. Vols. I, II, VIII.
(Translation) Ancient and Modern Constantinople. from
Patriarch Constantine's Greek Guidebook. London:
1868.
(Translation) The Turkish version of Al-Tabaris' Conquest
of Persia By the Arabs. Journal of the American Ori-
ental Society. Vols. I, II and VIII.

BROWN, Winthrop Gilman, 1907- . Lawyer, Exec. officer
Harriman Mission for Economic Affairs, London
1941-45; State Department official 1945-51; Foreign
Service Reserve Officer 1951-56; Foreign Service Officer 1956- . Served in London (Superior Service
Award), New Delhi, Kathmandu, Ambassador to Laos
1960, Career Minister, National War College, (President's Award for Distinguished Federal Civil Service
1963); Ambassador to Korea 1964, State Department,
Career Ambassador, (Distinguished Honor Award 1972).
Wartime Diary. Diary kept while in England November
1941-May 1945. Privately printed. 450 p.
Postmark Asia. Letters from Delhi, Vientiane and Seoul

July 1957 through June 1967. Privately printed. 475 p.

BROWNE, John Ross, 1821-1875. Born in Dublin. Became
United States Senator. Minister to China 1868-69.
Spent many years traveling on whalers as a sailor.
Official reporter for California's first State Constitu-
tional Convention, 1849, for which he received $10,000.
As Minister to China he disagreed with the Burlingame
treaty and was recalled.
A Tour Through Arizona, 1864: or, Adventures in the
Apache Country. Illus. by author. Tucson, Ariz.:
Arizona Silhouette, 1950. 292 p. 500 copies.
An American Family in Germany. Illus. by author. New
York: Harper & Bros., 1866. 381 p.
Crusoe's Island: A Ramble in the Footsteps of Alexander
Selkirk. with sketches of adventure in California and
Washoe. New York: Harper & Bros., 1864. 436 p.
A Dangerous Journey. California 1849. Palo Alto,
Calif.: A. Lites Press, 1950. 93 p. First published
as two articles in Harper's Magazine, May and June
1862.
Etchings of a Whaling Cruise, with Notes of a Sojourn on
the Island of Zanzibar, To Which Is Appended a Brief
History of the Whale Fishery. New York: Harper &
Bros., 1846. 580 p.
Illustrated Mining Adventures: California and Nevada,
1863-1865. Balboa Island, Calif.: Paisano Press,
1961. 207 p.
The Indians of California. San Francisco: Colt Press,
1944. 73 p. Colt Press Series of California Classics.
No. 2.
J. Ross Browne: His Letters, Journals, and Writings.
Edit. with introd. and commentary by Lina Fergusson
Browne. Albuquerque: New Mexico University Press,
1969. 419 p.
The Land of Thor. Illus. by author. New York: Harp-
er & Bros., 1867. 542 p.
A Peep at Washoe, and Washoe Revisited. Illus. by au-
thor. Balboa Island, Calif.: Paisano Press, 1959.
240 p.
Yusef: or, the Journey of the Frangi: A Crusade in the
East. New York: Harper & Bros., 1853. 421 p.
A Report of the Debates in the Constitutional Convention
of California on the Formation of the State Constitution.
in September and October 1849. Washington: printed
by J. T. Towers, 1850. 479 p. In Spanish. Nuevo
York: Imprenta S. W. Benedict, 1851. 439 p.

Report of John Ross Brown on the Mineral Resources of
the States and Territories West of the Rocky Mountains.
Washington: Government Printing Office. (Treasury
Report) 1868.   674 p.
Mineral Resources of the United States, by Special Com-
missioners J. Ross Browne and James W. Taylor.
Washington: Government Printing Office, 1867.   360 p.
The Mariposa Estate: Its Past, Present and Future.
Comprising the official report of J. Ross Browne (U.S.
Commissioner) upon its mineral resources etc. etc.
New York: Russells' American Steam Printing House,
1868.   62 p.

BRUCE, David Kirkpatrick Este, 1898- . Lawyer, business and farming. Government official. Foreign Ser-
vice Officer 1926-28. Served in Rome. Member of
Virginia State Legislature. Banking. Red Cross.
Office of Strategic Services 1941-45. Assistant Secre-
tary of Commerce. Chief of Economic Cooperation
Administration mission to France 1948. Ambassador
to France 1949-52. Under-Secretary of State 1952.
U.S. Observer to European Defense Community in
Paris and to European Coal-Steel Community in Luxem-
bourg 1953. Ambassador to Germany 1957-59, to
Great Britain 1961-68, to Paris Peace Talks with North
Viet-Nam 1970-1971.
Sixteen American Presidents. Indianapolis: The Bobbs-
Merrill Co., 1962.   336 p.
Les Presidents des USA de George Washington a Abraham
Lincoln, 1789-1865. Translated by Pierre Singer.
Paris: Galimard, 1954.   462 p.
Seven Pillars of the Republic. Privately printed. Garden
City, N.Y.: Country Life, Printers. 1936.   337 p.
Revolution to Reconstruction. New York: Doubleday,
Doran & Co., Inc., 1939.   486 p.

BRUCE, James, 1892- . Business executive. Assistant
Military Attaché in Italy. Ambassador to Argentina
1947-49.
Those Perplexing Argentines. London: Longmans Green,
1953.   362 p.

BRYAN, Jack Yeaman, 1907- . Professor of journalism.
Foreign Service Reserve Officer 1948-68. Cultural
Affairs Officer. Served in Bombay, Madras, Cairo,
Tehran, Karachi.
Come to the Bower. New York: The Viking Press, Inc.,

1963. 406 p.

BUCHANAN, James, 1791-1868. Minister to Russia 1832-33, to Great Britain 1853-56. Secretary of State 1845-49. President 1857-61. While Secretary of State he negotiated and signed the "Oregon Treaty" of 1846 with Great Britain and directed the negotiation of the Treaty of Guadalupe Hidalgo of 1848 with Mexico, and sought unsuccessfully to purchase Cuba from Spain. He objected to Secretary of State Marcy's decision that American Ministers wear "only the simple dress of an American citizen." The British permitted him to appear at Court in "frock dress" with the addition of a plain sword.

The Works of James Buchanan Comprising his Speeches, State Papers, and Private Correspondence. collected and edit. by John Bassett Moore. Philadelphia: J. B. Lippincott Co., 1908-11. 12 vols.

The Administration on the Eve of Rebellion: A History of Four Years Before the War. London: S. Low Son & Marston, 1865. 296 p.

The Diary of a Public Man. Foreword by Carl Sandburg. Rutgers University Press, 1946. 137 p.

BUCHANAN, Wiley Thomas, Jr., 1914- . Business executive, politician. Minister to Luxembourg 1953-55. Ambassador to Luxembourg 1955-57. Chief of Protocol 1957-60.

Red Carpet at the White House: Four Years as Chief of Protocol in the Eisenhower Administration. with Arthur Gordon. Introd. by Arthur Krock. New York: E. P. Dutton Co., 1964. 256 p.

BUCHANAN, William-Insco, 1852-1909. Minister to Argentina 1894-99. (Arbitrator in special Boundary Commission between Chile and Argentina to fix the boundary in the Puno de Atacama.) First Minister to Panama 1903-04.

The Central American Peace Conference Held at Washington, D. C. 1907. Report of Mr. William-Insco Buchanan Representing the United States of America. Washington: Government Printing Office, 1908. 97 p.

Report of Mr. William-Insco Buchanan, High Commissioner, Representing the President of the United States to Attend the Inauguration of the Court of Justice for Central America at Cartago, Costa Rica, 1908. Washington: Government Printing Office, 1908. 42 p.

BULLITT, William Christian, 1891-1967. Editor, foreign
correspondent. Assistant to State Department 1917-18.
Attached to the American Commission to Negotiate
Peace, Paris 1918-19. Ambassador to Russia 1933-
36, to France 1936-41, Ambassador-at-Large 1941-42.
Thomas Woodrow Wilson. with Sigmund Freud. London:
Weldenfeld & Nicholson, 1967. 265 p.
The Great Globe Itself. New York: Charles Scribner's
Sons, 1946. 310 p.
It's Not Done Here. New York: Harcourt, Brace Co.,
1926. 374 p.
The Bullitt Mission to Russia: Testimony before the Com-
mittee on Foreign Relations, United States Senate, of
William C. Bullitt. New York: B. W. Huebsch, 1919.
151 p.
Papers, 1916-21. New Haven: Yale University Library,
2 ft.
For the President. Personal and Secret. Correspondence
Between Franklin D. Roosevelt and William C. Bullitt.
Edit. by Orville H Bullitt. Introd. by George F.
Kennan. Boston: Houghton Mifflin Co., 1972. 655 p.

BURGESS, Warren Randolph, 1889- . Banker, government
official. Federal Reserve Bank 1920-38. Under-Secretary of Treasury 1955-57. U.S. Permanent Representative to NATO 1957-64, Paris, with rank of Ambassador.
Europe and America: The Next Ten Years. with James
Robert Huntley. Introd. by Livingston T. Merchant.
New York: Walker & Co., 1970. 232 p.

BURLINGAME, Anson, 1820-1870. Congressman and orator.
Minister to China 1861-68. Promoted the policy of
cooperation among Western powers in China to secure
settlement of disputes with China by diplomacy rather
than by force. Upon resignation as Minister he was
appointed the imperial Chinese envoy to conduct China's
foreign relations. Negotiated the so-called Burlingame
Treaty with Secretary of State William Seward, on behalf of China, putting on record American respect for
China's territorial integrity.
Papers. 1 foot (550 items) in Library of Congress.

BURRITT, Elihu, 1812-1879. Consular Agent in Birmingham,
appointed by Abraham Lincoln. Sometimes called the
"Learned Blacksmith." Mastered 18 ancient and modern languages and 22 dialects. Wrote 30 books among

which are the following. An ardent abolitionist. Spent
several years intermittently in England.
The Children of the Bible. New Britain, Conn.: G. L.
Allen, 1871. 70 p.
Chips from Many Blocks. Toronto: Rose-Belford Pub-
lishers, 1878. 294 p.
Elihu Burritt: A Memorial Volume Containing a Sketch of
his Life and Labors, with Selections from his Writings
and Lectures, and Extracts from his Private Journals
in Europe and America. Edit. by Charles Northend.
New York: D. Appleton Co., 1879. 479 p.
Jacob and Joseph, and the Lesson of Their Lives for the
Young. London: S. Low, Son & Marston, 1870.
162 p.
The Learned Blacksmith: The Letters and Journals of
Elihu Burritt. Edit. by Merle Curti. New York:
Wilson-Erockson, 1937. 241 p.
A Voice from the Back Pews to the Front Seats, in An-
swer to "What Think Ye of Christ?" by a Backpews-
man. London: Longmans, Green, 1872. 450 p.
Journals. 28 vols. in Library of the Institute of New
Britain, Conn.
Sparks from the Anvil. Worcester, Mass.: H. J. How-
land, 1846. 96 p.
Ten Minute Talks on All Sorts of Subjects. with an auto-
biography of the author. Boston: Lee, Shepard &
Dillingham, 1874. 360 p.
Thoughts and Things at Home and Abroad. Boston: Phil-
lips, Sampson & Co., New York: J. C. Derby, 1854.
364 p.
A Walk from London to John O'Groats. London: S. Low,
Son & Marston, 1864. 420 p.
A Walk from London to Land's End and Back. London:
S. Low, Son & Marston, 1865. 464 p. Also in micro-
film in Library of Congress.
Walks in the Black Country, Etc. London: S. Low, Son
& Marston, 1868. 448 p.
Washington's Words to Intending English Emigrants to
America. London: S. Low, Son & Marston, 1870.
127 p.
The Western and Eastern Questions of Europe. Hartford,
Conn.: Hammersley & Co., 1871. 51 p.
The Yearbook of the Nations, for 1855. London: Long-
mans, Brown, Green & Longman's, 1855.

BUSHNELL, John A., 1933- . Foreign Service Reserve
and Foreign Service Officer 1959- . Served in Bogota,

Santo Domingo, San Jose, Geneva.
Australian Company Mergers 1946-1959. Melbourne,
    Australia: Melbourne University Press. London:
    Cambridge University Press, 1961. 223 p.

BUSS, Claude Albert, 1903- . Professor in Political Sci-
    ence. Foreign Service Officer 1929-34. Served in
    Peking, Nanking.
The Art of Crisis. Garden City, N.Y.: Doubleday &
    Co. Inc., 1961. 479 p.
The Far East. New York: The Macmillan Co., 1955.
    738 p.
Asia in the Modern World. New York: The Macmillan
    Co., 1964. 767 p.
The People's Republic of China. Princeton, N.J.: Van
    Nostrand Co., Inc., 1962. 190 p.
The Relation of Tariff Autonomy to the Political Situation
    In China. [thesis] Philadelphia: University of Penn-
    sylvania Press, 1927. 141 p.
Southwest Asia and the World Today. Princeton, N.J.:
    D. Van Nostrand Co., Inc., 1958. 192 p.
War and Diplomacy in Eastern Asia. New York: The
    Macmillan Co., 1941. 570 p.

BUTRICK, Richard Porter, 1894- . Foreign Service Offi-
    cer 1921-59. Served in Iquique, Guayaquil, Hankow,
    Washington, St. John (New Brunswick), Shanghai, Pe-
    king, (interned by the Japanese 1941), Santiago, For-
    eign Service Inspector, Minister to Iceland, Career
    Minister. Director General of the Foreign Service.
    Consul General with personal rank of Minister at Mon-
    treal and at Sao Paulo.
American University Club of Shanghai. Shanghai: Amer-
    ican University Club. Comacrib Press, 1936. 233 p.
(Translation) Orestes and I. a play in 3 acts by Juan
    Marin, Chilean Chargé d'Affaires in Peking. From
    Spanish to English. Tokyo: Asia-America, 1940.
    66 p.

BYERS, Samuel Hawkins Marshall, 1838-1933. Civil War
    veteran with rank of Major. In Consular Service from
    1869-93. Served in Zurich, Rome, St. Gall.
Iowa in War Times. Des Moines: W. D. Condit Co.,
    1888. 615 p.
Allatoona. a play staged in Des Moines. 1905. 122 p.
The Bells of Capistrano. Romance of the California mis-
    sions. Los Angeles: Grafton Publishing Corporation,

1915. 45 p.
The Happy Isles and Other Poems. New York: C. L.
Webster Co., 1891. 162 p.
A Layman's Life of Jesus. New York: Neale Publishing
Co., 1912. 108 p.
The March of the Sea. A poem. Boston: Arena Pub-
lishing Co., 1896. 149 p.
Pocahontas. Melodrama in 3 acts. 1875. 91 p. staged.
Poems. New York: Neale Publishing Co., 1914. 149 p.
The Pony Express and Other Poems, New and Old. Los
Angeles: Times-Mirror Printers, 1925. 95 p.
Switzerland and the Swiss, By an American Resident.
Zurich: Orell, Fussli & Co., 1875. 203 p.
Twenty Years in Europe - A Consul General's Memories,
Etc. Chicago: Rand, McNally & Co., 1900. 320 p.
What I Saw in Dixie: Or Sixteen Months in Rebel Prisons.
Dansville, N.Y.: Robbins & Poore, 1868. 126 p.
With Fire and Sword. New York: Neale Publishing Co.,
1911. 203 p.

CABOT, John Moors, 1901- . Foreign Service Officer
1926-67. Served in Callao-Lima, Santo Domingo,
Mexico City, Rio de Janeiro, The Hague, Stockholm,
Guatemala City, Washington, Buenos Aires, Belgrade,
National War College, Shanghai, Minister to Finland
1950, Ass't Secretary of State for Inter-American Af-
fairs 1953, Ambassador to Sweden 1954, to Colombia
1957, to Brazil 1959, to Poland 1962, Deputy Com-
mandant National War College 1965-67. Career Min-
ister.
The Racial Conflict in Transylvania. [Thesis.] Philip
C. Washburn Prize. Rewritten and revised. Boston:
Beacon Press, 1926. 206 p.
Toward Our Common American Destiny: Speeches and
Interviews. Medford, Mass.: Fletcher School of Law
and Diplomacy, 1956. 214 p.

CALDWELL, John Cope, 1913- . Born in China of Ameri-
can parents. Specialist conservation education, 1935-
43. Office of War Information, China Branch 1943-45.
State Department and Foreign Service Reserve Officer
1945-50. Served in Seoul, Washington.
American Agent. with Mark Gayn. New York: Henry
Holt, 1947. 220 p. The story of John Caldwell,
American Agent in China 1943-44.
Children of Calamity. New York: The John Day Co.,
Inc., 1957. 191 p.

China Coast Family. Chicago: Henry Regnery Co., 1953.
228 p.
Communism in Our World. Foreword by Harry D. Gide-
onese. New York: The John Day Co. Inc., 1956.
126 p.
Far East Travel Guide. New York: The John Day Co.
Inc., 1959. 246 p.
John C. Caldwell's Far Pacific Travel Guide. New York:
The John Day Co. Inc., 1966. 384 p.
The Korea Story. with Lesley Frost. Chicago: Henry
Regnery Co., 1952. 180 p. [QV Leslie Frost Bal-
lantine]
The Let's Visit series. All published by the John Day
Co. Inc. in New York: all 96 p.
Afghanistan 1968; Australia 1963; Central America 1964;
Ceylon 1960; Americans Overseas: The Story of For-
eign Aid, Voice of America, Military Assistance and
Bases 1958; Brazil 1961; Canada 1964; Chile 1963;
China 1959; Colombia 1960; Formosa 1956; France
1967, joint author; Indonesia 1960; Italy, with Bartlett
Vernon 1968; Japan 1959; Korea 1959; Malaysia 1968;
Mexico 1968; Middle East, Central Africa, the Congo
1958; New Zealand 1963; Pakistan 1960; Peru 1962;
Russia, with Julian Popescu 1968; Scotland, with Angus
MacVicar 1967; South Africa, with Bernard Newman
1968; Southeast Asia and Hong Kong 1957; Thailand
1967; Middle East 1958 and 1966; Philippines 1961;
South Pacific 1963; West Indies 1966; Venezuela 1962;
Vietnam 1966; West Africa 1959 and 1962.
Massage Girl and Other Sketches of Thailand. New York:
The John Day Co., 1968. 255 p.
Our Friends the Tigers. London: Hutchinson, 1954.
176 p.
Our Land and Our Living. with James L. Bailey and
Richard W. Watkins. Syracuse, N.Y.: L. W. Singer
Co., 1941.
Our Neighbors in Africa. with Elsie F. Caldwell. Illus.
by Heidi Ogawa. New York: The John Day Co., 1961.
48 p.
Our Neighbors in Brazil. with Elsie F. Caldwell. Draw-
ings by Barbara Ewald. New York: The John Day
Co., 1962. 48 p.
Our Neighbours in Central America. with Elsie F. Cald-
well. Drawings by Barbara Ewald. New York: The
John Day Co., 1967. 48 p.
Our Neighbors in India. with Elsie F. Caldwell. Draw-
ings by Heidi Ogawa. New York: The John Day Co.,

1960. 48 p.
Our Neighbors in Japan. with Elsie F. Caldwell. Draw-
  ings by Heidi Ogawa. New York: The John Day Co.,
  1960. 48 p.
Our Neighbors in Korea. with Elsie F. Caldwell. Draw-
  ings by Heidi Ogawa. New York: The John Day Co.,
  1961. 48 p.
Our Neighbors in Australia and New Zealand. with Elsie
  F. Caldwell. Drawings by Barbara Ewald. New
  York: The John Day Co., 1967. 48 p.
Same series: Peru 1969; Philippines 1961; Thailand 1968.
South Asia Travel Guide. New York: The John Day Co.,
  1960. 252 p.
South China Birds. with Harry R. Caldwell. Color illus.
  plates by Professor Andrew Allison. Stories and leg-
  ends by Muriel E. Caldwell. Shanghai: H. M. Van-
  derburgh, 1931. 447 p.
South of Tokyo. Chicago: Henry Regnery Co., 1957.
  100 p.
Still the Rice Grows Green: Asia in the Aftermath of
  Geneva and Panmujon. Chicago: Henry Regnery Co.,
  1955. 312 p.

CAMBRELENG, Churchill Caldom, 1786-1862. Congressman.
  Minister Russia 1840-41.
The American Chancery Digest: Being a Digested Index
  of All Important Decisions in Equity in the United States
  Courts of the Several States. with John D. Campbell.
  New York: Gould and Banks. Albany: W. Gould Co.,
  1828. 581 p.
Report of the Chairman of the Committee on Commerce
  and Navigation. Washington: Government Printing Office, 1840. 72 p.
An Examination of the New Tariff Proposed by the Honorable Henry Baldwin. New York: Gould & Banks, 1821.
  268 p.

CAMPBELL, John Franklin, 1940-1971. Foreign Service
  Officer 1962- . Served in Bonn, State Department,
  Asmara.
The Foreign Affairs Fudge Factory. New York: Basic
  Books, Inc., 1971. 292 p.

CARMICHAEL, William, -1795. Assistant to Silas Deane,
  secret agent of Congress at Paris, spring of 1776,
  went to Berlin in American interests, fall of 1776.
  Secretary to commissioners in France, commissioned

in 1777 but did not act and returned to United States in 1778. Secretary to John Jay, Minister Plenipotentiary to Spain, 1779. Chargé d'Affaires ad interim to Spain, assumed office 1782, formally received 1783. Served till 1794.
Letters of William Carmichael. Manuscript Room of Library of Congress.

CARTER, John Franklin, 1897-1967. (Pseud: "Diplomat, " "Franklin") Employed in American embassies in Rome and Constantinople 1918-19. Private secretary to Ambassador in Rome 1920-21. Economic specialist in State Department 1928-32. Newspaper correspondent in Rome and Washington. Columnist and radio commentator.
American Messiahs, by the Unofficial Observer. with others. Introd. by Donald Stewart. Port Washington, N.Y.: Kennikat Press, 1969. 238 p. reprint of 1935 edit.
Brain Trust Murder. by Diplomat. New York: Coward McCann, 1935.
Catoctin, Etc. Introd. by Sumner Welles. Imaginary conversation between Roosevelt and Churchill, "Putzi" Hanfstaengl, Bernard Baruch, Harry Hopkins and Jay Franklin. by Franklin. New York: Charles Scribner's Sons, 1947. 283 p.
Champagne Charlie. by Jay Franklin. New York: Buel, Sloan, Pearce, 1950. 190 p.
Conquest: America's Painless Imperialism. New York: Harcourt, Brace Co. , 1928. 348 p.
Corpse on the White House Lawn. by Diplomat. New York: Covia, Friede, 1931. 274 p.
Death in the Senate. by Diplomat. New York: Covia, Friede, 1953. 325 p.
The Future is Ours. (study of racial survival) New York: Modern Age Books, 1939. 208 p.
Bible. New Testament Gospels. English Harmonics 1961. American Standard. A Layman's Harmony of the Gospels. Nashville: Broadman Press, 1961. 364 p.
LaGuardia: A Biography. research by Joseph C. Bailey. New York: Modern Age Books, 1937. 176 p.
Man Is War. Indianapolis: The Bobbs-Merrill Co. , Inc. , 1926. 398 p.
Murder in the Embassy. by Diplomat. New York: J. Cape & H. Smith, 1930. 250 p.
Murder in the State Department. by Diplomat. New York: J. Cape & H. Smith, 1930. 253 p.

The New Dealers. by Unofficial Observer. New York:
    Simon & Schuster, 1934. 414 p. The lowdown on the
    higher ups. With others.
1940. by Franklin. New York: The Viking Press, Inc.,
    1940. 319 p.
Our Lords and Masters: Known and Unknown Rulers of
    the World. by Unofficial Observer. New York: Simon
    & Schuster, 1935. 389 p.
Power and Persuasion. New York: Durell, Sloan &
    Pearce, 1960. 200 p.
The Rat Race. by Franklin. Los Angeles: Fantasy
    Publishing Co., 1950. 371 p.
The Rectory Family. Illus. by Oscar Howard. New
    York: Coward & McCann, 1937. 275 p.
Remaking America. by Franklin. Boston: Houghton
    Mifflin Co., 1942.
Republicans on the Potomac: The New Republicans in
    Action. by Franklin. New York: McBride Co., 1953.
    288 p.
Scandal in the Chancery. New York: J. Cape & H.
    Smith, 1931. 272 p.
Slow Death to Geneva. by Diplomat. New York: Coward
    & McCann, 1934. 305 p.
What This Country Needs. by Franklin. New York:
    Covici-Friede, 1931. 256 p.
What We Are About to Receive. New York: Covici-
    Friede, 1932. 282 p. Also Freeport, N.Y.: Books
    for Libraries Press, 1968. 243 p.
The Drew Pearson Story. by Jay Franklin (pseud.) with
    Frank L. Kluckhohn. Chicago: C. Hallberg, 1967.
    181 p.

CASS, Lewis, 1782-1866. Governor of the Territory of
    Michigan 1813-31; Secretary of War 1831-36; Minister
    to France 1836-42; Senator from Michigan 1845-48,
    1849-57; joined Union Forces during Civil War. Sec-
    retary of State 1857-60.
France, Its King, Court, and Government, by an Ameri-
    can. [Collection of essays during his mission to
    France.] New York: Wiley & Putnam, 1840. 191 p.
The Cass Code or Digest of Laws of the Territory of
    Michigan in Force in 1816. Lansing, Mich.: Printers
    to the State. Vol. 1, pp. 107-230. 1871.
An Examination of the Question, Now in Discussion, Be-
    tween the American and British Governments Concern-
    ing the Right of Search. by an American. Baltimore:
    W. Hickman, 1842. 55 p. Paris: H. Fournier.

82 p. [In French.]
Letter from Secretary of War re Indian Affairs in the
     Territory of Michigan during 1820-21. Washington:
     Gales & Seaton, 1822. 132 p. (17th Congress. First
     Session of the House.)
The Life of General Lewis Cass, with his Letters and
     Speeches on Various Subjects. Baltimore: N. Hick-
     man, 1848.

CATHCART, James Leander, 1767-1843. Seaman. Captured
     by Algerians in 1785 and sold into slavery. Became
     clerk of the galley slaves, keeper of the prison tavern,
     clerk to the Prime Minister, chief Christian secretary
     to the Dey and Regency. Appointed American Consul
     at Tripoli and Special Diplomatic Agent in 1798 to ac-
     company William Eaton to Tunis and on to Tripoli.
     Appointed Consul General at Algiers in 1802, then
     Tunis 1803, Consul at Madeira 1807-15, Cadiz 1815-17.
The Captives. (The journal of his captivity compiled and
     published by his daughter, Mrs. Jane B. Newkirk.)
     LaPorte, Ind.: LaPorte Herald Press, 1899. 312 p.
Tripoli, First War with the United States, Inner History,
     Letter Book by James Leander Cathcart, First Consul
     to Tripoli, and Last Letters from Tunis. Compiled
     by his daughter, J. B. Cathcart Newkirk. Daughters
     of the American Revolution. LaPorte, Ind.: LaPorte
     Herald Press, 1901. 355 p.
The Diplomatic Journal and Letter Book of James Leander
     Cathcart, 1788-1796. Worcester, Mass.: American
     Antiquarian Society. Vol. 64. pp. 303-346.

CERWIN, Herbert, 1908- . Foreign Service Reserve officer
     1951-53. Served in Rio de Janeiro.
Bernal Diaz, Historian of the Conquest. Norman, Okla.:
     Oklahoma University Press, 1963. 239 p.
Famous Recipes by Famous People. Illus. by Sinclair
     Ross. San Francisco: Sunset Magazine and Hotel del
     Monte, 1940. 62 p.
In Search of Something: Memoirs of a Public Relations
     Man. Introd. by Frank H. Bartholomew. Los Angeles:
     Sherbourne Press, 1966. 318 p.
These Are the Mexicans. New York: Reynal & Hitchcock,
     1947. 384 p.

CHAMBERLAIN, George Agnew, 1879-1966. Novelist. Born
     in Sao Paulo, Brazil, of American parents. Foreign
     Service Officer 1902-19. Served in Rio, Bahia, Per-

nambuco, Lourenco Marques, Mexico City.
African Hunting Among the Thongas.   Photo. illus. by
Charles Anderson Cass and author.   New York: Harper
Bros. , 1923.   286 p.
The Auction.   Indianapolis: Bobbs-Merrill Co. , 1933.
296 p.
Bride of Bridal Hill.   Indianapolis: Bobbs-Merrill Co. ,
1942.   229 p.
Cobweb.   New York: Harper Bros. , 1921.   312 p.
The Great Van Suttart Mystery.   New York: G. P. Put-
nam's Sons, 1925.   315 p.
Highboy Rings Down the Curtain.   Bridgeton, N. J. :
Evening News Co. , 1923.   55 p.
Home.   Illus. by Reginald B. Birch.   New York: Century
Co. , 1914.   337 p.
In Defense of Mrs. Mason.   Indianapolis: Bobbs-Merrill
Co. , 1938.   320 p.
Is Mexico Worth Saving?   Indianapolis: Bobbs-Merrill
Co. , 1920.   251 p.
John Bogardus.   Illus. by W. T. Benda.   New York:
Century, 1916.   344 p.
Knoll Island.   Indianapolis: Bobbs-Merrill Co. , 1943.
299 p.
The Lantern on the Plow.   New York: Harper Bros. ,
1924.   409 p.
Lip Malvy's Wife.   New York: Harper Bros. , 1923.
307 p.
Lord Buff and the Silver Star.   Illus. by Wesley Dennis.
New York: A. S. Barnes & Co. , Inc. , 1955.   116 p.
Lost.   play in 7 settings.   New York: G. P. Putnam's
Sons, 1926.   239 p.
Lovely Reason: A Story to Dispel Dull Care.   Mexico
City: Privately printed by Blan Bros. , 1918.   81 p.
Man Alone.   New York: G. P. Putnam's Sons, 1926.
349 p.
Marriage for Revenue.   Indianapolis: Bobbs-Merrill Co. ,
1934.   314 p.
Midnight Boy.   Indianapolis: Bobbs-Merrill Co. , 1949.
258 p.
Mr. Trumper Bromleigh Presents no Ugly Duckling.   New
York: G. P. Putnam's Sons, 1926.   387 p.
Night at Lost End.   New York: Brewer, Warren & Put-
nam, 1931.   273 p.
Not All the King's Horses.   Indianapolis: Bobbs-Merrill
Co. , 1919.   309 p.
Overcoat Meeting.   New York: A. S. Barnes & Co. Inc. ,
1949.   185 p.

The Phantom Filly. Indianapolis: Bobbs-Merrill Co.,
    1942.   241 p.
Pigs to Market. Indianapolis: Bobbs-Merrill Co., 1920.
    319 p.
Rackhouse. New York: Harper Bros., 1922.   302 p.
The Red House. Indianapolis: Bobbs-Merrill Co., 1945.
    221 p.
River to the Sea. New York: Brewer & Warren, 1936.
    241 p.
Scudda-Hoo! Scudda-Hay! Indianapolis: Bobbs-Merrill
    Co., 1946.   208 p.
The Silver Cord. New York: G. P. Putnam's Sons,
    1927.   389 p.
The Stranger at the Feast. New York: G. P. Putnam's
    Sons, 1928.   352 p.
The Taken Child. New York: G. P. Putnam's Sons,
    1928.   374 p.
Taxi. Illus. by Lejaren A. Hiller. Indianapolis: Bobbs-
    Merrill Co., 1920.   222 p.
Through Stained Glass. New York: Century, 1915.
    354 p.
Two on Safari. Indianapolis: Bobbs-Merrill Co., 1935.
    314 p.
When Beggars Ride. New York: G. P. Putnam's Sons,
    1930.   344 p.
White Man. Illus. by W. H. D. Koerner. Indianapolis:
    Bobbs-Merrill Co., 1919.   299 p.

CHAMBERLIN, Charles Dean, 1926- . Teacher. Foreign
    Service Staff and Cultural Officer 1951- . United
    States Information Agency. Served in Frankfurt, Bonn,
    Stuttgart.
Did They Succeed in College? with Enid Chamberlin,
    Neal E. Drought and William E. Scott. Follow-up
    study of graduates of thirty schools. New York:
    Harper Bros., 1942.   291 p.
American Educational Fellowship. Evaluation of 8-year
    study. Chicago: Progressive Education Association,
    1941.   252 p.

CHANDLER, Joseph Ripley, 1792-1880. Journalist, Con-
    gressman. Editorial writer on Gazette of the United
    States, 1822. Minister to the Two Sicilies 1858-61.
The Beverly Family: or Home Influence of Religion.
    Philadelphia: P. F. Cunningham & Son, 1875.   166 p.
Chandler's Common School Grammar: a Grammar of the
    English Language: Adapted to the Schools of America.

Philadelphia: Thomas Copperthwaite, 1848. 208 p.
Outline of Penology. Philadelphia: Social Science Asso-
ciation of Philadelphia, 1874. 24 p.
Report Made to the Philadelphia Society for Alleviating the
Miseries of Public Prisons, on the Proceedings of the
International Congress. Philadelphia: Press of J. B.
Chandler, 1872. 101 p.

CHARLICK, Carl, 1907- . Born in Austria. Naturalized.
Travel agent, research writer. Chief translation editor
United States Military Government, Bonn. Foreign
Service Staff officer, High Commissioner's office,
Bonn. 1949-51.
The Metropolitan Club of Washington: the Story of the
Men and Its Place in City and Country. Washington:
1964. 307 p.

CHILD, Julia, 1913- . Wife of Cultural Affairs Officer
Paul Child. Mrs. Child joined the Office of Security
Services in World War II. She was sent to Asia where
she met and married Paul Child. He was later Cul-
tural Attache in France and in Norway 1945-63. Mrs.
Child has appeared on National Educational Television
in her own weekly half-hour program on French cook-
ing, titled "The French Chef" since 1967. With
Louisette Bertholle and Simone Beck she founded and
operated a cooking school in Paris, "L'Ecole des
Trois Gourmanes."
Mastering the Art of French Cooking. with Louisette
Bertholle and Simone Beck. New York: Alfred A.
Knopf, 1961. 684 p.
The French Chef Cookbook. New York: Alfred A. Knopf,
1968. 450 p. [This comprises 119 television pro-
grams.]
Mastering the Art of French Cooking. Volume Two. A
New Repertory of Dishes and Techniques Carries the
Reader into New Areas of Mastering the Art of French
Cooking. with Simone Beck. New York: Alfred A.
Knopf, 1970. 599 p.

CHILD, Maude Parker. (See Parker, Maude.) Wife of
Richard Washburne Child, Ambassador to Italy 1921-
24. [Q.V.]
The Social Side of Diplomatic Life. Indianapolis: Bobbs-
Merrill Co., 1926. 305 p.

CHILD, Richard Washburne, 1881-1935. Lawyer, editor,

author. Ambassador to Italy 1921-24. U. S. Delegate
to the Genoa and Lausanne conferences 1922.
Bodbank. New York: Henry Holt, 1916. 437 p.
A Diplomat Looks at Europe. New York: Duffield, 1925.
301 p.
The Hands of Nara. New York: E. P. Dutton & Co.
Inc., 1922. 326 p.
Jim Hands. Frontispiece by J. A. Dilliams. New York:
Macmillan Co., 1910. 358 p.
The Man in the Shadow. [short stories] New York: The
Macmillan Co., 1911. 372 p.
The Pitcher of Romance. [short stories] New York: J.
H. Sears Publishing Co., 1930. 300 p.
Potential Russia. New York: E. P. Dutton & Co. Inc.,
1916. 221 p.
The Vanishing Men. New York: E. P. Dutton & Co.
Inc., 1920. 324 p.
The Velvet Black. [short stories] New York: E. P.
Dutton & Co. Inc., 1921. 387 p.
The Writing on the Wall: Who Shall Govern Us Next?
New York: J. H. Sears Publishing Co., 1929. 274 p.

CHILDS, James Rives, 1893- . Foreign Service Officer
1923-53. Served in Jerusalem, Bucharest, Cairo,
Teheran, State Department, Tangier, Gibraltar, Paris,
Minister to Saudi Arabia and to Yemen 1946; Career
Minister, Ambassador to Saudi Arabia 1949, to Ethi-
opia 1951-53.
Reliques of the Rives (Ryves). Lynchburg, Va. : J. P.
Bell, 1929. 750 p. Genealogy of the Ryves family of
Dorset, England, and the Rives of Virginia. Two sup-
plements published in Virginia Magazine of History and
Biography, July 1957 and July 1963.
Before the Curtain Falls. Indianapolis: Bobbs-Merrill
Co., 1932. 333 p. Anonymous--fictionalized auto-
biography.
German Military Ciphers from February to November,
1918. Signal Intelligence Section, War Department.
Washington: Government Printing Office, 1935.
The Pageant of Persia. A Record of Travel by Motor in
Persia with an Account of Its Ancient and Modern
Ways. by Henry Filmer (pseud.). Indianapolis:
Bobbs-Merrill Co., 1936. 422 p.
Escape to Cairo. by Henry Filmer (pseud.). Indianapo-
lis: Bobbs-Merrill Co., 1938. 280 p. [fiction]
American Foreign Service. New York: Henry Holt, 1948.
261 p. Foreword by Joseph C. Grew.

Restif de la Bretonne, Temoignages et Jugements, Bib-
liographie. Preface du Prof. Pasteur Vallery-Radot
de l'Academie Francaise. Paris: Briffant, 1949.
369 p.
Casanoviana, an Annotated World Bibliography of Jacques
Casanova de Seingalt and of Works Concerning Him.
Vienna: Nebehay, 1956. 396 p.
Casanova, a Biography Based on New Documents. Lon-
don: George Allen and Unwin, Ltd., 1961. 323 p.
Giacomo Casanova de Seingalt in Selbstzeugnissen und
Bildokumenten. Rowohlt: 1960. 178 p.
Casanova, Biographie Nouvelle d'Apres des Documents
Inedits. Paris: Chez Jean-Jacques Pauvert, 1962.
465 p.
Casanova. Milano: Area, 1962. 164 p.
Giacomo Casanova de Seingalt. Tokyo: Orion Press,
1968. 189 p. Also translated into Japanese from the
German edition of 1960.
Diplomatic and Literary Quests. Four lectures given at
Randolph-Macon College, Ashland, Va., first in the
Walter Hines Page Library Visiting Lecturer series.
Richmond, Va.: Whittet & Shepperson, 1966. 102 p.
Collector's Quest: The Correspondence of Henry J. Miller
and J. Rives Childs. 1947-65. with Henry J. Miller.
Introd. by Richard Clement Wood. Charlottesville,
Va.: published for Randolph-Macon College, Ashland,
Va. by the University Press of Virginia. 1968. 216 p.
Foreign Service Farewell: My Years in the Near East.
Charlottesville, Va.: University of Virginia Press,
1969. 192 p.
The Hidden Possibilities of Man. with Marcelle de Jou-
venel. Richmond: Whittet & Shepperson, 1966. 47 p.
[seminar papers.]
Memoirs of Casanova. Del Mar, Calif.: The Limited
Editions Club, 1972. 560 p.

CHOATE, Joseph Hodges, 1832-1917. Lawyer, public speak-
er. Ambassador to Great Britain 1899-1905. Head of
U. S. Delegation to the Second Hague Conference 1907.
Boyhood and Youth of Joseph Hodges Choate. New York:
privately printed by Scribner Press, 1917. 153 p.
Arguments and Addresses of Joseph Hodges Choate. col-
lected and edit. by Frederick C. Hicks. St. Paul:
West Publishing Co., 1926. 1189 p. Includes a
memorial by Elihu Root.
Abraham Lincoln and Other Addresses in England. New
York: Century Co., 1910. 293 p.

American Addresses.   New York: Century Co., 1911.
  360 p.
Case of General Fitz-John Porter, regarding the 2nd Battle of Bull Run 1862.   West Point: Courts Martial
  1862-63.   1879.   241 p.
The Choate Story Book: With a Biographic Sketch.   Will
  M. Clemens.   New York: Montgomery Publishing Co.,
  1899.   63 p.
Papers, 1745-1927.   Library of Congress, MSS Div. 20
  ft.
The Two Hague Conferences.   Princeton, N. J. :   Prince-
  ton University Press, 1913.   109 p.
Life of Joseph Hodges Choate as Gathered Chiefly from
  his Letters.   Edit. by Edward Sandford Martin.   New
  York: Charles Scribner's Sons, 1920.   2 vols.
Speeches and Literary Contributions.   1918.   246 p.

CHURCH, George Earl, 1835-1910.   Authority on South
  America, civil engineer, explorer, writer.   Appointed,
  1880, U. S. Commissioner to report on political, finan-
  cial and trade conditions of Ecuador.
Aborigines of South America.   Edit. by Clements R.
  Markham.   London: Chapman Hall, 1912.   314 p.
Mexico.   Its Revolutions: Are They Evidences of Retro-
  gression or of Progress?   A Historical and Political
  Review.   New York: Baker & Godwin, 1866.   84 p.
The Rapids of the Madeira Branch of the Amazon River.
  A Preliminary Report on the Madeira and Mamoré
  Railway.   London: Bates, Hendy Co., 1870.   32 p.
The Route to Bolivia Via the River Amazon.   A Report to
  the Governments of Bolivia and Brazil.   London:
  Waterlow & Sons, 1877.   216 p.
South America: An Outline of its Physical Geography.
  London: W. Clowes & Sons, 1901.   77 p.

CLARK, Joshua Reuben, Jr., 1871-1961.   Lawyer.   Coun-
  selor of the Church of Jesus Christ of Latter-Day
  Saints, Judge Advocate General, Under-Secretary of
  State 1928-29, Ambassador to Mexico 1930-33.
Behold the Lamb of God: Selections from the Sermons
  and Writings, Published and Unpublished, of J. Reuben
  Clark, Jr., on the Life of the Savior.   Salt Lake City:
  Deseret Book Co., 1962.   382 p.
Memorandum on the Monroe Doctrine.   Washington: Gov-
  ernment Printing Office, 1930.   238 p.
On the Way to Immortality and Eternal Life: A Series of
  Radio Talks.   with append.   Salt Lake City: Deseret

Book Co., 1949. 469 p.

Stand Fast by our Constitution. Salt Lake City: Deseret
Book Co., 1962. 214 p.

Why the King James Version: A Series of Study Notes,
Neither Treatises nor Essays, Dealing with Certain
Elementary Problems and Specific Scriptural Passages
Involved in Considering the Preferential English Trans-
lations of the Greek New Testament Text, Etc. Etc.
Salt Lake City: Deseret Book Co., 1956. 473 p.

Emergency Legislation Passed Prior to December, 1919,
Etc. Etc. Collected and annotated and indexed by J.
Reuben Clark. Washington: Government Printing Of-
fice, 1918. 1150 p.

CLARK, Velma B. Clerk in Embassy, Santiago, Chile in
early 1940's.

Not Looked Upon With Favor. Denver: Allan Swallow,
1951. 132 p.

CLAY, Cassius Marcellus, 1810-1903. Slavery abolitionist,
orator. Minister to Russia 1861-62, remained in Russia till 1869.

The Writings and Addresses of Cassius Marcellus Clay,
Including Speeches and Addresses. Edit. with Preface
and Memoir by Horace Greeley. New York: Harper
Bros., 1848. 535 p.

The Life of Cassius Marcellus Clay, Memoirs, Writings
and Speeches, Showing his Conduct in the Overthrow of
American Slavery, the Salvation of the Union, and the
Restoration of the Autonomy of the States: Written
and Compiled by Himself. Cincinnati: J. F. Brennan
Co., 1886. Vol. 1 [no more published].

CLAY, Henry, 1772-1852. Lawyer, politician, Speaker of
Kentucky Legislature, Congressman, Senator, Secretary
of State 1825-29. One of the Commissioners to negotiate the Treaty of Ghent, with Great Britain, 1814.

Works of Henry Clay, Comprising His Life, Correspondence and Speeches. Edit. by Calvin Colton. New
York: Henry Clay Publishing Co., 1897. 7 vols.

The Life and Speeches of Henry Clay. Edit. by Daniel
Mallory. Hartford: S. Andrus & Co., 1855. 2 vols.

Papers. Edit. by James F. Hopkins, Mary W. Har-
greaves, Assoc. Editor. Lexington, Ky.: University
of Kentucky Press, 1959-61. 2 vols.

Speeches of the Honorable Henry Clay in the Congress of
the United States. Edit. by Richard Chambers.

Cincinnati: Stereotyped by Shepard & Stearns, 1842. 504 p.

CLAYTON, Powell, 1833-1914. Politician, Governor of Arkansas, Minister to Mexico 1897-1905. Aftermath of the Civil War in Arkansas. [A defense of his governorship.] New York: Neale Publishing Co., 1915. 378 p.

CLEVELAND, Harlan, 1918- . Writer, publisher, educator. State Department and Economic Cooperation Administration 1942-65. Ass't Secretary of State 1961. Ambassador to NATO, Paris, 1965-68. The Art of Overseasmanship. Edit. by Harlan Cleveland and Gerard J. Mangone. Syracuse: Syracuse University Press, 1957. 150 p. The Overseas Americans. with Gerard J. Mangone and John Clarke Adams. New York: McGraw-Hill Book Co. Inc., 1960. 316 p. The Obligations of Power: American Diplomacy in the Search for Peace. New York: Harper & Row, 1966. 188 p. Conferences on World Tensions. Edit. by Harlan Cleveland. Chicago: University of Chicago Press, 1960. 157 p. Nato: The Transatlantic Bargain. New York: Harper & Row, Publishers, 1970. 204 p. The Future Executive: A Guide for Tomorrow's Managers. New York: Harper & Row, 1972. 144 p.

CLUBB, Oliver Edmund, 1901- . Foreign Service Officer 1928-51. Chinese language officer. Served in Peking, Hankow, Tientsin, Nanking, Shanghai, Saigon, Chungking, Kunming, Tiwa, State Department, Vladivostok, Mukden, Harbin, Changchun. Chinese Development Programs in Manchuria. with Supplement on Inner Mongolia. New York: Institute of Pacific Relations, 1954. 46 p. 20th Century China. New York: Columbia University Press, 1964. 470 p. map. Revised 1972. 526 p. China and Russia: The "Great Game." New York: Columbia University Press, 1971. 578 p. Communism in China, As Reported from Hankow in 1932. New York: Columbia University Press, 1968. 124 p. (Editor and major contributor) Biographical Dictionary of Republican China. New York: Columbia University Press, 1967-70. 4 vols.

CODY, Morrill, 1909- . Foreign correspondent in France
and Spain 1924-34. Art director of a magazine. Foreign Service Officer 1941-64. United States Information Agency. Served in Asuncion, Buenos Aires, Mexico City, State Department, Paris, Stockholm, Madrid.
This Must Be the Place. sub-titled Memoirs of Montpar-
nasse by Jimmie the Barman. Edit. by Morrill Cody.
Illus. by Ivan Opfer and Hilaire Hiler. Introd. by
Ernest Hemingway. Describes many of the writers,
artists and hangers-on of Montparnasse in the 1920's.
"Jimmie the Barman" was James Charters. New
York: Lee Furman, Inc., 1937. 300 p.
Passing Stranger. A novel of the Depression in the
1930's. New York: Lee Furman, Inc., 1936. 254 p.
The Favorite Restaurants of an American in Paris. Paris:
Nouveau Quartier Latin. Illus. by Man Ray. 1966.
228 p.
Hemingway's Paris. New York: Temple, 1965. 221 p.

COERR, Eleanor (Hicks). Wife of Wymberly De R. Coerr.
Mr. Coerr is a Foreign Service Officer 1939- . He
served in Montreal, Mexico City, Suva, Batavia,
Tegucigalpa, Guatemala, National War College, La
Paz, State Department, Ambassador to Uruguay 1962,
to Ecuador 1965, Cornell Univ. 1969, State Department
1972.
The Mystery of the Golden Cat. Rutland, Vermont: C.
E. Tuttle Co., 1968. 68 p.
Circus Day in Japan. Rutland, Vermont: C. E. Tuttle
Co., 1958. 47 p.
Twenty Five Dragons. Illus. by Joann Daley. Chicago:
Follett Publishing Co., 1971. 95 p.

COGGESHALL, William Turner, 1824-1867. Journalist, au-
thor, editor. Minister to Ecuador 1866-69. Obtained
the right of Protestant burial for foreigners in opposi-
tion to the Papal Nuncio in Ecuador.
The Poets and Poetry of the West. Columbus, Ohio:
Follett, Foster, 1860. 688 p.
Index to Ohio Laws, and Resolutions, 1845 to 1857. Co-
lumbus, Ohio: State Printer, 1857. 302 p.
Easy Warren and His Contemporaries: Sketched for Home
Circles. New York: Redfield, 1854. 332 p.
Five Black Arts. A Popular Account of the Historic Pro-
cesses of Manufacture and Uses of Printing, Pottery,
Glass, Iron. Columbus, Ohio: Follet, Foster & Co.,
1861. 392 p.

Lincoln Memorial. Columbus, Ohio: Ohio State Journal,
    1865. 327 p.
The Newspaper Record. United States, Canada, Great
    Britain. Philadelphia: Lay & Bro., 1856. 194 p.
The Signs of the Times: Comprising a History of the
    Spirit Rappings in Cincinnati and Other Places. Cin-
    cinnati: 1851. 144 p.
Cash and Character: A Lecture on High Life. Cincin-
    nati: Moore, Wilstach, Keys & Co., 1855. 62 p.

COLE, Charles Woolsey, 1906- . Professor of history and
    economics. President of Rockefeller Foundation. Am-
    bassador to Chile 1961-64.
Colbert and a Century of French Mercantilism. New
    York: Columbia University Press, 1939. 2 vols.
Economic History of Europe. with Shepard Bancroft
    Clough. Boston: D. C. Heath & Co., 1952. 917 p.
French Mercantilism 1683-1700. New York: Octagon
    Books, 1965. 354 p.
French Mercantilism Doctrines Before Colbert. [1931
    thesis] New York: Octagon Books, 1969. 243 p.
History of Western Civilization. with Carlton J. H.
    Hayes and Marshall Whithed Baldwin. New York:
    Macmillan Co., 1967. 2 vols.

COLLIER, William Miller, 1867-1956. Lawyer, teacher,
    author. Special Assistant Attorney General. Depart-
    ment of Commerce and Labor, Solicitor. Minister to
    Spain 1905-09. President George Washington Univer-
    sity 1917-21. Ambassador to Chile 1921-28.
At the Court of His Catholic Majesty. Chicago: A. C.
    McClurg & Co., 1912. 330 p.
Bankruptcy Act (U. S. Code, Title 11) as Amended to
    February 7, 1938. Albany: M. Bender & Co. Inc.,
    1938. 397 p.
The Civil Service Law of the State of New York. Albany:
    M. Bender & Co., 1901. 440 p.
Gilbert's Collier on Bankruptcy. Albany: M. Bender &
    Co., 1927. 1614 p.
The Official Rules, Forms and General Orders in Bank-
    ruptcy Prescribed by the Supreme Court of the United
    States and Promulgated November 28, 1898. Albany:
    M. Bender & Co., 1899. 663 p.
The Paternal Ancestry of William Miller Collier, former
    Ambassador to Chile. Auburn, N.Y.: 1946.

CONANT, James Bryant, 1893- . Chemistry scientist,

educator, author. President of Harvard 1933-53. U. S. High Commissioner to Germany 1953-55. Ambassador to Germany 1957-58.

The American High School Today. New York: McGraw-Hill Book Co., 1959. 140 p.

The Chemistry of Organic Compounds. New York: The Macmillan Co., 1933. 623 p.

The Child, the Parent and the State. Cambridge: Harvard University Press, 1959. 211 p.

The Citadel of Learning. New Haven: Yale University Press, 1956. 79 p.

The Comprehensive High School. 2nd report to interested citizens. New York: McGraw-Hill Book Co., 1967. 95 p.

Education and Liberty: The Role of Schools in a Modern Democracy. Cambridge: Harvard University Press, 1953. 168 p.

Education for a Classless Society. with Francis T. Spaulding. Cambridge: Harvard University Press, 1940. 43 p.

Education in a Divided World: The Function of the Public Schools In Our Unique Society. Cambridge: Harvard University Press, 1948. 249 p.

The Education of American Teachers. New York: McGraw-Hill Book Co., 1963. 275 p.

Fundamentals of Organic Chemistry. with Harold H. Blatt. New York: The Macmillan Co., 1950. 413 p.

Germany and Freedom: A Personal Appraisal. Cambridge: Harvard University Press, 1958. 117 p.

Harvard Case Histories in Experimental Science. with others. Cambridge: Harvard University Press, 1957. 2 vols.

Modern Science and Modern Man. New York: Columbia University Press, 1952. 111 p. Garden City, N. Y.: Doubleday, 1953. 187 p.

On Understanding Science: An Historical Approach. New Haven: Yale University Press. London: G. Cumberlege, Oxford University, 1947. 145 p.

Organic Chemistry: A Brief Introductory Course. New York: The Macmillan Co., 1928. 291 p. Revised 1936.

Our Fighting Faith. Cambridge: Harvard University Press, 1942. 105 p.

Science and Common Sense. New Haven: Yale University Press, 1951. 371 p.

Shaping Education Policy. New York: McGraw-Hill Book Co., 1964. 139 p.

Slums and Suburbs: A Commentary on Schools in Metro-
  politan Areas. New York: McGraw-Hill Book Co.,
  1961. 147 p.
Thomas Jefferson and the Development of American Public
  Education. Berkeley: University of California Press,
  1962. 164 p.
Two Modes of Thought. My Encounters with Science and
  Education. New York: Trident Press, 1964. 96 p.
My Several Lives: Memoirs of a Social Inventory. New
  York: Harper & Row, 1970. 701 p.

CONGER, Sarah P. Wife of Edwin Hurd Conger, who was
  Minister to Brazil 1890-93 and 1897-98; Minister to
  China 1898-1900; to Mexico 1905-06.
Letters from China with Particular Reference to the Empress Dowager and the Women of China. Illus. and
  map. Chicago: A. C. McClurg, 1909. 392 p.
Old China and Young America. Chicago: F. G. Browne
  Co., 1913.
Catalogue of the Important Private Collection of Mrs. Edwin Hurd Conger. To be sold at unrestricted public
  sale at the American Art Galleries on February 19-22,
  1909. Sale will be conducted by Mr. Thomas E. Kirby
  of the American Art Association, Mgrs. New York:
  American Art Association. J. J. Little & Co., Press.
  145 p.

CONKLING, Alfred, 1789-1874. Congressman, judge, author, lawyer. Minister to Mexico 1852-53.
The Admiralty Jurisdiction, Law and Practice of the
  Courts of the United States: With an Appendix Containing the New Rules of Admiralty Practice Prescribed
  by the Supreme Court of the United States, Those of
  the Circuit and District Courts of the United States and
  for the Northern District of New York, and Numerous
  Practical Forms. Boston: C. C. Little & J. Brown.
  Albany: W. C. Little, 1849. 950 p.
The Powers of the Executive Department of the Govern-
  ment of the United States, and the Political Institutions
  and Constitutional Law of the United States. Albany:
  W. C. Little Co., 1882. 195 p.
A Treatise on the Organization and Jurisdiction of the
  Supreme, Circuit and District Courts of the United
  States, Etc. Etc. New York: Gould, Banks Co. Al-
  bany: W. & A. Gould. 2nd edit. 1882. 634 p.
The Young Citizen's Manual: Being a Digest of the Laws
  of the State of New York and of the United States, Etc.

Etc. New York: W. E. Dean, 1839. 279 p.

CONRAD, Barnaby, Jr., 1922- . Author, artist. Vice
Consul 1943-46. Served in Vigo, Malaga, Seville,
Barcelona. Studied bullfighting and fought bulls in
Spain, Mexico and Peru.
Dangerfield. New York: Harper Bros., 1961. 208 p.
The Death of Manolete. Boston: Houghton Mifflin Co.,
1958. 148 p.
Encyclopaedia of Bullfighting. Boston: Houghton Mifflin
Co., 1961. 269 p.
Famous Last Words. Foreword by Clifton Fadiman.
Garden City, N.Y.: Doubleday, 1961. 208 p.
La Fiesta Brava: The Art of the Bull Ring. Boston:
Houghton Mifflin Co., 1953. 184 p.
Gates of Fear. New York: Thomas Y. Crowell Co.,
1957. 337 p.
How to Fight a Bull. Garden City, N.Y.: Doubleday,
1968. 224 p.
The Innocent Villa. [fiction.] New York: Random House
Inc., 1948. 246 p.
Matador. Illus. by author. Boston: Houghton Mifflin
Co., 1952. 213 p.
San Francisco: A Profile with Pictures. New York:
The Viking Press, Inc., 1959. 218 p.
Tahiti. New York: The Viking Press, Inc., 1962.
164 p.

COOLIDGE, Archibald Cary, 1866-1928. Historian. Acting
Secretary of Legation St. Petersburg 1890-91; Private
Secretary to American Minister to France 1892; Sec-
retary of Legation Vienna 1893; U.S. Delegate (also
representing Harvard University) to Pan American Sci-
entific Congress Santiago 1908-09; Special Agent in
Sweden and Northern Russia 1918. Chief of Mission
at Peace Conference in Paris and Vienna 1919.
The United States, a World Power. New York: The
Macmillan Co., 1908. 385 p. Also in French with
Preface by Anatole Leroy-Beaulieu. Paris: A. Colin,
1908. 415 p. Also in German, Berlin: E. S. Mittler
und Sohn, 1908. 367 p.
Origins of the Triple Alliance. New York: Charles
Scribner's Sons, 1917. 236 p.
Ten Years of War and Peace. Cambridge: Harvard Uni-
versity Press, 1927. 275 p.
Theoretical and Foreign Elements in the Formation of the
American Constitution. Freiburg (Germany): Buchdr.

von C. Lehmann, 1892. 65 p.
(Edited) with Edward Channing. The Barrington-Barnard
   Correspondence and Illustrative Matter, 1760-1770,
   Drawn From the Papers of Sir Francis Bernard.
   Cambridge: Harvard University Press, 1912. 306 p.
(Edited) Turkey. by Sir Edward S. Cressy. Reviewed
   and edited with Harold Claflin. New York: P. F.
   Collier & Son, 1916. 534 p.
(Edited) The Secret Treaties of Austria-Hungary, 1789-
   1914. by Alfred Franzis Pribram. New York: H.
   Fertig, 1967. 2 vols.

COOLIDGE, John Gardner, 1863-1936. World traveler 1887-
   1900. Vice consul Pretoria 1900-01; Secretary of
   Legation and Chargé d'Affaires Peking 1902-06; Sec-
   retary Legation Mexico City 1907-08; Special Agent
   Paris 1914-17; State Department 1918-19.
   Random Letters from Many Countries. Boston: Marshall
      Jones, 1924. 408 p.
   A War Diary in Paris 1914-1917. Private printed. Cam-
      bridge: Riverside Press, 1931. 283 p.

COOLIDGE, Thomas Jefferson, 1831-1920. Merchant, financier. Minister to France 1892-96. Joint High Commissioner of United States, with Great Britain, Canada
   and Newfoundland on the Alaskan boundary, fisheries,
   destruction of fur seals, armaments upon the lakes and
   transportation of goods in bond.
   Thomas Jefferson Coolidge 1831-1920, an Autobiography.
      (Drawn in great part from his diary and brought down
      to the year 1900.) Boston: Privately printed. Merry-
      mount Press, 1902. 410 p.
   Autobiography of Thomas Jefferson Coolidge 1831-1920.
      Boston: Houghton Mifflin Co., 1923. 311 p.

COOPER, James Fenimore, 1789-1851. First major American novelist. Entered Yale at 13, expelled in his
   junior year. Apprentice seaman in 1806. Midshipman
   in U. S. Navy 1808. Resigned 1811 and married.
   First novel published in 1820. Produced 50 separate
   works, of which 31 were novels. Consul at Lyons
   1826.
   The Works of James Fenimore Cooper. Household Edi-
      tion. Boston: Houghton Mifflin Co., 1880. 32 vols.
   Works. Illus. with wood engravings. New York: P. F.
      Collier, 1891-3. 10 vols.
   The Works of James Fenimore Cooper. Mohawk Edit.

New York: G. P. Putnam's Sons, 1912. 32 vols.

Oevres de James Fenimore Cooper. Trans. par A. J. B.
Depau Co. Paris: Furne et Cie., 1839. 24 vols.

Correspondence of James Fenimore Cooper. Edit. by his
grandson. New Haven: Yale University Press, 1922.
2 vols.

Afloat and Ashore. Introd. by Susan Fenimore Cooper.
Boston: Houghton Mifflin Co., 1884. 528 p.

The American Democrat: or Hints on the Social and
Civic Relations of the United States of America.
Cooperstown, N.Y.: H. & E. Phinney, 1838. 192 p.

Autobiography of a Pocket Handkerchief. Notes and Introd. by Walter Lee Brown. Evanston, Ill.: Golden
Book Publishers, 1897. 257 p.

The Battle of Lake Erie, or Answers to Messrs. Burges,
Duer & MacKenzie. Cooperstown: H. & E. Phinney,
1843. 117 p.

The Bravo. London: H. Colburn & R. Bentley, 1831.
3 vols.

The Chainbearer: or the Little Page Manuscript. New
York: Burgess, Stringer & Co., 1845. 2 vols.

The Chronicles of Cooperstown. Cooperstown, N.Y.:
H. & E. Phinney, 1838. 100 p.

The Crater: or Vulcan's Peak. A Tale of the Pacific.
New York: Burgess, Stringer & Co., 1847. 2 vols.

The Cruise of the Somers: Illustrative of the Despotism
of the Quarter-Deck: and of the Unmanly Conduct of
Commodore Mackenzie. New York: J. Winchester,
1844. 132 p.

Gleanings from Europe. Philadelphia: Carey, Lea &
Blanchard, 1837. 2 vols.

Excursions in Italy. Paris: Baudry's European Library,
1838. 335 p.

The Headsman: or the Abbaye des Vignerons. London:
B. Bentley, 1833. 3 vols.

The Heidenmauer: or the Benedictines: a Legend of the
Rhine. Philadelphia: Carey & Lea, 1832. 2 vols.

The Deerslayer. Philadelphia: Lea & Blanchard, 1841.
2 vols.

History of the Navy of the United States. Philadelphia:
Lea & Blanchard, 1839. 2 vols.

Eve Effingham: or, Home. London: R. Bentley, 1838.
3 vols.

Jack Tier: or the Florida Reef. New York: Burgess,
Stringer & Co., 1848. 2 vols.

The Last of the Mohicans: a Narrative of 1757. Philadelphia: H. C. Carey & I. Lea, 1826. 2 vols. Over

35 editions to 1965. Also in Dutch, German, French,
Hebrew, Russian, Norwegian, Portuguese and Spanish.
The Leather Stocking Tales. Riverside Edition. Boston:
Houghton Mifflin Co., 1898-99. 5 vols.
Lionel Lincoln or the Leaguer of Boston. New York: C.
Wiley, 1825. 2 vols.
Mercedes of Castile, or the Voyage to Cathay. Philadel-
phia: Lea & Blanchard, 1840. 2 vols.
Lives of Distinguished Americans. Philadelphia: Carey
& Hart, 1846. 2 vols.
Lucy Harding. London: R. Bentley, 1854. 399 p.
The Monikins. Philadelphia: Carey, Lea & Blanchard,
1835. 2 vols.
Ned Myers: or a Life Before the Mast. Philadelphia:
Lea & Blanchard, 1843. 232 p.
Notions of Americans: Picked Up by a Travelling Bache-
lor. Philadelphia: Lea & Co., 1828. 2 vols.
The Oak Openings, or the Bee Hunter. New York: Bur-
gess, Stringer, 1848. 2 vols.
The Pathfinders: or the Inland Sea. Philadelphia: Lea
& Blanchard, 1840. 2 vols.
The Pilot: a Tale of the Sea. New York: C. Wiley,
1823. 2 vols.
The Pioneers, or the Sources of the Susquehanna. Paris:
Baudry's, 1835. 404 p.
The Prairie. London: H. Colburn, 1827. 3 vols.
Precaution. New York: A. T. Goodrich Co., 1820. 2
vols.
Red Rover. Philadelphia: Carey, Lea & Carey, 1828.
2 vols.
The Redskins, or Indian and Injin. New York: Burgess
& Stringer, 1846. 2 vols.
Satan's Toe: or the Littlepage Manuscripts. New York:
Burgess & Stringer, 1845. 2 vols.
The Sea Lions: or, the Lost Sealers. New York:
Stringer, 1849. 2 vols.
Sketches of Switzerland. Philadelphia: Carey, Lea &
Blanchard, 1836. 2 vols.
The Spy. London: J. T. Davison, 182?. 3 vols.
The Two Admirals. Philadelphia: Lea & Blanchard,
1842. 2 vols.
The Water Witch, or, the Skimmer of the Seas. London:
Colburn & Bentley, 1830. 3 vols.
The Ways of the Hour. New York: G. P. Putnam, 1850.
512 p.
The Wept of Wish-Ton-Wish. Philadelphia: Carey, Lea
& Carey, 1829. 2 vols. Published as "The Borderers"

in 1849.
The Wing-and-Wing, or, Le Feu-follet.   Philadelphia:
Lea & Blanchard, 1842. 2 vols.
Wyandotte, or, the Hutted Knoll.   Philadelphia: Lea &
Blanchard, 1843. 2 vols.

COPELAND, Miles Axe, Jr., 1916- . International business consultant. Foreign Service Staff officer 1947-
50. Served in Damascus as Political Attaché.
The Game of Nations: the Amorality of Power Politics.
New York: Simon & Schuster, Inc., 1970. 318 p.

CORRIGAN, Francis Patrick, 1881-1968. Surgeon. Minis-
ter to Salvador 1934-37, to Panama 1937-39. Special
Ambassador to Venezuela to attend inauguration of the
President 1938.
South America. with Franklin H. Martin. Westwood,
N.J.: Fleming H. Revell Co., 1927. 435 p.

CORRY, Andrew Vincent, 1904- . Geologist. Foreign
Service Officer 1947-70. Served in State Department,
New Delhi, Colombo, Karachi, Rangoon, Katmandu,
Madrid, Lahore, Foreign Service Institute. Ambassa-
dor to Sierra Leone 1964, to Ceylon and Maldive Is.
1967-70.
Grade of Ore. with O. E. Kiessling. Work Projects
Administration in cooperation with the Department of
Interior, Bureau of Mines. Philadelphia: 1938.
114 p.

CORWIN, Thomas, 1794-1865. Lawyer, Governor of Ohio,
Senator, Secretary of the Treasury, politician, orator.
Minister to Mexico 1861-66.
Speeches of Thomas Corwin with a Sketch of his Life. by
Isaac Strohm. Dayton, Ohio: W. F. Comley & Co.,
1859. 518 p.
Corwin Papers. 12 vols. Library of Congress.
Correspondence 1850-1852. 4 ft. Library of Congress.
Life and Speeches of Thomas Corwin, Orator, Lawyer
and Statesman. Edit. by Josiah Morrow. Cincinnati:
W. H. Anderson Co., 1896. 477 p.

CORYELL, John Russell, 1851-1924. Pseudonyms--Nick
Carter, Julia Edwards, Geraldine Fleming and Margaret Grant. Vice Consul in Shanghai and Canton
about 1870-75. Returned to U.S. and after trying
itinerant journalism began his career as a writer of

juvenile and then thriller fiction. Creator of the "Nick Carter" detective stories in the 1880's which continued until his death in 1924. Produced a million words a year, under his pseudonyms, sometimes simultaneously appearing in as many as six different magazines. He turned out 2,740 words (ten pages of finished narrative) a day, every working day of his life, an average short story every two days, eleven book length novels a year.

Among the Nihilists: or, a Plot Against the Czar. New York: Street & Smith, 1898. 187 p.

An Australian Klondike. New York: Street & Smith, 1897. 222 p.

Beautiful But Poor. (Julia Edwards) New York: Street & Smith, 1890. 211 p.

Brought to Bay. (Nick Carter) New York: Street & Smith, 1901. 210 p.

A Child of Love: A Startling Story of the Struggles of a Girl Born Out of Wedlock Against the Sins and Perversions of Today. (Margaret Grant) New York: Physical Culture Publications, 1904. 407 p.

A Dead Man's Grip. New York: Street & Smith, 1899. 232 p.

Denman Thompson's Old Homestead. New York: Street & Smith, 1889. 232 p.

The Detective's Pretty Neighbor (Carter) New York: Street & Smith, 1899. 233 p.

The Diamond Mine Case. (Carter) New York: Street & Smith, 1899. 210 p.

Diccon the Bold, A Story of the Days of Columbus. New York: G. P. Putnam's Sons, 1893. 279 p.

Diego Pinzo and the Fearful Voyage He Took into the Unknown Ocean, A.D. 1492. New York: Harper Bros., 1892. 259 p.

Entrapped. (Fleming) New York: N. L. Munro, 1886. 187 p.

False. (Fleming) New York: John W. Lovell, 1888. 318 p.

Fedora. New York: Street & Smith, 1890. 211 p.

$5,000 Reward: or, The Missing Bride. (Fleming) New York: N. L. Munro, 1887. 168 p.

The Great Enigma: or, Nick Carter's Triple Puzzle. New York: Street & Smith, 1892. 189 p.

How He Won Her, and a False Friend. (Fleming) New York: N. L. Munro, 1888. 93 p.

Lady Velvet: or, the Stroke of a Lifetime. (Carter) New York: Street & Smith, 1900. 215 p.

Laura Brayton: or, a Struggle to Rise. (Edwards) New
York: Street & Smith, 1890. 208 p.

The Little Widow: or, the Fortune Hunter's Doom. (Edwards) New York: Street & Smith, 1890. 210 p.

The Man from India. (Carter) New York: Street & Smith,
1898. 169 p.

Marjorie's Child: or, Shadowed for Years. New York:
N. L. Munro, 1884. 155 p.

Nick Carter and the Green-Goods Men, or, the Great
Detective's Thrilling Adventures in a New Field. New
York: Street & Smith, 1890. 305 p.

Nick Carter's Clever Protege, or, the Making of a Detective. New York: Street & Smith, 1899. 245 p.

Nick Carter's Star Pupil: or, "Roxy" and Bob Ferrett
after Big Game. (Carter) New York: Street & Smith,
1900. 219 p.

Only a Girl's Love. (Fleming) New York: Street & Smith,
1897. 317 p.

The Piano Box Mystery. (Carter) New York: Street &
Smith, 1892. 199 p.

The Prettiest of All. (Edwards) New York: Street &
Smith, 1889. 208 p.

A "Queer" Case. (Carter) New York: Street & Smith,
1890. 245 p.

Sadie the Rose Bud. (Edwards) New York: Street &
Smith, 1890.

A Sinless Crime. (Fleming) New York: John W. Lovell,
1888. 250 p.

A Sister's Sacrifice. (Fleming) New York: N. L. Munro,
1885. 189 p.

The Stolen Pay Train: the Case of the Burned Car: the
Passengers in Stateroom Thirty-three. (Carter) New
York: Street & Smith, 1899. 216 p.

The Stolen Racehorse, Etc. New York: Street & Smith,
1899. 241 p.

Sunlight & Gloom, or, From the Workhouse to the Peer-
age. (Fleming) New York: N. L. Munro, 1885. 250 p.

A Terrible Secret. (Fleming) New York: N. L. Munro,
1885. 141 p.

Tommy's Money: Adventures in New York & Elsewhere.
Illus. by W. A. Rogers. New York: Harper & Bros.,
1911. 218 p.

La Tosca. New York: Street & Smith, 1889. 198 p.

The Twelve Wise Men: or, Patsy's Long Chase. New
York: Street & Smith, 1900. 212 p.

The Van Alstine Case. New York: Street & Smith, 1899.
200 p.

Who Was the Heir? (Fleming) New York: John W. Lov-
ell, 1888.   237 p.
Wild Margaret.   New York: Street & Smith, 1900.   285 p.
The Crime of a Countess, or, The American Detective
and the Russian Nihilist.   by Nick Carter.   New York:
Street & Smith, 1892.   229 p.

COSTELLO, William Aloysius, 1904-1969.   News corres-
pondent, White House correspondent, Columbia Broad-
casting Corp., Ambassador to Trinidad and Tobago
1967.
Democracy Versus Feudalism in Post-War Japan.   Tokyo:
Itagaki Shoten, 1948.   237 p.
The Facts About Nixon, An Unauthorized Biography.   New
York: The Viking Press, Inc., 1960.   306 p.

COULTER, Eliot Brewster, 1892-1965.   Foreign Service Officer 1917-1926.   Served in St. Nazaire, Nantes Helsinki, London.
(Translated) Memoirs of the Duc de Sully, Finance Minister for Henry IV, King of France 1597-1610.   ?
George Hoefnagel, Flemish Artist of the 16th Century.
Arlington, Va.: 1960.   ?
Visa Work of the Department of State and the Foreign
Service, 1949.   Washington: Government Printing Office.   Department of State and Foreign Service Series,
8, 31, 69.

COX, Samuel Sullivan, 1824-1889.   Congressman, author.
Minister to Turkey 1885-86.
Eight Years in Congress, from 1857 to 1865.   Memoirs
and Speeches.   New York: Appleton & Co., 1865.
442 p.
Diversions of a Diplomat in Turkey.   New York: C. L.
Webster & Co., 1887.   685 p.
Why We Laugh.   New York: Harper Bros., 1876.   387 p.
Free Land and Free Trade: The Lessons of the English
Corn Laws Applied to the United States.   New York:
Putnam's Sons, 1880.   126 p.
Arctic Sunbeams, or, From Broadway to the Bosphorus
by Way of the North Cape.   New York: Putnam's
Sons, 1882.   2 vols.
Orient Sunbeams: From the Porte to the Pyramids By
Way of Palestine.   New York: Putnam's Sons, 1882.
Vol. II of "Artic Sunbeams."
Union - Disunion - Reunion.   Three Decades of Federal
Legislation From 1855 to 1885.   Providence, R.I.:

J. A. & R. A. Reid, 1886. 726 p. New York:
Books for Libraries Press, 1970.
A Buckeye Abroad, or, Wandering in Europe and the Ori-
ent. New York: Putnam's Sons, 1852. 444 p.
The Isles of the Princes: or, The Pleasure of Prinkipo.
New York: G. P. Putnam's Sons, 1887. 381 p.
Search for Winter Sunbeams in the Riviera, Corsica, Al-
giers and Spain. New York: Appleton & Co., 1870.
442 p.
Personal and Historical Memories of Events Preceding,
During and Since the Civil War, Involving Slavery,
Secession, Emancipation and Reconstruction. Washing-
ton: J. M. Stoddart & Co., 1885.
Papers. 1,000 items, in Brown University.

CRAMER, Michael John, 1835-1898. Methodist clergyman.
Consul Leipzig 1867; Minister to Denmark 1878-81;
Minister-Resident and Consul General in Switzerland
1881-85.
Conversations and Unpublished Letters of Ulysses S.
Grant. Cincinnati: Curts & Jennings, 1897. 207 p.

CRAWFORD, John Martin, 1845-1916. Physician, translator.
Consul General in Russia 1889-1894.
(Translated) Kalevala. (Ancient Finnish epic.) 1887.
Cincinnati: The Robert Clarke Co., 1904. 2 vols.
(Translated) Industries of Russia. (From the Russian.)
1893. St. Petersburg: Trenke & Fusnot, printers,
1893. 5 vols. in 4.
(Translation) Kalevipoeg. Esthonian epic. 1904.

CRAWFORD, William Rex, 1898- . Professor of romance
languages. Cultural Affairs Officer at Rio de Janeiro
1943-45.
A Century of Latin American Thought. Cambridge: Harvard University Press, 1944. 320 p.
Cuatro Conferencias en la Universidad de Chile: La Cultura de Los Estados Unidos. Santiago, Chile: Prensa
de la Universidad de Chile, 1941. 114 p.
Panorama de Cultura Norteamericana, Conferencias Lidas
en Brazil. Sao Paulo: Emprenta Grafica de Revista
dos Tribunals, 1945. 315 p.

CRESSON, William Penn, 1873-1932. Writer, architect.
Foreign Service Officer 1909-1917. Served in Lima,
London, Quito, Panama, Petrograd, Tiflis.
The Cossacks, Their History and Country. New York:

Brentano's, 1919.   239 p.
Diplomatic Portraits: Europe and the Monroe Doctrine
    One Hundred Years Ago.   Boston: Houghton Mifflin
    Co., 1923.   370 p.
Francis Dana, A Puritan Diplomat at the Court of Cath-
    erine the Great.   New York: L. McVeigh, Dial Press,
    1930.   397 p.
The Holy Alliance: The European Background of the
    Monroe Doctrine.   New York: Oxford University Press,
    1922.   147 p.
James Monroe.   Chapel Hill: University of North Caro-
    lina Press, 1946.   577 p.
Persia: The Awakening East.   Illus.   Philadelphia: J.
    B. Lippincott Co., 1908.   274 p.

CROMWELL, James Henry Roberts, 1896- .   Business.
    Minister to Canada, January-May 1940.
In Defense of Capitalism.   with Hugo E. Czerwonky.   New
    York: Charles Scribner's Sons, 1937.   373 p.
Pax Americana.   American Democracy and World Peace.
    Chicago: A. Kroch & Son, 1941.   94 p.
The Voice of Young America.   New York: Charles
    Scribner's Sons, 1933.   191 p.
What Is Sound Money?   And Who Will Control it, England
    or America?   New York: Economic Forum, 1934.
    64 p.

CROOK, William Herbert, 1925- .   Variously with Office
    of Economic Opportunity, Executive Offices, Volunteers
    Service to America, United States Mexican Border De-
    velopment Commission, Task Force for Retired Cent-
    ers, Texas City Planning Commission.   Ambassador
    to Australia 1968.
Warriors for the Poor: The Story of Vista, Volunteers
    Service to America.   with Ross Thomas.   New York:
    William Morrow & Co. Inc., 1969.   192 p.

CROWE, Philip Kingsland, 1908- .   Stock-broker, explorer,
    big game hunter, author.   Economic Cooperation Ad-
    ministration in China 1948-49.   Ambassador to Ceylon
    1953-56.   Special Assistant to Secretary of State 1957-
    59.   Ambassador to Union of South Africa 1959-61, to
    Norway 1969.
Diversions of a Diplomat in Ceylon.   Foreword by Vis-
    count Soulbury.   Illus. by P. E. P. Deraniyagala.
    Princeton: Princeton University Press, 1956.   318 p.
Sport is Where you Find It.   New York: D. Van Nostrand

Co., Inc., 1953. 189 p. Illus. by Paul Brown.
Sporting Journeys in Africa and Asia. Barre, Mass.:
Barre Publishers, 1966. 183 p.
The Empty Ark. New York: Charles Scribner's Sons,
1967. 301 p.
World Wildlife: The Last Stand. New York: Charles
Scribner's Sons, 1970. 308 p.
Out of the Mainstream. New York: Charles Scribner's
Sons, 1970. 212 p.

CUDAHY, John, 1887-1943. Lawyer, meat-packing, real
estate. Ambassador to Poland 1933-37, Minister to
Irish Free State 1937-40, Ambassador to Belgium and
Minister to Luxemburg 1940-43.
Archangel, the American War with Russia. Chicago:
A. C. McClurg & Co., 1924. 216 p.
American Horizons. New York: Duffield & Co., 1930.
159 p.
The Armies March: A Personal Report by John Cudahy.
New York: Charles Scribner's Sons, 1941. 304 p.
Mañanaland: Adventuring with Camera and Rifle Through
California in Mexico. New York: Duffield & Co.,
1928. 250 p.

CULBERTSON, William Smith, 1884-1966. Lawyer, Federal
Trade Commission, United States Tariff Commission,
writer, lecturer. Minister to Rumania 1925; Ambas-
sador to Chile 1928-33.
Alexander Hamilton: An Essay. New Haven: Yale Uni-
versity Press, 1911. 153 p.
Commercial Policy in War Times and After--. New
York: D. Appleton, 1919. 478 p. Introd. by Henry
C. Emery.
International Economic Policies: A Survey of the Eco-
nomics of Diplomacy. New York: D. Appleton, 1925.
575 p.
Liberation, The Threat and Challenge of Power. Atlanta:
Tupper & Love, 1953. 208 p.
Raw Materials and Foodstuffs in the Commercial Policies
of Nations. Philadelphia: American Academy of Politi-
cal and Social Sciences, 1924. 298 p.
Reciprocity, a National Policy for Foreign Trade. New
York: Whittlesey House and McGraw-Hill, 1937.
298 p. Papers in the Library of Congress, Washington: 1963.

CURRY, Jabez Lamar Monroe, 1825-1903. Statesman,

author, educator. Confederate officer, orator. Presi-
dent of Howard College (Ala.) 1865-68. Minister to
Spain 1885-88. Ambassador to Spain 1902 (requested
by King Alfonso at latter's coming of age).
Constitutional Government in Spain. New York: Harper
Brothers, 1889. 222 p.
William Ewart Gladstone. Richmond: B. F. Johnson &
Co., 1891. 239 p.
The Southern States of the American Union Considered in
Their Relations to the Constitution of the United States
and to the Resulting Union. New York: G. P. Put-
nam's Sons, 1894. 248 p.
A Brief Sketch of George Peabody and a History of the
Peabody Education Fund Through Thirty Years. Cam-
bridge: Harvard University Press, 1898. 161 p.
Civil History of the Government of the Confederate States,
With Some Personal Reminiscences. Richmond: B. F.
Johnson, 1901. 318 p.

CURTIS, William Eleroy, 1850-1911. Journalist, globe-
trotter, publicist, Special Commissioner to the Repub-
lics of Central and South America. First Director of
the Bureau of American Republics--now the Pan Amer-
ican Union--1889-93. Special Commissioner to Madrid
during the Chicago Exposition, also "Special Envoy to
the Queen Regent of Spain" and in 1892 to Pope Leo
XIII.
The Capitals of Spanish America. New York: Harper
Brothers, 1888. 715 p.
A Summer Scamper Along the Old Santa Fe Trail and
Through the Gorges of Colorado to Zion. Chicago:
Inter-Ocean Publishing Co., 1883. 113 p.
The Yankees of the East: Sketches of Modern Japan.
New York: Stone & Kimball, 1896. 2 vols.
Between the Andes and the Ocean. Chicago: H. S.
Stone, 1900. 442 p.
Today in Syria and Palestine. Chicago: F. H. Revell
Co., 1903. 529 p.
Egypt, Burma and British Malayasia. Chicago: F. H.
Revell Co., 1905. 399 p.
Modern India. Chicago: F. H. Revell Co., 1905. 513 p.
(First appeared in the Chicago Record-Herald in winter
of 1903-04.)
Turkestan: The Heart of Asia. New York: Hodder &
Stoughton, George Doran Co., 1911. 344 p. Illus. by
John T. McCutchen.
Children of the Sun. Chicago: Inter-Ocean Publishing

Co., 1883. 154 p.

Christopher Columbus: His Portraits and His Monuments. A descriptive catalogue. Washington: W. H. Loudermilk Co., 1893. 72 p.

Columbus and the Discovery of America. Chicago(?): Illus. plates, photos, plans, facsimiles, coats of arms. 1893? 25 vols.

Denmark, Norway and Sweden. Akron: The Saalfield Publishing Co., 1903. 505 p. plates.

The Land of the Nihilist. Russia: Its People, Its Palaces, Its Politics. A Narrative of Travel in the Czar's Dominions. Chicago: Belford, Clarke & Co., 1888. 323 p.

Letters on Canada. by William Eleroy Curtis, Special Correspondent of the Chicago "Record-Herald" and which appeared in that paper from August 25 to October 8, 1911. Printed by the Library of Congress. 173 p.

Abraham Lincoln. Philadelphia: J. B. Lippincott Co., 1902. 409 p.

The True Lincoln. Philadelphia: J. B. Lippincott Co., 1903. 409 p.

One Irish Summer. New York: Duffield & Co., 1909. 482 p.

The Relics of Columbus: An Illustrated Description of the Historical Collection in the Monastery of La Rabida. Washington: W. H. Loudermilk, 1893. 216 p.

Trade and Transportation Between the United States and Spanish America. Washington: Government Printing Office, 1889. 342 p.

The True Thomas Jefferson. Philadelphia: J. B. Lippincott Co., 1901. 395 p.

The Turk and His Lost Provinces: Greece, Bulgaria, Servia, Bosnia. Chicago: F. H. Revell, 1903. 396 p.

The United States and Foreign Powers. Meadville, Penna.: Flood & Vincent, 1892. 313 p.

Venezuela: A Land Where it's Always Summer. New York: Harper & Bros., 1896. 315 p.

Around the Black Sea, Asia Minor, Armenia, Caucasus, Circassia, Daghestan, The Crimea, Roumania. New York: Hodder & Stoughton, George H. Doran Co., 1911. 456 p.

La Mas Pequeña Republica de las Republicas Americanas. San José, Costa Rica: Imprenta Nacional, 1887. 60 p.

CUSHING, Caleb, 1800-1879. Editor, public speaker, linguist, lawyer, Congressman. "Most eminent scholar

of his day" (Emerson).   Brig. General in Mexican
War.   Commissioner to China 1843-44 (first U.S. dip-
lomatic representative to China).   Arranged commer-
cial treaty which included extraterritorial rights--
"Treaty of Wang Hiya. " Senior Counsel for the United
States on the Tribunal for Arbitration between United
States, Great Britain, Italy, Switzerland and Brazil at
Geneva, 1872--"Treaty of Washington" 1873.   Minister
to Spain 1874-77.   Attorney General 1853-57.
The History and Present State of the Town of Newbury-
   port. Newburyport, Mass. : E. W. Allen, 1826.
Opinion of the Attorney General on so much of the Act
   to Remodel the Diplomatic and Consular Systems of
   the United States, Approved March 1, 1855, and the
   Section III of the Act Approved March 3, 1855, Amend-
   atory Thereof, as Relates to Consuls.   Washington:
   A. O. P. Nicholson, pub. printer. 1855.   48 p.
Outline of the Life and Public Services of William Henry
   Harrison of Ohio.   Boston: Weeks, Jordan & Co. ,
   1840.   71 p.
Reminiscences of Spain, the Country, Its People, History,
   and Monuments.   Boston: Carter, Hendee & Co. ,
   1833.   2 vols.
Reply to a Letter of J. Fenimore Cooper by One of his
   Countrymen. Boston: J. T. Buckingham, 1834. 76 p.
Review, Historical and Political, of the Late Revolution
   in France, and the Consequent Events in Belgium,
   Poland, Great Britain, and Other Parts of Europe.
   Boston: Carter, Hendee & Co. , Newburyport, Mass. :
   T. B. White, 1833.   2 vols.
Summary of the Practical Principles of Political Economy
   with Observations on Smith's "Wealth of Nations" and
   Say's "Political Economy, " by a Friend of Domestic
   Industry.   Cambridge: Hilliard & Metcalf, 1826. 88 p.
Tracts on Sundry Topics of Political Economy.   Boston:
   Russell Odiorne & Co. , 1834.   156 p.
The Treaty of Washington: Its Negotiation, Execution,
   and the Discussions Relating Thereto.   New York:
   Harper & Bros. , 1873.   280 p.   On microfilm, Ann
   Arbor.
Opinion of the Attorney General (Caleb Cushing) Concern-
   ing the Judicial Authority of the Commissioner or Min-
   ister and of Consuls of the United States in China and
   Turkey. Washington: A. O. P. Nicholson, 1855.
   36 p.
Opinion of the Attorney General (Caleb Cushing) on the
   Act to Remodel the Diplomatic and Consular Systems

of the United States. 2 parts in 1. Washington:
A. O. P. Nicholson, Printer, 1855. 55 p.
Ambassadors and Other Public Ministers of the United
States, Opinion of Honorable Caleb Cushing, Attorney
General May 25, 1855. Washington: Government
Printing Office, 1907. 34 p.
[The catalogue of his Law Library had 31 pages and of
his Private Library had 68 pages.]

CUSHING, Caroline Elizabeth (Wilde), 1802-1832. Wife of
Caleb Cushing. [Q. V.]
Letters, Descriptive of Public Monuments, Scenery, and
Manners in France and Spain. Newburyport, Mass.:
E. W. Allen & Co., 1832. 2 vols.

DALLAS, George Mifflin, 1792-1864. Minister to Russia
1837-39, to Great Britain 1856-61.
A Series of Letters from London Written during the Years
1856, '57, '58, '59, '60. Ed. by his daughter, Julia
Dallas. Philadelphia: J. B. Lippincott & Co., 1869.
229 p.
Diary of George Mifflin Dallas while United States Minister to Russia, 1837-39 and to England 1856-61. Ed.
by Susan Dallas. Philadelphia: J. B. Lippincott &
Co., 1892. 443 p.
Life and Writings of Alexander James Dallas, 1759-1817.
by his son, George Mifflin Dallas. Philadelphia: J.
B. Lippincott & Co., 1871. 487 p.

DANIEL, John Moncure, 1825-1865. Chargé d'Affaires in
Sardinia 1853, and Minister 1854.
Richmond Examiner during the War: or, Writings of
John M. Daniel with Memoir of his Life by his Broth-
er, Frederick S. Daniel. New York: Printed for the
author, 1868. 232 p.

DANIELS, Adelaide Worth (Bagley). Wife of Ambassador
Josephus Daniels. [Q. V.]
Recollections of a Cabinet Minister's Wife 1913-1921.
Raleigh, N. C.: 1945. 199 p. ?

DANIELS, Josephus, 1862-1948. Lawyer, editor, politician,
writer. Secretary of the Navy 1913-21. Ambassador
to Mexico 1933-41.
The Cabinet Diaries of Josephus Daniels, 1913-1921. Ed.
by E. David Cronon. Lincoln, Nebraska: University

of Nebraska, 1963.   648 p.
Editor in Politics.   Chapel Hill, N. C. :   University of
North Carolina, 1941.   644 p.
The First Fallen Hero, A Biographic Sketch of Worth
Bagley, Ensign U. S. Navy.   Norfolk, Va. :   S. W.
Bowman, 1898.   88 p.
The Life of Woodrow Wilson 1856-1924.   Philadelphia:
John C. Winston Co. , 1924.   381 p.
The Navy and the Nation: War-Time Addresses.   Introd.
by John Wilber Jenkins.   New York: George A. Doran,
1919.   348 p.
Our Navy at War.   with photographic illus.   Washington,
D. C. :   Pictorial Bureau, 1922.   374 p.
Papers 1863-1942.   410 feet.   Library of Congress MSS
Division.
Shirtsleeve Diplomat.   Chapel Hill, N. C. :   University of
North Carolina Press, 1947.   547 p.   Also in Spanish,
Mexico City: Talleres Grafica la Nacion, 1949.
623 p.
Tar Heel Editor.   Chapel Hill: University of North Caro-
lina Press, 1932.   544 p.
The Wilson Era: Years of Peace 1910-1917.   Chapel
Hill: University of North Carolina, 1944.   615 p.
The Wilson Era: Years of War and After, 1917-1923.
Chapel Hill: University of North Carolina Press, 1946.
654 p.

DARLINGTON, Charles Francis and Alice B. , 1904-   .
Charles Francis, a banker, with the League of Nations,
Bank for International Settlements, Office of the President, Oil corporation, State Department.   First Ambassador to Gabon 1961-63.   Alice B. Darlington is his
wife.   Co-authors.
African Betrayal.   New York: David McKay Co. , 1968.

DAVIES, John Patton, Jr. , 1908-   .   Born in China of
American parents.   Foreign Service Officer 1931-54.
Chinese language officer.   Served in Windsor, Yunnanfu,
Peiping, Mukden, Hankow, State Department, Kunming,
Chungking (political officer on the staff of General
Stilwell), Moscow, Policy Planning staff in State De-
partment, Bonn-Bad Godesberg, Lima.   Forced out of
the Service by the political attacks against the State
Department and the Foreign Service by Senator Joseph
R. McCarthy, in 1951.   Record was cleared in 1968.
Foreign and Other Affairs: A View From the Radical
Center.   New York: W. W. Norton Co. , 1964.   219 p.

Dragon By the Tail: American, British, Japanese and Russian Encounters With China and With One Another. New York: Norton Publishers, 1972. 448 p. photos.

DAVIES, Joseph Edward, 1876-1958. Lawyer, politician, consultant. Ambassador to Soviet Union 1936-38, Ambassador to Belgium and Minister to Luxembourg 1938-39.
Mission to Moscow. New York: Simon & Schuster, 1941. 660 p.

DAVIS, John Chandler Bancroft, 1822-1907. Lawyer, politician, newspaper correspondent. Chargé d'Affaires and Secretary of Legation at London 1849-52. Assistant Secretary of State 1869.
Mr. Fish and the Alabama Claims. A Chapter in Diplomatic History. Boston: Houghton Mifflin Co., 1893. 158 p.
(Edited) The Massachusetts Justice. A Treatise on the Powers and Duties of Justices of the Peace. Vols. 108-186. United States Reports. Worcester, Mass.: W. Lazell, 1847. 553 p.

DAVIS, John Ker, 1882-1969. Born in Soochow, China, of American parents. Foreign Service Officer (Chinese language officer) 1910-43. Served in Shanghai, Canton, Chefoo, Antung, Nanking, State Department, Peking, London, Amsterdam, Seoul, Vancouver, Warsaw, Dublin.
(Co-author) Manual of Probate Procedure in American Consular Courts in China. with Walter Smith. Washington: Government Printing Office, 1923. 32 p.

DAVIS, Michael, 1940- . University instructor. Foreign Service Officer 1971- .
The Image of Lincoln in the South. Knoxville: University of Tennessee, 1971. 240 p. Benjamin Barondess Award by the Civil War Round Table of New York.

DAVIS, Nathaniel Penniston, 1895- . Foreign Service Officer 1919-51. Served in Berlin, Pernambuco, London, Foreign Service Inspector, State Department, Manila (interned by the Japanese 1941-43), Ambassador to Costa Rica 1947, to Hungary 1949-51.
Few Dull Moments. Philadelphia: Dunlap Printing Co., 1967. 158 p. (200 copies. Foreign Service reminiscenses.)

Internment Interludes. 24 poems on the lighter side of
    life in a Japanese prison camp. Glossary of Japanese
    and Tagalog words. List of names of American For-
    eign Service internees. [Privately printed.] Princeton
    University Press.

DAVIS, William Brownlee, 1852- . Editor, publisher,
    member of Texas Legislature. U. S. Pension Examin-
    er. Consular Agent at Guadalajara 1904; Vice and
    Deputy Consul 1908; Vice Consul 1915-16.
    Experiences and Observations of an American Consular
        Officer During the Recent Mexican Revolution. Los
        Angeles: 1920. 248 p.

DAWES, Charles Gates, 1865-1951. Lawyer, banker, busi-
    nessman. Vice President of the United States 1925-29.
    Ambassador to Great Britain 1929-32. Nobel Peace
    Prize 1925.
    The Banking System of the United States. Chicago: Rand
        McNally & Co., 1894. 83 p.
    Essays and Speeches. Boston: Houghton Mifflin Co.,
        1915. 427 p.
    A Journal of the Great War. Boston: Houghton Mifflin
        Co., 1921. 2 vols.
    The First Year of the Budget of the United States. New
        York: Harper & Bros., 1923. 436 p.
    Notes as Vice President. 1928-29. Boston: Little,
        Brown & Co., 1935. 329 p.
    How Long Prosperity. Chicago: A. N. Marquis, 1937.
        45 p.
    A Journal of Reparations. Foreword by Lord Stamp and
        H. Bruning. London: MacMillan Co., 1939. 527 p.
    A Journal as Ambassador to Great Britain. Foreword by
        Herbert Hoover. New York: Macmillan Co., 1939.
        442 p.
    A Journal of the McKinley Years. Foreword by Basom
        M. Timmons. Chicago: Lakeside Printing Co., 1950.
        458 p.

DAWSON, Owen, 1892- . Agriculturist, teacher. Depart-
    ment of Agriculture Foreign Service 1922-37. Foreign
    Service Officer 1937-50. Served in Berlin, Bucharest,
    El Golea, Shanghai, Washington, Chungking.
    Food and Agriculture in Communist China. with others.
        Stanford, California: Hoover Institute, 1966. 171 p.
    Communist China's Agriculture: Its Development and
        Future Potential. New York: Frederick A. Praeger,

Inc., 1970. 213 p.

DAWSON, Thomas Cleland, 1865-1912. Secretary of Legation Brazil 1897-1904. Minister Resident and Consul
General Dominican Republic 1904-07. Minister to
Colombia 1907, to Chile 1909, to Panama 1910, also
to Nicaragua 1910-11, to State Department 1911-12.
The South American Republics. New York: G. P. Putnam's Sons, 1903-04. 2 vols.

DEAN, Arthur Hobson, 1898- . Lawyer, Government offi-
cial. Special Deputy Secretary of State and Special
Ambassador to negotiate peace between the United
States and Korea, 1953-54.
A Review of the Law of Corporate Reorganizations. Lec-
ture delivered before the Association of the Bar of the
City of New York on March 6, 1941, under the auspices
of the Committee on Post-Admission Legal Education.
New York: Bowne & Co. Inc., c1941. 64 p.
Test Ban and Disarmament: the Path of Negotiation.
New York: Published for the Council on Foreign Re-
lations by Harper & Row, 1966. 153 p.
William Nelson Cromwell, 1854-1948: an American Pio-
neer in Corporation, Comparative, and International
Law. New York? 1957. 237 p.

DEANE, Silas, 1737-1789. Secret agent of the Continental
Congress in France, May 1776. Joint Commissioner
with Benjamin Franklin and, later, with Arthur Lee to
the Court of France. Signed treaties of Commerce
and Alliance in Paris in 1778.
Papers. New York: New York Historical Society Collection. vols. XIX-XXIII.
Paris Papers: or, Mr. Silas Deane's Late Intercepted
Letters. New York: 1872.

DEARBORN, Henry, Sr., 1751-1829. Minister to Portugal
1822-25.
Journal While on Arnold's Expedition to Quebec. Pro-
ceedings of the Massachusetts Historical Society.
Series 2, Vol. III 1886-87.
Revolutionary War Journals of Henry Dearborn, 1775-
1783. Ed. by Lloyd A. Brown and Howard Packham.
Chicago: Caxton Club, 1939. 284 p.

DELANEY, Robert Finley, 1925- . Foreign Service Staff
Officer 1950-62. Served in Kuala Lumpur, Rome,

State Department, United States Information Agency,
Budapest, Vienna, San Salvador.
Your Future in the Foreign Service.   New York: Richard
    Rosen Press, 1961.   158 p.
The Literature of Communism in America: A Selected
    Guide.   Washington Cathedral: University of America
    Press, 1962.   433 p.
This Is Communist Hungary.   Chicago: Henry Regnery
    Co. , 1958.   260 p.

DE LEON, Edwin, 1828-1891.   Newspaper publisher in South
    Carolina.   Appointed Diplomatic Agent and Consul
    General in Cairo by President Pierce and continued
    under President Buchanan, 1853-61.
The Khedive's Egypt, or the Old House of Bondage Under
    New Masters.   London: Sampson Low, Marston,
    Searle and Rivington, 1877.   435 p.
Thirty Years of My Life on Three Continents.   with a
    chapter on the life of women in the East by Mrs. De
    Leon.   London: Ward & Downey, 1890.   2 vols.
The Purchase of Camels.   Report of the Secretary of
    War.   Washington: Executive Document No. 62, 34th
    Congress, 3rd Session.   238 p.
Outrages at Jaffa.   Washington: Executive Document No.
    54.   35th Congress, 1st Session.   30 p.
Askaros Kassis, The Copt. A Romance of Modern Egypt.
    Philadelphia: J. B. Lippincott & Co. , 1870.   462 p.
Under the Stars and Under the Crescent, a Romance of
    East and West.   London: S. Low, Marston, Searle
    & Rivington, 1887.   2 vols.

DENBY, Charles, 1830-1904.   Lawyer, Civil War veteran.
    Minister to China 1885-98.
American Missionaries in China.   New York: Missionary
    Review of the World.   Feb. 1888.   Funk & Wagnalls.
China and Her People, Being the Observation, Reminis-
    cences and Conclusions of an American Diplomat.
    Boston: L. C. Page, 1906.   2 vols.   (published
    posthumously)
Report of the Philippine Commission To the President,
    January 31, 1900, to December 20, 1900.   Washington:
    Government Printing Office, 1900-01.   4 vols.
Judge John Law.   Indianapolis: Bowen Merrill, 1897.
    213 p.

DENBY, James Orr, 1896- . Born in China of American
    parents.   Foreign Service Officer 1921-51.   Served in

Tokyp, Athens, Peking, Dublin, Capetown, Pretoria,
United States Political Advisor to the Mediterranean
Theater Supreme Allied Command, Vienna, State De-
partment.
Society of the Cincinnati and Its Museum.   Washington:
The Society of the Cincinnati, 1967.   37 p.   illus.

DENISON, Charles Wheeler, 1809-1881.   Author and editor
of "Emancipator" the first anti-slavery journal published in New York.   Appointed Consul in British
Guiana in 1841 where he and his wife, a prolific author, lived until the Civil War.   They returned to the
United States, he to serve as an Army Chaplain and
she as a nurse.
The Yankee Cruiser: A Story of the War of 1812.   Il-
lustrative of Scenes in the American Navy.   Boston:
J. E. Fairwell & Co., 1848.   50 p.
The Tanner-Boy and How He Became Lieutenant-General.
by Major Penniman (pseud.).   Boston: Roberts Bro-
thers, 1864.   316 p.
Illustrated Life, Campaigns and Public Services of Philip
H. Sheridan.   Philadelphia: J. B. Peterson & Bro-
thers, 1865.   197 p.
Winfield, The Lawyer's Son, and How He Became a Major-
General.   by Major Penniman (pseud.).   Philadelphia:
Ashmead & Evans, 1865.   323 p.   Also published un-
der his own name, Rev. C. W. Denison.
Hancock, 'The Superb.'   The Early Life and Public Ca-
reer of Winfield S. Hancock, Major-General U. S. A.
Including also a Sketch of the Life of Hon. William H.
English.   by Rev. C. W. Denison with Capt. G. B.
Herbert.   Philadelphia: H. W. Kelly, 1880.   431 p.
The Child-Hunters.   By a Friend of Italy.   New York:
J. W. Lovell Co., 1885.   188 p.
(Edited) Old Slade: or, Fifteen Years Adventures of a
Sailor: Including a Residence Among Cannibals on
Wallace Islands, and, Sketches of Other Parts of the
North and South Pacific Oceans.   Boston: J. Putnam,
1844.   108 p.

DENISON, Mary Andrews, 1826-1911.   (Pseud. N. I. Edson
and Clara Vance.)   Wife of Reverend Charles Wheeler
Denison [Q. V.].   Mrs. Denison lived with her husband
in British Guiana until the outbreak of Civil War when
they returned to the United States.   He served as an
Army chaplain and she as an Army nurse.
Barbara.   Boston: D. Lothrop, 1876.   361 p.

Barbara Triumphs. New York: F. A. Munsey, 1887.
197 p.

A Brave Little Woman. New York: F. M. Lupton, 1892.
121 p.

Captain Molly - A Love Story. Boston: Lee & Shepard,
1897. 251 p.

Carrie Hamilton: or The Beauty of True Religion. Philadelphia: American Baptist Publishing Society, 1855.
296 p.

The Daughter of the Regiment. New York: A. L. Burt,
1888. 310 p.

The Days and Ways of the Cocked Hats: or, the Dawn of
the Revolution. New York: S. A. Rollo, 1860. 383 p.

Erin Go Bragh. Washington, D. C. : Glove Printing Co.,
1879. 354 p.

Ethel's Triumph: From Fifteen to Twenty Five. Boston:
Bradley & Woodruff, 1890. 422 p.

An Every-Day Heroine. Illus. by Ida Waugh. Philadelphia: Penn Publishing Co., 1896. 329 p.

The Frenchman's Word. New York: Street & Smith,
1902. 212 p.

Glennandale. Philadelphia: American Baptist Publishing
Society, 1882. 320 p.

Grandmother Normandy. Boston: D. Lothrop, 1882.
264 p.

The Guardian's Trust. New York: Street & Smith, 1902.
283 p.

Her Secret: A Story for Girls. Illus. by Isobel Lyndalls.
Philadelphia: The Penn Publishing Co., 1903. 316 p.

Hidden Treasure. Dover, New Hampshire: G. T. Day
& Co., 1877. 301 p.

His Triumph. New York: G. T. Dillingham, 1883.
248 p.

Home Pictures. New York: Harper & Bros., 1853.
417 p.

How She Helped Him. Boston: I. Bradley & Co., 1889.
212 p.

If She Will She Will. Boston: Lee & Shepard, 1891.
351 p.

John Dane. Boston: H. Holt, 1874. 451 p.

A Late Repentance: or, The Little White Hand. New
York: Street & Smith, 1889. 230 p.

Led Back. Philadelphia: American Baptist Publication
Society, 1891. 272 p.

Led To The Light. A sequel to Opposite the Jail. Philadelphia: J. S. Claxton, 1867. 352 p.

Like a Gentleman. New York: C. T. Dillingham, 1882.

213 p.

The Little Folks of Redbow.   Boston: H. A. Young &
    Co., 1875.   362 p.

The Mad Hunter: or, The Downfall of the Le-Forests.
    New York: Beadle & Co., 1863.   106 p.

The Man in Blue: or, Which Did He Love?   New York:
    Street & Smith, 1889.   214 p.

The Master.   Boston: Walker, Wise & Co., 1862. 270 p.

Mr. Peter Crewitt.   New York: C. T. Dillingham, 1878.
    221 p.

No Mother Like Mine.   Boston: J. Bradley Co., 1880.
    273 p.

Noble by Birth.   Philadelphia: The Union Press, 1879.
    306 p.

A Noble Sister.   Philadelphia: J. S. Claxton, 1868.
    373 p.

The Old Folly, and Its Inhabitants.   Philadelphia: Amer-
    ican Baptist Publishing Society, 1882.   308 p.

Old Hepsy.   Illus. from designs by the author, engraved
    by N. Orr.   New York: A. B. Burdick, 1858.   459 p.

Old Slip Warehouse.   New York: Harper Bros., 1878.
    145 p.

Orange Leaves.   Illus. with engravings from designs by
    White.   Philadelphia: J. B. Lippincott & Co., 1856.
    384 p.

Out of Prison.   New York: Sheldon & Co., 1864.   358 p.

The Prisoner of La Vintresse: or, The Fortunes of a
    Cuban Heiress.   New York: J. P. Beadle & Co.,
    1860.   126 p.

Raphael Inglesse: or, The Jew of Milan.   A thrilling tale
    of the Victories of Virtue, and the Punishments of
    Vice.   Boston: J. E. Furwell & Co., 1848.   113 p.

The Romance of a Schoolboy.   Illus. by John Henderson
    Garnesey.   St. Paul: The Price-McGill Co., 1893.
    266 p.

Ruth Margerie.   A Romance of the Revolt of 1689.
    (Beadle's Dime Novels) New York: Beadle & Co.,
    1861.   111 p.

Sequel to Opposite the Jail: or, On Trial For His Life.
    Boston: I. Bradley & Co., 1883.   279 p.

Silent Tom.   Boston: D. Lothrop & Co.   Dover, New
    Hampshire: G. T. Day & Co., 1872.   377 p.   (N. I.
    Edson, pseud.)

Stolen From Home.   Boston: H. Holt, 1873.   399 p.

Strawberry Hill.   Dover, New Hampshire: G. T. Day &
    Co., 1870.   432 p.   (Clara Vance, pseud.)

The Talbury Girls.   Dover, New Hampshire: G. T. Day

& Co. , 1871.   487 p.   (Clara Vance, pseud.)
That Husband of Mine.   Boston: Lee & Shepard.   New
    York: C. T. Dillingham, 1877.   227 p.
That Wife of Mine.   Boston: Lee & Shepard.   New York:
    C. T. Dillingham, 1877.   228 p.
Tim Bumble's Charge; or, Mrs. Lattison's One Great
    Sorrow.   New York: Beadle & Co. , 1862.   103 p.
Victor Norman, Rector.   Philadelphia: J. B. Lippincott
    Co. , 1873.   262 p.
What Not.   Illus. with engravings from designs by White.
    Philadelphia: Lippincott, Grambo & Co. , 1855.   384 p.
What One Boy Can Do.   Boston: I. Bradley & Co. ,
    1886.   267 p.
The Yellow Violin.   Illus. by W. H. Fry.   Akron, Ohio:
    The Saalfield Publishing Co. , 1902.   311 p.
Revolution.   New York: S. A. Rollo, 1860.   383 p.

DENNIS, Lawrence, 1893- .   Writer.   Foreign Service Of-
    ficer 1920-27.   Served in Port-au-Prince, State De-
    partment, Bucharest, Tegucigalpa, Publisher and editor
    of the Weekly Foreign Letter 1939-43, and Appeal to
    Reason news letter 1946- .
The Coming American Fascism.   New York: Harper &
    Bros. , 1936.   320 p.
The Dynamics of War and Revolution.   New York: Weekly
    Foreign Letter, 1940.   259 p.
A Trial on Trial: The Great Sedition Trial of 1944.   with
    Maximilian John St. George.   New York?:   National
    Civil Rights Committee, 1946.   503 p.
Las Conferencias del'Denver' Etc.   Managua, Nicaragua:
    Encuadernacion Nacional, 1926.   79 p.
Is Capitalism Doomed?   New York: Harper Bros. , 1932.
    328 p.

DICKINSON, Charles Monroe, 1842-1924.   Journalist, lawyer,
    writer.   Consul General in Turkey 1897.   Diplomatic
    Agent in Bulgaria 1901.   Consul General-at-large for
    the Middle East 1906-08.   Was on the Board which
    drafted the Consular Regulations of 1906.
The Children and Other Verses.   New York: Cassell &
    Co. Ltd. , 1889.   138 p.

DIX, John Adams, 1798-1879.   Minister to France 1866-69.
A Winter in Madeira; and a Summer in Spain and Florence.
    4th ed.   New York: W. Holdridge, 1851.   377 p.
Speeches and Occasional Addresses.   New York: D. Ap-
    pleton & Co. , 1864.   2 vols.

Memoirs of John Adams Dix. Compiled by Morgan Dix.
New York: Harper & Bros., 1883. 2 vols.

DIZARD, Wilson Paul, 1922- . Foreign Service Reserve
Officer 1951- . Served with United States Information
Service in Istanbul, Washington, Athens, Dacca, War-
saw.
The Strategy of the Truth: The Story of the United States
Information Service. Washington: Public Affairs
Press, 1961. 213 p.
(Edited) Television: A World Review. Syracuse, N.Y.:
Syracuse University Press, 1966. 349 p.

DODD, William Edward, 1869-1940. Educator. Professor
of history at University of Chicago 1909-33. Author.
Ambassador to Germany 1933-37.
Ambassador Dodd's Diary, 1933-38. Edit. by William E.
Dodd, Jr. and Martha Dodd. Introd. by Charles A.
Beard. New York: Harcourt, Brace & Co., 1941.
464 p.
The Days of the Cotton King. with Jesse-Macy. New
Haven: Yale University Press, 1926. 245 p.
Chief Justice Marshall and Virginia, 1813-1821. London:
Macmillan Co., 1907. 776 p.
The Cotton Kingdom: A Chronicle of the Old South. New
Haven: Yale University Press, 1919. 161 p.
Expansion and Conflict. Boston: Houghton Mifflin Co.,
1915. 329 p.
Jefferson Davis. Philadelphia: G. W. Jacobs, 1907.
396 p.
Lincoln or Lee: Comparison and Contrast of the Two
Greatest Leaders in the War Between the States. The
Narrow Accidental Margins of Success. New York:
Century Co., 1928. 177 p.
The Old South: Struggles for Democracy. New York:
The MacMillan Co., 1937. 312 p.
Statesmen of the Old South. From Radicalism to Conser-
vative Revolt. New York: The MacMillan Co., 1911.
242 p.
Woodrow Wilson and His Work. Garden City, N.Y.:
Doubleday, 1920. 369 p.
(Edited) Woodrow Wilson's Public Papers. with Ray Stan-
nard Baker. New York: Harper Bros., 1925-27. 6
vols.
Dodd Papers. Washington, D.C.: Library of Congress,
MSS Division 26 ft.

DOERFLINGER, William Main, 1910- . Editor, war correspondent, Office of War Information. Information
Officer at Embassy, Rome 1950-53.
Shantymen and Shantyboys: Songs of the Sailor and Lum-
berman. (Songs of sailors on deep-water windjammers,
on fishing schooners, of western North Atlantic and
West Indies trade; and ballads of American and Canadian lumbermen.) New York: The Macmillan Co.,
1951. 374 p.
(Edited) The Young Traveler in Italy. by David Raymon.
Illus. with photos and map sketches by Winifred Maza-
rian. New York: E. P. Dutton & Co., Inc., 1955.
224 p.

DORSEY, Stephen Palmer, 1913-1968. Banking. War Pro-
duction Board. Foreign Service Officer 1944- .
Served at UNESCO, Technical Cooperation Administra-
tion, State Department, International Cooperation Ad-
ministration, Foreign Service Institute, in Beirut,
Khartoum, Genoa, Rome.
Early English Churches in America, 1607-1807. New
York: Oxford University Press, 1952. 206 p.
Alexandria Houses, 1750-1850. with Deering Davis, Ralph
Cole Hall and Nancy McClelland. New York: Archi-
tectural Book Publishing Co., 1946. 128 p.
Georgetown Houses of the Federal Period. Washington,
D.C. 1780-1830. with Deering Davis, Ralph Cole Hall
and Nancy McClelland. New York: Architectural
Book Publishing Co., 1944. 130 p.

DOUGLASS, Fredrick, 1817(?)-1895. Born a slave with the
name Fredrick Augustus Washington Bailey of an unknown white father and a slave, Harriet Bailey, who
had some Indian blood. He was appointed Minister
and Consul General in Haiti 1889-1901. An abolition-
ist, orator and journalist. A famous negro leader.
Fredrick Douglass. Selections from His Writings. Edit.
and with an introd. by Philip S. Foner. New York:
International Publishers, 1964.
The Life and Writings of Fredrick Douglass. by Philip
S. Foner. New York: International Publishers, 1950-
55. 4 vols.
The Mind and Heart of Fredrick Douglass, Excerpts from
Speeches of the Great Negro Orator. Adapted by
Barbara Ritchie. New York: Thomas Y. Crowell
Co., 1968. 201 p.
My Bondage and My Freedom. Introd. by Dr. James

McCune.   New York: Miller, Orton & Mulligan, 1855.
464 p.

Life and Times of Fredrick Douglass, as Written by Himself.   His Early Life as a Slave, His Escape from
Bondage and His Complete History to the Present Time,
Including His Connection with the Anti-Slavery Movement.   Introd. by George L. Ruffin.   Hartford, Conn.:
Park Publishing Co., 1881.   516 p.   (microfilm--new
edition 1962)

The Life and Times of Fredrick Douglass from 1817 to
1882, Written by Himself.   Introd. by Right Honorable
John Bright, M. P.   Edit. by John Lobb.   London:
Christian Age Office, 1882.

Narrative of the Life of Fredrick Douglass, an American
Slave, Written by Himself.   Boston: Published at the
Anti-Slavery Office, 1845.

DRAPER, William Franklin, 1842-1910.   Civil war veteran,
on Union side.   Textile industrialist.   Ambassador to
Italy 1897-1900.

Recollections of a Varied Career.   Boston: Little, Brown,
1908.   411 p.

DREIER, John C., 1906- .   Teacher.   Department of the
Interior.   Emergency Relief Administration.   Department of Agriculture.   State Department.   Ambassador
to the Organization of American States 1941-48.   Served
in Washington, Caracas, Bogota.   Superior Service
Award 1958.

The Alliance For Progress: Problems and Perspectives.
Baltimore: The Johns Hopkins Press, 1962.   146 p.

The Organization of American States and the Hemisphere
Crisis.   New York: Harper & Row, for the Council
on Foreign Relations, 1962.   147 p.

Taking Stock of Inter-American Relations.   Washington:
Government Printing Office for the Department of
State, 1951.   693 p.

(Co-author) International Organization in the Western Hemisphere.   with others.   Ed. and introd. by Robert W.
Gregg.   Syracuse, N. Y.:   University Press, 1968.
262 p.

(Co-author) International Peace Observations.   A History
and a Forecast.   with David W. Wainhouse, Bernard
G. Bechhoeffer, Benjamin Gerig and Harry R. Turkel.
Baltimore: Johns Hopkins University Press, in cooperation with the Washington Center of Foreign Policy Research School of Advanced International Studies, 1966.
663 p.

DRUMRIGHT, Florence Bergen (Teets). Pseudonyms: Florence Bergen (for fiction), Florence Teets (for columns and feature writing). Wife of Foreign Service Officer Everett Francis Drumright, b. 1906, who was in the foreign Service 1930-62 and Career Minister, Ambassador to China (Taiwan) 1958-62.
She's Going Abroad. by Florence Teets. New York: Ives Washburn, Inc., 1953. 132 p. (A travel guide for women.)
The Men Who Loved Lucinda. by Florence Bergen. Taipei: Four Seas Cultural Co., 1961. 355 p.
Taiwan, Eden in Asia. by Florence Drumright. Taipei: Caves Book Co., 1969. 88 p. (Complete travel guide to Taiwan.)

DU BOIS, Coert, 1881-1960. United States Forestry Service 1901-17; United States Army 1917-18; Foreign Service Officer 1919-45. Served in Naples, Paris, Port Said, State Department, Batavia, Genoa, Havana, Anglo-American Commission 1942-45.
Trail Blazers. Stonington, Conn.?: 1957. 85 p.
Caribbean Tourist Trade, a Regional Approach. Washington: Anglo-American Caribbean Commission, 1945. 171 p.

DU BOIS, James T., 1851-1920. Lawyer, banker, editor. Foreign Service Officer 1877-86, and 1897-1913. Served in Aix-la-Chapelle, Callao, Leipzig, St. Gall, State Department, Singapore, Minister to Colombia 1911-13.
The Centennial of Susquehanna County. with William J. Pike. Washington: Gray & Clarkson, 1888. 138 p.
Fun and Pathos of One Life. New York: Neale Publishing Co., 1908. 187 p.
Galusha A. Grow, Father of the Homestead Law. with Gertrude S. Mathews. Boston: Houghton Mifflin Co., 1917. 305 p.

DULLES, Allen Welsh, 1893-1969. Foreign Service Officer 1916-26. Lawyer. Legal Advisor of American Delegation to Naval Conference at Geneva 1932-33. European Director of Office of Strategic Services during World War II. Director of Central Intelligence Agency 1953-61. Served in Vienna, Berne, Paris, Berlin, State Department, Constantinople, Geneva.
Secret Surrender. New York: Harper & Row, 1966. 268 p. In Portuguese, Sao Paulo, Brazil: Ibrasa,

1967.

Can America Stay Neutral? with Hamilton Fish Armstrong. New York: Harper & Bros. , 1939. 277 p.

Can We Be Neutral? with Hamilton Fish Armstrong. New York: Harper & Bros. for the Council of Foreign Relations, 1936. 191 p.

The Craft of Intelligence. New York: Harper & Row, 1963. 177 p.

Germany's Underground. New York: The Macmillan Co. , 1947. 207 p.

The United Nations. with a statement by Edward R. Stettinius, Jr. New York: Foreign Policy Association, 1946. 96 p.

(Edited) Great True Spy Stories. New York: Harper & Row, 1968. 393 p.

DULLES, Eleanor Lansing, 1895- . Research. Educator, lecturer, writer, Economic officer State Department 1942-45; Financial Attaché Vienna 1945-49. Sister of John Foster Dulles. [Q. V.]

The Bank for International Settlements At Work. New York: The Macmillan Co. , 1932. 631 p.

John Foster Dulles: The Last Year. Foreword by Dwight D. Eisenhower. New York: Harcourt, Brace & World, Inc. , 1963. 244 p.

Berlin: The Wall Is Not Forever. Chapel Hill, N. C. : University of North Carolina Press, 1967. 245 p.

Depression and Reconstruction: A Study of Causes and Controls. Philadelphia: University of Pennsylvania Press, 1936. 340 p.

Detente: Cold War Strategies in Transition. with others. Preface by Admiral Arleigh Burke. Foreword by Robert Murphy. New York: Frederick A. Praeger, Inc. for Georgetown University, Washington, Center of Strategic Studies, 1965. 307 p.

The Dollar, the Franc and Inflation. New York: The Macmillan Co. , 1933. 106 p.

Financing the Social Security Act. Washington: Social Security Board, 1936. 67 p.

The French Franc 1914-1928: The Facts and Their Interpretation. New York: The Macmillan Co. , 1929. 570 p.

DULLES, John Foster, 1888-1959. Lawyer. Advisor to President Wilson at Peace Conference in Paris. Reparations Commission. Supreme Economic Council 1919. Delegate to Berlin Debt Conferences 1933.

Delegate to United Nations General Assembly 1946-50.
Special Ambassador to negotiate the Peace Treaty with
Japan 1950-51. Secretary of State 1951-59.
War, Peace and Change. New York: Harper & Bros.,
　　1939. 170 p.
War or Peace. New York: The Macmillan Co., 1957.
　　274 p.
Spiritual Legacy of John Foster Dulles: Selections from
　　his Articles and Addresses. Introd. by Henry P. Van
　　Dusen. Philadelphia: Westminister Press, 1960.
　　232 p.
A Peace Treaty in the Making: Japanese Peace Confer-
　　ence, San Francisco, September 4-8, 1951. Washing-
　　ton: Government Printing Office, 1951. 55 p.

DUNHAM, Donald Carl, 1908- . Foreign Service Officer
　　1931-39, 1946-55. Served in Berlin, Hong Kong,
　　Athens, Aden, Bucharest, Bern, State Department.
Envoy Unextraordinary. New York: John Day Co., 1944.
　　166 p.
Kremlin Target: U. S. A. New York: Ives Washburn,
　　Inc., 1961. 274 p.
Political Aspects of Press Reporting of Crisis of Novem-
　　ber 1953. Trieste: Free Territory of Trieste, 1954.
　　332 p.
Zone of Violence: The Brutal, Shocking Story Lived by
　　an American Diplomat Behind the Red Curtain. New
　　York: Belmont Books, 1962. 188 p. Also published
　　in German under the title Die Schatten Werden Langer.
　　Zurich: Thomas Verlag, 1961.

DUNLAP, Maurice Pratt, 1882-1965. Editorial writer.
　　Philippine Civil Service, Department of Agriculture.
　　Foreign Service Officer 1915-1942. Served in Copen-
　　hagen, Odense, Malmo, Bangkok, Port-au-Prince,
　　Stockholm, State Department, Dundee, Bergen.
Stories of the Vikings. Indianapolis: The Bobbs-Merrill
　　Co., Inc., 1923. 342 p.
Viking Knights: A Story of the Pagan North. Edinburgh:
　　Moray Press, 1933. 308 p.

DUNN, James Clement, 1890- . Foreign Service Officer
　　1919-1956. Career Ambassador. Assistant Secretary
　　of State. Served in Washington, Madrid, Port-au-
　　Prince, Brussels, London, Ambassador to Italy 1946,
　　to France 1952, to Spain 1953, to Brazil 1955-56.
One book in two parts. The first part--"DISCORSI IN

ITALIA 1947-1950. " The second part--"ADDRESSES
IN ITALY 1947-1950. " The two parts are, respective-
ly, in Italian and in English. Published in Rome by
the American Daily Publishing Co. Inc. 1950. 192 p.

DUNN, William Edward, 1888-1966. History professor.
Department of Commerce 1919-24. Director General
Internal Revenue, Haiti 1924-27. Kemmerer Financial
Commission to Colombia 1930. International Banking
1927-31. Financial Advisor to Dominican Republic
1931-33. Bureau Foreign and Domestic Commerce
1934-37. Foreign Service Officer 1937-49. Director
Inter-American School Service 1949-55. Served in
Buenos Aires, Guatemala, Bogota, Port-au-Prince,
Santo Domingo.
The James McMurry Dunn Family of Texas and Kentucky:
the Migration of Their Ancestors from County Derry,
Northern Ireland to Pennsylvania, Thence to the Pro-
vince of Maryland and Their Further Migration to Ken-
tucky and Texas. Washington, D. C. :? 1960. 124 p.
Peru: A Commercial and Industrial Handbook. by W. E.
Dunn, U. S. Commercial Attaché, Lima and with oth-
ers. Washington: Government Printing Office, 1925.
530 p.
Spanish and French Rivalry in the Gulf Region of the
United States, 1678-1702: The Beginning of Texas and
Pensacola. Austin: University of Texas Press, 1917.
238 p.

DUNNELL, Mark Boothby, 1864-1940. Lawyer, book pub-
lisher, author, Member of Congress. Deputy Consul
General at Shanghai 1889-92.
(Edited) Minnesota Digest Decisions of the Supreme Court,
Minnesota. Reports, 1-109. Owatonna, Minn. :
Minnesota Law Book Co. , 1910. 3 vols.
(Edited) Suppl. Owatonna: Minnesota Law Book Co. ,
1912. 234 p.
(Edited) Suppl. Owatonna: Minnesota Law Book Co. ,
1921. 1263 p.
(Edited) complete prior to July 1, 1927. Owatonna:
Minnesota Law Book Co. , 6 vols.
(Edited) Suppl. Owatonna: Minnesota Law Book Co. ,
1930. 410 p.
(Edited) Suppl. Owatonna: Minnesota Law Book Co. ,
1932. 920 p.
(Edited) Suppl. Owatonna: Minnesota Law Book Co. ,
1934. 537 p.

(Edited) Suppl. Owatonna: Minnesota Law Book Co.,
    1937. 583 p.
Minnesota Pleading. Minneapolis: Goodyear Book Co.,
    1899. 578 p. 2nd edit. Owatonna: Minnesota Law
    Book Co., 1914. 1047 p.
Persig's Dunnell on Minnesota Pleading. 3rd edit. new
    and rev. St. Paul: Mason Publishing Co., 1944. 3
    vols.
Minnesota Tax Law, Etc. St. Paul: F. P. Dufresne,
    1904.
Minnesota Trial Book. Minneapolis: Goodyear Book Co.,
    1898. 457 p.

EAGLETON, William L., Jr., 1926- . Foreign Service
    Officer 1949- . Served in Damascus, Beirut, State
    Department, Tabriz, Nouakchchett, London, Aden,
    Algiers.
The Kurdish Republic of 1946. London: Oxford Univer-
    sity Press, 1963. 142 p.

EATON, Charles Edward, 1916- . Vice Consul Rio de
    Janeiro 1942-46.
The Bright Plain. Chapel Hill: University of North Caro-
    lina Press, 1942. 92 p.
The Shadow of the Swimmer. [poems] New York: Fine
    Editions Press, 1951.
Write Me From Rio. Winston-Salem, North Carolina:
    John F. Blair, 1961. 214 p.

EATON, John Henry, 1790-1856. Minister to Spain 1836-
    40. [Q. V. O'Neale]
The Life of Andrew Jackson, Major General in the Ser-
    vice of the United States. Comprising a history of the
    war in the South. From the commencement of the
    Creek campaign, to the termination of hostilities be-
    fore New Orleans. Commenced by John Reid, Brevet
    Major, U. S. Army. Completed by John Henry Eaton.
    Philadelphia: M. Carey & Son. For the benefit of
    the children of John Reid. Lydia R. Bailey, printer,
    1817. 425 p.
The Complete Memoirs of Andrew Jackson, Seventh Pre-
    sident of the United States, Containing a Full Account
    of His Military Life and Achievements, With His Ca-
    reer as President. Philadelphia: Claxton, Remson &
    Haffelfinger, 1878. 362 p.

ECHOLS, James R., 1924- . Teacher. United States

Information Agency 1951- . Served in Port-au-
Prince, Sao Paulo, Lima, Milan, Santiago. (Co-au-
thor, with James H. McGillivray, of the following:)
Ten Great Americans. New York: American Book Co.,
    1960. 116 p.
People at Work. New York: American Book Co., 1961.
    104 p.
Toward a Better World. New York: American Book
    Co., 1962. 122 p.
Let's Take a Trip. New York: American Book Co.,
    1963. 120 p.

EGAN, Maurice Francis, 1852-1924. Editor, professor,
    writer, translator. Minister to Denmark 1907-18.
    He was Dean of the Diplomatic Corps in Denmark by
    1916. Negotiated the treaty for the purchase of the
    Danish West Indies (Virgin Islands).
Recollections of a Happy Life. New York: George H.
    Doran Co., 1924. 374 p.
The Life Around Us. New York: F. Pustet Co., 1885.
    409 p.
Ten Years on the German Frontier. New York: George
    H. Doran Co., 1919. 364 p.
The Adventurers. Philadelphia: H. L. Kilner Co.,
    1922. 224 p.
Amelie in France. Philadelphia: H. L. Kilner Co.,
    1912. 202 p.
Belinda: A Story of New York. Philadelphia: H. L.
    Kilner, 1901. 276 p.
Belinda's Cousins--A Tale of Town and Country. Phila-
    delphia: H. L. Kilner, 1903. 315 p.
The Boys in the Block. New York: Benziger Bros.,
    1897. 85 p.
The Chatelaine of the Roses. A Romance of St. Bartholo-
    mew's Night, and Other Tales. Philadelphia: H. L.
    Kilner, 1895. 218 p.
Confessions of a Book-Lover. Garden City, N.Y.: Page
    & Co., 1922. 249 p.
Everybody's St. Francis. New York: The Century Co.,
    1912. 191 p.
The Flower of the Flock, and the Badgers of Belmont.
    New York: Benziger Bros., 1895. 279 p.
A Garden of Roses. Stories and Sketches. Boston: T.
    B. Noonan Co., 1887. 278 p.
A Gentleman. New York: Benziger Bros., 1893. 207 p.
The Ghost in Hamlet and Other Essays in Comparative
    Literature. Chicago: A. C. McClurg, 1906. 325 p.

(Edited) Glories of the Catholic Church in Art, Architecture and History. Chicago: D. H. McBride, 1895. 508 p. Illustrated.

(Edited) The Hierarchy of the Roman Catholic Church in the United States. Philadelphia: G. Barrie, 1888. 2 vols.

How They Worked Their Way, and Other Tales. New York: Benziger Bros., 1892. 256 p.

In a Brazilian Forest, and Three Brave Boys. Philadelphia: H. L. Kilner Co., 1898. 219 p.

An Introduction to English Literature. Boston: Marlier Co., 1901. 241 p.

The Ivy Hedge. New York: Benziger Bros., 1914. 331 p.

Jack Chumleigh at Boarding School. Philadelphia: H. L. Kilner Co., 1899. 280 p.

Jack Chumleigh, or, Friends and Foes. Baltimore: J. Murphy Co., 1896. 251 p.

Jasper Thorn: A Story of New York Life. Philadelphia: H. L. Kilner Co., 1897. 303 p.

The Knights of Columbus in Peace and War. with John B. Kennedy. New Haven: Knights of Columbus, 1920. 2 vols.

The Leopard of Lancianus, and Other Stories. Philadelphia: H. L. Kilner Co., 1898. 229 p.

A Marriage of Reason. Baltimore: J. Murphy Co., 1893. 344 p.

St. Martin's Summer. Philadelphia: H. L. Kilner Co., 1905. 307 p.

Short Stories. Series II. New York: C. Wildermann, 1900. 3 vols.

Some Pleasant Talks for Boys and Girls. New York: C. Wildermann, 1898. 64 p.

Songs and Sonnets, and Other Poems. Chicago: A. C. McClurg Co., 1892. 201 p.

Studies in Literature. Some Words About Chaucer and Other Essays. St. Louis: B. Herder, 1899. 130 p.

The Success of Patrick Desmond. Notre Dame: Office of the "Ave Maria," 1893. 418 p.

That Girl of Mine. Philadelphia: T. B. Peterson & Bro., 1877. 294 p.

That Lover of Mine. Philadelphia: T. B. Peterson & Bro., 1877. 248 p.

The Vacation of Edward Conway. New York: Benziger Bro., 1896. 322 p.

The Watson Girls - A Washington Story. Philadelphia: H. L. Kilner Co., 1900. 196 p.

The Watsons of the Country. Philadelphia: H. L. Kilner
    Co. , 1905. 303 p.
The Wiles of Sexton Maginnis. New York: The Century
    Co. , 1909. 380 p.
(Edited) The Best Stories by the Foremost Catholic Au-
    thors. New York: Benziger Bros. , 1910. 10 vols.

EHLERS, Joseph Henry, 1892- . Civil engineer, lawyer,
    writer, publisher. Professor of structural engineering
    at Pei Yang Univ. in China 1920-24. Construction en-
    gineer on diversion of Yellow River 1923. Commer-
    cial Attaché Tokyo 1929 on earthquake reconstruction
    Japan 1926-30. Housing Coordinator International Co-
    operation Administration 1960-61.
Far Horizons. The Travel Diary of an Engineer. New
    York: The Carlton Press, 1966. 189 p.

EINSTEIN, Lewis, 1877-1967. Historian. Diplomatic Ser-
    vice 1903-30. Served in Paris, London, Morocco,
    Constantinople, Peking, Bucharest. Minister to Costa
    Rica 1911-13, to Czechoslovakia 1921-30.
American Foreign Policy by a Diplomatist. Boston:
    Houghton Mifflin Co. , 1909. 192 p.
Divided Loyalties: Americans in England During the War
    of Independence. Boston: Houghton Mifflin Co. , 1933.
    469 p. Freeport, N.Y. : Books for Libraries Press,
    1969.
Inside Constantinople: A Diplomatist's Diary During the
    Dardanelles Expedition. April - September 1915.
    London: J. Murray, 1917. 291 p.
Holmes-Einstein Letters. Edited by James Bishop Pea-
    body. New York: St. Martin's Press, 1964. 377 p.
    [Mr. Justice Holmes]
A Diplomat Looks Back. Edited by Lawrence E. Gelfand.
    Foreword by George Kennan. New Haven: Yale Uni-
    versity Press, 1968. 269 p.
Historical Change. Cambridge, England: Cambridge Uni-
    versity Press, 1946. 132 p.
The Italian Renaissance in England: Studies. New York:
    Columbia University Press, 1902. 420 p.
Looking at Italian Pictures in the National Gallery of Art.
    Washington: National Gallery of Art, Smithsonian In-
    stitute, 1951. 116 p.
Luigi Pulci and the Morgante Maggiore. Berlin: E.
    Felber, 1902. 68 p.
A Prophecy of the War, 1913-1914. Foreword by Theo-
    dore Roosevelt. New York: Columbia University

Press, 1918. 94 p.

Roosevelt, His Mind in Action.   Boston: Houghton Mifflin
Co., 1930. 259 p.

Scattered Verse.   Florence: Tip. Giuntina, 1949.   140 p.

Tudor Ideals.   New York: Harcourt, Brace, 1921.
366 p.

The Winged Victory.   London: De La Mare Press, 1941.
51 p.

(Edited) Thoughts on Art and Life, by Leonard Da Vinci.
Translated by Maurice Baring.   Boston: The Merry-
mount Press, 1906.   200 p.

EISENHOWER, John S. D., 1922-   .   United States Army
1944-63.   Writer 1965-69.   Son of President Eisenhower.   Ambassador to Belgium 1969-71.

The Bitter Woods: The Dramatic Story, Told at All
Echelons, From Supreme Command to Squad Leader,
of the Crisis That Shook the Western Coalition: Hitler's Surprise Ardennes Offensives.   New York: G. P.
Putnam's Sons, 1969.   506 p.

ELLIS, George Washington, 1875-1919.   Lawyer, sociologist,
author.   Secretary of Legation at Liberia 1902-10.
Instructed to find out all he could about that part of
Africa, he became an authority on the ethnology,
linguistics, sociology and economy of West Africa.
Returned to America to practice law.

Negro Culture in West Africa.   Introd. by Fredrick Starr.
New York: Neale Publishing Co., 1914.   290 p.

The Leopard's Claw.   [a novel] New York: International
Author's Association, 1917.   172 p.

Negro Achievements in Social Progress.   ?   ?   ?   1915.

ELLSWORTH, Henry William, 1814-1864.   Lawyer.   Chargé
d'Affaires in Sweden and Norway 1845-49.

Valley of the Upper Wabash, Indiana, With Hints on its
Agricultural Advantages, Etc.   New York: Pratt,
Robinson Co., 1838.   175 p.

The American Swine Breeder, a Practical Treatise on the
Selection, Rearing and Fattening of Swine.   Boston:
Weeks, Jordan & Co., 1840.   304 p.

EMMERSON, John Kenneth, 1908-   .   Foreign Service Offi-
cer 1935-68.   Served in Tokyo, Osaka, Taihoku, Lima,
Chungking, Political Advisor to Commander-in-Chief
Pacific, to Supreme Commander Tokyo, Washington,
Moscow, National War College, Karachi, Beirut, Paris,

Lagos, Salisbury, Stanford University, Personal rank of Minister.

Arms, Yen, and Power: The Japanese Dilemma. New York: The Dunellen Co., Inc., 1971. 420 p.

EMMONS, Arthur Brewster III, 1910-1962. Sikong Expedition to Southeastern Tibet 1931-33. British-American Himalayan Expedition 1936. Burma-China Expedition 1936. Foreign Service Officer 1939-62. Served in Montreal, Hankow, Keijo, State Department, Montevideo, SCAP (Office of Supreme Command for Allied Powers) Japan, Seoul, Madrid, Canberra, Dublin, Kuala Lumpur.

Men In The Clouds. with Richard L. Burdsall and others. New York: Harper Brothers, 1935. 292 p.

ENGLISH, George Bethune, 1787-1828. Writer. Lieutenant in Marines. Became a Mohammedan and an officer in the Egyptian Army. Left for home after a campaign to the Sudan 1820-21. Appointed American secret agent in Turkey 1823-24. Left when suspected by Turks of being a Greek spy. Sent to Levant as interpreter for Commodore John Rogers 1825-26.

The Grounds of Christianity Examined by Comparing the New Testament with The Old. Boston: Printed for the author, 1813. 182 p.

A Letter to the Reverend Mr. Cary, Containing Remarks Upon his Review of the Grounds of Christianity Examined, by Comparing the New Testament With the Old. By the Author of That Work. Boston: Printed for the author, 1813. 133 p.

A Narrative of the Expedition to Dongola and Sennaar, Under the Command of His Excellence Ismael Pasha, Undertaken by Order of His Highness Mohammed Ali Pasha, Viceroy of Egypt. By an American in the Service of the Viceroy. London: J. Murray, 1822. 232 p.

Five Pebbles From the Brook. Philadelphia: Printed for the author, 1824. 124 p.

EPERNAY, Mark, (pseud.). See John Kenneth Galbraith.
The McLandress Dimension. Illus. by James Stevenson. Boston: Houghton Mifflin Co., 1963. 126 p.

ERVING, George William, 1769-1850. Diplomatic agent in London. Chargé d'Affaires in Madrid 1804-09. Minister to Spain 1814-19.

(Translated) The Alphabet of the Primitive Language of
Spain and a Philosophical Investigation of the Antiquity
and Civilization of the Basque People.   by Juan Bautista de Erro.   1829.   89 p.

EVANS, F. Bowen, 1916- . Lecturer.   State Department
official and Foreign Service Reserve Officer with United
States Information Administration 1951-71.   Served in
London, Bogota and Rio de Janeiro.
Worldwide Communist Propaganda Activities.   New York:
The Macmillan Co., 1955.   222 p.

EVANS, John Walker, 1904- . Investment banker.   Department of State 1941-45; United States Commercial
Company 1945-46; Department of Commerce 1947-48;
State Department 1949-57; Foreign Service Officer
1957-65; Harvard University 1965-67; Executive Office
of the President 1967-71; Johns Hopkins University
1967- . Served in London, Madrid, Geneva.   Personal rank of Minister.
United States Trade Policy.   New York: Harper & Row,
for the Council on Foreign Relations, 1967.   112 p.
The Kennedy Round in American Trade Policy: The Twilight of the GATT?   Cambridge: Harvard University
Press, 1971.   383 p.

EVERETT, Alexander Hill, 1790-1847.   Editor.   Private
Secretary to John Quincy Adams in Russia 1809-11.
Secretary of Legation at The Hague 1815-16, Chargé
d'Affaires at The Hague 1818-24, Minister to Spain
1825-29, Commissioner to China 1845-47.
Europe.   Boston: O. Everett, 1822.   451 p.
America.   Philadelphia: H. C. Carey & I. Lea, 1827.
364 p.
New Ideas on Population with Remarks on the Theories of
Malthus and Godwin.   Boston: O. Everett, 1823.
125 p.
Critical and Miscellaneous Essays.   Boston: J. Monroe
& Co., 1845-46.   2 vols.
The Poems.   Boston: J. Monroe & Co., 1845.   105 p.

EVERETT, Edward, 1794-1865.   Clergyman, teacher, ora-
tor, Congressman, Senator.   President of Harvard.
Minister to Great Britain 1841-45.   Secretary of State
1852-53.
An Address at Gettsburg Published with Lincoln's Address.
Boston: by Little, Brown & Co. for the benefit of the

Cemetery Monument Fund, 1864.   87 p.
Eulogy of Lafayette.   at Faneuil Hall.   Boston: N. Hale
    and Allen, 1834.   104 p.
Life of George Washington.   (Orations and speeches.)
    New York: Sheldon Co.   Boston: Gould & Lincoln,
    1860.   348 p.
The Mount Vernon Papers.   New York: D. Appleton Co.,
    1860.   490 p.   [The author received $10,000 from the
    New York Ledger for the Mount Vernon Ladies Associ-
    ation toward the purchase of Mount Vernon.]
Orations and Speeches on Various Occasions.   Boston:
    American Stationers Co., 1836.   637 p.

EWING, Hugh Boyle, 1826-1905.   Army officer.   Minister
    to the Netherlands 1866-70.   Writer.
A Castle in the Air.   New York: H. Holt Co., 1888.
    273 p.
The Black List: A Tale of Early California.   New York:
    P. F. Collier, 1893.   288 p.

FAIRBANK, John King, 1907- .   Historian, authority on
    China.   Professor at Harvard.   Office of Strategic
    Services in Washington 1941-42; special assistant to
    American Ambassador in Chungking 1942-43; Office of
    War Information, Washington, 1944-45; Director of
    United States Information Service in China 1945-46.
China: the People's Middle Kingdom and the U.S.A.
    Cambridge: Belknap Press of Harvard University
    Press, 1967.   145 p.
China's Response to the West: a Documentary Survey,
    1839-1923.   with Ssu-yu Teng, E-tu Zen Sun, Chaoying
    Fang and others.   Cambridge: Harvard University
    Press, 1954.   296 p.   Prepared in cooperation with
    the International Secretariat of the Institute of Pacific
    Relations.
Research Guide to the above by the same authors.   Cam-
    bridge: Harvard University Press, 1954.   84 p.
(Edited) Chinese Communist Publications: an Annotated
    bibliography of Material in the Chinese Library at Har-
    vard University.   with E-tu Zen Sun for the Russian
    Research Center and mimeographed for private distri-
    bution.   Cambridge: Russian Research Center, Har-
    vard University, 1949.   122 p.
Chinese Thought and Institutions.   with contributions by
    T'ung-tsu Ch'u and others.   Chicago: University of
    Chicago Press, 1957.   428 p.
Ch'ing Administration: Three Studies by John K. Fairbank

and Ssu-yu Teng. Cambridge: Harvard University
Press, 1960. 218 p. Originally published in Harvard
Journal of Asiatic Studies 1939-41.
Ch'ing Documents: An Introductory Syllabus. Compiled
    by John King Fairbank, For Use in the Seminar in
    Modern Chinese History at Harvard University. Cam-
    bridge: Published with the assistance of Harvard-
    Yenching Institute and distributed by Harvard University
    Press, 1952. 2 vols. 2nd edit. 1959. 3rd edit.
    (rev. and enl.) 1965. 2 vols.
A Documentary History of Chinese Communism. with
    Conrad Bradt and Benjamin Schwartz. New York:
    Atheneum Publishers, 1966. 552 p.
Japanese Studies of Modern China: a Bibliographical
    Guide to Historical and Social-Science Research on the
    19th and 20th Centuries. with Masataka Banno. Rut-
    land, Vt.: Published for the Harvard-Yenching Insti-
    tute by C. E. Tuttle Co., 1955. 331 p. 2nd edit.
    Cambridge: Harvard University Press, 1971. 331 p.
Trade and Diplomacy on the China Coast: the Opening of
    the Treaty Ports 1842-1854. Stanford, Calif.: Stan-
    ford University Press, 1969. 583 p. 1st edit. Cam-
    bridge: Harvard University Press, 1953. 2 vols.
Modern China: a Bibliographical Guide to Chinese Works,
    1898-1937. with Kwang-ching Liu. Cambridge: Har-
    vard University Press, 1950. 608 p.
New Views of China's Tradition and Modernization. Wash-
    ington: Service Center for Teachers of History, 1968.
    59 p.
The United States and China. Cambridge: Harvard Uni-
    versity Press, 1948. 384 p. 3rd edit. 1971. 500 p.

FAIRBANK, Wilma (Cannon), 1909- . Mrs. Fairbank is
    the wife of John King Fairbank. [Q. V.] Chinese
    language study Peiping 1932-36. Researcher American
    Council of Learned Societies 1941. Divisional Assistant
    in State Department 1942. Cultural Relations Officer
    at Chungking 1945, Nanking 1946-47.
Adventures in retrieval. Harvard-Yenching Institute
    Studies XXVIII. Han murals and Shang bronze molds.
    Cambridge: Harvard University Press, 1972. 201 p.
(Edited) Directory of Organizations in America Concerned
    with China. Washington, D. C.: American Council of
    Learned Societies, 1942. 116 p.

FAIRCHILD, Lucius, 1831-1896. Union soldier. Governor
    of Wisconsin. Consul at Liverpool 1872-78. Consul

General at Paris 1878-80.   Minister to Spain 1880-81.

The California Letters of Lucius Fairchild.   Edit. by
Joseph Schafer.   Madison, Wisconsin: State Historical
Society of Wisconsin, 1931.   212 p.

Fairchild Papers, 1819-1923.   116 vols. and 85 boxes.
State Historical Society of Wisconsin.   Includes business and financial papers of his father, brothers and
sister.   Also includes consular correspondence from
Fairchild's posts at Liverpool, Paris and Madrid, with
11 volumes of consular letter books.

FAY, Theodore Sedgewick, 1807-1898.   Writer.   Clerk in
Embassy, London.   Secretary of Legation in Berlin
1837-53.   Minister Resident in Switzerland 1853-61.
Retired in Berlin where he remained until his death.

Dreams and Reveries of a Quiet Man.   New York: J. &
J. Harper, 1832.   2 vols.   (His early articles in the
New York Mirror.)

Norman Leslie: A Tale of Pleasant Times.   New York:
Harper Bros. , 1835.   2 vols.   (A best seller until
Edgar Allen Poe attacked it in the Southern Literary
Messenger, which started a verbal battle between Poe
and New York Literati.)

Sydney Clifton.   New York: Harper & Bros. , 1839.   2
vols.

The Countess Ida.   A tale of Berlin.   New York: Harper
& Bros. , 1840.   2 vols.

Hoboken: A Romance.   New York: Harper & Bros. ,
1843.   2 vols.

Ulric, or, The Voices.   (narrative poem) New York: D.
Appleton Co. , 1851.   189 p.

A Great Outline of Geography.   New York: G. P. Putnam
& Sons, 1871.   396 p.

Die Sklavenmacht: Blicke in die Gaschichte der Vereinigten Staaten von Amerika.   Berlin: Stilke & Van May-
den, 1865.   158 p.

The Three Germanys.   New York: Published for the author, 1889.   2 vols.

Atlas of Universal Geography for Libraries and Families.
New York: G. P. Putnam, 1869.   238 p.

Atlas to Fay's Great Outline of Geography for High
Schools and Families, With a Textbook.   New York:
G. P. Putnam, 1867.   238 p.

Statement Relative to Some Business Transactions With
the Messrs. Harper & Brothers of New York, With
Correspondence.   Berlin: 1845.   78 p.   Ms. note on
cover "Confidential Theo. S. Fay to C. C. Jewett,

Esquire. "

FEAREY, Robert Appleton, 1918- . Private Secretary to
    Ambassador Grew in Tokyo 1941-42. State Department
    and Foreign Service Officer 1942- . Served in Tok-
    yo, State Department, Office of Supreme Commander
    for Allied Powers, (Tokyo), North Atlantic Treaty Or-
    ganization (London), Paris, National War College,
    Political Advisor to Commander in Chief Pacific (Hono-
    lulu) with personal rank of Minister.
The Occupation of Japan - Second Phase: 1948-50. New
    York: The Macmillan Co. , 1950. 239 p.

FEIS, Herbert, 1893-1972. Economist, teacher, writer.
    Council on Foreign Relations. Economic Advisor to
    State Department 1931-37. Attended 1st meeting Ex-
    perts Preparatory Commission for Monetary and Eco-
    nomic Conference, Geneva 1932. Chief Technical Ad-
    visor to American Delegation, London 1933. Special
    Advisor Inter-American Conference for Maintenance of
    Peace, Buenos Aires 1936, to American Delegation to
    Eighth International Conference of American States,
    Lima 1938, and to Meeting of Foreign Ministers of
    American Republics for Consultation, Panama 1939.
    Foreign Service Reserve Officer 1950.
Seen from E. A. New York: Alfred A. Knopf Inc. ,
    1946. 313 p. Republished under the title The Three
    International Episodes, New York: W. W. Norton Co. ,
    1966.
The Spanish Story: France and the Nations at War.
    New York: Alfred A. Knopf Inc. , 1948. 282 p.
The Diplomacy of the Dollar: First Era, 1919-1932.
    Baltimore: Johns Hopkins Press, 1950. 81 p.
The Road to Pearl Harbor. Princeton, N. J. : Princeton
    University Press, 1950. 365 p.
The China Tangle - The American Effort in China from
    Pearl Harbor to The Marshall Mission. Princeton,
    N. J. : Princeton University Press, 1953. 445 p.
Churchill, Roosevelt, Stalin. The War They Waged and
    the Peace They Sought. Princeton, N. J. : Princeton
    University Press, 1957. 692 p.
Between War and Peace: The Potsdam Conference.
    Princeton, N. J. : Princeton University Press, 1960.
    367 p.
Japan Subdued. 1962. 199 p. Revised edit. published
    under the title The Atomic Bomb and The End of World
    War II. Princeton, N. J. : Princeton University

Press, 1966. 213 p.
1933: Characters in Crisis. Boston: Little, Brown &
    Co., 1966. 366 p.
Foreign Aid and Foreign Policy. New York: St. Martin's
    Press, 1964. 246 p.
Contest Over Japan. New York: W. W. Norton Co.,
    1967. 187 p.
The Birth of Israel: The Touseled Diplomatic Bed. New
    York: W. W. Norton & Co., 1969. 90 p.
The Changing Pattern of International Economic Affairs.
    New York: Harper & Bros., 1940. 132 p.
Europe the World's Banker, 1870-1914: An Account of
    European Foreign Investment and the Connection of
    World Finance with Diplomacy Before The War. In-
    trod. by Charles P. Howland. New Haven: Yale Uni-
    versity Press for the Council on Foreign Relations,
    1931. 469 p.
The International Trade of Manchuria. New York: Car-
    negie Endowment for International Peace. Division of
    Intercourse and Education, 1931. 68 p.
The Settlement of Wage Disputes. New York: The Mac-
    millan Co., 1921. 289 p.
The Sinews of Peace. New York: Harper & Bros., 1944.
    271 p.
From Trust to Terror: The Onset of the Cold War,
    1945-1950. New York: W. W. Norton & Co., Inc.,
    1971. 412 p.
The Historian and the Diplomat: The Role of History and
    Historians In American Foreign Policy. with others.
    Edit. by Francis L. Lowenheim. New York: Harper
    Bros., 1967. 213 p.
(Edited) A Collection of Decisions Presenting Principals
    of Wage Settlement. with introd. New York: H. W.
    Wilson Co., 1924. 452 p.

FENZI, Jewell (Tickle), 1927- . Mrs. Fenzi is the wife
    of Foreign Service Officer Guido C. Fenzi, b. 1927,
    who entered the Foreign Service in 1956 and has served
    in the State Department, Rotterdam, Freetown (Sierra
    Leone), Rabat and Curaçao. Mrs. Fenzi has accom-
    panied her husband to all his foreign posts.
This Is the Way We Cook: Recipes from Outstanding
    Cooks of the Netherlands Antilles. with Helen Dovale.
    Curaçao: Thayer-Sargent Publications, 1972. 64 p.
    Original title in 1971: This Is the Way We Cook -
    Recipes from Outstanding Cooks of Aruba, Curaçao and
    Bonaire. Curaçao: Thayer-Sargent Publications, 1971.
    48 p.

FIFIELD, Russell Hunt, 1914- . Professor of history and
Far East expert. State Department and Foreign Ser-
vice Officer 1945-47. Served in Hankow.
The Diplomacy of Southeast Asia: 1945-58. New York:
Harper Bros., 1958. 584 p.
Geopolitics in Principle and Practice. with G. Etzel
Pearcy. Boston: Ginn & Co., 1944. 203 p.
The Lower Mekong: Challenge to Cooperation in Southeast
Asia. with C. Hart Schaaf. Princeton, N.J.: D. Van
Nostrand Co. Inc., 1963. 136 p.
Southeast Asia in United States Policy. New York: Fred-
erick A. Praeger Inc. for the Council on Foreign Re-
lations, 1963. 488 p.
Woodrow Wilson and the Far East: the Diplomacy of the
Shantung Question. New York: Thomas F. Crowell
Co., 1952. 383 p.
World Political Geography. with G. Etzel Pearcy and
others. Cartography by Robert J. Voskuil. New
York: Thomas Y. Crowell Co., 1948. 653 p.

FISHER, Glen H., 1922- . Foreign Service Information
Agency 1953-57. Foreign Service Officer 1957- .
Served in State Department, Caracas, Cebu, Manila,
Foreign Service Institute, Cochabamba.
Public Diplomacy and the Behavioral Sciences. Blooming-
ington: Indiana University Press, 1972. 192 p.

FISHER, Roger Drummer, 1922- . Lawyer, educator, As-
sistant Deputy United States Special Representative,
Economic Cooperation Administration, Paris 1948-49.
International Conflict for Beginners. Foreword by Edward
M. Kennedy. Illus. by Robert C. Osborn. New York:
Harper & Row, 1969. 231 p.
(Edited) International Conflict and Behavioral Science: The
Craigville Papers. New York: Basic Books, 1964.
290 p.

FLAGG, Edmund, 1815-1890. Author, editor. Secretary to
American Minister, Berlin, 1894. Consul in Venice.
Statistician in the State Department. (A list of the published writings of Edmund Flagg is in the Library Bulletin of Bowdoin College, Brunswick, Maine. 1895.
pp. 36-38.)
The Far West: or, A Tour Beyond the Mountains, Em-
bracing Outlines of Western Life and Scenery: Sketches
of the Prairies, Rivers, Ancient Mounds, Early Settlements of the French. New York: Harper & Brothers,

1838. 2 vols.
The Howard Queen: A Romance of History. By Edmund
   Flagg, Esq. to which the Prize of 100 Dollars Offered
   by the Proprietors of the St. Louis Union, for the
   Best Original Story, Was Awarded. St. Louis: 1848.
   78 p.
Venice: The City of the Sea, From the Invasion by Napo-
   leon in 1797 to the Capitulation to Radetzky, in 1849.
   New York: Charles Scribner, 1853. 2 vols.
Edmund Dantes: A Sequel to the 'Count of Monte Cristo'
   by Alexandre Dumas. Philadelphia: T. B. Peterson
   & Brothers, 1872. 203 p.
De Molai: The Last of the Military Grand Masters of the
   Order of Templar Knights. A Romance of History.
   Philadelphia: T. B. Peterson & Brothers, 1888.
   378 p.
Report of the Commercial Relations of the United States
   with all Foreign Nations. A. O. P. Nicholson, Print-
   er, 1856-57. 4 vols.
[The names of the publishers and the number of pages of
   each of the following titles are not available.]
The Duchess of Ferrara. Louisville: 1839.
Beatrice of Padua. Louisville: 1839.
Mary Tudor. New York: 1842.
Marion de Lorme. New York: 1842.
The Brigand. New York: 1842.
Gabrielle de Vergi. New York: 1842.
Francis of Valois. New York: 1843.
Carrero: or, the Prime Minister. New York: 1843.
Mary Tudor. (a play) New York: 1844.
Ruy Blas. (a play based on Victor Hugo's drama) New
   York: 1845.
Catherine Howard. (a play) St. Louis: 1847.
Panorama of the Mississippi. St. Louis: 1849.
Report on Immigration. Washington: 1854.
Report on Cotton Trade. Washington: 1855.
Report on Tobacco Trade. Washington: 1856.
Report of the Constitution Convention. St. Louis: 1845.

FLETCHER, James Cooley, 1823-1901. Missionary in
   Brazil. Secretary of Legation at Rio de Janeiro 1852-
   53. Consul in Oporto 1869-73. Chargé d'Affaires
   Lisbon 1870.
   Brazil and the Brazilians. with the Reverend D. P. Kid-
      der. Boston: Little, Brown & Co. , 1879. 646 p.
   Also in Portuguese, transl. by Elias Dolianiti, revised
   from notes of Edward Sussekind de Mendonça. Sao

Paulo: Companhia Editora Nacional, 1941. 2 vols.

FOLSOM, George, 1802-1869. Author, antiquarian. Chargé
    d'Affaires at The Hague 1850-53.
  History of Sacco and Biddeford. Saco, Maine: A. C.
    Putnam, 1830. 331 p.
  Mexico in 1842. To which was added an account of Texas
    and Yucatan and of the Santa Fe Expedition. New
    York: C. J. Folsum, 1842. 256 p.
  (Translated) Despatches of Hernando Cortez. New York:
    Wiley & Putnam, 1843. 431 p.
  (Edited) 2nd volume of the American Antiquarian Society's
    Transactions and Collections. 1836.

FOLSOM, Robert Slade, 1915- . Foreign Service Officer
    1941-67. Served in Port-au-Prince, Budapest, Canton,
    Saigon, Mexico City, National War College, State De-
    partment, Thessalonika, Cyprus.
  Handbook of Greek Pottery: A Guide for Amateurs.
    London: Faber & Faber, Ltd., 1968. 84 p. Illus.
    by the author.

FOOTE, Lucius Harwood, 1826-1913. Lawyer. Consul at
    Valparaiso 1879. Acting Chargé d'Affaires at Santiago
    1881-82. To Colombia on a special mission 1883.
    Minister to Korea 1883-84.
  The Wooing of the Rose and Other Poems. New York:
    Platt & Peck, 1911. 189 p.
  Red Letter Day, and Other Poems. Boston: A. Williams
    & Co. 113 p.

FORBES, John Murray, 1771-1831. Consul at Hamburg and
    Copenhagen 1801-19. Diplomatic Agent in Chile and
    Chargé d'Affaires at Buenos Aires 1820-31.
  Once Anos en Buenos Aires, 1820-1831. Las Cronicas
    Diplomaticas de John Murray Forbes. Traducidas por
    Felipe A. Espil. Buenos Aires: Emecé, 1956.
    662 p.

FORBES, William Cameron, 1870-1959. Finance, business,
    public official Governor General of the Philippine Is-
    lands 1909-13. Chairman of the President's Commis-
    sion to study conditions in Haiti 1930. Ambassador to
    Japan 1930-32.
  As To Polo. Seattle: Metropolitan Printing Co., 1911.
    134 p. Privately printed.
  Journals 1904-46. Library of Congress. 3 ft. Manuscript

Division.

The Philippine Islands. Boston: Houghton Mifflin Co.,
1928. 2 vols.

Romance of Business. Boston: Houghton Mifflin Co.,
1921. 258 p. Illus. by A. L. Ripley.

The Friar Land Inquiry, Philippine Government. with
Dean C. Worcester and Frank W. Carpenter. Manila:
Bureau of Printing, 1910. 208 p.

Report of the President's Commission for the Study and
Review of Conditions in the Republic of Haiti. March
26, 1930. Washington: Government Printing Office.
34 p.

FORESTI, Eleutario Felice, 1793-1858. Born in Italy where
he lived until 1836. Editor, professor, political agita-
tor, imprisoned in Italy until exiled to United States in
1836. Naturalized 1841. Sent as Consul to Genoa 1858
where he died four months later.

(Edited) Learning to Read, Write and Speak Italian. by
Ollendorff. 1846. Edited with additions and correc-
tions.

(Edited) Crestonnazia Italiana. Prose selections of Italian
writers. Class reading book for beginners in the study
of Italian. New York: D. Appleton & Co., 1846.
298 p.

FORMAN, Elbert Eli, 1831-1911. Jurist. Diplomatic Agent
and Consul General at Cairo 1876-1884. Simultaneously
one of the delegates on the International Commission
for Revision of Judicial Codes of International Mixed
Tribunals in Egypt, and one of the judges. Arranged
for the gift from Egypt to New York City of "Cleo-
patra's Needle."

Along the Nile With General Grant. New York: Grafton
Press, 1904. 339 p.

Egypt and Its Betrayal: or, An Account of the Country
During the Periods of Ismail and Tewfik Pashas and
of How England Acquired a New Empire. New York:
The Grafton Press, 1908. 349 p.

FOSTER, John Watson, 1836-1917. Minister to Mexico
1873-80, to Russia 1880-81, to Spain 1883-85. Special
plenipotentiary to negotiate reciprocity agreements
1890-91. United States Agent in Fur-seal Arbitration
1892-93. Secretary of State 1892-93. Commissioner
for China in negotiation of peace treaty of 1895 with
Japan. Ambassador on Special Mission to Great

Britain and Russia in 1897. United States Agent before
Alaska Boundary Tribunal in 1903. He represented
China at the Second Hague Conference in 1907.
American Diplomacy in the Orient. Boston: Houghton
Mifflin Co. , 1903. 498 p.
Biographic Sketches of Matthew Watson Foster, 1800-1865.
Washington: J. J. Little Co. , 1896. 86 p.
A Century of American Diplomacy: Being a Brief Review
of the Relations of the United States. 1776-1876. Bos-
ton: Houghton Mifflin Co. , 1900. 497 p.
Las Memorias Diplomaticas de Mr. Foster Sobre Mexico,
con un Prologo de Genaro Estrada. Mexico City:
Publicaciones de la Secretaria de Relaciones Extran-
jeras, 1929. 143 p.
The Practice of Diplomacy as Illustrated in the Foreign
Relations of the United States. Boston: Houghton
Mifflin Co. , 1906. 401 p.
Diplomatic Memoirs. Boston: Houghton Mifflin Co. ,
1909. 2 vols.
Venezuelan Claims. Senate Foreign Relations Committee.
Washington: Government Printing Office. Apr. 14,
1908. 428 p.
War Stories For My Grandchildren. Cambridge, Mass. :
Riverside Press, 1918. 192 p. Privately printed.

FOX, Ernest F. , 1902- . Mining, Geology Professor.
Military Attaché in Kadul 1943-46. Department of
State and Foreign Service Reserve Officer 1947-53.
Department of Defense 1953-57. Foreign Service Re-
serve Officer 1957-59. Served in Kabul, Tehran,
Kathmandu, State Department.
Travels in Afghanistan. New York: The Macmillan Co. ,
1943. 300 p.
By Compass Alone. Philadelphia: Dorrance & Company,
1971. 280 p. Maps and photos by author, drawings
by Merle M. Fox. Narrative of exploration in Northern
Rhodesia and the Congo.

FRANCIS, Charles Spencer, 1853-1911. Son of John Morgan
Francis, diplomat and editor. Private secretary to
his father in Athens and Vienna. Minister to Greece,
Rumania and Serbia 1900-02.
Sport Among the Rockies. Troy, N. Y. : Troy Daily
Times. Job Printing Establishment, 1889. 134 p.

FRANCIS, David Rowland, 1850-1927. Merchant, Governor
of Missouri 1889-93. President of the St. Louis

World's Fair 1904. Ambassador to Russia 1916-18.
The Universal Exposition of 1904. St. Louis: Louisiana
Purchase Exposition Co., 1915. 2 vols.
Russia from the American Embassy. April 1916 - November 1918. New York: C. Scribner's Sons, 1921.
361 p.
A Tour of Europe in Nineteen Days. St. Louis? 1903.
107 p.

FRANKLIN, Albert Barnes, 3rd, 1909- . Teacher and
professor of romance languages 1930-43. Foreign
Service Officer 1943-67. Cultural Affairs Officer.
Served in Montevideo, Havana, Buenos Aires, Rangoon,
Washington (Dean of the School of International Studies
at the Foreign Service Institute), Jerusalem, Tegucigalpa, Madras.
Ecuador: Portrait of a People. New York: Doubleday,
Doran, 1943. 325 p.

FRANKLIN, Benjamin, 1706-1790. Printer, author, philanthropist, inventor, statesman, diplomat, scientist.
The first "career" diplomat of the United States.
Most of the time from 1757 to 1762 and again from
1764 to 1775, a total of 16 years, he represented the
Colony of Pennsylvania in London. Simultaneously
from 1768 he represented Georgia, from 1769 New
Jersey and from 1770 Massachusetts in London. He
returned to Philadelphia in 1775 as the Revolutionary
War drew near. From the outbreak of the war in 1776
until 1785 he was mostly in Paris, representing the
new republic of the United States of America, jointly,
at times, with Thomas Jefferson, John Adams, John
Jay and Henry Laurens, conducting negotiations not
only with Great Britain and France but also with
Sweden, Prussia and the Barbary States. Returned to
Philadelphia for good in 1785, a total of 28 years
abroad in a represtative capacity.
During this time, beside his other activities, he
never ceased to write important and historical letters,
speeches, articles and essays of political, scientific,
philosophical and social significance. Franklin wrote
126 articles for British newspapers from 1765 to 1775,
defending the cause of the American colonies. In February 1766 he answered 174 questions before the House
of Commons.
His official appointments in Europe for the United
States were as follows:

Joint Commissioner, 1776-78, with Silas Deane and, later, Arthur Lee, to the Court of France, with full powers to negotiate treaties. He signed treaties of commerce and alliance in 1778.

He was assigned Commissioner to the Court of Spain in 1777 but did not enter upon that mission.

Appointed Minister Plenipotentiary to the Court of France 1778-1785.

Joint Commissioner with John Adams, John Jay and Henry Laurens to negotiate a peace treaty with Great Britain 1781; signed preliminary articles in 1782 at Paris; signed definitive treaty 1783 in Paris.

Franklin was Minister Plenipotentiary to negotiate a treaty of amity and commerce with Sweden 1782; signed the treaty 1783 in Paris.

He was joint Minister Plenipotentiary with Thomas Jefferson and John Adams to negotiate a treaty of amity and commerce with European countries and with the Barbary States 1784. Signed a treaty with Prussia 1785 at Passy. He served simultaneously under his several commissions.

Among Franklin's thousands of writings are the following:

Modest Enquiry into the Nature and Necessity of a Paper Currency. 1729. ? ?

Poor Richard's Almanac - Collected Sayings of Poor Richard Saunders. Philadelphia: Printed and sold by Benjamin Franklin at the New Printing Office near the market, 1732-1757.

Plain Truth, or Serious Considerations on the Present State of the City of Philadelphia and Province of Pennsylvania. Philadelphia: Printed by Benjamin Franklin, 1747. 22 p.

Proposals Relating to the Education of Youth in Pennsylvania. Philadelphia: B. Franklin & D. Hall, 1749. 32 p.

Experiments and Observations on Electricity. 1st. Edit. London: E. Cave, 1751-53.

The Interest of Great Britain Considered with Regard to Her Colonies and the Acquisition of Canada and Guadaloupe. London: MDCCLX. Boston: reprinted by B. Mecom and sold at the New Printing Office, near the Towne House, 1760.

Rules By Which a Great Empire May Be Reduced to a Small One. London: Gentleman's Magazine, Sept. 1773. Vol. 43 pp. 441-445.

The Franklin Manuscripts are chiefly to be found in:

(1) The Library of the American Philosophical Society at Philadelphia. 76 vols., 13,000 documents in nine languages.

(2) The Library of Congress, Washington, D.C., Stevens Collection. 14 Vols. nearly 3,000 documents. See A List of Benjamin Franklin Papers in the Library of Congress. Washington: Government Printing Office, 1905. 322 p.

(3) The Library of the University of Pennsylvania. 800 documents. See Calendar of Papers of Benjamin Franklin in the Library of the University of Pennsylvania.

(4) The Library of the Historical Society of Pennsylvania. 660 documents.

FROST, Wesley, 1884-1967. Foreign Service Officer 1909-44. Served in Charlottetown, Cork, State Department, Marseilles, Montreal, Rio de Janeiro, Santiago, Wellington, Minister and Ambassador to Paraguay 1941-44. German Submarine Warfare: A Study of Its Methods and Its Spirit, Including the Crime of the Lusitania, a Record of Observations and Evidence. Introd. by Frank Lyon Polk. New York: D. Appleton, 1918. 243 p. In Spanish, Caracas, 1917.

FRY, William Henry, 1815-1864. Composer, music critic, journalist. Secretary of Legation in Turin 1861. His compositions include program symphonies, choral works and operas. See "The Musical Works by William H. Fry" by William Treat Upton, 1946. 33 p. in the Library of Philadelphia. Also "William Henry Fry" by the same author, New York: Thomas Crowell Company, 1954. 346 p.

Leonora. An opera on the libretto from Bulwer Lytton's "Lady of Lyons." First performed at the Chestnut Street Theatre in Philadelphia, June 4, 1845. Said to be the first publicly performed grand opera written by a native American. New York: E. Ferrett & Co., 1846. 439 p.

Notre Dame de Paris. An opera, written in 1863, produced at the Philadelphia Festival on May 3, 1864. 65 p.

Santa Claus, or the Christmas Symphony. A symphony, performed by Julien, 1853.

Niagara. A symphony, produced in New York, May 4, 1854.

The Breaking Heart. A symphony, performed by Julien,

1853.

A Day in the Country.   A symphony performed by Julien, 1853.

Complete Treatise on Artificial Fish Breeding.   New York: D. Appleton & Co. , 1854.   188 p.

GADE, John Allyne, 1875- .   Architect.   Member of Commission for Relief of Belgium 1916-17.   Naval Attaché in Denmark and Sweden 1917-19.   State Department representative in Baltic provinces.

All My Born Days.   Experiences of a Naval Intelligence Officer in Europe.   New York: Charles Scribner's Sons, 1942.   408 p.

Book-Plates: Old and New.   New York: M. F. Mansfield & Co. , 1898.   52 p.

Cathedrals of Spain.   Boston: Houghton Mifflin Co. , 1911. 279 p.

Christian IV, King of Denmark and Norway: a Picture of the Seventeenth Century.   Boston: Houghton Mifflin Co. , 1928.   319 p.

(Translation) Charles the Twelfth, King of Sweden.   From the manuscript of Carl Gustafson Klingspor.   Boston: Houghton Mifflin Co. , 1916.   370 p.

The Hanseatic Control of Norwegian Commerce During the Late Middle Ages.   Thesis Columbia University.   Ann Arbor, Mich. :   University Microfilms.   Publication No. 1635.   1950.   Leiden: E. J. Brill, 1951.   139 p.

The Life of Cardinal Mercier.   New York: Charles Scribner's Sons, 1934.   312 p.

The Life and Times of Tycho Brahe.   Princeton, N. J. : Princeton University Press for the American-Scandinavian Foundation.   New York: 1947.   209 p.

Luxemburg in the Middle Ages.   Leiden: E. J. Brill, 1951.   238 p.

Under the Golden Lilies.   Leiden: E. J. Brill, 1955. 287 p.

GALBRAITH, John Kenneth, 1908- .   (Pseud. :   Mark Epernay and Julian K. Prescott) Professor of economics, author.   Ambassador to India 1961-63.

The Affluent Society.   Boston: Houghton Mifflin Co. , 1958.   368 p.

American Capitalism.   The Concept of Countervailing Power.   Boston: Houghton Mifflin Co. , 1952.   217 p.

A China Passage.   Boston: Houghton Mifflin Co. , 1973. 143 p.

Economic Power in Perspective.   Cambridge: Harvard

University Press, 1962. 76 p. Revised and enlarged.
Boston: Houghton Mifflin Co., 1964. 109 p.
Economics and the Art of Controversy. New Brunswick,
N.J.: Rutgers University Press, 1955. 111 p.
The Great Crash--1929. Boston: Houghton Mifflin Co.,
1961. 212 p.
How to Control the Military. Garden City, N.Y.: Dou-
bleday, 1969. 64 p.
Indian Painting, the Scene, Themes and Legends. with
Mohinder Singh Randhawa. Boston: Houghton Mifflin
Co., 1968. 142 p.
Journey to Poland and Yugoslavia. Cambridge: Harvard
University Press, 1958. 118 p.
The Liberal Hour. Boston: Houghton Mifflin Co., 1961.
107 p.
Made to Last. London: H. Hamilton, 1964. 144 p.
Marketing Efficiency in Puerto Rico. with Richard H.
Holton and others. Cambridge: Harvard University
Press, 1955. 204 p.
The New Industrial State. Boston: Houghton Mifflin Co.,
1967. 427 p.
The Scotch. Illus. by Samuel H. Bryant. Boston:
Houghton Mifflin Co., 1964. 145 p.
Resources For the Future. with others. Edit. by Henry
Jarrett. Baltimore: Johns Hopkins Press, 1958.
260 p.
Economic Development. Boston: Houghton Mifflin Co.,
1964. 109 p.
The Triumph: a Novel of Modern Diplomacy. Boston:
Houghton Mifflin Co., 1968. 239 p.
Ambassador's Journal. Boston: Houghton Mifflin Co.,
1969. 656 p.
The McLandress Dimension. by Mark Epernay. Boston:
Houghton Mifflin Co., 1963. 126 p. Illus. by James
Stevenson.
Economics, Peace and Laughter. Boston: Houghton
Mifflin Co., 1971. 382 p.
A History of the Modern Age. by Julian K. Prescott.
Garden City, N.Y.: Doubleday & Co., Inc., 1971.
407 p.

GALLATIN, Abraham Alphonse Albert, 1761-1849. Born in
Switzerland of aristocratic family. Emigrated to United
States against family wishes when under 19 years of
age, 1779. By 1795 he was in politics and a member
of Congress. He showed remarkable ability in finance
and wanted to make United States solvent, feeling that

this was the way to greater power and stability.   Secretary of the Treasury under Jefferson 1801-13 and
the result was a Treasury surplus.   He was appointed
one of the Commissioners to negotiate peace with
Great Britain in 1813, along with James Bayard, John
Quincy Adams (then Minister to Russia), and Jonathon
Russell and Henry Clay.   The resulting Treaty of
Ghent was signed December, 1814.   Served as Minister to France 1815-23, and as Minister to Great Britain
1826-28.   He was opposed to commercial treaties and
diplomatic intercourse but believed that all commercial
intercourse could be protected by the consular system.

Autobiography.   Portland: Maine Historical Collections,
Vol. 6, pp. 93-105.   For the Society, 1859.

The Oregon Question.   New York: Bartlett & Welford,
1846.   75 p.

The Right of the United States of America to the North-
eastern Boundry Claimed by Them.   Principally Ex-
tracted From the Statements Laid Before the King of
the Netherlands, and Revised By Albert Gallatin.   New
York: S. Adams, printer, 1840.   179 p.   Append. and
8 maps.

Considerations on the Currency and Banking System of the
United States.   Philadelphia: Carey & Lea, 1831.
106 p.

Notes on the Semi-Civilized Nations of Mexico, Yucatan
and Central America.   (transactions of the American
Ethnological Society) New York: Bartlett & Welford,
1845.

The Writings of Albert Gallatin.   Edit. by Henry Adams.
Philadelphia: J. B. Lippincott & Co., 1879.   3 vols.

GALLATIN, James, 1791-1876.   Secretary to his father,
Albert Gallatin, United States Minister to France 1815-
23, to Great Britain 1826-28.

The Great Peacemaker.   The diary of James Gallatin,
Secretary to Albert Gallatin, United States Minister to
France and to Great Britain.   Edited by Count Galla-
tin.   Introd. by Viscount Bryce.   London: William
Heinemann, 1914.   316 p.

GALLMAN, Waldemar John, 1899- .   Foreign Service Officer 1922-1961.   Served in Havana, Washington, San
José, Quito, Riga, Warsaw, Danzig, London.   Ambassador to Poland 1948-50.   National War College
1950.   Ambassador to Union of South Africa 1951, to
Iraq 1954, Director General of the Foreign Service

1959-61. Career Minister.
Iraq Under General Nuri: My Recollections of Nuri Al-
Said, 1954-58. Baltimore: Johns Hopkins Press,
1964. 241 p.

GANTENBEIN, James Watson, 1900-1960. Foreign Service
Officer 1929-1960. Served in Milan, Santo Domingo,
Buenos Aires, Quito, Berlin, Bucharest, Copenhagen.
Appointed to Marseilles as Consul General just before
his death.
Continuous Voyage Particularly as Applied to Contraband
and Blockade. Portland, Ore.: Columbia University
thesis, 1929. 207 p.
Documentary Background of World War II, 1931-1941.
New York: Columbia University Press, 1948. 1122 p.
Financial Questions in United States Foreign Policy. New
York: Columbia University Press, 1939. 246 p.
The Evolution of Our Latin American Foreign Policy.
New York: Columbia University Press, 1950. 979 p.

GAUSS, Clarence Edward, 1887-1960. Foreign Service Offi-
cer 1906-44. Spent most of his career in the Far
East. Served in Shanghai, Tientsin, Amoy, Tsinan,
Mukden. He was Consul General in Shanghai during
the Japanese-Chinese hostilities in 1935. Minister to
Australia 1940, Ambassador to China 1941-44.
A Notarial Manual for Consular Officers. Washington:
Government Printing Office, 1921. 84 p.

GAVIN, James Maurice, 1907- . United States Army 1929-
58. Lieutenant General. Ambassador to France 1961-
63.
Airborne Warfare. Washington: Infantry Journal Press,
1947. 186 p. Special Spanish edition, with assistance
of the War Ministry, Buenos Aires: 1948.
Crisis Now. with Arthur T. Hadley. New York: Random House, 1968. 184 p.

GERARD, James Watson, 1867- . Lawyer, mine owner,
Associate Justice Supreme Court of New York. Am-
bassador to Germany 1913-17.
My Four Years in Germany. New York: Hodder &
Stoughton, 1917. 320 p.
Face to Face with Kaiserism. New York: George H.
Doran, 1918. 380 p.
Memoires de L'Ambassadeur Gerard. Paris: Payot,
1918-19. 2 vols.

My First 83 Years in America.   New York: Doubleday,
   1951.   372 p.

GEREN, Paul Francis, 1913- . Professor. Lecturer at
   University of Rangoon and at Lahore 1941-42.   At
   Berea College 1946-47.   Foreign Service Officer 1947-
   68.   Served in Bombay, Damascus, Amman, Washing-
   ton (Deputy Director of Peace Corps), Salisbury,
   Tripoli.
Burma Diary.   Drawings by Cyrus LeRoy Baldridge.
   New York: Harper, 1943.   57 p.
Christians Confront Communism.   Nashville Convention
   Press, 1962.   149 p.
New Voices, Old Worlds.   New York: Friendship Press,
   1958.   166 p.
Pilgrimage, Etc.   Drawings by Cyrus LeRoy Baldridge.
   New York: Harper, 1948.   229 p.
Doughboy Poems.   Dallas: Story Book Press, 1948.
   37 p.

GERIG, Orie Benjamin, 1894- .   League of Nations Sec-
   retariat 1930-39.   Professor of Government.   Department of State official 1942-61.   Served in Washington
   and London.
International Peace Observations.   A History and a Forecast.   with David W. Wainhouse, Bernard G. Bechhoeffer, John C. Dreier and Harry R. Turkel.   Baltimore: Johns Hopkins Press, in cooperation with the
   Washington Center of Foreign Policy Research School
   of Advanced International Studies, 1966.   663 p.
The Open Door and the Mandates System.   George Allen
   & Unwin Ltd. , 1930.   236 p.

GIBSON, Hugh Simons, 1883-1954.   Foreign Service Officer
   1908-38.   Served in Tegucigalpa, London, State De-
   partment, Havana, Santo Domingo, Brussels, Paris,
   Minister to Poland 1919, to Switzerland 1924, to Bel-
   gium 1927, Ambassador to Brazil 1933, to Belgium
   and Minister to Luxemburg 1937-38.   While in Switzer-
   land he was delegate to many conferences.   He was
   Chairman of the American Delegation to the Tripartite
   Naval Conference at Geneva and Acting Chairman of
   American Delegation to the Disarmament Conference at
   GENEVA 1932-33.   American representative to Chaco
   Mediation Conference, Buenos Aires 1935-37.   During
   World War I he was closely associated with Herbert
   Hoover in feeding the civilian population through the

Commission for Relief in Belgium. He was charged
with the defense of Nurse Cavell who was shot by the
Germans in October, 1915. In 1952, following retire-
ment, he served as Director of the Intergovernmental
Committee for European Migration.

(Edited) The Ciano Diaries, 1939-43. (Count Galeazo
Ciano was Italian Minister of Foreign Affairs 1936-43,
and son-in-law of Benito Mussolini.) Introd. by
Sumner Welles. New York: Garden City Publishing
Co., 1947. 582 p.

The Basis of Lasting Peace. with Herbert Hoover. New
York: D. Van Nostrand Co., Inc., 1954. 44 p.

A Journal From Our Legation in Belgium. Garden City,
N.Y.: Doubleday, Page Co., 1917. 380 p.

Belgium, The Country and Its People. New York: Doubleday, Doran Co., 1939. 347 p.

The Problems of Lasting Peace. with Herbert Hoover.
Garden City, N.Y.: Doubleday, Doran & Co. Inc.,
1942. 303 p.

The Road to Foreign Policy. New York: Doubleday,
Doran Co., 1944. 252 p.

Rio. New York: Doubleday, Doran Co., 1937. 263 p.

Hugh Gibson, 1883-1954: Extracts From His Letters and
Anecdotes From His Friends. Introd. by Herbert
Hoover. Edit. by Perrin C. Galpin. New York:
Belgian American Educational Foundation, 1956. 163 p.

A Diplomatic Diary. London: Hodder & Stoughton, 1917.
296 p.

GIESECKE, Albert Anthony, 1880- . Educator. President
of the University of Cuzco, Peru, 1910-23. Director
General of Public Education, Peru, 1924-30. Special
Assistant to American Embassy Lima 1934-53 and
1958-64. Distinguished Service award 1951.

American Commercial Legislation Before 1789. Philadelphia: University of Pennsylvania. New York: Appleton, 1910. 167 p.

Questions in Municipal Civics. Syracuse, N.Y.: C. W.
Bordeen, 1911. 114 p.

GILLIAM, Albert M., ?-1859. Editor of the Dover Intelli-
gencer, of Dover, Tennessee. Commissioned by
President Tyler as Consul of the Port of San Francisco, Upper California, in the Republic of Mexico. He
left his home for his post on October 15, 1843, did
not serve long.

Travels in Mexico, 1843-44: Including a Description of

California. The Principal Cities and the Mining Dis-
tricts of the Republic: The Oregon Territory, Etc.
A new and complete edition: Aberdeen: G. Clark &
Son, 1847. 312 p. Now on microfilm.
Travels Over the Table Lands and Cordilleras of Mexico,
During the Years 1843-44: Including a Description of
California and the Biographies of Iturbide and Santa
Anna. Philadelphia: J. W. Moore etc., etc., 1846.
455 p. 1st edition.

GILMORE, Eugene Allen, Jr., 1902-1971. Professor of
economics. Foreign Service Officer 1941-61. Served
in Montevideo, Washington, Calcutta, Nepal, New Delhi, Tehran, Lima, La Paz, Havana.
The Adequacy of Deposit Banking Facilities in Nebraska.
Nebraska Studies in Business. No. 39. Lincoln:
University of Nebraska Press, 1937. 45 p.

GILOANE, William, 1907- . Born in Germany, educated
in Germany and United States. Farmer in Germany
and United States. Foreign Economic Administration
(U. S.) in Prague 1943-45. State Department official
1946-55. Foreign Service Officer 1955-67. Served in
Washington, Saigon, Paris. Merit Service Award 1967.
Co-author, with others, of a series of Area Handbooks
prepared by Foreign Area Studies of the American Uni-
versity, Washington, D. C. for the Department of the
Army. Mr. Giloane contributed economic chapters.
Area Handbook for Iraq. Washington: Government Print-
ing Office, 1969. 411 p.
Area Handbook for Lebanon. Washington: Government
Printing Office, 1969. 352 p.
Area Handbook for Israel. Washington: Government
Printing Office, 1970. 457 p.
Area Handbook for Albania. Washington: Government
Printing Office, 1971. 233 p.
Area Handbook for Cyprus. Washington: Government
Printing Office, 1971. 241 p.
Area Handbook for The Soviet Union. Washington: Gov-
ernment Printing Office, 1971. 827 p.
Area Handbook for Czechoslovakia. Washington: Govern-
ment Printing Office, 1972. 321 p.
Area Handbook for East Germany. Washington: Govern-
ment Printing Office, 1972. 329 p.
Area Handbook for Romania. At the printers.
Area Handbook for Poland. Draft being completed.
Area Handbooks for Hungary and Bulgaria are next on the
program.

GOOD, Robert C. , 1924- . Teacher. State Department
   1961-65. Ambassador to Zambia 1965-68.
   Foreign Policy in the Sixties: The Issues and the Instru-
      ments. with Roger Hilsman. Baltimore: Johns Hop-
      kins Press, 1965. 299 p.

GOODFRIEND, Arthur, 1907- . Author, foreign corres-
      pondent. Editor-in-Chief of Stars and Stripes in Europe
      and China 1944-46. Foreign Service Reserve Officer,
      New Delhi 1957-60.
   If You Were Born in Russia. New York: Farrar,
      Strauss, 1950. 192 p.
   The Only War We Seek. Foreword by Chester Bowles.
      New York: Published for Americans For Democratic
      Action, by Farrar, Strauss & Young, 1951. 128 p.
   What Can A Man Believe? New York: Farrar, Strauss
      & Young, 1952. 127 p.
   What Can A Man Do? Introd. by Carlos P. Romulo.
      New York: Farrar, Strauss & Young, 1953. 128 p.
   Something Is Missing. Postscript by James Michener.
      New York: Farrar, Strauss & Young, 1955. 117 p.
   What Is America? New York: Simon & Schuster, 1954.
      123 p.
   Rice Roots. Photos by Bambang. New York: Simon &
      Schuster, 1958. 209 p.
   Stand Fast In Liberty. Introd. by Allan Nevins. New
      York: St. Martin's Press, 1959. 131 p.
   Two Sides of One World. A report on an international
      discussion. United States National Commission for
      UNESCO. Washington: 1957. 79 p.
   Defense Against Chemical War. What To Do When the
      Enemy Uses Gas. Washington: Infantry Journal,
      1944. 90 p.
   The German Soldier. Washington: Infantry Journal,
      1944. 96 p.
   How To Shoot the U. S. Army Rifle. Washington: Infantry
      Journal, 1943. 122 p.
   The Jap Soldier. Washington: Infantry Journal, 1943.
      124 p.
   Map Reading For the Soldier. Washington: Infantry
      Journal, 1944. 101 p.
   Scouting and Patrolling: the Soldier, the Enemy, the
      Ground. Washington: Infantry Journal, 1943. 126 p.
   The Twisted Image. New York: St. Martin's Press,
      1963. 264 p.

GORDON, Lincoln, 1913- . Educator. Economist 1936-49.

Consultant on economic affairs to various Government
departments. Chief of the Economic Cooperation Administration in London 1955-61. Ambassador to Brazil
1961-65. Assistant Secretary of State 1966-68.
Government and the American Economy. with Merle
Fainsod. New York: W. W. Norton, 1948. 985 p.
The Public Corporation in Great Britain. London: Oxford University Press, 1938. 351 p.
United States Manufacturing Investment in Brazil 1946-
1960. with Engelbert L. Grommers. Cambridge:
Harvard Graduate School of Business Administration,
1962. 177 p.
The Alliance for Progress: A New Deal for Latin America. Cambridge: Harvard University Press, 1964.
146 p.

GRADY, Henry Francis, 1882-1957. Economist, author,
U. S. Trade Commissioner to London and Continental
Europe 1919-20. Commercial Attaché at London and
Holland 1919-20. At the Hague 1920. Professor at
University of California 1921-37. State Department
1934-36. Chairman U. S. Tariff Commission 1937-39.
Assistant Secretary of State 1939, Ambassador to India
1947, also Minister to Nepal 1948, Ambassador to
Greece 1948, to Iran 1950-51.
British War Finance 1914-1919. Ph. D. thesis. New
York: Columbia University Press, London: P. S.
King & Son, 1927. 316 p.
The Port of San Francisco. A Study of Traffic Competi-
tion 1921-33. with Robert M. Carr. Berkeley: Uni-
versity of California Press, 1934. 501 p.
Inter-American Maritime Conference, Washington, Nov.
25, 1940. Report with Max O'Rell Truit. Washington:
Government Printing Office, 1941. 479 p.
A Survey of India's Industrial Production for War Pur-
poses. Report to the Government of India and to the
United States, 1942. 62 p.

GREEN, James Fredrick, 1910- . State Department 1943-
55. Foreign Service Officer 1955-69. Served in State
Department, Leopoldville, Accra, Casablanca.
The United Nations and Human Rights. (bibliographical
notes) Washington: Brookings Institution, 1956. 195 p.
The British Empire Under Fire. New York: Foreign
Policy Association. Headline Books Series, 1940.
96 p. Maps and charts by Bunji Tagawa.

GREW, Joseph Clark, 1880-1959. Clerk at Consulate General in Cairo 1904-06. Diplomatic Service 1906-24. Foreign Service Officer 1924-45. Served in Mexico City, St. Petersburg, Berlin, Vienna, State Department. Secretary General, with rank of Minister, to American Commission to Negotiate Peace at Paris 1918-19. Minister to Denmark 1920, to Switzerland 1921-24, Under-Secretary of State 1924-27, Ambassador to Turkey 1927, to Japan 1932-42, Under-Secretary of State 1944-45. An excellent biography is American Ambassador by Waldo H. Heinrichs, Jr. Boston: Little, Brown & Co., 1960. 460 p.
Invasion Alert: The Red China Drive for a United Nations Seat. Baltimore: Maran Publishing Co., 1956. 81 p.
Report From Tokyo - A Message to the American People. New York: Simon & Schuster, Inc., 1942. 88 p.
Sport and Travel in the Far East. Photos by author. Foreword by Theodore Roosevelt. Boston: Houghton Mifflin Co., 1910. 264 p.
Ten Years in Japan. A contemporary record drawn from the diaries and private and official papers of Joseph C. Grew, United States Ambassador to Japan 1932-42. New York: Simon & Schuster, Inc., 1944. 555 p.
Turbulent Era - A Diplomatic Record of Forty Years - 1904-1945. Edit. by Walter Johnson, assisted by Nancy Harvison Hooker. Cambridge: Riverside Press. Boston: Houghton Mifflin Co., 1952. 2 vols.

GRIEVE, Miller, 1801-1878. Journalist. Chargé d'Affaires in Denmark 1852.
Memoirs of Georgia: Containing Historical Accounts of the State's Civil, Military, Industrial and Professional Interests, and Personal Sketches of Many of its People. Atlanta, Ga.: The Southern Historical Association, 1895. 2 vols. Microfilmed. Library of Congress.

GRIFFIS, Stanton, 1887- . Investment banker. Ambassador to Poland 1947, to Egypt 1948, to Argentina 1949, to Spain 1951-52.
Lying in State. Garden City, N.Y.: Doubleday & Co., Inc., 1952. 315 p.

GRIFFITHS, John Lewis, 1855-1914. Lawyer. Consul at Liverpool 1905. Consul General at London 1909-14.
Inland Waterways and Canals and Railway Rates of the United Kingdom. Report by John L. Griffiths, American Consul General at London. Washington: Govern-

ment Printing Office, 1910.   83 p.
The Greater Patriotism: Public Addresses by John Lewis
Griffiths, American Consul General at London.   Delivered in England and America.   with a memoir by
(Mrs.) Caroline Henderson Griffiths and an introduction
by Hilaire Belloc.   New York: John Lane Co., 1918.
230 p.

GRIMKE, Archibald Henry, 1849-1930.   Consul in Santo
Domingo 1899-1903.   Second black graduate of Harvard
Law School, in 1874.   Lawyer, publisher (The Hub).
Leader of Boston radicals and of the NAACP.   Presi-
dent of the Washington D. C. branch.
William Lloyd Garrison, the Abolitionist.   New York:
Funk & Wagnalls Co., 1891.   405 p.
The Life of Charles Sumner, the Scholar in Politics.
New York: Funk & Wagnalls Co., 1892.   415 p.

GRISCOM, Lloyd C., 1873- .   Secretary to Ambassador at
London 1893-94.   Deputy District Attorney, New York
1896.   Secretary Legation Constantinople 1899, Minis-
ter to Persia 1901, to Japan 1902, Ambassador to
Brazil 1906, to Italy 1906-09.
Diplomatically Speaking.   New York: Literary Guild of
America, 1940.   476 p.   [autobiography]

GROSS, Christian Channing, 1895-1933.   Foreign Service
Officer 1923-32.   Served in Paris and Port-au-Prince.
Pseudonym: Fairfax Channing.
Siberia's Untouched Treasure.   by Fairfax Channing.
New York: G. P. Putnam's Sons, 1923.   475 p.   82
illus., 15 maps.

GROSS, Ernest Arnold, 1906- .   Lawyer.   State Depart-
ment 1946-49.   Assistant Secretary of State 1949.
Ambassador to the United Nations 1949-53.
The New United Nations.   New York: Foreign Policy
Association, 1957.   62 p.
The United Nations: Structure For Peace.   New York:
Council on Foreign Relations.   Harper Bros., 1962.
132 p.

GROTH, Edward Miller, 1893- .   Foreign Service Officer
1920-52.   Served in Rotterdam, Belgrade, Beirut,
Damascus, Aleppo, Baghdad, Surabaya, Copenhagen,
Capetown, Calcutta, Kabul, State Department, Pretoria,
Hamburg, Nairobi.

To Give Room for Wandering. Los Altos, Calif.: Pacifica Publishing Co., 1972. 324 p.

GROVER, John C., 1921- . Embassy guard, Lima, 1941-46. State Department Courier 1946-70. Headquarters variously at Cairo, Manila, Frankfort, Panama, Washington. Chief of Courier Service 1953. Meritorious Service Award 1965.
Defend Yourself. New York: Ronald Press, 1958. 82 p.

GRUMMON, Stuart Edgar, 1901-1960. Foreign Service Officer 1923-42. Served in Mexico City, The Hague, Madrid, Stockholm, Port-au-Prince, Dairen, Moscow, Tokyo.
Tres Meses En Mexico. with Alfredo de Noriega. A Spanish conversational reader. Illus. by Carmen Diez and Ernesto Cabral. New York: Charles Scribner's Sons, 1928. 321 p.
(Translated) The Three Roses. by Blasco Ibañez. New York: E. P. Dutton & Co., Inc., 1932. 348 p.
(Translated) Bewitched Lands. by Adolfo Costa do Rels. New York: Alfred A. Knopf, Inc., 1945. 203 p.
(Translated) The Bay of Silence. by Edwardo Mallea. New York: Alfred A. Knopf, Inc., 1944. 339 p.
(Translated) A Sarmiento Anthology. Introd. and notes by Allison Williams Bunkley. Princeton, N.J.: Princeton University Press, 1948. 336 p.

GUGGENHEIM, Harry Frank, 1890-1971. Copper mining, nitrate and tin. Founder of the Guggenheim Fund for the Promotion of Aeronautics. Ambassador to Cuba 1929-33.
The United States and Cuba. New York: The Macmillan Co., 1934. 268 p.
The Seven Skies. New York: G. P. Putnam's Sons, 1930. 216 p.

GUINN, Paul Spencer, 1896-1963. Commerce Department 1915-18, 1920-33, 1936-39. Served in Washington, Johannesburg, London, The Hague, Boston, Brussels. Foreign Service Officer 1939-47. Served in Vienna, Berlin, Caracas, Istanbul, London.
British Strategy and Politics - 1914-1918. Oxford: Clarendon Press, 1965. 359 p.

GULLION, Edmund Asbury, 1913- . Foreign Service Officer 1937-63. Served in Marseilles, Salonika, London, Algiers, Helsinki, Stockholm, State Department, Na-

tional War College, Saigon, Foreign Service Inspector.
Ambassador to the Congo 1961-63.
(Edited) Uses Of The Sea. Englewood Cliffs, N.J.: for
the American Assembly of Columbia University. Prentice-Hall Co., 1968. 202 p. Intended as background
for the 33rd American Assembly at Arden House,
May 2-5, 1968.

HAEBERLE, Arminius T., 1874-1943. School teacher 1897-
1908. Foreign Service Officer 1908-1936. Served in
Manzanillo, Tegucigalpa, St. Michael's, Pernambuco,
Rio de Janeiro, Sao Paulo, Dresden.
Old Pewter. [German pewter.] Boston: Richard G.
Badger. The Garden Press, 1931. 128 p.

HAGER, Alice Rogers, 1915- . Aviation reporter for news-
paper syndicate 1934-40. Information officer for the
Civil Aeronautics Board. Correspondent for aviation
magazine. Writer. Foreign Service Reserve Officer
with United States Information Agency 1948-57. Served
in Brussels, Luxembourg, Department of State.
Washington: City of Destiny. Photos by Jackie Martin.
New York: The Macmillan Co., 1949. 72 p.
Brazil: Giant of the South. Photos by Jackie Martin.
New York: The Macmillan Co., 1945. 80 p.
Frontier By Air: Brazil Takes the Sky Road. Photos by
Jackie Martin. New York: The Macmillan Co., 1942.
243 p.
Dateline: Paris. (Romances for moderns.) New York:
J. Messner, 1954. 190 p.
Janice, Air Line Hostess. Foreword by Gill Wilson.
New York: J. Messner 1948. 190 p.
Love's Golden Circle. New York: J. Messner, 1962.
189 p.
Washington Secretary. New York: J. Messner, 1958.
192 p.
Wings for the Dragon: The Air War in Asia. New York:
Dodd, Mead & Co., 1945. 307 p.
Wings Over the Americas. New York: The Macmillan
Co., 1940. 162 p.
Wings To Wear. New York: The Macmillan Co., 1938.
96 p.
The Wonderful Ice Cart. Illus. by Mimi Korach. New
York: The Macmillan Co., 1955. 149 p.
Big Loop and Little: The Cowboy's Story. New York:
The Macmillan Co., 1937. 96 p.
The Canvas Castle. Illus. by Mary Stevens. New York:

J. Messner, 1949. 179 p.

Cathy Whitney, President's Daughter. New York: J. Messner, 1966. 192 p.

HAGERMAN, Herbert James, 1871-1935. Secretary of Embassy at St. Petersburg 1898.

Letters of a Young Diplomat. Santa Fe, New Mexico: Rydal Press, 1937. 191 p.

A Statement in regard to Certain Matters Concerning the Governorship and Political Affairs in New Mexico in 1906-07. Roswell, N.M.: 1908. 112 p. Printed for private circulation.

HALDERMAN, John William, 1907- . Lawyer, educator. Assistant Legal Advisor State Department 1937-42. General Services Officer, State Department 1942-53. Foreign Service Reserve Officer 1953-55. Foreign Service Officer 1955-60. Served in Bonn, Berlin, National War College, Casablanca, Colombo.

The United Nations and the Rule of Law: Charter Development Through the Handling of International Disputes and Situations. Dobbs Ferry: Oceana Publications, 1966. 248 p.

(Edited and contributed one chapter) The Middle East Crisis: Test of International Law. Dobbs Ferry, N.Y.: Oceana Publications, 1969. 193 p.

HALE, Franklin Darius, 1854-1940. Lawyer, Vermont State Legislator. Consular officer 1902-18. Served in Coaticook, Quebec; Charlottetown, Prince Edward Island, Trinidad, Huddersfield, England.

Reveries of Vermont, and Other Poems. Rutland, Vermont: Tuttle College, 1929. 143 p.

HANNA, Willard Anderson, 1911- . School teacher in China 1932-36. Foreign Service Reserve Officer 1947-54. Served in Manila, Batavia, Djakarta, National War College, Tokyo.

Bung Karno's Indonesia: Collection of 25 Reports Written for American Universities Field Staff. New York: American University Field Service, 1960. 1 vol. map.

Destiny Has Eight Eyes. New York: Harper & Bros., 1941. 305 p.

Eight Nation Makers: Southeast Asia's Charismatic Statesmen. New York: St. Martin's Press, 1964. 307 p.

The Formation of Malaysia, Etc. New York: American
University Field Staff, 1964. 247 p.
Indonesia, a "Guided" Republic. New York: Foreign
Policy Association World Affairs Center, 1961. 61 p.
Sequel to Colonialism: The 1957-1960 Foundations for
Malaysia, Etc. New York: American University Field
Service, 1965. 288 p.

HAPGOOD, Norman, 1868-1937. Drama critic, editor, au-
thor. Minister to Denmark 1919-20.
Literary Statesmen and Others: Essays on Men Seen
From a Distance. Chicago: H. Stone & Co., 1897.
208 p.
The Stage in America 1897-1900. New York: The Mac-
millan Co., 1901. 408 p.
Up From the City Streets: Alfred E. Smith, A Biograph-
ical Study in Contemporary Politics. New York: Har-
court, Brace Co., 1927. 349 p.
Why Janet Should Read Shakespeare. New York: Century
Co., 1929. 257 p.
Daniel Webster. Boston: Small, Maynard & Co., 1899.
119 p.
George Washington. New York: Macmillan Co., 1901.
419 p.
Industry and Progress. New Haven: Yale University
Press, 1911. 123 p.
The Advancing Hour. New York: Boni & Liveright,
1920. 262 p.
The Changing Years. New York: Farrar & Rinehart,
Inc., 1930. 321 p.
(Edited) Professional Patriots. with Sidney Howard and
John Hearlay. New York: A. & C. Boni, 1927.
210 p. Bibliography.

HARDY, Arthur Sherburne, 1847-1930. Mathematician,
novelist, professor. Minister Resident to Persia 1897-
99. Minister to Greece, Roumania and Servia 1899-
1901. Minister to Switzerland 1901-03, to Spain 1903-
05.
But Yet A Woman. Boston: Houghton Mifflin Co., 1883.
348 p.
Diane and Her Friends. Illus. by Elizabeth Shippen
Green. Boston: Houghton Mifflin Co., 1914. 298 p.
Duality. (a poem) New York: Liber Scriptorum, 1893.
272 p.
Elements of Analytic Geometry. Boston: Ginn Co.,
1889. 229 p.

Elements of Quaternions. Boston: Ginn Heath Co., 1881.
230 p.
Francesca of Rimini. (a poem) Philadelphia: J. B. Lip-
pincott Co., 1878. 46 p.
Helen. Boston: Houghton Mifflin Co., 1916. 314 p.
His Daughter First. Boston: Houghton Mifflin Co.,
1903. 349 p.
Life and Letters of Joseph Hardy Neesima. Boston:
Houghton Mifflin Co., 1891. 350 p.
No. 13 Rue de Bon Diable. Boston: Houghton Mifflin
Co., 1917. 212 p.
Passe Rose. Boston: Houghton Mifflin Co., 1889. 361 p.
Things Remembered. Boston: Houghton Mifflin Co.,
1923. 311 p.
The Wind of Destiny. Boston: Houghton Mifflin Co.,
1886. 307 p.
Topographical Surveying. with others. New York: Van
Nostrand Co., 1884. 210 p.
(Translated) Imaginary Quantities: Their Geometrical In-
terpretation. From the French. by M. Argand. New
York: Van Nostrand Co., 1881. 135 p.

HARR, John Ensor, 1926- . Personnel management spe-
cialist. Foreign Service Reserve Officer 1963-67.
Served in Bonn, Washington.
The Anatomy of the Foreign Service - A Statistical Pro-
file. New York: Carnegie Endowment for International
Peace, 1965. 89 p.
The Development of Careers in the Foreign Service. New
York: Carnegie Endowment for International Peace,
1965. 104 p.
The Professional Diplomat. Princeton, N.J.: Princeton
University Press, 1969. 404 p.
Programming Systems and Foreign Affairs Leadership.
with Frederick Mosher. London: Oxford University
Press, 1970.

HARRIMAN, Florence Jaffray (Hurst). (Mrs. J. Borden
Harriman) 1870-1967. Active in women's organiza-
tions, in Democratic politics, in Red Cross. Minister
to Norway 1937-41.
From Pinafores to Politics. New York: H. Holt Co.,
1923. 359 p.
Mission to the North. Philadelphia: J. B. Lippincott
Co., 1941. 331 p. 17 illus. Foreword by Johan
Nygaarsvold. In Norwegian, Oslo: Bergendahl, 1946.
228 p. Titled Pa Post I Norge.

Florence Jaffray Harriman: A Register of Her Papers
in the Library of Congress. Washington: 1958.

HARRIMAN, William Averell, 1891- . Banker, railway
   interests, Governor of New York, Minister to England
   1941, Chairman of Mission to Russia, 1941, with rank
   of Ambassador. Ambassador to Russia 1943-46; to
   Great Britain 1946. Secretary of Commerce 1946-48.
   Economic Cooperation Agency representative in Europe
   with rank of Ambassador 1948-50. Ambassador-at-
   Large 1961. Under Secretary of State 1963. Head of
   American Peace Talks Mission in Paris with North
   Vietnamese 1968.
   America and Russia in a Changing World: a Half Century
      of Personal Observation. New York: Doubleday &
      Co. Inc., 1970. 218 p.
   Peace With Russia? New York: Simon & Schuster, Inc.,
      1959. 174 p.
   Public Papers of Averell Harriman, Fifty-second Governor
      of New York. Albany: 1955-58. 4 vols.
   United States President's Committee on Foreign Aid.
      Washington: Government Printing Office, 1947. 286 p.

HARRIS, George Sellers, 1931- . English instructor and
   student at University of Ankara 1954-55. Assistant
   Foreign Affairs Officer, Department of the Air Force
   1956-57. Foreign Service Staff Officer. Attaché at
   Ankara 1957-60.
   The Origins of Communism in Turkey. Stanford, Calif.:
      Hoover Institute. Stanford University Press, 1967.
      215 p.

HARRIS, Townsend, 1804-1878. New York merchant ship
   owner engaged in Far Eastern trade. President of the
   Board of Education of New York City for several
   years. Appointed American Consul at Ningpo, China
   in 1855 but did not serve. Appointed American Consul
   General at Shimoda, Japan, by President Pierce, arrived 1856, departed 1862. En route to Japan he
   stopped at Bangkok to obtain a treaty of friendship and
   commerce with the Kings of Siam, and to arrange for
   the appointment of an American Consul there.
   The Complete Journal of Townsend Harris, First Ameri-
      can Consul General and Minister to Japan. Introd.
      and notes by Mario Emilio Cosenza, Ph.D. Professor
      of Classical Languages. The College of the City of
      New York. Published for the Japan Society. New

York: Doubleday, Doran & Co., Garden City, N.Y.:
1930. 616 p.
Some Unpublished Letters of Townsend Harris. Edit. by
Shio Sakanshi. New York: Japan Reference Library,
1941. 72 p.

HARRISON, William Henry, 1773-1841. Politician, Army
officer, Governor of Indiana, United States Senator.
Ninth President of the United States--died one month
after taking office in 1841. Minister to Colombia
1828-29. Became involved in Colombian politics and
was forced to return to the United States by the Colombian Government.
Governor's Messages and Letters. Messages and Letters
of William H. Harrison. Indiana Historical Collections, 1922. 2 vols.
Remarks of General Harrison, Late Envoy to the Republic
of Colombia, On Certain Charges Made Against Him by
that Government. To Which Is Added an Unofficial
Letter from General Harrison to General Bolivar, on
the Affairs of Colombia; with Notes, Explanatory of
his Views of the Present State of that Country. Washington: Printed by Gales & Seaton, 1830. 69 p.

HART, Joseph C., ?-1855. Consul at Santa Cruz de Tener-
ife, Canary Island, 1854-55. Died at his post.
Geographic Exercises Containing 10,000 Questions For
Practical Examinations on the Most Important Features
on the Maps of the World and the United States by
Melish, Lay's Map of the State of New York, and the
Maps of America, Europe, Asia and Africa by Arrow-
smith. New York: W. A. Mercein, Printer, 1824.
155 p.
An Abridgement of (the above) 2nd. Edition Improved.
New York: R. Lockwood, 1827. 108 p.
A Popular System of Practical Geography For the Use of
Schools and the Study of Maps. New York: Cady &
Burgess, 1851. 132 p.
A Modern Atlas of Fourteen Maps. 7th edition, revised
and corrected. New York: R. Lockwood, 1830.
Introduction to Geography Written For the Department of
New York High Schools. New York: R. Lockwood,
1826. 54 p.
Miriam Coffin, or the Whale Fisherman: A Tale. New
York: G. & C. & H. Carvill. Philadelphia: Carey
& Hart, 1834. 2 vols.
The Romance of Yachting: Voyage the First. New York:
Harper Bros., 1848. 322 p.

HARTE, Francis Brett, 1836-1902. Born in Albany, N.Y.
Published his first verses at age 11. Moved to California. One trip to the mining country made a lasting
impression. He supported minority groups, i.e., Indians and Mexicans. Worked for a weekly paper, the
"Northern Californian. " Wrote for the "Golden Era"
and published popular novels as parodies of famous authors including James Fenimore Cooper, Charles
Dickens, Victor Hugo which were then very popular.
Edited a weekly paper, the "Californian," then the
"Overland Monthly. " His The Luck of Roaring Camp
and The Outcasts of Poker Flat made him famous
across the nation. He moved to New England. Success went to his head and his production and reputation
slumped. He succeeded in getting an appointment as
American Consul at Crefeld, Germany in 1878 and then
to Glasgow in 1880 where he served until 1885. He
then moved to London where he spent the remaining 17
years of his life.
The Works of Bret Harte. Collected and revised by the
    author. Riverside Edition. Boston: Houghton Mifflin
    Co. , 1894-1900. 6 vols.
Autograph Edition: The Writings of Bret Harte with In-
    troduction, Glossary and Indexes. Boston: Houghton
    Mifflin Co. , 1896-1903. 19 vols.
The Best of Bret Harte. Selected by Wilhelmina Harper
    and Aimé M. Peters. Illus. by Paul Brown. Boston:
    Houghton Mifflin Co. , 1947. 434 p.
Ah Sin. A dramatic work by Mark Twain and Bret Harte.
    Edit. by Frederick Anderson. San Francisco: Book
    Club of California, 1961. 90 p.
The Ancestors of Peter Atherly and Other Tales. Copy-
    right edition. Leipzig: B. Tauchnitz, 1897. 279 p.
    Also Boston: Houghton Mifflin Co. , 1900.
The Argonauts of North Liberty. Boston: Houghton Mif-
    flin Co. , 1888. 206 p.
Barker's Luck and Other Stories. Boston: Houghton
    Mifflin Co. , 1896. 256 p.
The Bell Ringer of Angels and Other Stories. Boston:
    Houghton Mifflin Co. , 1894. 334 p.
The Best Short Stories of Bret Harte. Edit. and introd.
    by Robert H. Linscott. New York: Modern Library,
    1947. 517 p.
Bret Harte's Deadwood Mystery and Mark Twain's Night-
    mare. with other tales, sketches and poetry. London:
    Creame & Co. , 189?. 167 p.
By Shore and Sedge. Boston: Houghton Mifflin Co. ,

1885. 260 p.

Captain Jim's Friends and the Argonauts of North Liberty.
Leipzig: B. Tauchnitz, 1889. 256 p.

Clarence. Boston: Houghton Mifflin Co., 1895. 270 p.

Colonel Starbottle's Client and Some Other People. Boston: Houghton Mifflin Co., 1892. 283 p.

Condensed Novels and Stories. Boston: Houghton Mifflin Co., 1882. 480 p.

Cressy. Boston: Houghton Mifflin Co., 1889. 290 p.

Crusade of the Excelsior. Boston: Houghton Mifflin Co., 1887. 250 p.

Drift From Two Shores and Other Stories. Boston: Houghton Mifflin Co., 1878. 266 p.

East and West. [poems] Boston: J. R. Osgood, 1871. 171 p.

Echos of the Foothills. Boston: J. R. Osgood, 1875. 146 p.

An Episode of Fiddletown and Other Sketches. London: G. Routledge and Sons, 1873. 137 p.

A First Family of Tasajora. Leipzig: B. Tauchnitz, 1891. 280 p.

Flip and Found at Blazing Star. Boston: Houghton Mifflin Co., 1882. 192 p.

The Fool of Five Forks. London: G. Routledge, 1875. 128 p.

From Sand Hill to Pine. Boston: Houghton Mifflin, 1900. 327 p.

Frontier Stories. Boston: Houghton Mifflin Co., 1887. 452 p.

Gabriel Conroy. Hartford, Conn.: American Publishing Co., 1876. 400 p.

Gabriel Conroy, Bohemia Papers, Stories Of and For the Young. Boston: Houghton Mifflin Co., 1896. 2 vols.

An Heiress of Red Dog and Other Sketches. Leipzig: B. Tauchnitz, 1879. 288 p.

Heritage of Deadlow Marsh and Other Tales. Boston: Houghton Mifflin Co., 1889. 259 p.

Idylls of the Foothills. In Prose and Verse. Leipzig: Tauchnitz, 1874. 279 p.

In a Hollow of the Hills and Other Tales. Boston: Houghton Mifflin Co., 1896. 447 p.

In the Carquinez Woods. Hamburg: K. Gradener & J. F. Richter, 1883. 265 p.

Jeff Briggs' Love Story and Other Tales. Leipzig: B. Tachnitz, 1880. 286 p.

Jinny. London: G. Routledge & Sons, 1878. 124 p.

The Lectures of Bret Harte. Compiled from Various

Sources to Which Is Added The Piracy of Bret Harte's
Fables. by Charles Meeker Kozlay. Brooklyn: C. M.
Kozlay, 1909. 53 p.
The Letters of Bret Harte. Edit. by Geoffrey Bret Harte.
Boston: Houghton Mifflin Co. , 1926. 515 p.
The Lost Galleons and Other Tales. San Francisco:
Towne & Bacon, 1867. 108 p.
The Luck of Roaring Camp and Other Sketches. Boston:
J. R. Osgood Co. , 1871. 256 p.
Maruja. London: Chatto & Windus, 1885. 266 p.
A Millionaire of Rough and Ready and Devil's Ford. Bos-
ton: Houghton Mifflin Co. , 1887. 299 p.
Mr. Jack Hamlin's Meditation and Other Stories. Boston:
Houghton Mifflin Co. , 1889. 289 p.
Mrs. Skagg's Husband and Other Sketches. Boston: J.
R. Osgood, 1873. 352 p.
A Niece of Snapshot Harry's and Other Tales. Boston:
Houghton Mifflin Co. , 1903. 355 p.
On the Frontier. Boston: Houghton Mifflin Co. , 1884.
288 p.
Openings In the Old Trail. Boston: Houghton Mifflin
Co. , 1902. 332 p.
Outcroppings: Being Selections of California Verse. San
Francisco: A. Roman & Co. New York: W. J.
Middleton, 1866. 144 p.
A Phyllis of the Sierras and Adrift from 'Redwood Camp. '
Boston: Houghton Mifflin Co. , 1888. 215 p.
Poems, and Two Men of Sandy Bar. (a drama) Boston:
Houghton Mifflin Co. , 1896.
Poems. Boston: Fields, Osgood Co. , 1871. 152 p.
A Protegée of Jack Hamlin's and Other Stories. Boston:
Houghton Mifflin Co. , 1894. 292 p.
The Queen of the Pirate Isle. Illus. by Kate Greenway.
Printed by Edmund Evans. London: Chatto & Windus,
1886. 58 p.
Sally Dows and Other Stories. Boston: Houghton Mifflin
Co. , 1893. 299 p.
Salome Jane. Illus. by Harrison Fisher and Arthur Kel-
ler. Boston: Houghton Mifflin Co. , 1910. 78 p.
Snowbound at Eagle's. A Novel. London: Ward &
Downey, 1886. 254 p.
A Sapho of Green Springs and Other Stories. Boston:
Houghton Mifflin Co. , 1891. 294 p.
Sensation Novels, Condensed. London: J. G. Hotten,
1871. 215 p.
Some Later Verses. London: Chatto & Windus, 1898.
118 p.

Stories in Light and Shadow. Boston: Houghton Mifflin
  Co., 1898. 304 p.
Stories of the Sierras and Other Sketches, With a Story
  of Wild Western Life by Joaquin Miller. London:
  J. C. Hotten, 1872. 152 p.
The Story of a Mine. Leipzig: B. Tauchnitz, 1877.
  271 p.
Suzy, A Story of the Plains. Boston: Houghton Mifflin
  Co., 1893. 264 p.
Tales of Trail and Town. Boston: Houghton Mifflin Co.,
  1898. 248 p.
Thankful Blossom, A Romance of the Jerseys. Boston:
  J. R. Osgood, 1877. 158 p.
That Heathen Chinee and Other Poems, Mostly Humorous.
  Music by Stephen Tucker. London: J. C. Hotten,
  1871. 140 p.
Three Partners, or, the Big Strike on Heavy Tree Hill.
  Boston: 1897. 342 p.
A Treasure of the Redwoods and Other Tales. Boston:
  Houghton Mifflin Co., 1903. 363 p.
Trent's Trust and Other Stories. London: E. Nash,
  1903. 321 p.
Twins of Table Mountain, A Ghost of the Sierras, Views
  From a German Spion, Peter Schroeder, Cadet Grey.
  Leipzig: B. Tauchnitz, 1879. 224 p.
Two Men of Sandy Bar. (a drama) Boston: J. R. Os-
  good, 1876. 151 p.
Under the Redwoods. Boston: Houghton Mifflin Co.,
  1901. 334 p.
A Waif of the Plains. Boston: Houghton Mifflin Co.,
  1890. 231 p.
A Ward of the Golden Gate. Boston: Houghton Mifflin
  Co., 1890. 249 p.

HARTLEY, Harry Livingston, 1900- . Foreign Service
  Officer 1928-33. Served in London, Pernambuco,
  Buenos Aires.
Atlantic Challenge. Foreword by Elmer Roper. Dobbs
  Ferry, N.Y.: Oceana Publications, 1965. 111 p.
Is America Afraid? A New Foreign Policy for United
  States. New York: Prentice-Hall Inc., 1937. 462 p.
Our Maginot Line: The Defense of the Americas. New
  York: Carrick & Evans, 1939. 315 p.
Yankee Viking. (a novel) New York: Exposition Press,
  1951. 155 p.

HARVEY, George Brinton McCelland, 1864-1928. Journalist,

politician. Editor of New York World, Harper's Weekly, North American, Harvey's Weekly. Ambassador to Great Britain 1921-23.
Henry Clay Frick, The Man. New York: Charles Scribner's Sons, 1928. 382 p.
The Power of Tolerance and Other Speeches. New York: Harper Bros., 1911. 325 p.
Women Etc., Some Leaves From an Editor's Diary. New York: Harper Bros., 1908. 231 p.
On Track and Diamond. with Van Tassel Sutphen, James M. Hallowell, J. Conover and S. Scoville, Jr. New York: Harper Bros., 1909. 220 p.

HAWKINS, Harry Calvin, 1894- . Teacher. Department of State and Foreign Service Officer 1924-25. Professor at University of Oregon 1925-27. Department of State 1931-44. Foreign Service Officer 1944-48. Professor at Tufts College 1948-49. State Department 1949-51. Served in the State Department and London.
Commercial Treaties and Agreements: Principles and Practice. with Nan Grindle and others. New York: Rinehart, 1951. 254 p.
International Trade Policy Issues. Report for the Chamber of Commerce of the United States. Washington: Fletcher School of Law and Diplomacy. Medford, Mass.: 1953. 68 p.
Merchant Shipping Industry. Co-authored under the pen names of H. C. Calvin and E. G. Stewart. New York: John Wiley & Sons, Inc., 1925. 373 p. [This title is under H. C. Calvin in the Library of Congress catalogue.]

HAWTHORNE, Nathaniel, 1804-1864. Writer. Friend of President Pierce who appointed him Consul at Liverpool 1853-57. Liverpool was then a lucrative consular post and he saved $30,000 from his consular income during his five-year assignment. His book Our Old Home includes memoirs of his consular service.
His best-known works include:
Fanshaw. Boston: Marsh and Capen, 1828.
Twice-Told Tales. Boston: American Stationers Co., 1837.
Mosses from an Old Manse. New York: Wiley and Putnam, 1846.
The Scarlet Letter. Boston: Ticknor, Reed, and Fields, 1850.
The House of Seven Gables. Boston: Ticknor, Reed and

Fields, 1851.
The Snow-Image and Other Twice-Told Tales.   Boston:
    Ticknor, Reed and Fields, 1851.
The Blithesdale Romance.   Boston: Ticknor, Reed and
    Fields, 1852.
The Life of Franklin Pierce.   Boston: Ticknor, Reed
    and Fields, 1852.
A Wonder Book for Girls and Boys.   Boston: Ticknor,
    Reed and Fields, 1852.
Tanglewood Tales for Girls and Boys.   Boston: Ticknor,
    Reed and Fields, 1853.
The Marble Faun.   Boston: Ticknor and Fields, 1860.
Our Old Home.   Boston: Ticknor and Fields, 1863.
Passages from the American Note-Books.   Edit. by
    Sophia Hawthorne.   Boston: Ticknor and Fields, 1868.
    (The American Note-Books.   Edit. by Randall Stewart,
    New Haven: Yale University Press, 1932.)
Passages from the English Note-Books.   Edit. by Sophia
    Hawthorne.   Boston: Fields, Osgood, 1870.
Dr. Grimshaw's Secret.   Edit. by Julian Hawthorne.
    Boston: Osgood, 1883.
Hawthorne as Editor: Selections from His Writings in the
    American Magazine of Useful and Entertaining Knowl-
    edge.   Edit. by Arlin Turner.   Baton Rouge: Louisi-
    ana State University Press, 1941.
The Century Edition of the Works of Nathaniel Hawthorne.
    Edit. by William Charvat, Roy H. Pierce.   Columbus,
    Ohio: Ohio State University Press, 1963.
Works of Nathaniel Hawthorne.   Introductory bibliographi-
    cal notes by Charles Curtis Bigelow.   New York:
    Bigelow & Brown, 1923.   10 vols.
The Complete Writings of Nathaniel Hawthorne.   Boston:
    Houghton Mifflin, 1900.   22 vols.

HAY, John Milton, 1838-1905.   Poet, historian, lawyer.
    Private Secretary to President Lincoln 1861-65.   Sec-
    retary of Legation at Paris 1865-67.   Chargé d'Af-
    faires ad interim Vienna 1867-68.   Secretary of Lega-
    tion Madrid 1869-70.   Ambassador to Great Britain
    1897-98.   Secretary of State 1898-1905.
Papers, 1856-1914.   30 feet.   1 reel microfilm in Li-
    brary of Congress, Manuscript Division.
Microfilm of Diary and Notebooks at Brown University.
Pike County Ballads and Other Pieces.   Boston: J. R.
    Osgood, 1871.   167 p.
Poems.   Boston: Houghton Mifflin Co., 1890.   272 p.
A Poet in Exile: Early Letters.   Edit. by Caroline

Ticknor. Boston: Houghton Mifflin Co., 1910. 48 p.
Democracy: An American Novel. (16th edition) Hay is
the supposed author. New York: H. Holt Co., 1908.
340 p.
The Life and Letters of John Hay. by William Roscoe
Thayer. Boston: Houghton Mifflin Co., 1915. 2
vols.
Abraham Lincoln: A History. with John G. Nicolay.
Appeared first serially in the Century Magazine, for
which the authors received $50,000. Vols. 33-39
(1886-90).
Castilian Days. Boston: J. R. Osgood, 1871. 414 p.
The Breadwinners. An anonymous satirical attack on
labor unions. New York: Harper & Bros., 1884.
319 p.
Addresses of John Hay and Extracts From His Diary.
Collected by Henry Adams and Edit. by Mrs. Hay.
The Century Co., 1906. 353 p.
The Complete Poetical Works of John Hay. with an in-
troduction by his son, Clarence Hay. Boston: Hough-
ton Mifflin Co., 1916. 271 p.
The Life and Letters of John Hay. by William Roscoe
Thayer. Boston: Houghton Mifflin Co., 1915.

HAYES, Carlton Joseph Huntley, 1882-1964. Historian.
Professor at Columbia University 1907-42 and 1945-
64. Ambassador to Spain 1942-45.
Ancient and Modern History. with Parker Thomas Moon.
New York: The Macmillan Co., 1929. 893 p.
A Brief History of the Great War. New York: Macmillan
Co., 1920. 461 p.
British Social Politics. Boston: Ginn & Co., 1913.
580 p.
Contemporary Europe Since 1870. New York: Macmillan
Co., 1953. 785 p.
Essays on Nationalism. New York: Macmillan Co.,
1926. 279 p.
France, A Nation of Patriots. New York: Columbia Uni-
versity Press, 1930. 487 p.
A Generation of Materialism: 1871-1900. New York:
Harper Bros., 1941. 390 p.
The Historical Evolution of Modern Nationalism. New
York: R. R. Smith, 1931. 327 p.
History of Europe. with Marshal Whithed Baldwin and
Charles Woolsey Cole. New York: Macmillan Co.,
1949. 1049 p.
History of Western Civilization. with Marshall Whithed

Baldwin and Charles Woolsey Cole. New York: Macmillan Co., 1962. 919 p.
An Introduction to the Sources Relating to the Germanic Invasions. New York: Columbia University. Longman's Green, 1909. 229 p.
Modern Europe to 1870. New York: Macmillan Co., 1953. 837 p.
Nationalism: A Religion. New York: Macmillan Co., 1960. 187 p.
A Political and Cultural History of Modern Europe. New York: Published for the United States Armed Forces Institute by Macmillan Co., 1944. 4 vols.
A Political and Cultural History of Modern Europe...Vol. 2. A Century of Predominantly Industrial Society Since 1850. New York: Macmillan Co., 1939. 865 p.
A Political and Social History of Modern Europe. New York: Macmillan Co., 1916. 2 vols.
A Syllabus of Modern History. with Parker Thomas Moon and Austin P. Evans. New York: Columbia University Press, 1916. With map studies.
The United States and Spain: An Interpretation. New York: Sheed & Ward, 1951. 198 p. Madrid: in Spanish 1952.
Wartime Mission in Spain: 1942-1945. New York: Macmillan Co., 1945. 313 p. Madrid: 1946, in Spanish. 397 p.
World History. with Parker Thomas Moon and John W. Wayland. New York: Macmillan Co., 1932. 912 p.
History and Nature of International Relations. with Stephen P. Duggan and others. Freeport, N.Y.: Books for Libraries Press, 1956. 299 p.
Ancient and Medieval History. New York: Macmillan Co., 1929. 893 p.
Modern History. with Parker Moon. New York: The Macmillan Co., 1923. 890 p.

HECK, Lewis, 1889-1965. Student Interpreter Turkey 1909. Foreign Service Officer 1909-20. Served in Jerusalem, Constantinople and Berne. Also U.S. Coast and Geodetic Service 1925-61.
Delaware Place Names. with others. Washington: Government Printing Office, 1966. Biological Survey Bulletin, 124 p.

HENDERSON, Gregory, 1922- . Foreign Service Officer 1947-65. Korean language officer. Served in Seoul, Frankfort, Kobe, State Department.

Korea: The Politics of Vortex. Cambridge: Harvard
    University Press, 1968. 479 p.

HENDERSON, John W., 1910- . Newspaper reporter 1932-
    48. Foreign Service Officer 1948-67. Served in
    Shanghai, Hong Kong, Manila, Tokyo, Bangkok, State
    Department, National War College, Djakarta, Taipei,
    United States Information Agency.
The United States Information Agency. New York: Fred-
    erick A. Praeger, 1969. 324 p.

HERTER, Christian Archibald, 1896-1966. Attaché Berlin
    1916-17. State Department 1917-18. Secretary to
    American Commission to Negotiate Peace, Paris, 1919.
    Editor, lecturer. Representative and Speaker of Mas-
    sachusetts Legislature 1931-43. Member of United
    States Congress 1943-53. Governor of Massachusetts
    1953-57. Under Secretary and Secretary of State 1957-
    61.
Toward an Atlantic Community. New York: Harper &
    Row for the Council on Foreign Relations, 1963.
    107 p.

HERZ, Martin Florian, 1917- . Foreign Service Officer
    1946- . Served in Vienna, Paris, Phnom Penh,
    Tokyo, State Department, United Nations, Addis Ababa,
    Tehran, Saigon.
Beginnings of the Cold War. Bloomington, Ind.: Indiana
    University Press, 1966. 214 p.
Short History of Cambodia: From the Days of Angkor to
    the Present. New York: Frederick A. Praeger, Inc.,
    1958. 141 p.
The Golden Ladle. with Zack Hanle. New York: Siff-
    Davis, 1945. 32 p. (A children's book.)

HILL, David Jayne, 1850-1932. Author, teacher. President
    of Bucknell University 1879-88, of Rochester Univer-
    sity 1888-96, Assistant Secretary of State 1888. Min-
    ister to Switzerland 1903, to the Netherlands and Lux-
    embourg 1905. Ambassador to Germany 1908-11.
American World Policies. New York: George H. Doran,
    1920. 257 p.
Americanism: What Is It? New York: D. Appleton Co.,
    1916. 280 p.
La Crise de la Democratie aus Etats Unis. Paris:
    Payot Cie., 1918. 242 p. Translated from the Eng-
    lish by Mme. Emile Boutroux. Preface by M. Boutroux.

Course in European Diplomacy. Synopsis. Washington:
  Columbian University, 1899. 153 p.
The Elements of Psychology: A Textbook. New York:
  Sheldon Co. , 1888. 419 p.
The Elements of Rhetoric and Composition: A Textbook
  for Schools and Colleges. New York: Sheldon & Co. ,
  1878. 276 p.
Genetic Philosophy. New York: The Macmillan Co. ,
  1893. 382 p.
A History of Diplomacy in the International Development
  of Europe. New York: Longman's, Green, 1905-14.
  3 vols.
Impressions of the Kaiser. New York: Harper Bros. ,
  1918. 367 p.
Lecture Notes on Economics and Politics. Lewisburg,
  Penn. : Bucknell University Press, 1884. 76 p.
Lecture Notes on Ethics. Rochester, New York: Printed
  for the Senior Class, Rochester University, 1891.
  62 p.
The People's Government. New York: D. Appleton,
  1915. 286 p.
Present Problems in Foreign Policy. New York: D.
  Appleton Press, 1919. 360 p.
Principles and Fallacies of Socialism. New York: J. W.
  Lovell, 1885. 96 p.
The Problem of a World Court: The Story of an Unreal-
  ized American Dream. New York: Longman's, Green,
  1927. 204 p.
The Rebuilding of Europe: A Survey of Forces and Con-
  ditions. New York: Century, 1917. 289 p.
The Science of Rhetoric: and Introduction to the Laws of
  Effective Discourse. New York: Sheldon & Co. , 1877.
  304 p.
Washington Irving. New York: Sheldon & Co. , 1879.
  234 p.
William Cullen Bryant. New York: Sheldon & Co. , 1879.
  240 p.
World Organization as Affected by the Nature of the Modern State. New York: Columbia University Press,
  1911. 214 p. Paris: E. Flammerion, 1912. in
  French.

HILLENBRAND, Martin Joseph, 1915- . Entered Foreign
  Service 1939. Served in Zurich, Rangoon, Calcutta,
  Washington, Lourenço Marques, Bremen, Paris, Berlin, Superior Service Award 1960. Career Minister
  1962. Ambassador to Hungary 1967. Assistant

Secretary of State 1969.
Power and Morals. New York: Columbia University
Press, 1949. 217 p.

HILLIARD, Henry Washington, 1808-1892. Lawyer, Con-
gressman, Confederate soldier. Educator. Chargé
d'Affaires in Belgium 1842-44. Minister to Brazil
1877-81. (Many Southerners migrated to Brazil during
this time.)
Speeches and Addresses, 1839-1854. New York: Harper
& Bros., 1855. 497 p.
Devane: A Story of Plebians and Patricians. New York:
Blelock Co., 1865. 2 vols.
Politics and Pen Pictures at Home and Abroad. New
York: G. P. Putnam, 1892. 445 p.

HILTON, Mary Kendall, 1916-1970. Wife of Ralph Hilton,
Foreign Service Officer. [Q. V.]
Old Homes and Churches of Beaufort County. Columbia,
S. C.: State Printing Co., 1970. 128 p. 111 photo-
graphs.

HILTON, Ralph, 1907- . Office of Inter-American Affairs
1943-46. Reserve Officer 1947-55. Foreign Service
Officer 1955-64. Served in San José, Buenos Aires,
Washington, Asuncion, United States Information Agency. Board of Examiners. From 1965-70 Mr. Hilton
published the Islander Magazine, Hilton Head Island,
South Carolina.
Worldwide Mission: The Story of the United States Foreign Service. New York: World Publishing Co.,
1970. 256 p.

HINCKLEY, Frank Erastus, 1871-1950. Clerk of United
States Court in China 1906. Disbursing Officer of the
Court 1909. District Attorney of the United States
Court for China 1916.
American Consular Jurisdiction in the Orient. Washing-
ton: W. H. Loudermilk, 1906. 283 p.

HINTON, Harold Boaz, 1898- . Author, journalist. Assistant to Ambassador Joseph P. Kennedy in London,
1938.
Air Victory: the Men and the Machines. Foreword by
Barton K. Yount. New York: Harper Bros., 1948.
428 p.
America Gropes for Peace. Richmond: Johnson

Publishing Co., 1937. 214 p.
Cordell Hull, a Biography. Foreword by Sumner Welles.
Garden City, N.Y.: Doubleday, Doran & Co. Inc.,
1942. 377 p.

HODGE, Max Edwin, 1925- . State Department and Foreign Service Officer 1950- . Served in Frankfort,
Salonika, Dacca, State Department, Bonn, Athens,
Johannesburg.
Catalogus Faunae Graeciae, Pars II: Aves. Thessaloniki
(privately printed) 1969. 203 p. In German with English nomenclature.

HOFFMAN, Wickham, 1821-1900. Army officer. Secretary
of Legation Paris 1866-74, at London 1874-77, at St.
Petersburg 1877-83. Minister to Denmark 1883-85.
Camp, Court and Siege. New York: Harper & Bros.,
1877. 285 p.
Leisure Hours in Russia. London: G. Bell & Sons,
1883. 184 p.

HOLCOMBE, Chester, 1844-1912. Missionary and part-time
interpreter at Legation in Peking 1871-76. Secretary
and Interpreter at Legation 1876-1883. Refused appoint-
ment as Secretary of Legation and Consul General in
Bogota, hoping for appointment as Minister to China.
Remained in China.
China's Past and Future. by Chester Holcombe and
Britain's Sin and Sin and Folly. by B. Broomhall.
London: Morgan & Scott, 1904. 298 p.
The Real Chinaman. New York: Dodd, Mead & Co.,
1895. 350 p.
The Real Chinese Question. New York: Dodd, Mead &
Co., 1900. 386 p.
Ancient Chinese Porcelains and Other Curios, Belonging
to Mr. George A. Hearn. New York: 1894. 177 p.

HOLLAND, Jerome H., 1916- . Sociologist, President of
Delaware State College 1953-60, of Hampton Institute
1960-70. Ambassador to Sweden 1970-72.
Black Opportunity. New York: Weybright and Talley,
1969. 274 p. In Swedish: Svart Framtid? Om
Negrernas Mojligheter i Framtidens Warld. Stockholm:
Broderna Lagerstrom AB. 1970. 269 p.

HOLLISTER, Gideon Hiram, 1817-1881. Lawyer, writer.
Minister to Haiti 1868-69.

Mount Hope: or, Philip, King of the Wampagoags. New
York: Harper Bros., 1851. 280 p.
History of Connecticut, From the First Settlement of a
Colony to the Adoption of the Present Constitution.
New Haven: Durrier & Peck, 1855. 2 vols.
Thomas A Becket. Tragedy in blank verse. Boston:
W. V. Spencer, 1866. 186 p.
Andersonville. A poem. 1866.
Kinley Hollow. A novel. New York: Henry Holt, 1882
(posthumously published). (His most successful work,
a vigorous indictment of a New England village of the
early 19th century.) 379 p.

HOPE, A. Guy, 1914- . Lawyer. U.S. Navy 1941-45.
Foreign Service Officer 1946-64. Served in Shanghai,
Dairen, Washington, Brussels, Tel Aviv, National War
College, Istanbul, Abidjan.
America and Swaraj: The United States Role in Indian
Independence. Washington: Public Affairs Press,
1968. 136 p. Reprint Bombay: Vora & Co. Publish-
ers Private Ltd., 1970.
Symbols of the Nations. with Janet Barker Hope, Q.V.
Washington: Public Affairs Press, 1972.

HOPE, Janet (Barker), 1916- . Mrs. Hope is the wife of
Foreign Service Officer A. Guy Hope. [Q.V.] Before
marrying Mr. Hope Janet Barker entered the Foreign
Service in 1940 and served in Niagara Falls, Cairo,
Albania and Shanghai. She left the Foreign Service to
marry Mr. Hope in 1949, after which she accompanied
him to Washington and Istanbul.
Symbols of the Nations. with A. Guy Hope. Washington:
Public Affairs Press, 1972.

HORNBECK, Stanley Kuhl, 1883-1967. Lecturer, author.
Technical expert on American Commission to Negotiate
Peace 1918; on military mission to Armenia 1919; on
American delegation to Conference on Limitation of
Armaments, Washington, 1921. State Department 1921-
24. Harvard University 1924-28. State Department
1928-44, Director of Far Eastern Affairs. Ambassador
to the Netherlands 1944-47.
Contemporary Politics in the Far East. New York: D.
Appleton, 1916. 466 p.
The Most Favored Nation Clause in Commercial Treaties,
Its Function in Theory and in Practice, And Its Rela-
tion to Tariff Policies. Madison, Wis., 1910. 121 p.

The United States and the Far East: Certain Fundamentals of Policy. Boston: World Peace Foundation, 1942. 100 p.

HOROWITZ, Daniel L., 1916- . Labor economist for State Department 1946-56. Foreign Service Officer 1956-69. Served in Santiago, Washington, Paris, New Delhi, National War College, The Hague, Foreign Service Institute.
The Italian Labor Movement. Cambridge: Harvard University Press, 1963. 356 p.

HORSTMANN, G. Henry. Consul at Munich 1869-80, at Nuremburg 1880-85.
Consular Reminiscences. Philadelphia: J. B. Lippincott Company, 1886. 420 p.

HORTON, George, 1859-1942. Newspaper reporter. Foreign Service Officer 1893-98, and 1905-24. Served in Athens, Saloniki, Smyrna, Budapest.
Aphroesa, a Legend of Argolis and Other Poems. London: T. F. Unwin, 1897. 91 p.
The Blight of Asia: An Account of the System of Extermination of Christian Populations by Mohammedans and the Culpability of Certain Great Powers. With the True Story of the Burning of Smyrna. Foreword by James W. Gerard. Indianapolis: Bobbs-Merrill Co. Inc., 1926. 292 p.
The Edge of Hazard. Pictures by C. M. Relyea. Indianapolis: Bobbs-Merrill Co. Inc., 1906. 429 p.
A Fair Brigand. Chicago: H. S. Stone, 1899. 320 p.
Home of the Nymph and Vampires: The Isles of Greece. Indianapolis: Bobbs-Merrill Co. Inc., 1929. 319 p.
In Argolis. Illus. with photos. Chicago: A. C. McLurg, 1902. 225 p.
Like Another Helen. Illus. by C. M. Relyea. Indianapolis: Bowen-Merrill, 1901. 379 p.
The Long Straight Road. Illus. by Roy and Margaret West Kinney. Indianapolis: Bowen-Merrill Co., 1902. 401 p.
Miss Schuyler's Alias. Boston: H. G. Badger, 1913. 333 p.
Modern Athens. Illus. by Corwin Knapp Linson. New York: C. Scribner's Sons, 1901. 91 p.
The Monk's Treasure. Frontispiece by C. M. Relyea. Indianapolis: Bobbs-Merrill Co. Inc., 1905. 391 p.
Poems of an Exile. Indianapolis: Bobbs-Merrill Co.

Inc., 1931. 276 p.

Recollections Grave and Gay, the Story of a Mediterranean
Consul. [autobiographical] Indianapolis: Bobbs-Merrill
Co. Inc., 1927. 331 p.

Songs of the Lowly and Other Poems. Chicago: F. J.
Schulte Co., 1892. 241 p.

The Tempting of Father Anthony. Chicago: A. C. Mc-
Clurg, 1901. 246 p.

In Unknown Seas. poetry. Cambridge University Press
by John Wilson & Son under the direction of Stone &
Kimball, Chicago: 1895. 38 p.

Constantine: a Novel of Greece under King Otto. Written
in Greek. Athens: Asty, 1896. 133 p. Chicago: in
English. Way & Williams, 1897. 232 p.

War and Mammon. Wasau, Wisconsin: Philosopher
Press "At the Sign of the Green Pine Tree." 1903.
[poetry]

HOWARD, Harry Nicholas, 1902- . Professor of history
1929-42. State Department officer 1942-55, Foreign
Service Officer 1955-63. Served in Washington, San
Francisco, Wiesbaden, United Nations Relief and Re-
habilization Administration, United Nations Commission
Investigating Frontier Incidents, Beirut.

The Partition of Turkey, 1913-1923. A Study in Diplomatic History. Norman: University of Oklahoma
Press, 1931. 486 p.

The Balkan Conferences and the Balkan Entente, 1930-
1936. A Study in the Recent History of the Balkan and
Near Eastern Peoples. with Robert J. Kerner. Berkeley: University of California Press, 1936. 271 p.

Military Government in the Panama Canal Zone. Norman:
University of Oklahoma Press, 1949. 86 p.

The Problem of the Turkish Straits. Washington: Department of State Publication 2752, Near Eastern Series
#5.   United States Government Printing Office, 1947.
68 p.

The United Nations and the Problem of Greece. Washington: Department of State Publication 2909, Near
Eastern Series 9. Government Printing Office, 1947.
97 p.

Yugoslavia. with R. J. Kerner, editor. Berkeley: University of California Press, 1949. 271 p.

United States Policy in the Near East, South Asia and
Africa - 1954. Washington: Department of State Pub-
lication 5801. Near and Middle Eastern Series 18.
Government Printing Office, 1955. 72 p.

The King-Crane Commission: An American Inquiry in the Middle East. Beirut: Khayats, 1963. 369 p.

HOWE, Fisher, 1914- . Salesman, teacher. Office of Strategic Services. Foreign Service Officer 1945-68. Served in Washington, National War College, Board of Examiners, Oslo, The Hague, University of Utah, Political Planning Council.
The Computer and Foreign Affairs: Some First Thoughts. Washington: Department of State, 1964. 88 p.

HOWELL, Joseph Morton, 1863-1937. Physician, lawyer, author of several books on hygiene and sanitation. Diplomatic Agent and Consul General in Cairo 1921. Minister to Egypt 1922-27.
Egypt's Past, Present and Future. Dayton, Ohio: Service Publishing Co., 1929. 378 p.

HOWELLS, William Dean, 1837-1920. Author and editor. Wrote a campaign biography of Abraham Lincoln which earned him appointment as Consul in Venice, 1861-65. He spent the time learning Italian, reading Dante, getting married, and collecting notes for a series of sketches on Venetian life. Became editor of the Atlantic Monthly in 1872.
Selected Writings. Edit. with introd. by Henry Steele Commager. New York: Random House, 1950. 946 p.
Selected Edition of William Dean Howells. Bloomington, Ind.: University of Indiana Press, 1968. 5 vols.
Annie Kilburn. Edinburgh: D. Douglas, 1888. 331 p.
April Hopes. New York: Harper Bros., 1888. 484 p.
Between the Dark and the Daylight. Romances. New York: Harper Bros., 1907. 184 p.
Florence in Art and Literature. Philadelphia: Booklovers Library, 1901. 124 p.
A Boy's Town. New York: Harper Bros., 1890. 247 p.
Certain Delightful English Towns. New York: Harper Bros., 1906. 289 p.
A Chance Acquaintance. Illus. by William L. Sheppard. Boston: J. R. Osgood, 1874. 271 p.
Christmas Every Day and Other Stories Told for Children. New York: Harper Bros., 1893. 150 p.
The Coast of Bohemia. New York: Harper Bros., 1892. 340 p.
Complete Plays. Edit. with introd. by William M. Gibson and George Arms. New York: New York University Press, 1960. 649 p.

Criticism and Fiction. New York: Harper Bros., 1890.
188 p.
The Day of Their Wedding. New York: Harper Bros.,
1896. 158 p.
A Day's Pleasure and Other Sketches. Boston: Houghton
Mifflin Co., 1881. 240 p.
Different Girls. (stories) New York: Harper Bros.,
1906. 271 p.
Doctor Breen's Practice. Boston: J. R. Osgood, 1881.
272 p.
Discovery of a Genius. with Henry James. Book reviews
and articles about Henry James's publishers. Edit. by
Albert Mordell. Introd. by Sylvia Bowman. New
York: Twayne Publishers, 1961. 207 p.
Doorstep Acquaintances and Other Sketches: With Bio-
graphic Introduction and Notes. Boston: Houghton Mif-
flin Co., 1906. 92 p.
European and American Masters. Edit. with introd. by
Clara Marburg Kirk and Rudolf Kirk. New York:
Collier Books, 1963. 225 p.
Familiar Spanish Travels. New York: Harper Bros.,
1913. 326 p.
A Fearful Responsibility and Other Stories. Boston: J.
R. Osgood, 1881. 255 p.
Fennel and Rue. (a novel) Illus. by Charlotte Harding.
New York: Harper Bros., 1908. 129 p.
The Flight of Pony Baker: A Boy's Town Story. New
York: Harper Bros., 1902. 222 p.
A Foregone Conclusion. Boston: J. R. Osgood, 1875.
265 p.
Great American Stories, An Anthropology. Compiled and
edit. with introd. by William Dean Howells. New
York: Boni & Liveright, 1920. 432 p.
A Hazard of New Fortunes. Edinburgh: D. Douglas,
1889. 2 vols.
Heroines of Fiction. Illus. by H. C. Christie and A. I.
Keller and others. New York: Harper Bros., 1901.
2 vols.
Hither and Thither in Germany. New York: Harper
Bros., 1920. 131 p.
Imaginary Interviews and Other Essays. New York:
Harper Bros., 1910. 358 p.
An Imperative Duty. Edinburgh: D. Douglas, 1891.
196 p.
Impressions and Experiences. New York: Harper Bros.,
1896. 281 p.
Indian Summer. Boston: Ticknor Co., 1886. 395 p.

Italian Journeys. New York: Hurd and Houghton, 1867.
320 p.

Judgement Day. (a poem) New York: Liber Scriptorem,
1893. 288 p.

The Kentons. New York: Harper Bros., 1902. 317 p.

The Lady of Aroostook. Boston: Houghton Mifflin Co.,
1907. 320 p.

The Landlord of Lion's Head. Illus. by W. T. Smedley.
New York: Harper Bros., 1897. 461 p.

The Leatherwood God. Illus. by Henry Raleigh. New
York: Century, 1916. 236 p.

Letters Home. New York: Harper Bros., 1903. 299 p.

Letters of an Altrurian Traveller, 1893-1894. Introd. by
Clara Kirk and Rudolph Kirk. Gainsville, Florida:
Facsimiles and reprints by Scholars Facsimiles and
Reprints, 1961. 127 p.

Library of Universal Adventure by Sea and Land: Including Original Narratives and Authentic Stories of Personal Prowess and Peril in All the Waters and Regions
of the Globe from the Year 79 AD to the Year 1888
AD. Compiled and edit. with Thomas Sergeant Perry.
New York: Harper Bros., 1888. 1023 p.

Life in Letters of William Dean Howells. Edit. by
Mildred Howells. Garden City, N.Y.: Doubleday
Doran, 1928. 2 vols. with bibliog. of William Dean
Howells's works.

Life of Abraham Lincoln. Campaign biography, corrected
by the hand of Abraham Lincoln in the summer of
1860. Reproduced with careful attention to the appear-
ance of the original volume. Springfield, Ill.: Abraham Lincoln Association, 1938. 94 p.

Literary Friends and Acquaintances: A Personal Retrospect of American Authorship. New York: Harper
Bros., 1900. 287 p.

Literature and Life Studies. New York: Harper Bros.,
1902. 322 p.

A Little Girl Among the Old Masters. Boston: J. R.
Osgood, 1884. 65 p. 54 plates. The pictures are
the work of a little girl of ten years--Mildred Howells.

A Little Swiss Sojourn. New York: Harper Bros., 1892.
119 p.

London Films. New York: Harper Bros., 1905. 240 p.

The Minister's Charge: or, the Apprenticeship of Lemuel
Barker. Boston: Ticknor, 1887. 463 p.

Miss Bellard's Inspiration. New York: Harper Bros.,
1905. 223 p.

A Modern Instance. Boston: J. R. Osgood, 1882. 514 p.

Modern Italian Poets: Essays and Versions.   Portraits.
New York: Harper Bros., 1887.   368 p.
The Mousetrap and Other Farces.   New York: Harper
Bros., 1889.   184 p.
My Literary Passions.   New York: Harper Bros., 1895.
261 p.
My Mark Twain: Reminiscences and Criticisms.   New
York: Harper Bros., 1910.   186 p.
My Year in a Log Cabin.   New York: Harper Bros.,
1893.   62 p.
New Leaf Mills.   New York: Harper Bros., 1913.   153 p.
An Open-Eyed Conspiracy: An Idyll of Saratoga.   New
York: Harper Bros., 1897.   181 p.
Out of the Question.   (a comedy) Boston: J. R. Osgood,
1877.   183 p.
A Pair of Patient Lovers.   New York: Harper Bros.,
1901.   368 p.
The Parlor Car.   (farce) Boston: J. R. Osgood, 1876.
74 p.
A Parting and a Meeting.   New York: Harper Bros.,
1896.   98 p.
Parting Friends.   (farce) New York: Harper Bros.,
1911.   57 p.
Poems.   Boston: J. R. Osgood, 1873.   172 p.
Prefaces to Contemporaries: 1882-1920.   Facsimile re-
production with introduction and bibliog. note by
George Arms, William M. Gibson and Fredrick C.
Marston, Jr.   Gainsville, Florida: Scholars' Fac-
similes and Reprints, 1957.   200 p.
A Previous Engagement.   (comedy) New York: Harper
Bros., 1897.   65 p.
The Quality of Mercy.   New York: Harper Bros., 1892.
474 p.
Questionable Shapes.   New York: Harper Bros., 1903.
219 p.
Ragged Lady.   Illus. by A. I. Keller.   New York: Harp-
er Bros., 1899.   357 p.
The Register.   (farce) Boston: J. R. Osgood, 1884.
91 p.
The Rise of Silas Lapham.   Boston: Houghton Mifflin,
1884.   515 p.
Roman Holidays and Others.   New York: Harper Bros.,
1908.   302 p.
Room 45.   (farce) Boston: Houghton Mifflin Co., 1900.
61 p.
The Seen and Unseen at Stratford-on-Avon: A Fantasy.
New York: Harper Bros., 1914.   111 p.

Seven English Cities. New York: Harper Bros., 1909.
200 p.
The Shadow of a Dream. New York: Harper Bros.,
1890. 218 p.
Shapes That Haunt the Dusk. (Harpers' Novelettes) New
York: Harper Bros., 1907. 301 p.
Sketch of the Life and Character of Rutherford B. Hayes
and Biographic Sketch of William A. Wheeler. New
York: Hurd & Houghton, 1876. 195 p.
The Sleeping Car and Other Farces. Boston: Houghton
Mifflin Co., 1892. 212 p.
The Smoking Car. (farce) Boston: Houghton Mifflin Co.,
1902. 70 p.
The Son of Royal Langbrith. New York: Harper Bros.,
1904. 368 p.
Stories of Ohio. New York: American Book Co., 1897.
287 p.
The Story of a Play. New York: Harper Bros., 1898.
312 p.
Suburban Sketches. Illus. by Augustus Hoppins. Boston:
Houghton Mifflin Co., 1898. 255 p.
Their Silver Wedding Journey. New York: Harper Bros.,
1899. 2 vols.
Their Wedding Journey. Illus. by Augustus Hoppins.
Boston: J. R. Osgood, 1872. 287 p.
Three Villages. Boston: J. R. Osgood, 1884. 198 p.
Through the Eye of the Needle. New York: Harper
Bros., 1907. 232 p.
A Traveler from Altruria. New York: Harper Bros.,
1894. 318 p.
Tuscan Cities. Illus. by Joseph Pennell and others.
Boston: Ticknor, 1886. 251 p.
The Undiscovered Country. Boston: Houghton Mifflin
Co., 1880. 419 p.
The Unexpected Guests. (farce) New York: Harper
Bros., 1893. 54 p.
The Vacation of the Kelwins: An Idyll of the Middle
Eighteen-Seventies. New York: Harper Bros., 1920.
256 p.
Venetian Life. Venetian social life and customs. London:
N. Trubner, 1866. 359 p.
A Woman's Reason. Boston: Houghton Mifflin Co., 1882.
466 p.
The World of Chance. New York: Harper Bros., 1893.
375 p.

The Writings of William Dean Howells. Library edit.
New York: Harper Bros., 1913. 6 vols.
Years of My Youth. New York: Harper Bros., 1916.
238 p.

HOYT, Jo Wasson, 1929- . Wife of Michael P. E. Hoyt,
a Foreign Service Officer who was appointed in 1956.
Mrs. Hoyt served with her husband at his posts at
Karachi, Casablanca, Washington, Leopoldville, Dou-
ala.
For the Love of Mike. with Frank Graham, Jr. New
York: Random House, 1966. 210 p. [This is an
autobiographical account of the Hoyt's Foreign Service
life up to 1966, including their experiences during the
rebellion and massacres in the Belgian Congo in
1964.]

HUMPHREYS, David, 1752-1818. Soldier, statesman, poet.
Introduced Merino sheep into the United States. Sec-
retary of Commission for Negotiating Treaties of Com-
merce with Foreign Powers 1784-86. Secret Agent in
London, Lisbon and Madrid 1790. Commissioner in
Algerian Affairs 1793. Minister to Spain 1796-1801.
The Miscellaneous Works of Colonel Humphreys. 1804.
Gainsville, Florida: Scholar's Facsimiles and Re-
prints, 1968. 394 p.
Life of Israel Putnam--On Basis of Memoirs of David
Humphreys, His Companion in Arms. New York:
Sheldon, Lamport & Blakeman, 1855. 256 p.
An Historical Account of the Incorporated Society for the
Propagation of the Gospel in Foreign Parts--and the
Success of Their Missionaries in the British Colonies
to the Year 1728. London: J. Downing, 1730. 356 p.

HUNTINGTON, William Chapin, 1884-1958. Commercial
Attaché Petrograd 1916, Teheran 1917, Paris 1920-22.
The Homesick Million, Russia-Out-Of-Russia. Boston:
Stratford Co., 1933. 307 p.
The Prospects of British and American Trade with the
Soviet Union. London: School of Slavonic and East
European Studies. University of London, 1935. 50 p.

HUNTINGTON-WILSON, Francis Mairs, 1875-1946. Lawyer,
newspaperman, banker, manufacturer. Secretary and

Chargé d'Affaires in Tokyo 1897-1906. Chairman of
the Board of Examiners of the Diplomatic Service, Assistant Secretary of State, Under Secretary of State
1909-13. Special Ambassador on mission to Turkey
in 1910. Reorganized the State Department's diplomatic
and consular services with the assistance of Wilber J.
Carr 1909-13.
Memoirs of an Ex-Diplomat. Boston: B. Humphries,
  1945. 373 p.
Money and the Price Level. New York: The Century
  Co., 1932. 221 p.
Stultitia, a Nightmare and an Awakening: In Four Discussions, by a Former Government Official. New
  York: Frederick A. Stokes Co., 1915. 180 p. Also
  published under the title "Save America."
The Peril of Hifalutin. New York: Duffield & Co.,
  1918. 263 p. Reprinted in part from the Public
  Ledger and Annals of the American Academy of Politi-
  cal and Social Science.

HUNTLEY, James Robert, 1923- . Recreation specialist.
  Foreign Service Staff Officer 1952-60. United States
  Information Agency. Served in Munich, Nurnberg,
  Frankfurt-on-the-Main, Harvard University, Brussels.
Europe and America - the Next Ten Years. with Warren
  Randolph Burgess. Introd. by Livingston T. Merchant.
  New York: Walker & Co., 1970. 232 p.

HURD, James Douglas, 1921- . Writer. Foreign Service
  Reserve Officer 1948- . Served in London, Singa-
  pore, Geneva, State Department. Superior Honor
  Award 1965.
Preludes and Other Poems. London: Christopher John-
  son, 1956. 63 p.

HURST, Carlton Bailey, 1887-1943. Born in Germany of
  American parents. Foreign Service Officer 1892-1903,
  and 1904-31.
The Arms Above the Door. New York: Dodd, Mead &
  Co., 1932. 377 p. [Foreign Service experiences.]

IMBRIE, Katherine (Gillespie). Widow of Foreign Service
  Officer Robert Whitney Imbrie. [Q.V.]
Data Relating to the Assassination of United States Con-
  sular Officer Robert Whitney Imbrie by the Military

Police of Persia. in Teheran, Persia, July 1939.
Frederick, Md.: Copyrighted by Katherine Imbrie,
1924. 45 p.

IMBRIE, Robert Whitney, 1884-1924. Lawyer. Foreign
   Service Officer 1917-24. Served in Viborg, Petrograd,
   Constantinople, Teheran. Murdered by a mob of reli-
   gious fanatics in Teheran, 1924. (See story by Kath-
   erine Gillespie Imbrie.) [Q. V.]
Behind the Wheel of a War Ambulance. (Experiences in
   World War I in French Army.) New York: McBride,
   1918. 248 p.

IRELAND, Philip Willard, 1904- . Educator. State De-
   partment and Foreign Service Officer 1942-65. Served
   in Washington, Cairo, Nation War College, Baghdad,
   Salonika, Aleppo.
Iraq: A Study in Political Development. London: J.
   Cape, 1937. 510 p. New York: Russell & Russell,
   1970. 510 p.
(Edited) The Near East: Problems and Prospects. by
   Count Carlo Sforza and others. Chicago: University
   of Chicago Press, 1942. 265 p.

IRVING, Washington, 1783-1859. Author. "Attached" to the
   American Legation in Madrid 1826-29. Secretary of
   Legation, London, 1829-32. Minister to Madrid 1842-
   46.
The Works of Washington Irving. New York: G. P. Put-
   nam's Sons, 1850-1880. 10 vols.
Abbotsford and Newstead Abbey. London: J. Murray,
   1835. 290 p.
Abu Hassan. Introd. by George S. Hellman. Boston:
   Bibliophile Society, 1924. 83 p.
The Adventures of Captain Bonneville, U. S. A., In the
   Rocky Mountains and the Far West. New York: G. P.
   Putnam's Sons, 1850. 428 p.
The Alhambra. New York: G. P. Putnam's Sons, 1832.
   511 p.
Astoria: or, the Anecdotes of an Enterprise Beyond the
   Rocky Mountains. New York: G. P. Putnam's Sons,
   1849. 519 p.
The Beauties of Washington Irving. Illus. with 6 etchings
   by William Heath. London: J. Bumpus, 1825. 316 p.
Biographies and Miscellanies. Edit. by Pierre M. Irving.

New York: G. P. Putnam's Sons, 1866. 579 p.
A Book of the Hudson, Collected From the Various Works
of Diedrich Knickerbocker. New York: G. P. Put-
nam's Sons, 1849. 215 p.
Bracebridge Hall: or, The Humorist. A Medley, by
Geoffrey Crayon, Gent. (pseud.). New York: Printed
by C. S. Van Winkle, 1822. 2 vols.
Chronicle of the Conquest of Granada, From the Manu-
script of Fray Antonio Agapida. Philadelphia: Carey,
Lea & Carey, 1829. 2 vols.
Contributions to the Corrector. Introd. by Martin Roth.
Minneapolis: University of Minnesota Press, 1968.
130 p.
The Crayon Miscellany. Philadelphia: Carey, Lea &
Blanchard, 1835. 3 vols.
The Crayon Reading Book. (selections) New York: G. P.
Putnam's Sons, 1849. 255 p.
The Devil and Tom Walker. Together with Deacon Grubb
and The Old Nick. (from Tales of a Traveller) Wood-
stock, Vermont: R. & A. Cole, 1830. 32 p.
Essays and Sketches. London: C. Tilt, 1837. 222 p.
The Gentleman in Black, & Tales of Other Days. Illus.
by George Cruikshank and others. London: C. Daly,
1840. 392 p.
A History of New York, From the Beginning of the World
to the End of the Dutch Dynasty. Containing Among
Many Surprising Matters the Unutterable Ponderings of
Walter, The Doubted, The Disastrous Projects of Wil-
liam the Testy, & the Chivalric Achievements of Peter
the Headstrong, the Three Dutch Governors of New
Amsterdam: Being the Only Authentic History of the
Time That Hath Ever Been or Ever Will Be Published.
By Diedrich Knickerbocker. New York: Inskeep &
Bradford, 1809. 2 vols.
Journal of Washington Irving: 1823-1824. Edit. by Stan-
ley T. Williams. Cambridge: Harvard University
Press, 1931. 278 p.
Legend of Sleepy Hollow. (from the Sketch Book). Illus.
by Huntington, Kenett, Darley, etc. New York: G.
P. Putnam's Sons, 1864. 50 p.
Legends of the Conquest of Spain. Philadelphia: Carey,
Lea & Blanchard, 1835. 276 p.
Letters From Sunnyside and Spain. Edit. by Stanley T.
Williams. New Haven: Yale University Press, 1928.
80 p.
Letters of Jonathan Oldstyle, Gent., With a Biographical
Notice. London: E. Wilson, 1824. 68 p.

Letters of Washington Irving to Henry Brevoort.   Edit.
  by George S. Hellman.   New York: G. P. Putnam's
  Sons, 1915.   2 vols.
History of the Life and Voyages of Christopher Columbus.
  Philadelphia: Carey, Lea & Blanchard, 1828.   2 vols.
Life of George Washington.   New York: G. P. Putnam's
  Sons, 1855-59.   5 vols.
Life of Mahomet.   London: H. Q. Bohn, 1850.   216 p.
Life of Oliver Goldsmith.   New York: J. W. Lovell,
  1883.   258 p.
Lives of the Successors of Mahomet.   London: H. Q.
  Bohn, 1858.   268 p.
Moorish Chronicles.   New York: Belford Co., 188?.
  131 p.
Notes and Journal of Travel in Europe, 1804-1805.   In-
  trod. by William P. Trent.   New York: Grolier Club,
  1921.   3 vols.
Old Christmas.   (from Sketch Book) 3rd Edit.   London:
  Macmillan Co., 1878.   165 p.
Oliver Goldsmith, A Biography.   New York: G. P. Put-
  nam's Sons, 1849.   448 p.
Reviews and Miscellanies.   New York: G. P. Putnam's
  Sons, 1897.   423 p.
Rip Van Winkle.   A Legend of the Kaatskill Mountains.
  A Posthumous Writing of Diedrich Knickerbocker.   (from
  the Sketch Book) New York: G. P. Putnam's Sons,
  1870.
Salmagundi: or, the Whim-Whams and Opinions of Launce-
  lott Langstaff, Esquire, and Others.   New York: D.
  Longworth at the Shakespeare Gallery, 1807-08.   2
  vols.
The Sketch Book of Geoffrey Crayon, Gent.   New York:
  C. S. Van Winkle, 1819-20.   2 vols.
Spanish Papers and Other Miscellanies Hitherto Unpub-
  lished.   New York: G. P. Putnam's Sons, 1866.   2
  vols.
Stories of the Hudson.   New York: Dodge Publishing Co.,
  1912.   289 p.
Tales of a Traveller, by Geoffrey Crayon, Gent.   London:
  J. Murray, 1824.   2 vols.
Tour in Scotland, 1817, and Other Manuscript Notes.
  Edit. by Stanley T. Williams.   New Haven: Yale Uni-
  versity Press, 1927.   146 p.
Voyages and Discoveries of the Companions of Columbus.
  Philadelphia: Carey & Lea, 1831.   350 p.
Washington Irving and the Storrows: Letters from England
  and the Continent, 1821-1828.   Edit. by Stanley T.

Williams. Cambridge: Harvard University Press, 1933. 136 p.

Washington Irving Diary, Spain 1828-29. New York: Hispanic Society of America, 1926. 142 p.

The Western Journals of Washington Irving. Norman, Okla.: University of Oklahoma Press, 1944. 200 p.

The Wild Huntsman. Boston: Bibliophile Society, 1924. 113 p.

Woolfert's Roost, and Other Papers. New York: G. P. Putnam's Sons, 1855. 383 p.

A Tour On the Prairies. London: J. Murray, 1835. 335 p.

IVES, Elizabeth Stevenson. Wife of Ernest L. Ives, 1887-1958. Foreign Service Officer 1909-39. Served in Frankfort-on-Main, Erfurt, Breslau, Budapest, Paris, Alexandria, Constantinople, Copenhagen, Pretoria, Callao-Lima, Algiers, Stockholm, Belfast. Mrs. Ives's brother was Adlai Stevenson who was Governor of Illinois, Presidential candidate against Dwight Eisenhower, and Ambassador to the United Nations 1960-64.

My Brother Adlai. New York: Morrow & Co., 1955. 308 p.

Back to Beginnings, Adlai E. Stevenson in North Carolina. Charlotte: Heritage Printers, 1969. 58 p. Privately printed, 1000 copies. Photographs.

IZARD, Ralph, 1741-1804. Revolutionary patriot. Senator. Commissioner to Tuscany 1777-79. Not recognized by that Government and went to France. Tried unsuccessfully to take over Benjamin Franklin's duties.

Correspondence of Mr. Ralph Izard of South Carolina. Edit. by Anne Izard Dess. New York: C. S. Francis & Co., 1844. 389 p. Vol. I, the only volume printed.

JACKSON, Henry Rootes, 1820-1898. Lawyer, soldier, editor. Chargé d'Affaires in Austria and Minister Resident 1853-58. Minister to Mexico 1885-86.

Tallulah and Other Poems. Savannah, Ga.: J. M. Cooper, 1850. 235 p.

JAY, John, 1745-1829. Lawyer. Member Continental Congress 1774-79. President Continental Congress 1779. Chief Justice New York State 1777-78. Minister to Spain 1779-82, was not formally received at Court and left Madrid for Paris in May 1782. Joint Commissioner with John Adams, Benjamin Franklin and Henry

Laurens to negotiate a peace treaty with Great Britain;
signed preliminary articles Nov. 30, 1782, at Paris;
signed definitive treaty September 3, 1783, at Paris.
Secretary of Foreign Affairs December 1784-March
1790. Minister to Great Britain 1794-95. Chief Justice 1789-95. Governor of New York 1795-1801.
Works by this author printed in America before
1801 are available in the Library of Congress in the
Readex Microprint editions of Early American Imprints,
published by the American Antiquarian Society.

The Correspondence and Public Papers of John Jay. Edit.
by Henry P. Johnston. New York: G. P. Putnam's
Sons, 1890-93. 4 vols.

The Diary of John Jay During the Peace Negotiations of
1782. Being a True and Faithful Rendering of the
Original Manuscript, Now Published for the First Time.
Introd. by Frank Monoghan. New Haven: Bibliographical Press, 1934.

The Federalist; a Commentary on the Constitution of the
United States, being a Collection of Essays Written in
Support of the Constitution Agreed Upon September 17,
1787, by the Federal Convention, from the Original
Text of Alexander Hamilton, John Jay and James
Madison. Introd. by Edward Mead Earle. New York:
The Modern Library, 1941. 618 p.

Letters, Being the Whole of the Correspondence Between
the Honorable John Jay, Esquire, and Mr. Lewis
Littlepage: a Young Man Whom Mr. Jay, When in
Spain, Patronized and Took Into His Family. New
York: Printed and sold by F. Childs, 1786.

The Life of John Jay, With Selections from his Correspondence and Miscellaneous Papers. by his son, William Jay. New York: J. & J. Harper, 1833. 2
vols.

JAY, John, 1817-1894. Lawyer, author. Minister to Austria 1869-74.

The Peace Negotiations of 1782-1783. New York: New
York Historical Society, 1884. 239 p.

Addresses and Letters. Including The American Foreign
Service. From the "International Review," May-June
1877. New York: A. S. Barnes, 1877. 15 p.

The Fisheries Dispute. New York: Dodd, Mead & Co.,
1887. 52 p.

The Great Conspiracy. The Civil War and England's
Neutrality. (an address) New York: J. G. Gregory,
1861. 50 p.

A Statistical View of American Agriculture. New York:
D. Appleton Co., 1859. 81 p.

JEFFERSON, Thomas, 1743-1826. Lawyer. Member Virginia House of Burgesses 1769-75. Continental Congress 1775-76. Prepared the first draft of the Declaration of Independence and signed the final Declaration.
Member of Virginia House of Delegates 1776-79. Governor of Virginia 1779-81. Continental Congress 1783-
84. Joint Minister Plenipotentiary with Benjamin
Franklin and John Adams to negotiate treaties of amity
and commerce with European nations and the Barbary
States. Commissioned May 12, 1784, signed treaty
with Prussia July 28, 1785 at Paris. Signed treaty
with Morocco January 1, 1787 at Paris. Minister to
France 1785-89. Secretary of State 1790-93. President 1801-1809.

Works printed in America before 1801 are available
in the Library of Congress in the Readex Microfilm
edition of Early American Reprints published by the
American Antiquarian Society.
Autobiography of Thomas Jefferson. Introd. and notes by
Paul Leicester Ford, and Fore. by George Haven Put-
nam. New York: G. P. Putnam's Sons, 1914. 162 p.
Basic Writings of Thomas Jefferson. Edit. by Philip S.
Forner. Garden City, N.Y.: 1950. 816 p.
Calendar of the Correspondence of Thomas Jefferson.
Washington: Department of State, 1894-95.
2 vols.
Catalogue: President Jefferson's Library. Copied from
original manuscript in his handwriting, as arranged by
himself, to be sold at auction at the Long Room,
Pennsylvania Avenue, Washington: Gales & Seaton,
1829.
The Complete Jefferson. Containing his major writings
published and unpublished, except his letters, assem-
bled and arranged by Saul K. Padover, will illustrations
and analytic index. New York: Duell, Sloan and
Pearce, 1943. 1322 p. Freeport, N.Y.: Books for
Libraries Press, 1969. 1323 p.
The Jefferson Cyclopedia. A comprehensive collection of
the views of Thomas Jefferson, classified and arranged
in alphabetical order under 9,000 titles relating to government, politics, law, education, political economy,
finance, science, art, literature, religious freedom,
morals, etc. Edit. by John P. Foley. New York:
Funk & Wagnalls, 1900. 1009 p.

Letters and Addresses of Thomas Jefferson.   Edit. by
William B. Parker, Jonas Viles.   New York: The
Unit Book Publishing Co., 1905.   323 p.
The Writings of Thomas Jefferson.   Definitive edition
containing his "Autobiography," 'Notes on Virginia,"
"Parliamentary Manual," official papers, messages and
addresses and other writings, official and private,
now collected and published in their entirety for the
first time, including all of the original manuscripts
deposited in the Department of State and published in
1853 by order of the joint Houses of the Congress;
with numerous illustrations and a comprehensive analytical index.   Andrew J. Lipscomb, Editor-in-Chief.
Albert Ellery Bergh, Managing Editor.   Washington:
Issued under the auspices of the Thomas Jefferson
Memorial Association of the United States, 1905.   20
vols.
Democracy.   Edit. by Saul K. Padover.   New York: D.
Appleton-Century Co., 1939.   291 p.
Notes on the State of Virginia: Written in the Year 1781,
Somewhat Corrected and Enlarged in the Winter of 1782
for the Use of a Foreigner of Distinction.   In Answer
to Certain Inquiries Proposed by Him 1782.   Paris:
Printed 1784-85.   391 p.
The Writings of Thomas Jefferson.   Edit. by Paul L.
Ford, 1892-99.   New York: G. P. Putnam's Sons,
1892-1900.   10 vols.
Correspondence Between Thomas Jefferson and Pierre
Samuel Dupont de Nemours, 1798-1817.   with a Supple-
ment by Gilbert Chinard.   Edit. by Dumas Malone.
Boston: Houghton Mifflin, 1930.   210 p.
Declaration of Independence.   Philadelphia: Continental
Congress, July 4, 1776.

JESSUP, Philip Caryl, 1897- .   Jurist.   Professor Colum-
bia University 1925-51.   Judge International Court of
Justice 1961- .   Ambassador-at-Large 1949-53.
American Neutrality, Etc.   Boston: World Peace Founda-
tion, 1928.   170 p.
Controls for Outer Space and the Antartic Analogy.   with
H. J. Taubenfield.   New York: Columbia University
Press, 1959.   379 p.
Modernes Volkerrecht.   (Modern Law of Nations) Vienna:
Humboldt-Verlag, 1950.   311 p.
Opinion of Philip C. Jessup and Oliver J. Lissitzyn With
Respect to the U.S. Senate's Attempt to Repeal the
Federal Power Act In Its Relation to the Niagara

Through the Use of the Treaty-Making Power. New
York: Power Authority of the State of New York,
1955. 96 p.
Outlines of the Law for Bar Examination and Law School
Review. Washington: Hayworth Printing Co., 1925.
149 p.
The Use of International Law. 5 lectures. Foreword by
Eric Stein. Ann Arbor: University of Michigan Law
School, 1959. 164 p.
The Law of Territorial Waters and Maritime Jurisdiction.
New York: G. A. Jennings, 1927. 548 p.
The United States and the World Court. Foreword by
Elihu Root. New York: World Peace Foundation,
1929. 159 p.
American Neutrality and International Police. Boston:
World Peace Foundation pamphlet. Vol. XI, No. 3,
1928. 170 p.
International Security. New York: Council on Foreign
Relations, Inc., 1935. 157 p.
Neutrality: Its History, Economics and Law. Vol. I.
The Origins with Francis Deak. New York: Columbia
University Press, 1935-36. Vol. IV. Today and To-
morrow. New York: Columbia University Press,
1936.
Elihu Root. New York: Dodd, Mead, 1938. 2 vols.
A Modern Law of Nations. New York: The Macmillan
Co., 1948. 236 p.
International Regulation of Economic and Social Questions.
with Oliver J. Lissitzyn and Adolf Lande. New York:
Carnegie Foundation for International Peace, 1956.
173 p.
Transnational Law. New Haven: Yale University Press,
1956. 113 p.
The National Purpose. with others. Chicago: Holt,
Rinehart & Winston in LIFE 1960. 146 p.
(Edited) Columbia University Studies in History, Economics
and Law. 1929-33.
The Price in International Justice. New York: Columbia
University Press, 1971. 82 p.

JEWELL, J. Grey. American Consul in Singapore, 1869-
71.
Among Our Sailors. New York: Harper Bros., 1874.
311 p. (The author was American Consul in the Orient
for many years. In the book he describes the shocking
treatment of American seamen, including those on
whalers. With an appendix containing extracts from the

laws and consular regulations governing the United
States merchant service.)

JOHNSON, Edgar Augustus Jerome, 1900- . Professor of
economic history.   Civil Administrator of South Korean
interim government, 1946-48; Advisor to Economic
Cooperation Administration Mission to Greece 1951-52;
Deputy Chief U.S. Aid Program in Yugoslavia 1952-55.
American Economic Thought in the Seventeenth Century.
London: F. S. King & Son, Ltd., 1932. 292 p.
(Edited) The Dimensions of Diplomacy. by McGeorge
Bundy and others. Baltimore: Johns Hopkins Press,
1964. 135 p.
The American Economy, Its Origins, Development, and
Transformation: an Introduction to Economics. with
Herman E. Krooss. Englewood, N.J.: Prentice-Hall
Inc., 1960. 466 p.
American Imperialism in the Image of Peer Gynt: Mem-
oirs of a Professor-Bureaucrat. Minneapolis: Uni-
versity of Minnesota Press, 1971. 352 p.
An Economic History of Modern England. New York:
T. Nelson & Sons, 1939. 230 p.
The Origins and Development of the American Economy:
an Introduction to Economics. with Herman E. Krooss.
New York: Prentice-Hall Inc., 1953. 420 p.
The Organization of Space in Developing Countries. Cam-
bridge: Harvard University Press, 1970. 452 p.
Predecessors of Adam Smith: the Growth of British Eco-
nomic Thought. New York: A. M. Kelley, 1965.
426 p.
Some Origins of the Modern Economic World. New York:
The Macmillan Co., 1936. 163 p.

JOHNSON, Hallett, 1888-1968. Foreign Service Officer
1912-1947. Served in London, Constantinople, La
Paz, Santiago, State Department, Brussels, Stockholm,
Madrid, Berlin, Paris, Oslo, The Hague, Warsaw,
Ambassador to Costa Rica 1944-47.
Diplomatic Memoirs, Serious and Frivolous. New York:
Vantage Press, 1963. 207 p.

JOHNSON, James Weldon, 1871-1938. Lawyer, writer,
editor, educator, poet, song writer, champion of Negro
rights and culture, columnist, actor. With his brother, J. Rosamond Johnson, he wrote some 200 songs,
including "The Maiden with the Dreamy Eyes," "Under
the Bamboo Tree," "The Congo Love Song," "Lift

Every Voice and Sing" (Negro "National Anthem") and
shared in composing "The Shoofly Regiment. "
Consul at Puerto Cabello 1906, Corinto 1909-13.
Editor of "New York Age, " oldest Negro newspaper in
New York.

Fifty Years and Other Poems. Introduction by Brander
Matthews. Boston: The Cornhill Company, 1917.
92 p.

God's Trombones: Seven Negro Sermons in Verse.
Drawings by Aaron Douglas. Lettering by C. B. Falls.
New York: The Viking Press, 1927. 56 p.

Black Manhattan. (Negro musical and theatrical experiences.) New York: Alfred A. Knopf, 1930. 284 p.

Saint Peter Relates an Incident of the Resurrection Day.
(satirical poem on race prejudice and selected poems)
New York: The Viking Press, 1935. 105 p.

Negro Americans, What Now? (series of lectures) New
York: The Viking Press, 1934. 103 p.

The Autobiography of an Ex-Colored Man. (fiction, story
of a light-skinned negro who "passed over") Boston:
Sherman, French Co. , 1912. 207 p.

Along This Way. (autobiography) New York: The Viking
Press, 1933. 418 p.

Self-Determining Haiti. Four articles reprinted from the
"Nation" embodying a report of an investigation made
for the National Association for the Advancement of
Colored People, together with official documents. New
York: The Nation, 1920. 48 p. In French, Port-au-
Prince: Comité Central de l'Union Patriotique, 1921.
35 p.

(Translation) Gernandos Periquet's libretto "Goyescas" by
Enrique Granados. Presented at the Metropolitan
Opera House in 1916.

(Edited) The Book of American Negro Poetry: Chosen and
Edited with an Essay on the Negro's Creative Genius.
New York: Harcourt, Brace & Company, 1922. 217 p.

(Edited) The Book of American Negro Spirituals, Edited
with an Introduction by James Weldon Johnson: Musical
Arrangements by J. Rosamond Johnson. Additional
Numbers by Lawrence Brown. New York: The Viking
Press, 1925. 187 p.

(Edited) The Second Book of Negro Spirituals, Edited With
an Introduction by James Weldon Johnson: Musical
Arrangements by J. Rosamond Johnson. New York:
The Viking Press, 1926. 189 p.

(Edited) The Books of American Negro Spirituals, Including the Book of American Negro Spirituals and the

Second Book of Negro Spirituals, by James Weldon
Johnson and J. Rosamond Johnson. New York: The
Viking Press, 1940. 2 vols.
Johnson's MSS is in the James Weldon Johnson Memorial
Collection of Negro Arts and Letters at Yale Univer-
sity.

JOHNSON, Nelson Trusler, 1887-1954. Foreign Service Officer 1907-1952. Chinese language officer. Served in
Peking, Mukden, Harbin, Hankow, Shanghai, Chungking, Changsha, State Department. Assistant Secretary
of State. Foreign Service Inspector. Minister to
China 1929-35. Ambassador to Australia 1941-46.
Secretary General to the Far Eastern Commission
1946-52.
Papers 1916-1950. Library of Congress, Manuscript Division, 11 ft. The main body of the Papers consists of
personal correspondence 1916-37. Also includes a
large group of memoranda of conversations and twelve
engagement books (1927-35), articles, speeches and
other material relating to the State Department and the
Far East, 1920-30. When Johnson was Secretary General of the Far Eastern Commission his correspondents
include Stanley Hornbeck, Owen Lattimore and Henry
Morganthau, Jr.

JOHNSON, Richard Abraham, 1910- . Educator, historian,
lecturer 1935-40 and 1965- . Foreign Service Officer
1940-65. Served in Naples, London, La Paz, Guada-
lajara, Ciudad Trujillo, State Department, National
War College, Madrid, Director Board of Examiners,
Monterrey.
The Administration of United States Foreign Policy. Aus-
tin: University of Texas Press, 1971. 415 p.
The Mexican Revolution of Ayutla, 1854-1855. An Analy-
sis of the Evolution and Destruction of Santa Anna's
Last Dictatorship. Rock Island, Ill.: Agustant College
Library, 1939. 125 p.

JOHNSON, Robert Underwood, 1853-1937. Editor, author,
poet. Ambassador to Italy 1920-21.
Remembered Yesterdays. Boston: Little, Brown & Co.,
1923. 624 p.
The Winter Hour and Other Poems. New York: The Century Co., 1892. 87 p.
Songs of Liberty and Other Poems. New York: The Century Co., 1897. 107 p.

Poems. New York: The Century Co., 1908. 319 p.
Saint Gaudens: an Ode and Other Verses. New York: The Century Co., 1910. 340 p.
The Coastwise Exemption: The Nation is Against It. New York: The Century Co., 1913. 68 p.
Poems of War and Peace. Indianapolis: The Bobbs-Merrill Co., 1916. 57 p.
Collected Poems, 1881-1919. New Haven: Yale University Press, 1920. 529 p.
Poems of the Longer Flight, Chiefly Odes and Apostrophes. New York: The author, 1928. 121 p.
Poems of Fifty Years, 1880-1930. New York: The author. Seven volumes in one. 1931. 560 p.
Aftermath. A supplement to his Poems of Fifty Years. New York: The author, 1933. 117 p.
Poems. New York: The Century Co., 1902. 270 p.
Heroes, Children and Fun. New York: The author, 1934. 136 p.
Papers, 1898-1937. New York: American Academy of Arts and Letters Library. 2 ft.
The Pact of Honor, and Other Poems, Grave and Gay. New York: The author, 1929. 75 p.

JONES, Arthur Griffith, 1913- . Tennessee Valley Authority 1937-47. State Department officer 1947-55. Foreign Service Officer 1956-68. Served in the State Department, National War College, New Delhi, Foreign Service Inspector.
The Evolution of Personnel Systems for United States Foreign Affairs. New York: Carnegie Endowment for International Peace, 1965. 136 p.

JONES, Chester Lloyd, 1881- . Commercial expert, professor of political science. Commercial Attaché 1919-27. Served in Madrid, Havana, Paris.
Caribbean Backgrounds and Prospects. Port Washington, N.Y.: Kennikat Press, 1971. 354 p.
Caribbean Interests of the United States. New York: D. Appleton & Co., 1916. 379 p.
The Caribbean Since 1900. New York: Russell & Russell, 1970. 511 p.
The Consular Service of the United States. Its History

and Activities. Philadelphia: University of Pennsyl-
vania, 1906.
Costa Rica and Civilization in the Caribbean. New York:
Russell & Russell, 1967. 172 p.
Guatemala, Past & Present. New York: Russell &
Russell, 1966. c1940. 420 p.
Readings on Parties and Elections in the United States.
Westport, Conn.: Negro Universities Press, 1970.
354 p. Reprint of the 1912 edition.

JONES, George Lewis, 1907-71. Newspaper reporter.
Foreign Service Officer 1930-1971. Served in London,
Cairo, State Department, National War College, Teh-
ran, Ambassador to Tunisia 1956-59, Special Negoti-
ator for Wheeler AFB, Libya, 1964. Foreign Service
Institute 1965. Foreign Service Inspector 1969-71.
Tidemarks, a Collection of Occasional Verses, 1930-70.
Quezon City, The Philippines: Bookman Printing
House, 1970. 103 p.

JONES, Howard Palfrey, 1899- . Professor at Columbia
University 1933-39. Authority on taxes and finance.
Chief of finance, Office of Military Government, Berlin, 1947-48. Foreign Service Officer 1948-65. Served
in Berlin, Taipei, Djakarta, Ass't Secretary of State
for Far Eastern Affairs 1957-58. Ambassador to Indonesia 1958-65. Career Minister.
Indonesia: The Possible Dream. New York: Harcourt,
Brace, Jovanovich, 1971. 473 p.

JONES, William Patterson, 1831-1886. Educator and author. Consul at Macao 1862-68.
The Myth of the Stone Idol. An epic poem, a love legend
of Dakota. Chicago: S. C. Griggs & Co., 1876.
74 p.

JORDAN, Yvonne (Mrs.), 1897- . Born in Brittany,
France. Wife of Curtis Calhoun Jordan, Foreign Ser-
vice Officer 1919-1950. He served in Port-au-Prince,
Helsingfors, Havana, Barcelona, Bilbao, Madrid, Mad-
ras, Vigo, San Luis Potosi, Lourenço Marques.
Culinary Gleanings From Here, There and Everywhere.
Madras: Diocesan Press, 1938. 454 p.

KALIJARVI, Thorsten Waino Valentine, 1897- . Government official, professor and writer on government and foreign affairs. Ambassador to El Salvador 1957-60.
Central America: Land of Lords and Lizards. Princeton, N.J.: Van Nostrand Co., 1962. 128 p.
The Government of New Hampshire. with William C. Chamberlin. Durham, New Hampshire: The University of New Hampshire, 1939. 283 p.
The Problem of Taxation in New Hampshire. Lectures delivered before the first Institute of Public Affairs of the University of New Hampshire. Foreword by Fred Engelhardt. Durham: 1938. 58 p.
The Memel Statute, Its Origin, Legal Nature, and Observation to The Present Day. London: R. Hale, Ltd., 1937. 256 p.
(Edited) Recent American Foreign Policy: Basic Documents 1941-51. with Francis O. Wilcox, Co-editor. New York: Appleton-Century Co., 1952. 927 p.
(Edited) Congress and Foreign Relations. with Chester E. Merrow, co-editor. Philadelphia: American Academy of Political and Social Science, 1953. 245 p.
(Edited) Peace Settlements of World War II. Philadelphia: American Academy of Political and Social Science, 1948. 271 p.
Modern World Politics. with Associates. Maps by Clifford H. MacFadden. New York: Thomas Y. Crowell Co., 1942. 853 p. Bibliography at end of each chapter.

KALISH, Betty McKelvey. Wife of Stanley E. Kalish. Mr. Kalish (1906-) served from 1951 to 1969 as Foreign Service Reserve officer in Washington, Djkarta, Dacca, Rawalpindi.
Siti's Summer. Illus. by Ipe Maaroef. New York: Macmillan Co., 1964. 152 p.

KASSON, John Adam, 1822-1910. Lawyer, politician, Congressman. Minister to Austria-Hungary 1877-81, to Germany 1884-85. Commissioner to Congo International Conference 1893.
History of the Formation of the Constitution. First published in 1889. Republished as The Evolution of the United States of America and the History of the Monroe Doctrine. Boston: Houghton Mifflin Co., 1904. 273 p.

KATZ, Milton, 1907- . Professor of law at Harvard 1904- . United States Special Representative, rank of

Ambassador, to Economic Commission for Europe
1950-51.
Cases and Materials in Administrative Law. St. Paul:
West Minnesota Publishing Co., 1947. 1108 p.
The Things That Are Caesar's. New York: Alfred A.
Knopf Inc., 1966. 227 p.

KEENE, Francis Bowler, 1856- . Newspaper editor.
Wisconsin State Legislator. Foreign Service Officer
1903-24. Served in Florence, Geneva, Zurich, Rome.
Lyrics of the Links. The Poetry, Sentiment and Humor
of Golf. Foreword by Grantland Rice. New York:
Appleton, 1923. 126 p.

KELLY, Dorothy (Smith). Mrs. Kelly, wife of Henry Warren Kelly, [Q. V.]. Dorothy Smith was a clerk in the
Consulate General in Shanghai when the Japanese took
over Shanghai and was transferred to Lima in 1942,
where she met "Hank" Kelly a newly arrived Foreign
Service Officer. They were married in Lima and assigned to Iquitos, the Peruvian port at the head of
ocean navigation on the Amazon River.
Dancing Diplomats. by Hank and Dot Kelly. Foreign
Service experiences in the Peruvian Amazon. Foreword by Oliver La Farge. Illus. by Gustave Baumann.
Albuquerque: University of New Mexico Press, 1950.
254 p.

KELLY, Henry Warren, 1917-47. Foreign Service Officer
1942-45. Served in Iquitos (Peru), Santiago and Punta
Arena (Chile). Husband of Dorothy Smith Kelly.
[Q. V.]
Dancing Diplomats. by Hank and Dot Kelly. Foreword
by Oliver La Farge. Illus. by Gustave Baumann.
Foreign Service experiences in the Peruvian Amazon.
Albuquerque: University of New Mexico Press, 1950.
254 p.

KENNAN, George Frost, 1904- . Diplomat, author, pro-
fessor, Foreign Service Officer 1927-53 and 1961-1963.
Served in Hamburg, Tallin, Riga, Kovno, Berlin,
Moscow, Vienna, State Department, Prague, Lisbon,
London, National War College, Deputy Counselor of the
State Department, Chief of the Policy Planning Staff,
Institute of Advanced Study, Ambassador to Russia
1952-53, to Yugoslavia 1961-1963. Professor at the
Institute of Advanced Studies at Princeton University

1956- .
American Diplomacy 1900-1950.   Chicago: University of
    Chicago Press, 1951.   146 p.   (1951 Freedom House
    Award)
Realities of American Foreign Policy.   Princeton: Prince-
    ton University Press, 1954.   119 p.   In Russian in
    1956.
Soviet-American Relations 1917-1920.   Princeton: Prince-
    ton University Press, 1956-58.   513 p.   Volume I.
    Russia Leaves the War.   Volume II.   Decision to
    Intervene.   Bancroft Prize 1956, National Book Award.
    Francis Parkman Prize.   Pulitzer Prize 1957.
Das Amerikanisch Russische Verhaltnis.   Stuttgart: 1954.
    95 p.
La Diplomatie Americaine 1900-1950.   Traduit de l'ameri-
    cain par Helene Claireau.   Preface de Raymond Aron.
    Paris: Calmann-Levy, 1952.   209 p.
Russia, the Atom and the West.   New York: Harper
    Bros., 1958.   125 p.
Soviet Foreign Policy 1917-1941.   Princeton: Van No-
    strand Co. Inc., 1960.   192 p.
Russia and the West Under Lenin and Stalin.   Boston:
    Little, Brown & Co., 1961.   411 p.
On Dealing With the Communist World.   New York:
    Harper Bros., 1964.   57 p.
Memoirs 1925-1950.   Boston: Little, Brown & Co.,
    1967.   583 p.
From Prague After Munich.   Princeton: Princeton Uni-
    versity Press, 1968.   266 p.   (Diplomatic Papers
    1938-1940.)
Democracy and the Student Left.   with students and teach-
    ers from Barnard, Brandeis, Brooklyn.   Boston: Lit-
    tle, Brown & Co., 1968.   239 p.
The Marquis de Custine and His Russia in 1839.   Prince-
    ton: Princeton University Press, 1971.   145 p.
Memoirs: Vol. II.   1950-1963.   Boston: Atlantic-Little,
    Brown Co., 1972.

KENNEDY, Joseph Patrick, 1888-1969.   Financier, business-
    man.   Ambassador to Great Britain 1937-40.   Father
    of President John F. Kennedy.
I'm For Roosevelt.   New York: Reynal & Hitchcock,
    1936.   149 p.
The Surrender of King Leopold.   with James M. Landis.
    Appendix containing the Keyes-Gort correspondence.
    New York: 1950.   61 p.
(Edited) The Story of Films.   As told by the leaders of

the industry to students of the Graduate School of Business Administration at Harvard University. Chicago: A. W. Shaw Co., 1927. 377 p.

KERBEY, Joseph Orton, 1837-1913. Major in the Union Army in the Civil War. Journalist. With Pan American Union. Consul in Belem, 1890-91. Visited Belem again in 1909. Travelled up the Amazon River valley and over the mountains to Lima.
The Boy Spy, A Civil War Episodes. New York: Bedford Clarke, 1890. 556 p.
On the Warpath. (a journey over the Civil War battlegrounds) Chicago: Donohue, Hennebery, 1890. 301 p.
Florida Rubber Culture Co. "The gold which grows on trees in the California of South America to be transplanted to South Florida. Secretary Blaine's foresight of the immense value of the rubber industry explained by Ex-Consul Kerbey." Pittsburgh: P. F. Smith Printing & Lithograph Co., 1896. 47 p.
The Land of Tomorrow. New York: W. F. Brainard, 1906. "A newspaper exploration up the Amazon River and over the Andes to the 'California of South America'." 405 p.
An American Consul in Amazonia. New York: William Edwin Rudge, 1911. 370 p.

KING, Jonas, 1792-1869. Missionary in Near East. Consular Agent at Athens 1851-57. Acting Consul 1857-58. Vice Consul at Piraeus 1868. Distributed books and tracts from his shop in Athens.
Farewell Letter. (his reasons for not joining the Catholic Church.) Written originally in Arabic, 1825, and later published by the Church Missionary Society of England. Two Popes prohibited it as defamatory. 467 p.
Defense. In Greek. A Defense Compiled by Certain Greek Newspapers with Certain Observations and Additions from the Writings of Saints Epifanios, Chrysostom, Basil, Irenaios, Clement and other Luminaries of the Church, Excelling during the First Five Hundred Years After the Coming of Christ. Athens: Nicholas Angelidon, 1845. 220 p.
Exposition of an Apostolic Church. In Greek. Cambridge, Mass.: 1851 and 1857. "80 or 100 pages."
Speech Before the Areopagus. In Greek. Partly delivered April 23, 1846--the President of the Court did not permit him to finish it. New York: 1847.

Hermaneutics of the Sacred Scriptures. In Greek. Athens: 1857. 2 vols.

Synoptical View of Palestine and Syria, with Various Viewpoints and Thoughts about the Evangelistic Apostles. In Greek. Written about the end of 1826 and the beginning of 1827. Translated from French to Greek. Athens: Laconia Press, 1859. 368 p.

Miscellaneous Works. In Greek. The charges against him and the King's order revoking sentence of exile. Athens: 1859 and 1860. 1 vol.

Answer to a Pamphlet Entitled "The Two Clergymen, by the Bishop of Karystis, Macarius, Kaliarchus. " 1863.

The Oriental Church, and the Latin. Farewell letter to his friends in Palestine and Syria. New York: J. A. Gray and Green, Printers, 1865. 134 p.

Inspection of Palestine and Syria. Athens: 1859. 368 p.

Composition of the Apostolic Church. In Greek. In Cantabrigia of New England. Metcalf and Sias. 1857. 54 p.

Various Written Verses from Different Periods and Locales. In Greek. Athens: Laconia Press, 1859. 843 p.

Speeches Delivered During Various Periods in Athens. In Greek. Athens: Laconia Press. 2 vols. in 1.

Religious Services of the Apostolic Church. In Greek. Athens: 1851. 96 p.

His letters are deposited at the Andover Theological Library at Harvard.

KING, Rufus, 1755-1827. Federalist statesman. Minister to Great Britain 1796-1803.

The Life and Correspondence of Rufus King. Edit. by Charles R. King (grandson). New York: G. P. Putnam's Sons, 1894-1900. 6 vols.

KING, Wilson, 1846- . Consul in Dublin 1872, Bremen 1876, Birmingham 1879-85.

Chronicles of Three Cities, Hamburg, Bremen, Lubeck. Introd. by J. P. Mahaffy. Illus. by Mrs. Wilson King and others. New York: E. P. Dutton & Co. , 1914. 464 p.

KINNEY, Elizabeth Clementine (Dodge) Stedman, 1810-1889. Wife of William Burnet Kinney. Chargé d'Affaires at Legation to Sardinia 1850-53.

Bianca Capello: A Tragedy. New York: Hurd & Houghton, 1873. 146 p.

Felicita: A Metrical Romance. New York: J. S. Dickerson, 1855. 188 p.
Poems. New York: Hurd & Houghton, 1867. 226 p.

KIRK, Lydia (Chapin). Wife of Alan Goodrich Kirk, U. S. Naval officer 1911-46. Retired with rank of Admiral. Ambassador to Russia 1949-52.
Postmarked Moscow. New York: Charles Scribner's Sons, 1952. 278 p.
The Man On the Raffles Verandah. Garden City, N. Y.: Doubleday & Co., Inc., 1969. 184 p.

KLAY, Andor C., 1912- . Born in Hungary. U. S. Army 1943-45. Office of Censorship 1942-43. Foreign Service Officer 1945- . Served in State Department, Belgrade, Frankfurt, Berlin.
Daring Diplomacy - The Case of the First American Ultimatum. St. Paul: University of Minnesota Press, 1957. 246 p. National Bancroft Prize.
(Translated in verse into Hungarian) The Rubaiyat of Omar Khayyam. Vienna: Occidental Press, 1949. 80 p. This is not a translation of Fitzgerald's transliteration into English. This is based on Persian texts, including those in 14th century MS discovered in 1930 and now at Cambridge University Library. It contains 286 stanzas (Fitzgerald's text contains 110 stanzas) and an analytical essay on the poet and his work.
Koszta Marton Esete. In Hungarian. Washington: American Hungarian Reformed Federation, 1953. 96 p. A brief version of Daring Diplomacy.
The Visitor Speaks. Washington: Williams & Heintz Co., 1950. 90 p. Three printings, one for overseas dissemination by the War Department. Backgrounds and speeches of the invited foreign guests of the joint Houses of Congress. 1800-1950.
Second Generation. Vol. 1, 1938, 96 p. Vol. 2, 1939, 96 p. Cleveland: Consolidated Press. Historical and cultural connections between the United States and Hungary. Prefaces by Governor Davey and Senator Bulkley.

KLEMMER, Harvey Joseph, 1900- . Newspaperman, publicist 1925-32. State Department 1936-37. Foreign Service Reserve and Foreign Service Officer 1947-60. Advisor to Thailand 1961- . Served in London, Berlin, Brussels, Copenhagen, Dublin, The Hague, Helsinki, Moscow, Oslo, Paris, Stockholm, Warsaw,

Madrid, Lisbon.

Harbor Nights. (an uninhibited account of the life seamen
lead ashore based on the author's experiences in the
Merchant Marine during and after World War I) Philadelphia: J. B. Lippincott Co., 1937. 338 p.

They'll Never Quit. (an eye-witness account of the Battle
of Britain) New York: Wilfred Funk, Inc., 1941.
321 p.

KNOX, Charles Frederick, Jr., 1906- . Writer. Commerce Department 1930-39. Foreign Service Officer
1939-51. Served in Havana, Buenos Aires, Santiago,
Washington, Caracas, National War College, Tel Aviv,
Curaçao. Resigned 1951. Free-lance economist
1951- .

Thirst: A Novel of Chile. New York: The John Day
Co., Inc., 1947. 207 p. Winner of the John Day
Foreign Service Book Contest, under the pseudonym of
Charles Lee Robinson.

KOCHER, Eric, 1912- . Born in Trinidad. B.W.I. Nat-
uralized 1925. Social scientist, writer, playright.
Foreign Service Officer 1947-67. Served in Brussels,
Luxembourg, National War College, Kuala Lumpur,
State Department, Amman, Belgrade, University of
Texas Senior Fellow.

Apocalypse. (half hour radio play) Boston: Yale Radio
Plays. Expression Company, Publishers, 1940.

Karma. (twenty minute drama with dance) New York:
Best Short Plays of 1953-54. Dodd, Mead & Co.

Shadow of the Cathedral. New York: Best One-Act Plays
of 1951-52. Dodd, Mead & Co.

A Medal for Julien. New York: Best Short Plays of
1954-55. Dodd, Mead & Co.

KOCHER, Margaret Helburn. Wife of Erich Kocher. [Q.V.]
The Traveller's Guide to Kuala Lumpur. Assisted by
other wives at the Consulate General. Singapore: Donald Moore MacDonald House, 1957. 86 p. Proceeds
for charitable work, mostly for books for needy schools
in Kuala Lumpur.

Selected Bibliography in Linguistics and the Uncommonly
Taught Languages. Washington: Center for Applied
Linguistics, 1968. 71 p.

KOERNER, Gustav Philip, 1809-1896. Jurist, statesman,
historian. Born in Germany. Came to the United

States in 1833. Minister to Spain 1862-64.
Das Deutsche Element in Den Vereinigten Staaten von
Nordamerika, 1818-1848. Cincinnati: A. E. Wilde &
Co., 1880. 461 p.
Memoirs of Gustav Koerner, 1809-1896: Life Sketches
Written at the Suggestion of his Children. Edit. by
Thomas J. McCormack. Cedar Rapids, Iowa: The
Torch Press, 1909. 2 vols.

KOHLER, Foy David, 1908- . Foreign Service Officer
1931-1968. Served in Windsor, Bucharest, Belgrade,
Athens, Italian Islands of Aegean Sea, Cairo, State
Department, London, Moscow, United States Mission to
Observe Elections in Greece, National War College,
Voice of America, Ankara, International Cooperation
Administration, Career Minister and Assistant Secretary
of State. Ambassador to Russia 1962-66. Deputy Un-
der Secretary of State. Center for Advanced Interna-
tional Studies, University of Miami.
Understanding the Russians - A Citizen's Primer. New
York: Harper & Row, 1970. 441 p.

KOHLER, Phyllis Penn. Mrs. Foy Davis Kohler. [Q. V.]
(Translated and edited) Journey For Our Time - The
Journals of the Marquis de Custine. New York: Pel-
legrini & Cudahy, 1951. 338 p.

KOLINSKI, Charles James, 1919- . Clerk, Staff Officer
and Foreign Service Officer 1940-60. Served in São
Vicente, Glasgow, State Department, Lisbon, Rio de
Janeiro, Guyaquil, Asunçion.
Independence or Death: The Story of the Paraguayan War.
Gainesville: University of Florida Press, 1965. 236 p.

KUPPINGER, Alice K. Wife of Eldred D. Kuppinger. Mr.
Kuppinger was born in 1911 and served in the State
Department 1934-44; was a Foreign Service Officer
1944-68. Served in London, São Paulo, Rio de Jan-
eiro, Edinburgh, Paramaribo.
Smakelijk Etan. A cookbook of Surinam, in Dutch and
English. Paramaribo: E. C. Ferrier-Vas, 1969.
73 p.

LA GUARDIA, Fiorello H., 1882-1947. Lawyer, writer,
commentator, politician. Member of Congress 1917-
19, 1923-33. Mayor of New York 1934-45. Consular
Service 1901-06. Served in Budapest, Trieste, Fiume.

Special Ambassador to Brazil 1946.
The Making of an Insurgent: Autobiography, 1882-1919.
Philadelphia: J. B. Lippincott Co. , 1948. 222 p.

LANCASTER, Bruce, 1896-1963. Business. Foreign Ser-
vice Officer 1927-33. Served in Kobe and Nagoya.
From Lexington to Liberty. The Story of the American
Revolution. Garden City, N. Y. : Doubleday & Co.
Inc. , 1955. 470 p.

LANCASTER, Jessie Bancroft (Payne). Wife of Foreign Service Officer Bruce Lancaster. [Q. V.] She wrote un-
der her own name.
Black Sheep. Philadelphia: Macrae Smith Co. , 1930.
318 p.
Guns of Burgoyne. New York: Fredrick A. Stokes,
1939. 424 p.
Roll, Shenandoah. Boston: Little, Brown & Co. , 1956.
316 p.
The Wide Sleeve of Kwannon. New York: F. A. Stokes,
1938. 307 p.
The Big Knives. Boston: Little, Brown & Co. , 1964.
371 p.
Night March. (historical) Boston: Little, Brown & Co. ,
1958. 341 p.
Bride of a Thousand Cedars. New York: Fredrick A.
Stokes Co. , 1939. 344 p.
Blind Journey. Boston: Little, Brown & Co. , 1953.
303 p.
Bright To the Wanderer. Boston: Little, Brown & Co. ,
1942. 451 p.
No Bugles Tonight. Boston: Little, Brown & Co. , 1948.
325 p.
Phantom Fortress. Boston: Little, Brown & Co. , 1950.
310 p.
The Scarlet Patch. Boston: Little, Brown & Co. , 1947.
477 p.
The Secret Road. Boston: Little, Brown & Co. , 1952.
259 p.
Trumpet to Arms. Boston: Little, Brown & Co. , 1944.
379 p.
Venture in the East. Boston: Little, Brown & Co. ,
1951. 317 p.

LANE, Arthur Bliss, 1894-1956. Foreign Service Officer
1916-1947. Served in Rome, Warsaw, London, Paris,
Bern, State Department, Mexico City, Minister to

Nicaragua 1933, to Esthonia, Latvia and Lithuania 1936,
to Yugoslavia 1937-41, to Costa Rica 1941, Ambassador to Colombia 1942, Ambassador to Polish Government in London 1944, to Warsaw 1945-47. Career
Minister.
I Saw Poland Betrayed: An American Ambassador Reports
    to the American People. Indianapolis: Bobbs-Merrill
    Co., Inc., 1948. 344 p. His papers were sent to
    Yale University.

LANGDON, William Russell, 1891-1963. Foreign Service
    Officer 1911-51. Japanese language officer. Served
    in Constantinople, Athens, Yokohama, Tokyo, Antung,
    Tsinan, Mukden, Dairen, Montreal, Seoul, Department
    of State, Kunming, State Department representative on
    the diplomatic prisoner exchange ship GRIPSHOLM.
    Political Adviser to U.S. Occupation Forces, Korea,
    Singapore.
(Translated and edited) Diplomatic Commentaries. by
    Viscount Kikujiro Ishii. Baltimore: Johns Hopkins
    University Press, 1931. 351 p.

LANGSTON, John Mercer, 1829-1897. Educator, lawyer.
    Born of slave parents. First negro chosen to an elec-
    tive office in the United States. Minister Resident and
    Consul General to Haiti 1877-83. First diplomatic
    representative, Chargé d'Affaires, to the Dominican
    Republic 1883-85.
From the Virginia Plantation to the Nation's Capital.
    Hartford, Conn.: American Publishing Co., 1894.
    534 p.
Freedom and Citizenship. Selected lectures and addresses
    of Honorable John Mercer Langston with introductory
    sketch by Reverend J. E. Rankin. Washington: R. H.
    Darby, 1883. 286 p.

LARKIN, Thomas Oliver, 1802-1858. Merchant, concurrent-
    ly with his appointment as American Consul in Mon-
    terey, California, from April 2, 1844 to May 30, 1848.
    The latter date was that of the ratification of the treaty
    of Guadalupe Hidalgo, which terminated hostilities be-
    tween the United States and Mexico. He was also Con-
    fidential Agent of the United States in Monterey from
    April 17, 1846 to May 30, 1848. He was Navy Agent
    1847-49 and Naval Storekeeper 1847-48. He was in-
    structed by the Secretary of State to guard against the
    machinations of England and France and "to arouse in

their (the Californians) bosoms that love of liberty and
independence so natural to the American Continent. "
In addition to his legitimate consular activities, his
status as American Consul in California was a conven-
ient cover for his activities as confidential agent to
deceive the local British and French consular officers
and the Mexican officials while he was working to
arouse the citizenry to demand independence from
Mexico and union with the United States.
Larkin Papers, Personal, Business and Official Correspondence of the Merchant and United States Consul in
California. Edit. by George P. Hammons. Berkeley:
University of California Press for the Bancroft Library, 1951. 10 vols.

LARSON, Gustav Edward, 1913-1969. Born in Sweden of
American parents. Government expert research as-
sistant. With Army Engineers 1936-41. War Produc-
tion Board 1942-43. Department of Agriculture 1943-
46. State Department and Foreign Service 1960-69.
Served in Washington, Stockholm and Ottawa.
Developing and Selling New Products. A Guidebook for
Manufacturers. Washington: Government Printing Of-
fice, 1949. 75 p.
Plastic Products and Processes: Available Patents. with
T. R. Reynolds and M. L. Towner. Washington:
Government Printing Office, 1949. 69 p.
Selecting and Operating a Business of Your Own: a Guide
for Choosing and Setting Up a Small Business Enter-
prise. with Robert H. Johnson and Walter Magnum
Teller. New York: Prentice-Hall Inc., 1946. 364 p.
Selling the United States Market: a Marketing Guidebook
for Manufacturers and Distributors. with Marshall N.
Poteat. Washington: Government Printing Office,
1951. 135 p.
Trade Association Industrial Research. Washington: Gov-
ernment Printing Office, 1948. 61 p.
(Edited) What Is Farming? by specialists in the Department of Agriculture. Madison: United States Armed
Forces Institute, 1944. 504 p.

LARSON, Joan Marie, 1927- . Private expert, director of
private school, newspaper columnist 1949-64. Office
of Equal Opportunity 1964-68. Foreign Service Reserve Officer. Peace Corps, 1968- . Served in
Tokyo, Washington.
Visit With Us in Japan. for children 8-11 years.

Inglewood, N. J. : Prentice-Hall Inc. Illus. by Dore
Singer. 71 p.

LARSON, Thomas Bryan, 1914- . Political science instruc-
tor. Foreign Service Staff officer 1947-57. Foreign
Service Officer 1957-66. Served in Moscow, Depart-
ment of State, Paris, National War College.
Disarmament and Soviet Policy, 1964-1968. Prepared
for the Russian Institute, Columbia University. New
York: Columbia University Press, 1969. 2 vols.
(Edited) Soviet Politics Since Khruschev. with Alexander
Dallin. Englewood Cliffs, N. J. : Prentice-Hall Inc. ,
1968. 181 p. (A Spectrum book.)

LATHROP, Lorin Andrews, 1858-1929. Consular officer
from 1882 to 1924, except for two years, 1889-1891,
when politics forced him out. He served otherwise
continuously at Bristol, England, 1882-1907; Cardiff,
Wales, 1907-1915; Nassau, Bahamas, 1915-1924. A
prolific writer of serial fiction for the London Mail
under the pseudonym of Andrew Loring, later for the
Saturday Evening Post under the pseudonym of Kenyon
Gambier. The record of his London Mail fiction is
not available. The Saturday Evening Post published
serially, between 1919 and 1926, eight full length
novels and his autobiography, of which the following
were also published in book form.
The Girl on the Hilltop. New York: George H. Doran
Co. , 1920. 319 p.
The Mad Masquerade. Boston: Houghton Mifflin Co. ,
1928. 297 p.
The Princess of Paradise Island. New York: George H.
Doran Co. , 1925. 305 p.
The White Horse and the Red-Haired Girl. New York:
George H. Doran Co. , 1919. 290 p.
(Edited) The Rhymer's Lexicon. Introd. by George
Saintsbury. New York: E. P. Dutton Co. , 1905.
879 p.

LATIMER, Rebecca H. Wife of Foreign Service Officer
Frederick Palmer Latimer, Jr. , 1904- . Served
1928-54, in San Salvador, Tallinn, Helsingfors, Istan-
bul, Ankara, Tegucigalpa, Panama, State Department.
(Turkish language officer.)
Susie and Leyla: Teenagers in Turkey. Indianapolis:
Bobbs-Merrill Co. , 1968. 206 p.

LAURENS, Henry, 1724-1792. Merchant, planter, Revolutionary statesman. Minister to the Netherlands 1779. Captured at sea by the British while on his way to his post in 1780. The British also captured his papers, including a draft treaty with Holland which he had thrown overboard too late, causing Great Britain to declare war on the Netherlands. He was taken to England and put in the Tower of London for 14 months, to December, 1781. Finally exchanged for General Burgoyne, he was sent to join Benjamin Franklin, John Adams and John Jay for the peace negotiations.

A Narrative of the Capture of Henry Laurens, of His Confinement in the Tower of London. South Carolina Historical Society Collection. Vol. I. 1857. pp. 18-68.

Correspondence of Henry Laurens, of South Carolina 1776-1782. New York: Printed for the Zenger Club, 1881. 240 p.

The Papers of Henry Laurens. Edited by Philip M. Hamer of Columbia. Published for the South Carolina Historical Society by the University of South Carolina Press. Columbia. 1968. Finished up to October 31, 1755.

A South Carolina Protest Against Slavery: Being a Letter from Henry Laurens, Second President of the Continental Congress, to His Son, Col. John Laurens: dated Charleston, S. C. August 14, 1776, Now first Published From the Original. New York: G. P. Putnam, 1861. 34 p. John Laurens was an aide to General Washington and special envoy to the French Court during the American Revolution.

Papers of Henry and John Laurens, 1732-1811. circa 90 items. Library of Congress, Manuscript Division.

Papers, 1747-1796. In South Carolina Historical Society collections.

The Papers of Henry Laurens, Vol. II, November 1, 1755 - December 31, 1758. Columbia, S. C.: University of South Carolina Press.

Papers, 1772-84. 44 items and 1 v. In New York Historical Society collections.

LAURENS, John, 1754-1782. Aide-de-camp to General Washington. Secretary of Legation in Paris, elected September 28, 1779. Special Minister to France to assist in negotiating loans. Commissioned December 23, 1780. Son of Henry Laurens.

A Succinct Memoir of the Life and Public Service of Colonel John Laurens, Aide-de-Camp to General Washington

185   LAWRENCE

of the American Revolution, Together with a Series of
Interesting Letters Written by Him Relating to that
Eventful Epoch, and Addressed to his Father, Henry
Laurens. Albany: Williamstadt, 1867. 250 p.

LAWRENCE, Abbott, 1792-1855. Merchant, manufacturer,
Member of Congress. Minister to Great Britain 1849-
52.
Memoirs of the Hon. Abbott Lawrence. Edit. by William
Hickling Prescott, for the National Portrait Gallery,
1856. 51 p.

LAY, Samuel Houston, 1912- . Lawyer, teacher of politi-
cal science. Foreign Service Staff Officer 1946-50.
Foreign Service Reserve Officer 1950-55. Foreign
Service Officer 1955-62. Foreign Service Inspector.
Served in Frankfurt, Bonn, Athens, State Department.
The Law Relating to Activities of Man in Space. with
Professor Howard J. Taubenfeld. Chicago: University
of Chicago Press, 1970. 333 p.
Documents and Comments on the Law of the Sea. with
Myron Nordquist. Dobbs Ferry, N.Y.: Oceana Pub-
lications, Inc., 1972. 500 p.

LAY, Tracy Hollingsworth, 1882-1964. Foreign Service Of-
ficer 1912-28. Served in London, Dublin, Paris, State
Department, Munich, Buenos Aires.
Beyond Our Limitations. New York: Philosophical Li-
brary, 1955. 114 p.
Foreign Service of the United States. Foreword by
Charles Evans Hughes. New York: Prentice-Hall Co.,
1925. 438 p.

LEAHY, William D., 1875-1959. United States Navy 1897-
1939. Advanced through ranks to Fleet Admiral.
Governor of Puerto Rico 1939. Ambassador to France
1940-42. Chief of Staff of the Army and Navy 1942-
49.
I Was There: The Personal Story of the Chief of Staff
to Presidents Roosevelt and Truman, Based on His
Notes and Diaries Made At The Time. Foreword by
President Truman. New York: Whittlesey House,
1950. 527 p.
Papers, 1893-1952. Library of Congress, MSS Division.
6 ft.

LEAR, Tobias, 1762-1816. Consul at Santo Domingo 1801-
02. Consul General at Algiers 1802-12, with power to
negotiate a treaty with Tripoli and the Barbary pirates.
He assisted in negotiations with Morocco 1803-05, which
were complicated by William Eaton's military expedition.
Observations on the River Potomac, the Country Adjacent,
and the City of Washington. New York: Samuel Lou-
den & Brower in Water Street, 1794. 30 p. Also at-
tributed to Andrew Ellicott.

LEE, Arthur, 1740-1792. Physician, lawyer, author,
pamphleteer. Secret agent of the Continental Congress
in London, appointed by Committee of Secret Correspondence, December 12, 1775. Joint Commissioner to
the Court of France with full powers to negotiate
treaties. Elected October 22, 1776 to replace Thomas
Jefferson, who declined the appointment. He signed,
with Silas Deane and Benjamin Franklin, treaties of
commerce and alliance, February 6, 1778. Commissioner also to the Court of Spain, elected May, 1777,
commissioned June 5, 1777, but never went to Spain
on this mission although he had been there previously
in the financial interests of the United States. He also
went to Berlin and back to france; quarrelled with Silas
Deane and Benjamin Franklin and was recalled in 1779.
Works printed in America before 1801 are available
in the Library of Congress in the Readex Microfilm
edition of early American imprints published by the
American Antiquarian Society.
The Monitor's Letters. Virginia Gazette. February-Ap-
ril 1768.
An Appeal to the Justice and Interests of the People of
Great Britain. By an Old Member of Parliament.
London: J. Almon, 1774. 63 p.
An Essay in Vindication of the Continental Colonies of
America From a Censure of Mr. Adam Smith, in His
Theory of Moral Sentiments. With Some Reflections
on Slavery in General. by an American. London:
Printed for the author, 1764. 40 p.
Extracts from a Letter To the President of Congress, by
The Honorable Arthur Lee, Esquire, in Answer to a
Libel Published in the Pennsylvania Gazette of the Fifth
of December, 1778, by Silas Deane, Esquire, in which
Every Charge or Insinuation Against Him in That Libel,
Is Fully and Clearly Refuted. (relating to Deane's con-
duct during his French mission.) Philadelphia:

Printed by F. Bailey, 1780.   74 p.

Observations on Certain Commercial Transactions in
    France, Laid Before Congress.   (relating to the con-
    duct of Benjamin Franklin and his nephew, Jonathan
    Williams, during the former's mission to France.)
    Philadelphia: Printed by F. Bailey, 1780.   51 p.

The Political Detection: or, the Treachery and Tyranny
    of Administration, Both at Home and Abroad: Displayed
    in a Series of Letters, signed Junius Americanus.
    (variously attributed to Lord Charham, to Benjamin
    Franklin and to Richard Glover.)   London: J. & W.
    Oliver, 1770.   151 p.

A Speech Intended to Have Been Delivered in the House of
    Commons, in Support of the Petition From the General
    Congress at Philadelphia.   By the Author of an Appeal
    to the Justice and the Interests of Great Britain.   Lon-
    don: Printed for J. Almon, 1775.   67 p.

A True State of the Proceedings in the Parliament of
    Great Britain, and in the Province of Massachusetts
    Bay, Relative to the Giving and Granting the Money of
    the People of That Province and of all America in the
    House of Commons, in which They are Not Represented.
    Philadelphia: Joseph Cruikshank in Market Street be-
    tween Second and Third streets, 1774.   39 p.

(Supposed author, Arthur Lee) The American Wanderer,
    Through Various Parts of Europe, in a Series of Let-
    ters to a Lady, (Interspersed With a Variety of Inter-
    esting anecdotes) by a Virginian.   (Written in 1776 and
    1777 "by a Loyalist refugee."   One letter "to a noble
    lord" is signed "A. W. L. ")   Dublin: Printed by B.
    Smith for W. & H. Whitestone, 1783.   288 p.

LEE, Henry, Jr., 1787-1837.   Son of Revolutionary General
    Henry Lee (Light Horse Harry) and half-brother of
    General Robert E. Lee of the Confederacy.   Appointed
    Consul General at Algiers by President Jackson about
    1833.   He proceeded to his post and entered upon his
    duties.   His appointment was not confirmed by the
    Senate and he went to Paris where he remained until
    his death.

The Campaign of 1781 in the Carolinas, Etc. Etc.   Phila-
    delphia: E. Littell, 1824.   511 p.

Exposition of Evidence in Support of the Memorial to Con-
    gress Setting Forth the Evils of the Existing Tariff of
    Duties, Etc.   Boston: 1832.   8 vols.

The Life of the Emperor Napoleon.   with an appendix
    containing an examination of Sir Walter Scott's Life of

Napoleon Bonapart and a notice of the principle errors
of other writers respecting his character and conduct.
New York: C. de Behr, 1835. Vol. I. 586 p.
Observations on the Writings of Thomas Jefferson, with
Particular Reference to the Attack They Contain on the
Memory of the Late General Henry Lee. A series of
letters. New York: C. de Behr, 1832. 237 p.
A Vindication of the Character and Public Service of An-
drew Jackson. Boston: True and Green, 1828. 51 p.

LEE, William, 1739-1795. Merchant. Sheriff of London,
1773. Alderman of London 1775, the only American
to hold that office. Appointed by the Secret Committee
of the Continental Congress in 1777 as American Commercial Agent at Nantes, also Commissioner to the
Courts of Vienna and Berlin and the Netherlands. He
distrusted Benjamin Franklin and Silas Deane and Arthur
Lee and was finally recalled in 1779. The draft treaty
he signed with the Dutch was seized by the British from
Henry Laurens. [Q. V.]
Letters of William Lee, Sheriff and Alderman of London:
Commercial Agent of the Continental Congress in
France: and Minister to the Courts of Vienna and
Berlin. 1766-1783. Collected and edited by Worthing-
ton Chauncey Ford. Brooklyn: Historical Printing
Club, 1891. 3 vols.
Reply of William Lee to the Charges of Silas Deane. 1779.
Edit. by Worthington Chauncey Ford. Brooklyn: His-
torical Printing Club, 1891. 60 p.

LEE, William, 1772-1840. Businessman. Consul in Bor-
deaux and Paris 1801-16, during which time he was
successfully engaged in business.
Les Etats-Unis et L'Angleterre. par William Lee.
Traduit sur le manuscrit de l'auteur. Bordeaux: P.
Coudert, 1814. 346 p. Lee was forced by the French
Government to add a chapter endorsing the Bourbons.
A Yankee Jeffersonian: Selections from the Diary and
Letters of William Lee of Massachusetts, Written from
1796 to 1840. Edit. by Mary Lee Mann, Lee's great-
granddaughter. Foreword by Allan Nevins. Cambridge,
Mass.: Belknap Press, Harvard University, 1958.
312 p.

LEGARE, Hugh Swinton, 1797-1843. First diplomatic representative (Chargé d'Affaires) in Belgium, 1832-37.
Writings of Hugh Swinton Legaré, Late Attorney General

and Acting Secretary of State of the United States.
Edit. by his sister.   Charleston: Burges & James,
1846.   2 vols.   Illus.
Some of his writings are included in the Papers, 1785-
1893 of George Frederick Holmes (1820-1897) in the
MSS Division of the Library of Congress.

LEGENDRE, Charles William, 1839-1899.   American Consul
at Amoy 1866-1872.   Counselor to Japanese mission to
China, 1872.   Arrested by American Consul at Amoy--
released by order of the State Department.   Continued
as Japanese advisor to 1875.
How to Deal With China.   A Letter to De. B. Rand.
Keim, Esq. Agent of the United States.   by General
Chas. William Legendre, Amoy: Rosario, Marcal
& Co., 1871.   141 p.
Progressive Japan, A Study of the Political and Social
Needs of the Empire.   New York: C. Levy, 1878.
398 p.
Is Aboriginal Formosa a Part of the Chinese Empire?
An Unbiassed Statement of the Question, with Eight
Maps of Formosa.   Shanghai: Lane, Crawford & Co.,
1874.

LESTER, Charles Edwards, 1815-1890.   Biographer, social
historian, clergyman, slavery abolitionist, news cor-
respondent.   Consul General at Genoa 1842-47.
America's Advancement: the Progress of the United
States During The First Century.   New York: Virtue
& Yorston, 1876.   412 p.
The Artists of America: a Series of Biographical Sketches
of American Artists: with Portraits and Designs on
Steel.   New York: Baker & Scribner, 1846.   257 p.
Chains and Freedom: or, the Life and Adventures of
Peter Wheeler, a Colored Man Yet Living.   By the
Author of the "Mountain Wild Flower."   New York:
E. S. Arnold & Co., 1839.   260 p.
The Condition and Fate of England.   2nd ed.   New York:
J. & H. G. Langley, 1943.   2 vols.
(Edited) The Gallery of Illustrious Americans, Containing
the Portraits and Biographical Sketches of Twenty-Four
of the Most Eminent Citizens of the American Republic,
Since the Death of Washington.   From Daguerreotypes
by Brady--engraved by D'Avignon.   Edit. by C. Ed-
wards Lester.   New York: M. B. Brady, F. D'Avig-
non, C. E. Lester, 1850.   26 p.
Glances at the Metropolis.   A Hundred Illustrated Gems.

New York: I. D. Guyer, 1854. 199 p.
The Glory and Shame of England. New York: Harper
  Bros. , 1841. 2 vols.
Lester's History of the United States. Illustrated in its
  five great periods: colonization, consolidation, de-
  velopment, achievement, advancement. New York:
  P. F. Collier, 1883. 3 vols. in 2.
Life and Achievements of Sam Houston: Hero and States-
  man. New York: J. B. Alden, 1883. 242 p.
Life and Character of Peter Cooper. New York: J. B.
  Alden, 1883. 116 p.
The Life and Voyages of Americus Vespucius: with Illus-
  trations Concerning the Navigator, and the Discovery
  of the New World. with Andrew Foster. New York:
  Baker & Scribner, 1846. 431 p.
The Life of Sam Houston. (The only authentic memoir of
  him ever published.) New York: J. C. Derby, 1855.
  402 p.
Sam Houston and His Republic. New York: Burgess,
  Stringer & Co. , 1846. 208 p.
The Light and Dark of the Rebellion. Philadelphia: G. W.
  Childs, 1863. 303 p.
Lives and Public Services of Samuel J. Tilden and Thomas
  A. Hendricks. 1776. A Revolution for Independence.
  1876. A Revolution for Reform. New York: Frank
  Leslie's Publishing House, 1876. 192 p.
The Mexican Republic, An Historic Study. New York:
  The American News Co. , 1878. 104 p.
The Mountain Wild Flower: or, Memoirs of Mrs. Mary
  Ann Bise, a Lady Who Died at the Age of Twenty-One,
  in the Valley of the Green River. New York: E.
  French, 1838. 243 p.
My Consulship. New York: Cornish, Lamport & Co. ,
  1853. 2 vols.
The Napoleon Dynasty: or, The History of the Bonaparte
  Family. An Entirely New Work. by the Berkeley
  Men. with Twenty Authentic Portraits. New York:
  Cornish, Lamport & Co. , 1852. 624 p.
Our First Hundred Years: The Life of the Republic of
  the United States of America Illustrated in its Four
  Great Periods: Colonization, Consolidation, Develop-
  ment, Achievement. New York: United States Publish-
  ing Co. , 1875. 2 vols.
Stanhope Burleigh. The Jesuits in Our Homes. A Novel,
  by Helen Dhu (pseud.) New York: Stringer & Town-
  send, 1855. 406 p.
(Edited) The Citizen of a Republic. What Are His Rights,

His Duties and Privileges, and What Should Be His
Education. by Ansaldo Ceba. Tr. and ed. by C. Edwards Lester. New York: Paine and Burgess, 1845.
190 p.

LEVY, Howard Seymour, 1923- . Teacher of oriental lan-
guages. Foreign Service Reserve and Foreign Service
Staff officer. Foreign Service Institute 1958- .
Served in Taipei, Tokyo, Yokohama, Washington.
Chinese Footbinding: The History of a Curious Erotic
Custom. Foreword by Arthur Waley. Introd. by
Wolfram Eberhard. New York: Walton Rawls, 1967.
352 p.
Harem Favorites of an Illustrious Celestial. Chung-t'ai,
Taichung: 1958. 198 p. Illus.
The Dwelling of Playful Goddesses. Tokyo: Dai-Nihon,
1965. 119 p. Illus.
The Illusory Flame. Tokyo: Kenkyusha, 1962. 100 p.
Illus.
Warm-Soft Village. Tokyo: Dai-Nihon, 1964. 142 p.
Illus.
(Translation) Biography of Huang Ch'ao. Chinese Dynastic
Histories Translations, No. 5. Berkeley: University
of California Press, 1st edit. 1955. 144 p. 3 maps,
no Chinese text. 2nd enlarged edition 1961. 153 p.
3 maps, no Chinese text.
(Translation) Biography of An Lu-Sham. Chinese Dynastic
Histories Translations. No. 8. Berkeley: University
of California Press, 1967. 122 p. Chinese text.
The Tao of Sex. with Dr. Akiro Ishihara. Annotated
translation of the Twenty-eighth Section of the Essence
of Chinese Medicine (I-Shimpo) on the Bedroom Arts.
Illus. , annotated bibliography of Sino-Japanese sexology:
appendices on Chinese medicine, acupuncture, and the
history of Chinese medicine in Japan; indices of sex
and medical terms. Printed in Japan, distributed in
U. S. by Paragon Book Gallery, New York: 1969.
273 p.

LIST, Georg Friedrich, 1789-1846. Economist, journalist,
editor. Born in Germany. A liberal, he was exiled
to the United States in 1825. Naturalized. Consul at
Baden 1831, Leipzig 1834-37, Stuttgart 1843-46.
Outlines of American Political Economy. Translated by
Sampson S. Lloyd, with introd. by J. Shield Nicholson.
1827. New impression. New York: Longmans, Green
& Co. , 1909. 366 p.

Uber Ein Sachsisches Eisenbahn-System. (About the train
  system in Saxony.) Leipzig: P. Reclam Jun., 1833.
Um Deutsche Wirklichkeit, Seine Schriften in Auswahl
  Herausgegeben Von Fritz Forschepiepe. (About German
  Reality. His Writings in Selections Published by Fritz
  Forschepiepe.) Stuttgart: A. Kroner, 1938. 283 p.
Friederich List - Volksbuch: Herausgegeben im Auftrag
  der Stadt Reutlingen mit 5 Kunstdrucktafeln. (Friedrich
  List, Popular Prose Romance: Published by Order of
  the City of Reutlingen, 5 Fine Arts Prints. Berlin:
  Publishing House for Social Legislation, Economics and
  Statistics) Paul Schmidt, 1938. 277 p.
Krafte und Machte, Grundsatze, Lehren, Gedanken: aus
  Schriften Ausgewahlt und Eingeleitet von Hartfrik Voss.
  (Strengths and Powers, Principles, Lectures, Thoughts:
  of Writings Selected and Introduced by H. Voss.)
  Ebenhausen bei Munchen: W. Langewiesche-Brandt.,
  1942. 237 p.
Schriften, Reden, Briefe - Im Auftrag der Friedrich List
  Gesellschaft E.V. (Writings, Orations, Letters: Com-
  missioned by the Friedrich List Society.) Berlin: R.
  Hobbing, 1927-36. 10 vols.
Staatsinteresse und Privatwirtschaft, Eine Auswahl aus
  den Schriften von Friedrich List. (Government Interests and Private Enterprise, a Selection of the Writings
  of Friedrich List.) Berlin: Deutsche Bibliothek Ver-
  lagsgesellschaft M.B.H., 1943. 280 p.
Grundlinien Einer Politischen Ekonomie und Andere Bei-
  trage der Amerikanischen Zeit. 1825-1832. (Principles
  of a Political Economy and Other Contributions of the
  American Time, 1825-32.) hrsg von William Notz.
  (published by William Notz.) Berlin: R. Hobbing,
  1931. 530 p.
Das Nationale System der Politischen Ekonomie. (The
  National System of Political Economy) 1841.

LIVINGSTON, Edward, 1764-1836. Congressman, Mayor of
  New York, Senator. Secretary of State 1831-33, Min-
  ister to France 1833-35.
The Complete Works of Edward Livingston on Criminal
  Jurisprudence. Consisting of systems of penal law for
  the State of Louisiana and for the United States of
  America with an introduction by Salmon P. Chase.
  New York: National Prison Association of the United
  States of America, 1873. 2 vols.
Address to the People of the United States. On the Meas-
  ures Pursued By the Executive With Respect to the

Batture at New Orleans: to Which Are Annexed a Full
Report of the Cause Tried in the Superior Court of the
Territory of Orleans: the Memoire of Mr. Derbigny:
an Examination of the Title of the United States: the
Opinion of Counsel Thereon: and a Number of Other
Documents Necessary to a Full Understanding of This
Interesting Case. New Orleans: Bradford & Anderson,
1808. 2 vols.

An Answer to Mr. Jefferson's Justification of His Conduct
in the Case of the New Orleans Batture. Philadelphia:
Printed by W. Fry, 1813. 187 p.

Code of Procedure, for Giving Effect to the Penal Code of
the State of Louisiana. Prepared Under the Authority
of a Law of the Said State. New Orleans: Printed by
B. Levy, 1825. 263 p.

A Code of Reform and Prison Discipline: To Which Is
Prefixed an Introductory Report to the Same. Introd.
by Salmon P. Chase. New York: National Prison Association of the United States, 1872. 140 p.

Commercial Code for the State of Louisiana. New Orleans: B. Levy, 1825. 260 p.

(Edited) Judicial Opinions Delivered in the Mayor's Court
of the City of New York, in the Year 1802. 1803.

MSS of Edward Livingston are privately owned: include
about 2,500 letters and documents.

A System of Penal Law for the United States of America:
Consisting of a Code of Crimes and Punishments, a
Code of Procedure in Criminal Cases; a Code of Prison
Discipline; and a Book of Definitions. Prepared and
Presented to the House of Representatives of the United
States, by Edward Livingston. Printed by order of the
House of Representatives. Washington: Printed by
Gales & Seaton, 1828. 446 p.

LIVINGSTON, Robert R., 1746-1813. Statesman, farmer.
Secretary of Foreign Affairs (antecedent of the State
Department) 1781-82. Minister to France 1801-04.

Examination of the Treaty of Amity, Commerce and Navi-
gation Between the United States and Great Britain.
New York: republished from the Argus by Thomas
Greenleaf, 1795. 96 p.

LODGE, Henry Cabot, Jr., 1902- . Newspaper reporter,
politician, Senator from Massachusetts 1936-53. Ambassador to United Nations 1953-60, to Viet Nam 1964-
65, at Large 1967, to Germany 1968, to the Viet Nam
Peace Talks at Paris 1968-69.

The Cult of Weakness. Boston: Houghton Mifflin Co.,
1932. 172 p.
You and the United Nations: U. S. Representative to the
U. N. Answers Your Questions. Washington: Government Printing Office, 1955. 50 p.

LONG, Breckenridge, 1881-1958. Assistant Secretary of
State 1917-20 and 1939-40. Ambassador to Italy 1933-
36, Ambassador on a special mission to Brazil, Ar-
gentina and Uruguay 1938. Delegate to Dumbarton
Oaks Conference 1944.
Genesis of the Constitution of the United States of America.
New York: The Macmillan Co., 1926. 260 p.
War Diary of Breckinridge Long. Edit. by Fred L. Isra-
el. Lincoln, Neb.: University of Nebraska Press,
1966. 410 p.

LONGSTREET, James, 1821-1904. Businessman. General
in the Confederate Army, Minister Resident to Turkey
1880-81.
From Manassas to Appomattox. Philadelphia: J. B.
Lippincott Co., 1896. 698 p.

LORING, George Bailey, 1817-1891. Physician, agriculturist, politician, orator, editor. Minister to Portugal
1889-90.
A Year in Portugal. New York: G. P. Putnam's Sons,
1891. 313 p.
The Farm-Yard Club of Jotham: An Account of the Families and Farms of that Famous Town. Boston: Lockwood, Brooks & Co., 1876. 603 p.

LOWELL, James Russell, 1819-1891. One of America's
most eminent nineteenth century poets. Minister to
Spain 1877-80, to Great Britain 1880-85.
The Complete Writings of James Russell Lowell. Cam-
bridge: Riverside Press, 1904. 16 vols.
Favorite Poems. Boston: J. R. Osgood, 1877. 108 p.
The Lowell Birthday Book. Boston: Houghton Mifflin
Co., 1883. 402 p.
The Complete Poetical Works of James Russell Lowell.
Cambridge edition. Boston: Houghton Mifflin Co.,
1917. 492 p.
Among My Books. Boston: Fields, Osgood, 1870. 380 p.
The Anti-Slavery Papers of James Russell Lowell. Bos-
ton: Houghton Mifflin Co., 1902. 2 vols.
Meliboeus-Hipponax. The Bigelow Papers. Cambridge:

G. Nichols, 1848. 163 p. An anthology.
A Bibliography of James Russell Lowell. by J. L. Liv-
ingston. 1914.
Conversations on Some of the Old Poets. Cambridge:
J. Owen, 1845. 263 p.
Democracy and Other Addresses. Boston: Houghton
Mifflin Co., 1887. 245 p.
The English Poets: Lessing, Rousseau. [essays.]
Toronto: W. J. Gage, 1888. 337 p.
Fireside Travels. Boston: Ticknor & Fields, 1864.
324 p.
Letters of James Russell Lowell. Edit. by Charles Eliot
Norton. New York: Harper Bros., 1894. 2 vols.
My Study Windows. Boston: J. R. Osgood, 1871. 433 p.
New Letters of James Russell Lowell. Edit. by M. A.
DeWolf Howe. New York: Harper Bros., 1932.
364 p.
Uncollected Poems. Edit. by Thelma M. Smith. Phila-
delphia: University of Pennsylvania Press, 1950.
291 p.
The Vision of Sir Launfall. Cambridge: George Nichols,
1848. 27 p.
A Bibliography of the First Editions in Book Form of the
Writings of James Russell Lowell. New York: Pri-
vately printed by The De Vinne Press, 1914. 136 p.
Political Essays. London: Macmillan Co., 1888. 326 p.

LUCE, Clare Boothe, 1903-   . Editor, playwright, politician,
Member of Congress 1943-47. Ambassador to Italy
1953-57. Married (2nd) publisher Henry R. Luce 1935.
Europe in the Spring. New York: Alfred A. Knopf, Inc.,
1940. 324 p.
Kiss the Boys Goodbye. (comedy) Foreword by Heywood
Broun. New York: Random House, 1939. 249 p.
Margin for Error. (satirical melodrama) Introd. by Henry
R. Luce. New York: Random House, 1940. 198 p.
Saints for Now. New York: Sheed & Ward, Inc., 1952.
312 p.
Stuffed Shirts. by Clare Boothe Brokaw. Illus. by Sher-
mund. New York: H. Liveright, 1931. 326 p.
The Women. (comedy) New York: Random House, 1937.
215 p.

MACMURRAY, John Van Antwerp, 1881-1963. Foreign Service Officer 1907-44. Served in Bangkok, St. Petersburg, State Department, Peking, Tokyo, Assistant Secretary of State 1924-25, Minister to China 1925-30,

Director of Walter Hines Page School of International
Relations 1930-35, Minister to Estonia, Latvia and
Lithuania 1933, Ambassador to Turkey 1936-42, Special
Assistant to the Secretary of State 1942-44.
(Edited) Treaties and Agreements With and Concerning
China, 1894-1919. New York: Oxford University
Press, 1921. 2 vols.
(Edited) Treaties and Agreements With and Concerning
China, 1919-1929. Washington: Carnegie Endowment
for International Peace, 1919. 282 p.
(Edited) Joint Preparatory Committee on Philippine Af-
fairs. Report of May 20, 1958. Washington: Govern-
ment Printing Office, 1938. 3 vols. in 4. John A.
MacMurray, Chairman.

MACVEAGH, Fanny Davenport (Rogers). Wife of Ambassador Charles Macveagh. He was Ambassador to Japan
1925-29.
Fountains of Papal Rome. Illus. by Rudolph Ruzicka.
New York: Charles Scribner's Sons, 1915. 312 p.

MACVEAGH, (Isaac) Wayne, 1833-1917. (Did not use the
name Isaac in his writings.) Minister Resident to
Turkey 1870-71. Ambassador to Italy 1893-97.
A Pleading Before the International Tribunal at the Hague
on Behalf of Venezuela Against Great Britain, Germany
and Italy. with Herbert W. Bowen and William L.
Renfield, counsel. Washington: 1905. 120 p.
Appendix to the Foregoing. with others. Washington:
1905. 230 p.
Venezuela Arbitration. October 3-5, 1903. Washington:
Judd & Detweiler, printers, 1903. 102 p.
Papers, 1833-1950. circa 3500 items. Historical Society
of Pennsylvania.

MACVEAGH, Lincoln, 1890-1972. Publisher. Minister to
Greece 1933, to Iceland 1941, to the Union of South
Africa 1942, Ambassador near the Government of Yugo-
slavia established in Egypt 1943, near the Government
of Greece established in Egypt 1943, Ambassador to
Portugal 1948, to Spain 1952-53.
Greek Journey. with Margaret Lewis MacVeagh. New
York: Dodd, Mead & Co. Inc., 1937. 270 p.
(Edited) Bible Selections, English. Poetry from the Bible.
New York: The Dial Press, 1925. 180 p.

MACVEAGH, Margaret (Lewis). Wife of Ambassador Lincoln

Macveagh.
Greek Journey. with Ambassador Lincoln Macveagh.
(Q.V.) New York: Dodd, Mead & Co., Inc., 1937.
270 p.

MADDOX, William Percy, 1901- . Educator. University
professor 1925-42. Foreign Service Officer 1946-64.
Served in Department of State (Director of Foreign
Service Institute), Lisbon, Port-of-Spain, Pretoria,
Singapore, United States Arms Control and Disarma-
ment Agency.
Foreign Relations in British Labour Politics. Harvard
University Press, 1934. 253 p.

MAGOON, Charles Edward, 1861-1920. Minister to Panama
1905-106: simultaneously General Counsel to the Panama Canal Commission: Law Officer, Bureau of Insular Affairs of the War Department and Governor of
the Canal Zone. Provisional Governor of Cuba 1906-
09.
The Municipal Code of Lincoln. Lincoln, Neb. : State
Journal Co., 1889. 589 p.
Report on the Legal Status of the Territory and Inhabitants
of the Islands Acquired by the United States During the
War With Spain. Washington: Government Printing Office, 1900. 72 p.
Reports on the Law of Civil Government in Territory Sub-
ject to Military Occupation by the Military Forces of
the United States. Washington: Government Printing
Office, 1902. 808 p.
Annual Report of Charles E. Magoon, Provisional Govern-
or of Cuba 1907. Washington: Government Printing
Office, 1908. 94 p.
Report of the Provisional Administration from October
13th, 1906 to December 1st, 1908. Havana: Rambla
& Bouza, printers, 1908-09. 2 vols.
Laws Against Treason, Sedition, Etc. United States Bu-
reau of Insular Affairs. Washington: Government
Printing Office, 1902. 42 p.

MANN, Ambrose Dudley, 1801-1889. Lawyer. Consul at
Bremen 1842-48. Appointed Special Commissioner to
the German States in 1846 for negotiating commercial
treaties. Special Agent to Kossuth in Hungary 1849
and to Switzerland 1850-53 when he negotiated and
signed a convention of friendship. Assistant Secretary
of State 1853-56. As Civil War drew on he identified

himself with the South and was appointed Joint Commis-
sioner, for the Confederacy, (with Yancy and Rost) and
Associate Commissioner (with Mason and Slidell) to
London (1 yr.) and Belgium (3 yrs.) 1861-63 and the
Vatican 1863-64. After the war he remained in Paris
till his death.
My Ever Dearest Friend. The letters of A. Dudley Mann
to Jefferson Davis 1869-89. Edit. by John Preston
Moore. Tuscaloosa, Ala.: Confederate Publishing
Co., 1960. 114 p. Limited edit. 450 copies.
Die Nordamericanischen Freistaaten. Bremen: C.
Schunemann, 1845. 326 p.

MARSH, Caroline Crane, 1816-1901. Wife of George Per-
kins Marsh, Minister to Turkey. [Q.V.]
Life and Letters of George Perkins Marsh. Compiled by
Caroline Crane Marsh. New York: Charles Scribner's
Sons, 1888. 2 vols. Projected, only one completed.
479 p.

MARSH, George Perkins, 1801-1882. Lawyer. Linguist.
Minister to Turkey 1849-53. First Minister to Italy
1861-62. While assigned to Turkey he was sent to
Greece to rescue a Hungarian revolutionist with the
assistance of an American Sloop-of-War.
The Camel. His organization, habits and uses, consid-
ered with reference to his introduction into the United
States. Smithsonian Institute Annual Report 1854.
pp. 98-122. Boston: Gould & Lincoln.
Lectures on the English Language. Prepared and deli-
vered at Columbia College 1858-59. New York:
Charles Scribner's Sons, 1860. 697 p.
Man and Nature: or, Physical Geography as Modified by
Human Action. London: S. Low, Son and Marston,
1864. 560 p. Cambridge: Belnap Press of Harvard
University Press, 1865. Includes bibliography.
Medieval and Modern Saints and Miracles. New York:
Harper & Bros., 1875. 307 p.
The Origin and History of the English Language and of the
Early Literature it Embodies. New York: Charles
Scribner's Sons, 1862. 574 p.

MARSHALL, George Catlett, 1880-1959. United States Army
1901-1945. General of the Army. Special Representative of the President, rank of Ambassador, to China
1945. Secretary of State 1947-49. United States member Council of Foreign Ministers at Moscow and London

in 1947.   President of the Red Cross.   Secretary of
   Defence 1950-51.
Selected Speeches and Statements of General of the Army
   George Catlett Marshall.   Edit. by Major H. A. De
   Weerd.   Washington: The Infantry Journal, 1945.
   263 p.
"Victory Is Certain, " being the Biennial Report of the
   Chief of Staff of the U. S. Army, General George C.
   Marshall, July 1, 1941, to June 30, 1943, to the Sec-
   retary of War.   New York: National Educational Alli-
   ance, 1943.   88 p.
Victory on the March: Reports on the Progress of the
   War by President Franklin D. Roosevelt, Prime Min-
   ister Winston Churchill, General George C. Marshall
   and the U. S. Navy.   New York: National Educational
   Alliance, Inc., 1944.   200 p.
Biennial Report of the Chief of Staff of the United States
   Army, July 1, 1943, to June 30, 1945 to the Secretary
   of War.   Washington: War Department.   General
   Staff, 1945.   122 p.
The War Reports of General Marshall, General Arnold,
   Admiral King.   Foreword by Walter Millis.   Philadel-
   phia: J. B. Lippincott Co., 1947.   801 p.   Illus.
   maps, etc.
La Vittoria en Europe e nel Pacifico.   con un comento
   del Mario Caracciola di Fereleto and translated by him
   from the Italian.   Torino: L. Rattero, 1948.   217 p.
   (Translated from the biennial report of 1945.)

MARSHALL, James Fowle Baldwin, 1818-1891.   Merchant,
   educator.   Minister to Great Britain 1843--specially to
   secure Great Britain's renunciation of annexation of
   Hawaii and to secure recognition of sovereignty of King
   Kamehameha III.
Report of the Proceedings and evidence in the Arbitration
   Between the King and Government of the Hawaiian Islands and Messrs. Ladd & Co.   with Stephen H. Williams.   Honolulu: C. F. Hitchcock, 1846.   548 p.

MARSHALL, Katherine Boyce Tupper Brown.   Wife of General George Catlett Marshall.   [Q. V.]
Together: Annals of an Army Wife.   Atlanta: Tupper &
   Love, 1946.   292 p.   London: Blandfurd Press, 1947.
   228 p.
Mon Mari, Le General Marshall.   Traduit de l'Americain
   par S. T. Vinoenot.   Paris: Amiot-Dumont, 1948.
   302 p.   Archives d'histoire contemporaine.

MARTIN, Edwin McCammon, 1908- . Government official.
Economist. Office of Strategic Services. State Department and Foreign Service Officer 1945- . Served
in Washington, Paris, London. Deputy Assistant Secretary of State for Economic Affairs. Assistant Secretary of State for Inter-American Affairs. Ambassador to Argentina 1964, Chairman Organization for Economic Cooperation and Development in Paris 1968.
Career Ambassador.
Allied Occupation of Japan. Stanford, Calif.: Stanford
University Press, American Institute of Pacific Relations, 1948. 155 p.
Development Assistance: Efforts and Policies of the Members of the Development Committee--1968 Review.
Paris: Organization for Economic Cooperation and De-
velopment. 278 p.
Development Assistance: Efforts and Policies of the
Members of the Development Committee--1969 Review.
Paris: Organization for Economic Cooperation and De-
velopment. 325 p.

MARTIN, John Bartlow, 1915- . Writer. Ambassador to
Dominican Republic 1962-64.
Adlai Stevenson. New York: Harper Brothers, 1952.
175 p.
Break Down the Walls: American Prisons: Past, Pre-
sent, Future. New York: Ballantine Books, 1954.
310 p.
Butcher's Dozen and Other Murders. New York: Harper
Brothers, 1950. 275 p.
Call It North Country: The Story of Upper Michigan.
New York: Alfred A. Knopf Co. Inc., 1944. 281 p.
The Deep South Says "Never." Foreword by Arthur
Schlesinger, Jr. New York: Ballantine Books, 1957.
181 p.
Jimmy Hoffa's Hot. A Crest Special. Greenwich, Conn.:
Fawcett Publications, 1959. 176 p. Originally pub-
lished in the Saturday Evening Post under the title
"The Struggle to Get Hoffa."
Indiana: An Interpretation. New York: Alfred A. Knopf
& Co., 1947. 300 p. Illus., bibliog.
Overtaken by Events: The Dominican Crisis from the
Fall of Trujillo to the Civil War. Memoirs of his
tour as Ambassador during the crisis. New York:
Doubleday & Co. Inc., 1966. 821 p. Illus., bibliog.
The Pane of Glass. New York: Harper & Row, 1959.
397 p. Portions of this book were published in the

Saturday Evening Post under the title, "Inside the Asylum. " Bibliog.
Why Did They Kill? New York: Ballantine Books, 1953.
131 p.
My Life in Crime. The Autobiography of a Professional
Criminal, Reported by John Bartlow Martin. New
York: Harper Bros. , 1952. 279 p.

MARVEL, Ik, 1822-1908. Pseud. for Donald Grant Mitchell.
[Q. V.]

MARX, Walter John, 1906- . Educator. Foreign Service
officer 1946-1966. Served in State Department, Le
Havre, Hamburg.
Mechanization and Culture: The Social and Cultural Implications of a Mechanized Society. St. Louis: B.
Herndon Book Co. , 1941. 243 p.
Twilight of Capitalism and the War: a Study of the Social
and Economic Effects of Modern Capitalism and of
Probable Post War Trends. St. Louis: B. Herndon
Book Co. , 1942. 294 p.
The Development of Charity in Medieval Louvain. Yonkers: Press of the author, 1936. 124 p.

MARYE, George Thomas, 1849-1933. Lawyer, banker.
Ambassador to Russia 1914-16.
Nearing the End in Imperial Russia. Philadelphia: Dorrance & Co. , 1929. 479 p.

MAURY, Dabney Herndon, 1822-1900. Minister to Colombia
1886.
Recollections of a Virginian in the Mexican, Indian and
Civil Wars. New York: Charles A. Scribner's Sons,
1894. 279 p.
A Young People's History of Virginia and Virginians.
Richmond: B. F. Johnson Publishing Co. , 1896.
246 p.

MAYER, Brantz, 1809-1879. Lawyer. First Secretary at
Mexico City 1841-42.
Adventures of an African Slaver: Being a True Account
of the Life of Captain Theodore Canot, Trader in Gold,
Ivory, and Slaves on the Coast of Guinea: His Own
Story as Told in the Year 1854 to Brantz Mayer and
now Edited with an Introduction by Malcolm Cowley.
New York: A. & C. Boni, 1928. 284 p. Illus. and
cover by Miguel Covarrubias. London, ed. by A. E.

Lawrence, 1940.
Mexico, As It Was and As It Is. New York: J. Winchester, 1844. 390 p.
Mexico, Aztec, Spanish and Republican. Hartford: S. Drake & Co., 1852. 2 vols.
Historical Sketches. An Account of Spaniards to the present time. Hartford: S. Drake & Co., 1852.
Three Tales from the Flemish of Hendrick Conscience. Baltimore: Murphy & Co., 1856. 156 p.
History of the War between Mexico and the United States, with a Preliminary View of Its Origin. New York: Wiley & Putnam, 1848. 188 p.
Mexico, Central America and the West Indies. Edit. from the work of Brantz Mayer by Frederick Albion Ober. New York: P. F. Collier & Son, 1939. 533 p.

McAFEE, Robert Breckenridge, 1784-1849. Chargé d'Affaires at Bogota 1833-37.
History of the Late War in the Western Country, Comprising a Full Account of All the Transactions in that Quarter from the Commencement of Hostilities at Tippecanoe, to the Termination of the Contest at New Orleans on the Return of Peace. Lexington, Kentucky: Worsley & Smith, 1916. 534 p.

McCAMY, James Lucian, 1906- . Newspaper reporter, professor of political science. Department of Agriculture 1939-41; Board of Economic Warfare 1942-43; Foreign Economic Administration 1943-45; Economic advisor to U. S. Forces in Austria 1945.
Government Publications for the Citizen: a Report of the Public Library Inquiry. with Julia B. McCamy. New York: Columbia University Press, 1949. 139 p.
The Administration of American Foreign Affairs. New York: Alfred A. Knopf Co., 1950. 364 p.
American Government. New York: Harper Bros., 1957. 866 p.
Conduct of the New Diplomacy. New York: Harper & Row, 1964. 303 p.
Government Publicity. Thesis (Ph. D.) Chicago: University of Chicago Press, 1939. 275 p.
Science and Public Administration. University, Ala.: University of Alabama Press, 1960. 218 p.

McCAMY, Julia B. (Mrs.). Wife of James Lucian McCamy. [Q. V.]
Government Publications for the Citizen: a Report of the

Public Library Inquiry. with James Lucian McCamy.
New York: Columbia University Press, 1949. 139 p.

McCARTEE, Divie Bethune, 1820-1900. Medical missionary in China. Educator. Consul in Ningpo 1844-57,
Vice Consul Chefoo 1862-65, Vice Consul Shanghai,
1872, where he was also interpreter and assessor to
the Mixed Court. Professor at Imperial University in
Tokyo 1872-75. Secretary to Chinese Legation in
Tokyo 1879. Counselor of the Japanese Legation in
Washington 1885-87.
A Missionary Pioneer in the Far East. Contains McCartee's memoirs. Edit. by Robert E. Speer. Westwood, N.J.: Fleming H. Revell Co., 1922. 224 p.

McCLINTOCK, Robert, 1909- . Foreign Service Officer
1931- . Served in Panama, Kobe, Santiago, Ciudad
Trujillo, Helsinki, Stockholm, State Department, United
Nations Affairs, Brussels, National War College, Cairo,
Saigon, Phnom Penh and Vientiane. Ambassador to
Cambodia 1954, to Lebanon 1957, to Argentina 1962,
Naval War College 1964, Foreign Service Inspector
1966, Ambassador to Venezuela 1970. Career Minis-
ter. Superior Service Award.
The Meaning of Limited War. Boston: Houghton Mifflin
Co., 1967. 239 p.

McCLOY, John Jay, 1895- . Banker, lawyer. President
of World Bank 1947-49. Military Governor and High
Commissioner to Germany 1949-52.
The Challenge to American Foreign Policy. The Godkin
Lectures. Cambridge: Harvard University Press,
1953. 81 p.
The Atlantic Alliance, Its Origin and Its Future. Ben-
jamin F. Fairless Memorial Lectures. New York:
Columbia University Press for Carnegie-Mellon Univer-
sity, 1969. 83 p.

McDONALD, James Grover, 1886-1964. History professor.
High Commissioner for German Refugees 1933-35.
News analyst. Special Representative to Israel 1948-
49. Ambassador to Israel 1949-51.
My Mission in Israel, 1948-51. New York: Simon &
Schuster, 1951. 303 p.

McGILLIVRAY, James Hale, 1918-1966. Teacher. United
States Information Administration 1946-66. Served in

Salvador, Bogota, Bahia, Sao Paulo, Madras, Recife, Rio de Janeiro.
(Co-author with James R. Echols of the following)
Ten Great Americans. New York: American Book Co., 1960. 116 p.
People At Work. New York: American Book Co., 1961. 104 p.
Toward a Better World. New York: American Book Co., 1962. 122 p.
Let's Take a Trip. New York: American Book Co., 1963. 120 p.

McKNIGHT, John Proctor, 1908- . Newspaper correspondent, chief of press association, free-lance writer-lecturer. Foreign Service Reserve Officer, United States Information Administration 1951-68. Served in Rome, Seoul, Rio de Janeiro, Washington, Brookings Institution, Buenos Aires.
The Papacy - A New Appraisal. New York: Rinehart, 1952. 437 p.

McLANE, Robert Milligan, 1815-1898. Commissioner to China 1853-55. Minister to Mexico 1859-60, to France 1885-89. Co-author of unratified McLane-Ocampo Treaty with Mexico.
Reminiscences, 1827-97. by Governor Robert M. McLane. Privately printed, 1903. 165 p. Original in Harvard College Library. Photostat copy reproduced from original, 1928.

MECKLIN, John M., 1918- . Newspaper writer, editor and correspondent. Foreign Service Reserve Officer 1961-64, on leave from TIME magazine.
Mission in Torment: An Intimate Account of the United States Role in Vietnam. Garden City, N.Y.: Doubleday, 1965. 318 p.

MEEKER, Claude, 1861-1929. Consul at Bradford, England, 1893-97.
Howarth, the Home of the Brontes. Bradford, England: Treweek & Co., 1895. 44 p.

MELADY, Margaret (Badum). Wife of Thomas Patrick Melady. [Q.V.] Mr. Melady is Ambassador to Republic of Burundi 1969- .
House Divided in the Family of Man. with Thomas Patrick Melady. New York: Sheed & Ward, Inc., 1970. 182 p.

MELADY, Thomas Patrick, 1927- . Educator, specialist
in African-Asian affairs, author-lecturer. Director of
development, Duquesne University. Ambassador to the
Republic of Burundi 1969- .
Profiles of African Leaders. New York: The Macmillan
    Co., 1961. 186 p.
White Man's Future in Black Africa. New York: Mc-
    Fadden-Bartell, 1962. 208 p.
Faces of Africa. New York: The Macmillan Co., 1964.
    298 p.
Revolution of Color. New York: Hawthorne Books, 1960.
    202 p. Spanish edition Madrid: Razon y Fe, 1967.
Western Policy and the Third World. New York: Haw-
    thorne Books, 1967. 199 p.
House Divided in the Family of Man. with his wife,
    Margaret Badum Melady. New York: Sheed & Ward,
    Inc., 1970. 182 p.
(Edited) Kenneth Kaunda of Zambia. New York: Freder-
    ick A. Praeger, Inc., 1964.

MERCHANT, Livingston Tallmadge, 1903- . Investments.
State Department and Foreign Service Officer 1942-62.
Served in Strasbourg, Paris, Nanking, Assistant Secretary of State for European Affairs 1953-56, Ambassador to Canada 1956-58 and 1961-62. Under Secretary
of State for Political Affairs 1959-61. Career Ambassador.
(Edited) Neighbors Taken For Granted: Canada and the
    United States. New York: Frederick A. Praeger,
    Inc. for the School of Advanced International Studies of
    Johns Hopkins University, Baltimore, 1966. 166 p.
    Bibliog. footnotes. Merchant wrote introd. and con-
    clusion. Other chapters mostly by Canadians. Chap-
    ter on American Business in Canada written by Foreign
    Service Officer Ivan B. White.

MERIWETHER, Lee, 1862-1966. Lawyer, author, politician,
Government official Special Assistant to American
Ambassador to France 1916-18.
Afloat and Ashore on the Mediterranean. New York:
    Charles Scribner's Sons, 1892. 363 p.
After-Thoughts, a Sequel to My Yesteryears. Webster
    Groves, Mo.: International Mark Twain Society, 1945.
    441 p.
Jim Reed, Senatorial Immortal. A Biography. Webster
    Groves, Mo.: Mark Twain Society, 1948. 273 p.
A Lord's Courtship: A Novel. Chicago: Laird & Lee,

1900. 288 p.
My Yesteryears: An Autobiography. Webster Groves,
   Mo. : Mark Twain Society, 1942. 440 p.
Seeing Europe by Automobile: A Five Thousand Mile
   Motor Trip Through France, Switzerland, Germany
   and Italy; with an Excursion into Andorra, Corfu, Dal-
   matia and Montenegro. New York: Baker & Taylor
   Co. , 1911. 415 p.
The Tramp At Home. New York: Harper Bros. , 1889.
   296 p.
A Tramp Trip: How To See Europe on Fifty Cents a
   Day. New York: Harper Bros. , 1887. 276 p.
The War Diary of a Diplomat. (Special Assistant to the
   American Ambassador to France, 1916, 1917, 1918.)
   New York: Dodd, Mead & Co. , Inc. , 1919. 303 p.
   In French, Paris: Payot & Cie. , 1922. 339 p.
   Preface by Edouard de Billy.

MERRILL, Selah, 1837-1909. Consul Jerusalem intermittent-
   ly for sixteen years between 1882-1907. Consul at
   Georgetown, British Guiana 1907-08.
Ancient Jerusalem, by Selah Merrill, for Sixteen Years
   American Consul in Jerusalem. New York: F. H.
   Revell & Co. , 1908. 419 p.
East of the Jordan: a Record of Travel and Observation
   in the Countries of Moab, Gilead and Rashan During
   1875-77. Introd. by Professor Roswell D. Hitchcock.
   New York: Charles Scribner's Sons, 1881. 549 p.
Galilee in the Time of Christ. by "Reverend" Selah
   Merrill, D. D. , Introd. by Reverend A. P. Peabody.
   Boston: Congregational Publishing Co. , 1881. 159 p.
A New Comprehensive Dictionary of the Bible. New
   York: J. Pott & Co. , 1922. 121 p.
(Collaborated in) Picturesque Palestine, Sinai and Egypt.
   Ed. by Sir Charles William Wilson. 1881-84. 2
   vols.

MESTA, Perle Skirvin. Daughter of William Skirvin (hotel-
   man) and widow of George Mesta, businessman. Active
   in American politics in both Republican and Democratic
   parties and famous as a Washington hostess. American Minister to Luxembourg 1949-53. Appointed by
   President Truman. Associated with the musical comedy Call Me Madam and its hit tune The Hostess with
   the Mostes' on the Ball by Irving Berlin.
Perle - My Story. with Robert Cahn. New York: Mc-
   Graw-Hill Book Co. Inc. , 1960. 251 p.

MEYER, George Von Lengerke, 1858-1918. Ambassador to
     Italy 1900-05, to Russia 1905-06.
  His papers, 1901-09, occupy 2 ft. on the Shelves of the
     Library of Congress.

MILLSPAUGH, Arthur Chester, 1883-1955. Professor of
     political science. State Department 1918-20. Consul,
     Acting Foreign Trade Advisor and Economic Advisor
     State Department 1920-22. Administrator of Finances,
     Persia 1922-27. Financial Advisor and General Re-
     ceiver, Haiti 1927-29. Brookings Institutiqn 1929-42.
     Administrator of Finances of Iran 1942-49.
  Party Organization and the Machinery in Michigan since
     1890. (thesis) Baltimore: Johns Hopkins University,
     1917. 189 p.
  The American Task in Persia. New York: The Century
     Co., 1925. 322 p. Washington: The Brookings In-
     stitution, 1946. 293 p.
  Haiti Under American Control. Boston: World Peace
     Foundation, 1931. 253 p. Reprint: Haiti Under
     American Control, 1915-1930. Westport, Conn.:
     Negro Universities Press, 1970. 253 p.
  Public Welfare Organization. Washington: The Brookings
     Institution, 1935. 700 p.
  Americans in Persia. Washington: The Brookings Insti-
     tution, 1946. 293 p.
  Local Democracy and Crime Control. Washington: The
     Brookings Institution, 1936. 263 p.
  Crime Control by the National Government. Washington:
     The Brookings Institution, 1937. 306 p.
  Democracy, Efficiency, Stability. Washington: The
     Brookings Institution, 1942. 522 p.
  Peace Plans and American Choices. Washington: The
     Brookings Institution, 1942. 107 p.
  Toward Efficient Democracy: The Question of Govern-
     mental Organization. Washington: The Brookings In-
     stitution, 1949. 307 p.

MITCHELL, Donald Grant, 1822-1908. (Pseudonym--Ik
     Marvel.) Agriculturist, landscape gardener, author.
     Consul at Venice 1853-54.
  The Works of Donald Grant Mitchell. New York: Charles
     Scribner's Sons, 1907. 15 vols.
  About Old Story Tellers: of How and When They Lived,
     and What Stories They Told. New York: Scribner,
     Armstrong & Co., 1878. 237 p.
  American Lands and Letters. The Mayflower to Rip Van

Winkle. Leatherstocking to Poe's Raven. New York:
  Charles Scribner's Sons, 1897-99. 2 vols.
The Battle Summer. Transcripts from personal observa-
  tions in Paris during 1848. by Ik Marvel (pseud.).
  New York: Baker & Scribner, 1850. 289 p.
Bound Together: A Sheaf of Papers. New York: Charles
  Scribner's Sons, 1884. 291 p.
Clarence's Courtship. by Ik Marvel (pseud.). In an
  anthology 1895.
Doctor Johns: Being a Narrative of Certain Events in the
  Life of an Orthodox Minister of Connecticut. New
  York: Charles Scribner's Sons, 1866. 2 vols.
Dream Life. by Ik Marvel (pseud.). A fable of the
  Seasons. New York: Charles Scribner, 1851. 265 p.
English Lands, Letters and Kings: From Celt to Tudor.
  New York: Charles Scribner's Sons, 1889-1897. 4
  vols.
Fresh Gleanings: or, a New Sheaf from Old Fields of
  Continental Europe. by Ik Marvel (pseud.). New
  York: Harper & Bros., 1847. 336 p.
Fudge Doings: Being Tony Fudge's Record of the same.
  by Ik Marvel (pseud.). New York: Charles Scribner,
  1855. 2 vols.
The Lorgnette: or, Studies of the Town. By an Opera
  Goer. 2nd edit. Set off with Mr. Darley's designs.
  New York: Printed for Stringer and Townsend, 1850.
  2 vols.
My Farm in Edgewood, a Country Book. Charles Scrib-
  ner, 1863. 319 p.
Out of Town Places: With Hints for Their Improvement.
  Charles Scribner's Sons, 1884. 295 p.
Reveries of a Bachelor. New York: Charles Scribner's
  Sons, 1900. 271 p.
Pictures of Edgewood. New Haven, Conn.: 1882. 62 p.
  Photographs.
Seven Stories, with Basement and Attic. New York:
  Charles Scribner's Sons, 1864. 314 p.
Wet Days at Edgewood: with Old Farmers, Old Gardners
  and Old Pastorals. New York: Charles Scribner's
  Sons, 1965. 324 p.

MITCHELL, Eleanor Swann. Wife of W. M. Parker Mitch-
  ell. Foreign Service Officer 1920-36. Served in
  Mexico City, San Luis Potosi, Chihuahua, Montreal,
  Riviere de Loup, Quebec, Ciudad Juarez, Ghent, Ali-
  cante.
Seven Homes Had I: Experiences of a Foreign Service

Wife. New York: Exposition Press, 1955. 172 p.
Postscript to Seven Homes. Francestown, New Hampshire: M. Jones Co. , 1960. 217 p.

MOFFAT, Abbot Low, 1901- . Attorney. State legislator.
  Foreign Service Reserve Officer 1943-61. Served in
  State Department, Chief of American Mission for Aid
  to Greece, in Athens and Washington 1947. Foreign
  Aid Operations in London and Rangoon. International
  Bank for Reconstruction and Development, Washington.
  International Cooperation Administration in Accra.
  Mongkut, the King of Siam. Ithaca, N.Y. : Cornell Uni-
  versity Press, 1961. 254 p.

MOFFAT, Jay Pierrepont, 1896-1943. Foreign Service Of-
  ficer 1919-43. Served in The Hague, Warsaw, Tokyo,
  Constantinople, Ottawa, Geneva, Sydney, Chief of the
  Division of European Affairs in the Department of
  State, Minister to Canada 1940-43.
  The Moffat Papers. Edit. by Nancy Hooker. Foreword
  by Sumner Welles. Cambridge: Harvard University
  Press, 1956. 408 p. Moffat's complete papers in-
  clude 52 vols. , diaries 15 vols. 1931-43.

MOMSEN, Richard Paul, Jr. , 1890-1964. Private secretary
  to Congressman 1909-13. Lawyer. Deputy Consul
  General at Rio de Janeiro 1913. Vice Consul Rio de
  Janeiro 1915-18.
  Argentina. with American Geographical Society. New
  York: Doubleday, 1965. 64 p.
  Brazil: A Giant Stirs. Princeton, N.J. : D. Van No-
  strand Co. , Inc. , 1968. 144 p.

MONROE, James, 1758-1831. Lawyer, member of Virginia
  House of Delegates, lieutenant in Revolutionary War,
  member of the Congress of the Confederation 1783-86.
  Minister to France 1803; to Great Britain 1803-07,
  Chief of the Diplomatic Mission to Spain 1804-05,
  Governor of Virginia 1811. Secretary of State 1811-
  17, President of the United States 1817-25.
    On the shelves of the Library of Congress there are
  discourses, papers, speeches, pamphlets, etc. com-
  prising 8 ft. of papers of James Monroe's years as
  President.
    The Library of Congress manuscript division has an
  index to the James Monroe papers. For sale at the
  Government Printing Office 1963. 25 p.

Views on the Subject of Internal Improvements.   The Li-
brary of Congress card says only "one of the most
formidable state papers on record. "
The Writings of James Monroe: Including a Collection of
His Public and Private Papers and Correspondence now
for the First Time Printed. Edit. by Stanilaus Murray
Hamilton. New York: G. P. Putnam's Sons, 1898-
1903. 7 vols. (750 copies.)
Autobiography. Edit. with an introd. by Stuart Gerry
Brown with assistance of Donald G. Baker. Syracuse,
N.Y.: Syracuse University Press, 1959. 236 p.
The Memoir of James Monroe, Esq., Relating to his Un-
settled Claims Upon the People and Government of the
United States. Charlottesville, Virginia: Gilver,
Davis Co., 1828. 60 p. "Claims for reimbursement
of expenses incurred during his two missions to
France, 1794-96 and 1803-07. "
The People the Sovereigns: Being a Comparison of the
Government of the United States with Those of the Re-
publics Which Have Existed Before, with the Causes of
their Decadence and Fall. Edit. by Samuel L. Gou-
verneur. Philadelphia: J. B. Lippincott & Co., 1867.
274 p.
The Value of the Diplomatic Service. A speech of the
Hon. James Monroe on the Diplomatic and Consular
appropriation bill. Delivered in the House of Repre-
sentatives, March 22, 1780. Washington: Government
Printing Office, 1880. 15 p.
A Diary of the French Revolution. Edit. by Beatrix Cary
Davenport. Boston: Houghton Mifflin Co., 1939. 2
vols.
See A Bibliography of James Madison and James Monroe.
Compiled by John William Cronin and W. Harvey Wise,
Jr. Washington: Riverford Publishing Co., 1935.
48 p.

MONTGOMERY, George Washington, 1804-1841. Translator
and diplomat. Born in Alicante, Spain, of American
parents. Was an attaché of the Legation in Madrid for
2 years during Washington Irving's first stay there.
Consul at San Juan, Puerto Rico 1835-38. Also served
at Tampico and Guatemala.
El Bastardo de Castilla, Novela Historica, Caballeresca,
Original. Madrid: Imprenta de I. Sancha, 1832.
2 vols. in 1.
Bernardo del Carpio. Trans. from Spanish of Montgomery by J. G. Marvia. Boston: J. Sly, 1843. 82 p.

(Same as El Bastardo de Castilla.)
Narrative of a Journey to Guatemala, in Central America,
 in 1838. New York: Wiley & Putnam, 1839. 195 p.
Novelas Españolas: El Serrano de las Alpujarras, y el
 Quadro Misterioso. Brunswick, Maine: Imprenta de
 Griffin, 1830. 80 p.
(Translated into Spanish) Washington Irving's Conquest of
 Granada. Madrid: Imprenta I. Sancha, 1831. 2 vols.
 in 1.

MONTI, Luigi, 1830-1914. Pseudonym, Samuel Sampleton.
 Consul at Palermo 1861. Vice Consul at Palermo
 1873.
Adventures of a Consul Abroad. by Samuel Sampleton,
 pseud. Boston: Lee & Shephard, 1878. 270 p.
A Grammar of the Italian Language. Boston: Little,
 Brown & Co. , 1855. 348 p.
A Reader of the Italian Language. Boston: Little, Brown
 & Co. , 1855. 252 p.
Leone. Published anonymously. Boston: J. R. Osgood
 & Co. , 1882. 370 p.
(Translated from the Italian) Beatrice Cenci. by F. D.
 Guerrazzi, of the 16th century. New York: Rudd &
 Carleton, 1858.
(Translated from the Italian) Manfred of the Battle of
 Benevento. by F. D. Guerrazzi, of the 16th century.
 New York: G. W. Carlton & Co. , 1875. 447 p.

MOOERS, Horatio, 1894- . Foreign Service Officer 1919-
 54. Served in Antwerp, Brussels, Glasgow, Edin-
 burgh, Horta, Lisbon, Turin, Quebec, Cherbourg,
 Toronto, San José, Mexicali, Manila, Prisoner of the
 Japanese Army in Manila 1942-44, Tijuana, Port-au-
 Prince, Lyons, St. Johns.
La Baie des Anges Pleureurs. Lyons: G. Bonnet, 1948.
 56 p. In French. Written during imprisonment in
 Manila by the Japanese.

MOORE, Helen Frances (Toland), 1867-1958. Wife of Ambassador John Bassett Moore. [Q. V.]
Old Family Receipts. New York: 1929. 102 p.

MOORE, John Bassett, 1860-1947. Lawyer, educator, author, Assistant Secretary of State. Secretary or delegate or member representing the United States on many
 international commissions. Counselor of the State Department. Personal title of Ambassador on the United

States delegation, and President of the International
Conference at the Hague 1922-23, on Rules for Aircraft
and Radio in Time of War.
Papers, 1866-1949. 118 ft. (ca. 100,000 items) in Li-
brary of Congress, Manuscript Division.
A Digest of International Law. Washington: Government
Printing Office, 1906. 8 vols.
Four Phases of American Development. Federalism,
democracy, imperialism, expansionism. Baltimore:
Johns Hopkins Press, 1912. 218 p.
International Law and Some Current Illusions and Other
Essays. New York: The Macmillan Co., 1924.
381 p.
American Diplomacy, Its Spirit and Achievements. New
York: Harper & Bros., 1905. 285 p.
The Principles of American Diplomacy. New York:
Harper & Bros., 1918. 476 p.
Asylum in Legations and Consulates and in Vessels. New
York: Ginn & Co., 1892. 297 p.
Report on Extradition, with Returns of All Cases from
August 9, 1842, to January 1, 1890, and an index.
Washington: Government Printing Office, 1890. 239 p.
Extradition and Interstate Rendition. Boston: Boston
Book Co., 1891. 2 vols.
The Monroe Doctrine. Its Origin and Meaning. New
York: The Evening Post Publishing Co., 1895. 21 p.
History and Digest of International Arbitrations. Wash-
ington: Government Printing Office, 1889. 6 vols.
Rights and Duties of Consuls. (Chapter 16 of Digest of
International Law) Washington: Government Printing
Office, 1906. 154 p. Published separately.
The Collected Papers of John Bassett Moore. New Haven:
Yale University Press. London: H. Milford, Oxford
University Press, 1944. 7 vols. Published, 1945, for
the trustees of John Bassett Moore Fund.
Boundaries of the United States. Berlin: W. Greve,
1900. 703 p.
En Defensa de la Validez y Fuerza Obligatorio del Laudo
del Rey de España. Tegucigalpa: Talleres Tipolito-
gráficos "Ariston," 1957. 190 p.
Essentials of Parliamentary Procedure. with Zoe Steen
Moore. New York: Harper & Bros., 1944. 221 p.
(Edited) International Adjudications, Ancient and Modern,
History and Documents: Together with Mediatorial Re-
ports, Advisory Opinions and the Decisions of Domestic
Commissions on International Claims. New York: Ox-
ford University Press, 1929. 8 vols.

(Edited) The Works of James Buchanan.   Philadelphia:
J. B. Lippincott Co. , 1908-11.   12 vols.

MORAN, Benjamin, 1820-1886.   Secretary of Legation in
London 1853-75.   Minister Resident in Portugal 1874-
82.
Moran's Manuscript Journals.   43 vols. including notes,
queries, clippings and drawings are in the MS. Division of the Library of Congress.
The Journal of Benjamin Moran, 1857-1865.   Edit. by
Sarah Agnes Wallace and Frances Elma Gillespie, from
14 volumes of his entire Journal.   Chicago: University
of Chicago Press, 1949.   2 vols.   1488 p.
The Footpath and Highway: or Wanderings of an American
in Great Britain in 1881-1882.   Philadelphia: Lippincott, Grambo & Co. , 1853.   391 p.

MORGAN, John Heath, 1901-   .   Foreign Service Officer
1925-60.   Served in Budapest, Berlin, Vienna, Madrid,
Bogota, Washington, Reykjavik, Paris, Quebec, Ottawa,
Helsinki, Army War College.
The Foreign Service of the United States: Origins, De-
velopment, and Functions.   with William Barnes.
Washington Historical Office, Bureau of Public Affairs,
Department of State, 1961.   430 p.   Illus.   Department
of State Publication No. 7050.   Foreign Service Series
#96.

MORGANTHAU, Henry, 1856-1946.   Born in Germany.   Edu-
cated in the United States.   Lawyer, banker.   Ambas-
sador to Turkey 1913-16.
Ambassador Morganthau's Story.   Garden City, N.Y. :
Doubleday Page & Co. , 1918.   407 p.   London: Hutch-
inson, 1918.   275 p.   Under title of Secrets of the
Bosphorus.
All in a Lifetime.   with French Strother.   Garden City,
N.Y. :   Doubleday Page & Co. , 1922.   454 p.   Ap-
pendix--report of the Mission of the United States to
Poland.
I Was Sent to Athens.   with French Strother.   Illus.
Garden City, N.Y. :   Doubleday Doran & Co. , 1929.
327 p.
An International Drama.   with F. Strother.   London:
Jarrolds Ltd. , 1930.   288 p.
My Trip Around the World.   New York: ?, 1928.   78 p.
Papers.   1834-1940.   29 ft. in the Library of Congress.

MORRIS, Edward Joy, 1815-1881. Minister to Turkey 1861-
   70. Chargé d'Affaires to the Two Sicilies 1850-53.
   Linguist.
   Notes of a Tour Through Turkey, Greece, Egypt, Arabia
      Petraea, to the Holy Land; Including a Visit to Athens,
      Sparta, Delphi, Cairo, Thebes, Mt. Sinai, Petra, Etc.
      Philadelphia: Carey & Hart, 1842. 2 vols.
   (Translated) The Turkish Empire. by Alfred de Bessé.
      Translated, reviewed and enlarged·from the 4th Ger-
      man edition, with memoirs of the reigning Sultan.
      Philadelphia: Lindsay & Blackistone, 1854. 216 p.
   (Translated) Corsica, Picturesque, Historical. by Ferdi-
      nand Adolf Gregorovius. From the German. Phila-
      delphia: Parray & Macmillan, 1855.

MORRIS, Gouverneur, 1752-1816. Lawyer. Member of the
   Continental Congress and the Constitutional Convention.
   Minister to France 1792. His hostility to the Revolu-
   tionary Government of France and his attempt to aid
   the King to escape led the French Government to re-
   quest his recall in 1794.
   The Diary and Letters of Gouverneur Morris. Edit. by
      Anne Cary Morris (his grand-daughter). New York:
      Charles Scribner, 1888. 388 p.
   A Diary of the French Revolution, 1789-1793. Edit. by
      Beatrix Cary Davenport. Cambridge: Houghton Mif-
      flin. The Riverside Press, 1939. 2 vols.
   United States Continental Congress, 1779. Observations
      on the American Revolution. Published According to
      a Resolution of Congress by their Committee. Com-
      piled by Gouverneur Morris, a member of the Com-
      mittee. Philadelphia: Styner & Cist, 1779. 122 p.

MORRIS, Ira Nelson, 1875-1942. Officer in several corporations. Commissioner to Italy 1913. Commissioner
   of the Panama-Pacific International Exposition. Minister to Sweden 1914-23.
   From an American Legation. New York: Alfred A.
      Knopf, 1923. 287 p.
   Heritage from My Father, An Autobiography. New York:
      Private printing, 1947. 263 p.
   With the Trade Winds: A Jaunt in Venezuela and the
      West Indies. New York: G. P. Putnam's Sons, 1897.
      157 p.

MORRIS, Lily Constance (Rothschild). Wife of Ira Nelson
   Morris, Minister to Sweden 1914-23. [Q. V.]

Maria Theresa, Empress of Austria, the Last Conservative. New York: Alfred A. Knopf, Inc. , 1937.
375 p.

On Tour with Queen Marie, an Account of the Queen of
Rumania's American Tour in 1926. New York: R. M.
McBride & Co. , 1927. 238 p.

(Edited and Translated) Behind Moroccan Walls. by
Celarié Henriette with pictures by Boris Artzybasheff.
Short stories from 2 vols. of Mme. Henriette Celarié's
Amour Marocaines and La Vie Mysterieuse des Harems.
New York: Macmillan Co. , 1931. 239 p.

MORRIS, Richard Valentine, 1768-1815.   Commodore Morris,
United States Navy, negotiated with Tripoli, Tunis and
Algiers in 1804 while in command of naval vessels in
the Mediterranean.

A Defence of the Conduct of Commodore Morris During
his Command in the Mediterranean, 1804. New York:
Riley & Co. , 1904. 98 p.

MORRISON, deLesseps S. , 1912- . Lawyer. Ambassador
to Organization of American States 1961-64.

Latin American Mission: an Adventure in Hemisphere
Diplomacy. Edit. and with an introd. by Gerold Frank.
New York: Simon & Schuster, 1965. 288 p.

MORROW, Dwight Whitney, 1873-1931. Banker. Ambassador to Mexico 1927-30.

The Society of Free States. New York: Harper Bros. ,
1919. 223 p.

MORROW, Elizabeth Reeve (Cutter), 1875-1955. Wife of
Ambassador Dwight Morrow. [Q. V.] Acting President
of Smith College 1939-40. Member of the Board of
the Union Theological Seminary.

All Gaul Is Divided. (letters from occupied france)
Anonymous, with foreword by Elizabeth Reeve Cutter
Morrow. New York: Greystone Press, 1941. 94 p.
London: Gollancz Ltd. , 1941. 119 p.

Beast, Bird and Fish, An Animal Alphabet. with René
d'Harnoncourt. Music by Eberhard d'Harnoncourt.
New York: Alfred A. Knopf, Inc. , 1933. 59 p.
(Children's song.)

Casa Mañana. Drawings by William Spratling. Croton
Falls, N. Y. : The Spiral Press, 1932. 74 p. (Including illus. plates, plans. "Our Street in Cuerna-
vaca" is reprinted by courtesy of the American

Mercury.)

The Mexican Years: Leaves from the Diary of Elizabeth Morrow. Reprint at the Spiral Press, 1953. 272 p.

My Favorite Age. Illus. by Susanne Suba. New York: The Macmillan Co. , 1943. 220 p.

The Painted Pig. A Mexican Picture Book. Pictures by René d'Harnoncourt. New York: Alfred A. Knopf, Inc. , 1930. 34 p.

Quatrains For My Daughter. New York: Alfred A. Knopf, Inc. , 1931. 47 p.

MORROW, John Howard, 1910- . Professor of languages in Talladega College 1945, Clark College 1954, Atlanta University 1950, North Carolina College 1956-59. Ambassador to Guinea 1959-61. United States Representative to UNESCO 1961-63. Foreign Service Institute 1963-64.

First American Ambassador to Guinea. New Brunswick, N. J. : Rutgers University Press, 1967-68. 291 p.

MORSE, Freedman Harlow, 1807-1891. Sculptor. Congressman. Consul at London, England, 1861-70. Retired as Consul General, but disappointed when not reappointed and became a British subject and continued helping Americans in England.

Chiriqui Isthmus, Panama. Washington: Naval Affairs Committee, 1860. 79 p.

MOSBY, John Singleton, 1833-1916. Colonel Mosby was a famous Confederate guerilla officer, during the Civil War, under General J. E. B. Stuart's 1st Virginia Cavalry. His group was referred to as "Mosby's Raiders. " He served as American Consul at Hong Kong 1878-85. When he returned home he was quoted as saying "Better fifty years of Europe than a cycle of Cathay. "

Memoirs of Colonel John Singleton Mosby. Edit. by Charles Wells Russell. Boston: Little, Brown & Co. , 1917. 414 p.

Mosby's War Reminiscences and Stuart's Cavalry Campaigns. Boston: G. A. Jones & Co. , 1887. 256 p. (Has been microfilmed.)

Stuart's Cavalry in the Gettysburg Campaign. New York: Moffat, Yard & Co. , 1908. 222 p.

MOSHER, John Stewart, 1901- . Born in Shanghai of American parents. Foreign Service Officer 1927-33.

Chinese language officer. Served in Havana, Canton, Peiping, Tientsin.

Liar Dice. New York: Simon & Schuster, Inc., 1939. 302 p. Inner Sanctum mystery. New York Times microfilm 1939.

MOTLEY, John Lathrop, 1814-1877. New England historian and intellectual. Secretary of Legation at St. Petersburg, 1841. Minister to Austria 1861-67, to London 1869-70.

The Writings of John Lathrop Motley. Netherlands edition. New York: Harper Bros., 1900. 17 vols.

The History of United Netherlands from the Death of William the Silent to the Twelve Years Truce, 1609. Paris: Michel Lévy Fréres, 1859-60. 4 vols.

John L. Motley and His family. Further letters and records, edit. by his daughter and Herbert St. John Mildmay. London: John Lane, 1910. 321 p.

John Lathrop Motley. Representative selections with introductory bibliography and notes by Chester Penn Higby and B. T. Schantz. New York: American Book Co., 1939. 482 p.

The Life and Death of John of Barneveld, Advocate of Holland. With a View of the Primary Causes and Movements of the Thirty Years War. London: J. Murray, 1874. 2 vols.

Merry Mount: A Romance of the Massachusetts Colony. Boston: J. Monroe & Co., 1849. 2 vols.

Morton of Morton's Hope: An Autobiography. London: H. Colburn, 1839. 3 vols.

Morton's Hope: or the Memoirs of a Provincial. New York: Harper & Bros., 1839. 2 vols.

Peter the Great. New York: Harper & Bros., 1877. 106 p. (Published also in raised type, for the blind.)

Rise of the Dutch Republic. New York: Harper & Bros., 1899. 3 vols.

MOYNIHAN, Daniel Patrick, 1927- . Educator. Assistant Secretary Labor 1963-65. Ambassador to India 1973.

Beyond the Melting Pot: The Negroes, Puerto Ricans, Jews, Italians and Irish of New York City. with Nathan Glazer. Cambridge: Massachusetts Institute of Technology Press, 1963. 300 p.

Maximum Feasible Misunderstanding. Community Action in the War on Poverty. New York: Free Press, 1969. 218 p.

(Edited) On Understanding Poverty: Perspective from the

Social Science. with Corinne Saposa Schelling. New
York: Basic Books, 1969. 425 p.
Politics of a Guaranteed Income. New York: Random
House, 1973.
(Edited) Toward a National Urban Policy. New York:
Basic Books, 1970. 348 p.

MUNRO, Dana Gardner, 1892- . Educator, research.
Foreign Service Officer 1919-32. Served in State De-
partment, Valparaiso, Panama, Managua, Minister to
Haiti 1930-32.
The Five Republics of Central America: Their Political
and Economic Development and Their Relations with the
United States. (Ph. D. thesis at University of Pennsyl-
vania) Edit. by David Kinley. New York: Oxford Uni-
versity Press, 1918. 332 p.
Intervention and Dollar Diplomacy in the Caribbean, 1900-
1921. Princeton, N. J.: Princeton University Press,
1964. 553 p.
The Latin American Republics. A History. New York:
D. Appleton Century Co., 1942. 650 p.
The United States and the Caribbean Area. World Peace
Foundation Publications, 1934. 322 p.

MURPHY, George M., 1860-1924. Entered Service after
examination in 1886 as consular clerk. Progressed to
Consul General, died in Service in 1924. Served in
Chemnitz, Berlin, Hanover, State Department, Colon,
Bremen, Magdeburg, Frankfort, St. Catherine's, Cape
Town, Zurich. Consular Inspector in Central America
and Colombia, Germany. Consul General-at-large.
Digest of Circular Instructions to Consular Officers.
Washington: Government Printing Office, 1904-06.
2 vols.

MURPHY, Robert Daniel, 1894- . Foreign Service Officer
1920-59. Served in Zurich, Munich, Seville, State
Department, Paris, Vichy, Algiers, Supreme Allied
Command, Allied Control in Italy. Political Advisor
German Affairs at Supreme Headquarters American Ex-
peditionary Force, Ambassador to Belgium 1949, to
Japan 1952, Assistant Secretary of State 1959. Career
Ambassador. Presidential Award for Distinguished
Federal Civil Service.
Diplomat Among Warriors. New York: Doubleday & Co.,
1964. 470 p.

MURRAY, William Vans, 1760-1803. Minister Resident to
the Netherlands 1797. Minister to France, with Oliver
Ellsworth and Governor W. E. Davie (North Carolina),
as Commissioners to negotiate a convention, signed in
1800.
Letters of William Vans Murray to John Quincy Adams,
1797-1803. Edit. by Worthington Chauncy Ford.
Washington: 1914. American Historical Association.
Annual Report for year 1912. pp. 341-715.
Political Sketches, Inscribed to His Excellency John
Adams, Minister Plenipotentiary from the United States
to the Court of Great Britain by a Citizen of the United
States. London: Printed for C. Dilly, 1787. 96 p.
Murray Manuscripts. In Library of Congress contains
Diary written at The Hague and Some Remarks on the
Stages of Our Negotiations at Paris, 1800.

NADLER, Seymour I., 1916- . Radio script writer. For-
eign Service Reserve Officer 1947- . Served in
Tientsin, Singapore, United States Information Agency,
Taipei, Buenos Aires, Ankara, State Department.
Life and Love in the Foreign Service. with Robert W.
Rinden. Washington: Foreign Service Journal, 1969.
60 p. Illus.

NAST, Thomas, 1840-1902. Famous American cartoonist
during and after the Civil War. From his pen came
the Democratic party's donkey, the Republican party's
elephant and Tammany's tiger. (Encyclopedia Britan-
nica) Consul General in Guayaquil, where he died in
1902.
Thomas Nast, His Period and His Pictures. New York:
Harper Bros., 1904. 583 p.
Thomas Nast's Christmas Drawings for the Human Race.
New York: Harpers, 1890. 60 p.
Nast's Illustrated Almanac. New York: McLoughlin
Bros., 1870. 1 vol. Illus. plates.
A three-volume scrapbook collection of Nast's pictures is
available in the New York Public Library.

NEWTON, Joseph Emerson, 1903- . Foreign Service Offi-
cer 1930-45. Served in Montreal, Nagoya, Singapore,
Yokohama, State Department, Nassau, Havana, Windsor.
Java Edge. Boston: Bruce Humphries, 1955. 205 p.
White Kimono. New York: Pageant Press, 1957. 202 p.
Years of Destruction. New York: Pageant Press, 1960.
222 p.

NICHOLSON, Meredith, 1866-1947. Author, lecturer. Minister to Paraguay 1933-34, to Venezuela 1935-38, to Nicaragua 1938-41.

And They Lived Happily Ever After. New York: Charles Scribner's Sons, 1925. 369 p.

Blacksheep! Blacksheep! Illus. by Leslie L. Benson. New York: Charles Scribner's Sons, 1920. 346 p.

Broken Barriers. New York: Charles Scribner's Sons, 1922. 402 p.

The Cavalier of Tennessee. Indianapolis: The Bobbs-Merrill Co., Inc., 1928. 402 p.

A Fifth Reader. with Will D. Howe and Myron T. Pritchard. New York: Charles Scribner's Sons, 1919. 372 p.

A Fourth Reader. with Will D. Howe and Myron T. Pritchard. New York: Charles Scribner's Sons, 1919. 344 p.

Honor Bright: A Comedy in Three Acts. with Kenyon Nicholson. New York: Charles Scribner's Sons, 1923. 105 p.

A Hoosier Chronicle. Illus. by F. C. Yohn. Boston: Houghton Mifflin Co., 1912. 605 p.

The Hoosiers. New York: The Macmillan Co., 1900. 277 p.

The Hope of Happiness. New York: Charles Scribner's Sons, 1923. 358 p.

The House of a Thousand Candles. Illus. by Howard Chandler Christy. Indianapolis: The Bobbs-Merrill Co., Inc., 1905. 382 p.

Lady Larkspur. New York: Charles Scribner's Sons, 1919. 171 p.

The Little Brown Jug at Kildare. Illus. by James Montgomery Flagg. Indianapolis: The Bobbs-Merrill Co. Inc., 1908. 422 p.

The Lords of High Decision. Illus. by Arthur I. Keller. New York: Doubleday, Page Co., 1909. 503 p.

The Madness of May. Illus. by Fredric Dorr Steele. New York: Charles Scribner's Sons, 1917. 187 p.

The Main Chance. Illus. by Harrison Fisher. Indianapolis: Bobbs-Merrill Co. Inc., 1903. 419 p.

The Man in the Street. New York: Charles Scribner's Sons, 1921. 271 p.

Old Familiar Faces. Indianapolis: Bobbs-Merrill Co. Inc., 1929. 189 p.

Otherwise Phyllis. Boston: Houghton Mifflin Co., 1913. 397 p.

Poems. Indianapolis: Bobbs-Merrill Co. Inc., 1906.

110 p.

The Poet.   Pictures by Franklin Booth, decorations by
W. A. Dwiggins.   Boston: Houghton Mifflin Co., 1914.
189 p.

The Port of Missing Men.   Illus. by Clarence F. Underwood.   Indianapolis: Bobbs-Merrill Co. Inc., 1907.
399 p.

The Proof of the Pudding.   Boston: Houghton Mifflin Co.,
1916.   372 p.

The Provincial American and Other Papers.   (essays)
Boston: Houghton Mifflin Co., 1912.   236 p.

A Reversable Santa Claus.   Illus. by Florence H. Minard.
Boston: Houghton Mifflin Co., 1917.   176 p.

Rosalind at Redgate.   Illus. by Arthur I. Keller.   Indianapolis: Bobbs-Merrill Co. Inc., 1907.   387 p.

Short Flights.   Indianapolis: Bowen-Merrill Co., 1891.
100 p.

The Siege of Seven Suitors.   Illus. by C. Coles Phillips
and Reginald Birch.   Boston: Houghton Mifflin Co.,
1910.   400 p.

A Third Reader.   with Will D. Howe and Myron T.
Pritchard.   New York: Charles Scribner's Sons, 1919.
310 p.

The Valley of Democracy.   Illus. by Walter Tillte.   New
York: Charles Scribner's Sons, 1918.   284 p.

Zelda Dameron.   Drawings by John Cecil Clay.   Indianapolis: Bobbs-Merrill Co. Inc., 1904.   411 p.

NICOLAY, John George, 1832-1901.   Nicolay and John Hay
were secretaries to Abraham Lincoln.   After Lincoln's
death John Nicolay was appointed consul in Paris, and
John Hay his secretary, 1865.

Abraham Lincoln: A History.   Co-author John Hay.   New
York: Century Co., 1890.   10 vols.

The Outbreak of Rebellion.   New York: Charles Scribner's
Sons, 1881.   220 p.

A Short Life of Abraham Lincoln.   Condensed from Abraham Lincoln: A History.   New York: Century Co.,
1902.   578 p.

Abraham Lincoln.   Complete Works.   Comprising his
speeches, letters, state papers and miscellaneous writings.   Edit. by John Nicolay and John Hay.   New
York: Century Press, 1902.   2 vols.

Papers of John George Nicolay.   Occupy 41 feet.   Library of Congress.

(Edited) Complete Works of Abraham Lincoln.   Edit. by
Nicolay and John Hay, with an introd. by Richard Wat-

son Gilder and special articles by other eminent persons. New and enlarged. New York: Francis D. Tandy, 1905. 12 vols.

NIGHSWONGER, William A., 1927- . Clergyman 1954-62. Foreign Service Reserve Officer. Agency for International Development, Saigon 1962-64.
Rural Pacification in Vietnam. New York: Frederick A. Praeger, Inc., 1966. 320 p.
War Without Guns: American Civilians in Rural Vietnam. with W. Robert Warne, Earle J. Young and George K. Tanham. New York: Frederick A. Praeger, Inc., 1966. 320 p.

NILES, Nathaniel, 1791-1869. Chargé d'Affaires, Paris 1830-33. Special Diplomatic Agent to Austria-Hungary 1837-38, to Sardinia 1838-39. Chargé d'Affaires in Sardinia 1848-50.
Nathaniel Niles Papers. Library of Congress. 2 vols.

NOEL, Edgar E., 1933- . Foreign Service Reserve Officer, 1960- . United States Information Agency.
Served in Bangkok, Seoul, Tokyo, Fukuoka, Washington.
Plum Blossoms. (Selected poems) Foreword by Edwin O. Reischauer. Fukuoka City, Japan: Kyushu Bungaku Sha, 1968. 79 p.
Heritage of Freedom. A Brief History of the United States. Washington: United States Information Agency, 1970-71. 4 vols.

NOSTRAND, Howard Lee, 1910- . Historian, professor of Romance languages and literature. Professor and President Emeritus of Yale 1911-37. Chief of Austro-Hungarian Division of American Commission to Negotiate Peace. United States delegate on Roumanian, Jugoslav, Czechoslovak Territorial Commission, Peace Conference, Paris 1919. Cultural Attaché in Lima, 1944-47.
The Cultural Attaché. New Haven: Hazen Foundation. n. d.
Background Data for the Teaching of French. Howard Lee Nostrand, Project Director. Seattle: Department of Romance Languages and Literature. University of Washington, 1967. 3 vols. in 4.
Research on Language Teaching: an Annotated International Bibliography. 1945-64. with David William Foster

and Clay Benjamin Christensen. 2nd ed. rev. Seattle: University of Washington Press, 1965. (i. e. 1966) 373 p.
Le Théatre Antique et à l'Antique en France de 1840 à 1900. Paris: E. Droz, 1934. 331 p.

OECHSNER, Frederick Cable, 1902- . Lawyer, newspaper correspondent. Office of Strategic Services 1942-46. Foreign Service Officer 1947-62. Served in State Department, Foreign Service Inspector, Warsaw, Monterrey.
This Is the Enemy. with Joseph W. Griggs, Jack M. Fleisher, Glen M. Stadler and Clinton B. Conger. Boston: Little, Brown & Co., 1942. 364 p.

OLIVARES, José De, 1867-1942. Newspaper reporter and foreign correspondent. Commissioner to South America for St. Louis World's Fair of 1904. Foreign Service Officer 1906-32. Served in Managua, Washington, Madras, Hamilton (Ontario), Kingston (Jamaica), Leghorn.
Our Islands and Their People as Seen with Camera and Pencil. Introd. by Major General Joseph Wheeler, with special descriptive matter and narratives by José de Olivares. Edit. and arranged by William S. Bryan. Photographs by Walter B. Townsend. St. Louis: N. D. Thompson Publishing Co., 1899-1900. 776 p.
The Parisian Dream City. A portfolio of the World's Exposition at Paris. Introd. by Fredrick Mayerand and by Hon. Ferdinand W. Peck. Descriptive features by José de Olivares. Photographs by Marius Bar, with Antoine and Etienne Neurdein. St. Louis: N. D. Thompson Publishing Co., 1900. 328 p.

OLSON, Theodore (Ted) Bernard, 1899- . Newspaper reporter and editor. Foreign Service Officer 1947-57. Served in Athens, Oslo, the State Department, Foreign Service Inspector. United States Information Agency.
Hawk's Way. (poems) New York: League to Support Poetry, 1941. 53 p.
A Stranger and Afraid. New Haven: Yale University Press, 1928. 50 p.

O'NEALE, Margaret (O'Neale) Timberlake Eaton Buchignani, 1796-1879. Daughter of a Washington tavern-keeper, William O'Neale. Married a Navy purser, John B. Timberlake. At his death she married, 1829, John H.

Eaton, Senator from Tennessee, whom President Jackson appointed Secretary of War, 1829-31, and then Minister to Spain 1836-40. Eaton died in 1856. Peggy married an Italian dancing master, Antonio Buchignani who, after running through her property eloped with her granddaughter. (Encyclopaedia Britannica.) She was the subject of a novel, Peggy O'Neale written by Alfred Henry Lewis, on which Stephen Vincent Benet and John Farrar wrote a play The Heart of Peggy O'Neill, in 1924. The name was variously spelled O'Neale, O'Neill and O'Neil.
The Autobiography of Peggy Eaton, Democracy's Mistress. "The story as she dictated it and read it in the year 1873. " Preface by Charles F. Deems. New York: Charles Scribner's Sons, 1932. 120 p.

O'SHAUGHNESSY, Edith Louise (Coues), 1870-1939. Wife of Nelson O'Shaughnessy, 1876-1932, Diplomatic Service 1904-16. He served in Copenhagen, Berlin, Vienna, Mexico City.
Alsace in Rust and Gold. New York: Harper & Bros., 1920. 183 p.
Diplomatic Days. New York: Harper & Bros., 1917. 337 p.
A Diplomat's Wife in Mexico. Letters from the Embassy at Mexico City covering the dramatic period between October 8, 1913 and the breaking off of Diplomatic relations on April 23, 1914; together with an account of the occupation of Vera Cruz. New York: Harper Bros., 1916. 335 p. In Spanish, Mexico City: 1962. 2 vols.
Intimate Pages of Mexican History. New York: George H. Doran, 1920. 351 p.
Marie Adelaide, Grandduchess of Luxemburg, Duchess of Nassau. London: J. Cope, 1932. 308 p.
Married Life. New York: Harcourt, Brace & Co., 1925. 299 p.
My Lorraine Journal. New York: Harper Bros., 1918. 195 p.
Other Ways and Other Flesh. New York: Harcourt, Brace & Co., 1929. 224 p.
Viennese Medley. New York: B. W. Huebsch, Inc., 1924. 295 p.

O'SHEEL, Patrick, 1914-   . United States Marine Corps 1942-46. Writer, editor, foreign correspondent. Foreign Service Reserve and Foreign Service Officer

1948-70. Served in Glasgow, London, Budapest, United States Information Agency, State Department, Cairo, Kaduna, Pretoria. Merit Honor Award.

Semper Fidelis - The United States Marines in the Pacific 1942-45. New York: William Sloane Associates, 1947. 360 p.

O'SULLIVAN, John L., 1813-1895. Minister Resident in Portugal 1854-58.

Union, Disunion, and Reunion: A Letter to General Franklin Pierce, Ex-President of the United States. London: R. Bentley, 1862. 122 p.

OWEN, Ruth (Bryan) Rohde, 1885-1954. Daughter of famous Democratic politician and former Secretary of State, William Jennings Bryan. Married Major Reginald Owen, a British Army officer 1910 (died 1927). Married in 1936 Captain Borge Rohde, Danish Royal Guards. Wrote under name of Ruth Owen. Minister to Denmark 1933-36.

Caribbean Caravel. Illus. by Leon Helguera. N. Y. : Dodd, Mead, 1949. 222 p.

The Castle in the Silver Wood and Other Scandian Fairy Tales. New York: Dodd, Mead & Co., 1939. 181 p.

Denmark Caravan. (Kammerjunkerinde Rohde) Illus. by Hedwig Collin. New York: Dodd, Mead & Co., 1936. 197 p.

Elements of Public Speaking. Preface by William Lyon Phelps. New York: H. Liveright Inc., 1931. 200 p.

Leaves From a Greenland Diary. New York: Dodd, Mead & Co., 1935. 166 p.

Look Forward, Warrior. New York: Dodd, Mead & Co., 1942. 108 p.

Picture Tales from Scandinavia: Selected and Retold. Illus. by Emma Brock. New York: Fredrick A. Stokes Co., 1939. 109 p.

PADDOCK, Paul Ezekiel, Jr., 1907- . Foreign Service Officer 1937-57. Served in Mexico City, Batavia, Medan, Melbourne, Auckland, Casablanca, Moscow, Kabul, Dairen, Denver Air Academy, Canadian National Defense College, Pusan, State Department, Valletta, Vientiane, Manila, United States Information Agency.

Hungry Nations. Boston: Little, Brown & Co., 1964. 344 p.

Famine 1975: America's Decision: Who Will Survive? Boston: Little, Brown & Co., 1967. 276 p.

PAGE, Thomas Nelson, 1853-1922. Lawyer, lecturer, author, poet. Ambassador to Italy 1913-20.
The Novels, Stories, Sketches and Poems of Thomas Nelson Page. New York: Charles Scribner's Sons, 1906-18. 18 vols.
Bred in the Bone. Freeport, N.Y.: Books for Libraries Press, 1969. 274 p.
Among the Camps, or, Young Peoples' Stories of the War. (Civil War) New York: Charles Scribner's Sons, 1891. 163 p.
Befo' de War. Joint Echos in Negro Dialect. New York: Charles Scribner's Sons, 1888. 131 p.
The Burial of the Guns. New York: Charles Scribner's Sons, 1894. 258 p.
A Captured Santa Claus. Illus. by W. L. Jacobs. New York: Charles Scribner's Sons, 1902. 81 p.
The Coast of Bohemia. (poems) New York: Charles Scribner's Sons, 1906. 126 p.
Danté and His Influences. (studies) New York: Charles Scribner's Sons, 1922. 239 p.
Elsket and Other Stories. New York: Charles Scribner's Sons, 1891. 208 p.
Gordon Keith. Illus. by George Wright. New York: Charles Scribner's Sons, 1903. 548 p.
In Ole Virginia: or Marse Chan and Other Stories. New York: Charles Scribner's Sons, 1887. 230 p.
Italy and the World War. with maps. New York: Charles Scribner's Sons, 1920. 422 p.
John Marvel, Assistant. Illus. by James Montgomery Flagg. New York: Charles Scribner's Sons, 1909. 573 p.
The Land of the Spirit. New York: Charles Scribner's Sons, 1913. 257 p.
Mount Vernon. The Acquisition and its Preservation, Restoration and the Care of, by the Mount Vernon Ladies Association of the Union for Over Half a Century. New York: Knickerbocker Press, 1910. 84 p.
The Negro: the Southerner's Problem. New York: Charles Scribner's Sons, 1904. 316 p.
The Old Dominion: Her Making and Her Manners. New York: Charles Scribner's Sons, 1908. 394 p.
The Old Gentlemen of the Black Stock. New York: Charles Scribner's Sons, 1897. 137 p. Illus. by Howard Chandler Christy.
The Old South: Essays Social and Political. New York: Charles Scribner's Sons, 1892. 344 p.
On Newfoundland River. New York: Charles Scribner's

Sons, 1891. 240 p.
The Page Story Book. Edit. by Frank E. Spaulding and
    Catherine T. Bryce. New York: Charles Scribner's
    Sons, 1906. 125 p.
Pastime Stories. Illus. by A. B. Frost. Freeport,
    N. Y. : Books for Libraries Press, 1969. 220 p.

PAGE, Walter Hines, 1855-1918. Editor of magazines, in-
    cluding The Forum, Atlantic Monthly, World's Work,
    and a member of Doubleday, Page & Co. , Publishers.
    Herbert Hoover called him "a great mind, a distin-
    guished scholar, a great editor, the soul of intellectual
    honesty, a man of sympathy and kindness, almost
    fanatically devoted to the service of his country. "
    Ambassador to Great Britain 1913-1918.
The Southerner, a Novel: Being the Autobiography of
    Nicholas Worth. Pseudonym. New York: Doubleday,
    Page & Co. , 1909. 424 p.
The Life and Letters of Walter Hines Page. by Burton
    J. Hendrick. Garden City, N. Y. : Doubleday, Page
    & Co. , 1923-26. 3 vols.
The Rebuilding of Old Commonwealths. (essays looking
    toward the training of the "forgotten man" in the South)
    New York: Doubleday, Page & Company, 1902. 153 p.

PALMER, Stephen E. , Jr. , 1923- . Teacher American
    Community School Tehran 1946-47. Foreign Service
    Officer 1951- . Served in Nicosia, State Department
    (Serbo-Croatian language training), Belgrade, Sarajevo,
    Tel Aviv, London (Superior Honor award), Rawalpindi,
    Madras (Merit Honor award).
Yugoslav Communism and the Macedonian Question. with
    Robert E. King. Hamden, Conn. : Shoe String Press
    (Archon Books), 1971. 247 p.

PARKER, Maude, ?-1959. Wife of Richard Washburn Child,
    Ambassador to Italy 1921-24. [Q. V.]
The Social Side of Diplomatic Life. (Child) Indianapolis:
    Bobbs-Merrill Co. , 1926. 305 p.
Impersonation of a Lady. Boston: Houghton Mifflin Co. ,
    1934. 270 p.
Secret Envoy. Indianapolis: Bobbs-Merrill Co. , 1930.
    302 p.
Which Mrs. Torr? (A Murray Hill Mystery) New York:
    Rinehart, 1951. 247 p.
The Intriguer. (A Murray Hill Mystery) New York:
    Rinehart, 1952. 248 p.

Invisible Red. New York: Rinehart, 1953. 247 p.
Murder in Jackson Hole. New York: Rinehart, 1955.
249 p.
Along Came a Spider. London: Hodder & Stoughton,
1957. 192 p.
Death Makes a Deal. London: Hodder & Stoughton, 1961.
224 p.

PARKER, Peter, 1804-1888. A medical missionary from
Massachusetts. Established a hospital in Canton,
China. Drawn into diplomatic service. In 1844 he
was one of the secretaries of Caleb Cushing, first
American Minister to China, 1843-45. Assisted in
negotiating the first treaty between the United States
and China. Was Secretary of Legation 1845, occasion-
ally Chargé d'Affaires. American Commissioner to
China 1855-57.
The Journal of Peter Parker. London: Smith, Elder,
1838. 75 p.
Statement Respecting Hospitals in China Preceded by a
Letter to John Abercrombie. Glasgow, Scotland:
Maclehose, 1842. 32 p.
Message of the President of the United States communi-
cating, in Compliance with a Resolution of the Senate,
the Correspondence of Messrs. McLane and Parker,
late Commissioners to China. Washington: W. A.
Harris, 1859. 2 vols. of which one is about Parker.
Journal of an Expedition from Singapore to Japan, With a
Visit to Loo-Chao: Descriptive of these Islands and
Their Inhabitants, in an Attempt with the Aid of Natives
Educated in England to Create an Opening for Mission-
ary Labours in Japan. London: Smith, Elder & Co.
Cornhill, 1838. Revised by Reverend Andrew Reed,
D. D. 75 p.
Report of the Medical Missionary Society Containing an
Abstract of its History and Prospects: and the Report
of the Hospital at Macao, for 1841-2: Together with
Dr. Parker's Statement of his Proceedings in England
and the United States in Behalf of the Society. Macao:
Press of S. W. Williams. (Under Medical Missionary
Society in China) 1843. 48 p.

PATTERSON, Jefferson, 1891- . Foreign Service Officer
1921-57. Served in State Department, Peking, Bogota,
Constantinople, Office of Protocol, Breslau, Oslo,
Berlin, Lima, Brussels, Cairo, Khartoum, Sao Paulo,
Ambassador to Uruguay 1956-57.

Diplomatic Duty and Diversion. Cambridge: Riverside
Press, 1956. 481 p. Privately printed.
Diplomatic Terminus, An Experience in Uruguay. Cambridge: Riverside Press, 1962. 113 p. Privately
printed.
Capitals and Captives. Cambridge: Riverside Press,
1966. 314 p. Privately printed.

PATTON, Kenneth Stuart, 1882-1960. Foreign Service Officer 1908-1945. Served in State Department, Marseilles, Rome, Ceiba, Lisbon, Cognac, La Rochelle,
Calais, Paris, Belgrade, Leipzig, Batavia, Amsterdam, Singapore, Calcutta. Minister to New Zealand
1944-45.
Kingdom of the Serbs, Croats and Slovenes. A commercial and industrial handbook for Yugoslavia. Washington: Government Printing Office, 1928. 261 p. Illus.
tables, maps. Department of Commerce.

PAYNE, John Howard, 1791-1852. Author, poet, playright,
actor, manager. Lived for many years in England and
France. Author of Home, Sweet Home. Consul at
Tunis 1842-45, again in Tunis 1851-52, where he died.
Wrote, translated or adapted more than 60 plays for
the English stage during 20 years residence there.
The Accusation: or, the Family of D'Anglade: A Melo-
drama in Three Acts. Translated from the French
with alterations by Payne. Boston: West, Richardson & Lord. Printed by J. H. A. Frost. 76 p.
Ali Pacha, or, the Signet Ring. (2 acts) printed from
the acting copy with remarks, etc. as performed at
the Theatre Royal, London: J. Cumberland, 1823.
36 p.
Brutus, or, the Fall of Tarquin. An historical tragedy
in five acts. Printed from the acting copy, with remarks. Cumberland Theatre, London: 1825-55. 52 p.
Reprinted and republished several times as performed
in London and New York and Philadelphia. Produced
by Edwin Booth in 1868.
Charles the Second, or, The Merry Monarch. A comedy
in three acts. London: Davidson, 45 p. Reprinted
1824, 66 p. for Covent Garden. London: Longman,
Hurst, Rees, Orme, Brown and Green. This play was
founded on Duval's La Jeunesse de Henri V. published
in London: J. Cumberland 1825 with engraving by
Mr. White from drawing by R. Cruikshank.
Clari: or, the Maid of Milan. (2 acts) Philadelphia:

Turner and Fisher, 1836? 40 p. This play contains
Home, Sweet Home. London: G. H. Davidson. 40 p.
The Fall of Algiers: A Comic Opera. (3 acts) Printed
from the acting copy, with remarks, etc. London:
J. Cumberland. 47 p.
John Howard Payne to His Countrymen. Edit. with an
introd. by Clemens de Baillou. Athens, Georgia:
University of Georgia Press, 1961. 61 p.
Julia, or, The Wanderer, A Comedy. (5 acts) performed
at New York Theatre from the prompt book. D. Long-
worth. Shakespeare gallery 1806. 70 p.
The Lancers: An Interlude. with remarks, from acting
copy. London: C. Cumberland. 27 p.
Lispings of the Music. Selections of Payne's juvenile
writings at or before 16 years of age. London: R.
& A. Taylor, 1815. 30 p.
The Last Duel in Spain, and Other Plays. Edit. by Cod-
man Hislop and W. R. Richardson. Princeton: Uni-
versity Press, 1940. 265 p.
Love in Humble Life: A Petite Comedy in One Act.
From the acting copy. London: G. H. Davidson, T.
Dolby, 1825. 31 p.
Richelieu: A Domestic Tragedy, Founded on Fact. (in
5 acts) printed from the author's manuscript. New
York: E. M. Murden, 1826. 79 p.
Trial Without Jury and Other Plays. Edit. by Codman
Hislop and W. R. Richardson. Princeton: Princeton
University Press, 1940. 264 p.
The Two Galley Slaves. A Melo-Drama. (2 acts) Lon-
don: Davidson. 33 p.
Therese, The Orphan of Geneva. Translated and adapted
by Victor Henri Joseph Brahain 1783-1838. 46 p.
Same in 3 acts printed by J. Tabby 1821. 57 p.
Archilla Smith. Indian Justice. A Cherokee murder trial
at Tahlequah in 1840, as reported by John Howard
Payne, edit. with introd. and footnotes by Grant Fore-
man, Oklahoma City. Harlow Publishing Co. 1934.
112 p. (The trial of Archilla Smith, Cherokee Indian,
charged with the murder of John MacIntosh in the late
fall of 1789. The defendant was tried in the Cherokee
Supreme Court at Tahlequah. Chief Justice Jessie
Bushyhead presiding; found him guilty, December 26,
1840, and sentenced him to die January 1, 1841. The
account of this important Indian case appeared in two
long installments in the New York Journal of Commerce for April 17 and April 29, 1841.)
Memoirs of John Howard Payne, The American Roscius:

With Criticisms on His Acting, In the Various Theatres
of America, England and Ireland. Compiled from au-
thentic documents. London: Printed for J. Miller,
1815. 131 p.
Catalogue of Stan V. Henkels, Auctioneers. Philadelphia:
1904. 65 p.
Papers of John Howard Payne, Author of Home, Sweet
Home, Including His Love Letters to and from Mary
Wollstoncroft Shelby and Valuable Autograph Letters
Belonging to the Estate of Howard T. Goodwin, De-
ceased, and From Other Sources. Also Peale's Oil
Portrait of Washington. (Etc.). To Be Sold. 65 p.

PELL, Claiborne, 1910- . Journalist, stockbroker, poli-
tician, Senator from Rhode Island 1961- . Secretary
to American Minister to Portugal 1940-41. State De-
partment and Foreign Service Officer 1945-52. Served
in Praha, Bratislava, Genoa.
Power and Policy: America's Role in World Affairs.
New York: W. W. Norton & Co., 1972. 171 p.
Megalopolis Unbound. New York: Frederick A. Praeger
Inc., 1966. 221 p.
Challenge of the Seven Seas. with Harold Goodwin. New
York: William Morrow & Co. Inc., 1966. 306 p.

PELL, Herbert Claiborne, 1884-1961. Author, lecturer,
politician. Member of Congress 1919-21. Minister
to Portugal 1937-41, to Hungary 1941, to United Nations War Crimes Commission 1943.
Glimpses of English History. Paintings by Oliver Bigelow
Pell. New York: A. S. Barnes, 1967. 63 p.
America and Its People. (light verse) New York: Vantage Press, 1969. 80 p.

PENDAR, Kenneth Whittemore, 1906- . Appointed an "observer" or "control officer" under the Murphy-Weygand
Economic Agreement in 1941, to North Africa. Offi-
cially designated as a non-career vice consul to pre-
pare for the Allied landings in North Africa in 1942.
Assigned to Casablanca 1941-43.
Adventure in Diplomacy: Our French Dilemma. New
York: Dodd, Mead & Co. Inc., 1945. 280 p. Republished as Adventure in Diplomacy: The Emergence
of General de Gaulle in North Africa. with new material. London: Cassell, 1966. 382 p.

PENFIELD, Frederick Courtland, 1855-1922. Vice-Consul-

General in London 1885; Diplomatic Agent and Consul
General in Cairo 1893-1897; Ambassador to Austria-
Hungary 1913-1917.
East of Suez: Ceylon, India, China and Japan.   Illus.
from drawings and photos.   New York: The Century
Co. , 1907.   349 p.
The Motor That Went to Court.   A fact-story, with ran-
dom illus.   New York: The De Vinne Press, 1909.
91 p.   Private printed.
Present-Day Egypt.   Illus. by Paul Philippoteaux and R.
Talbert Kelly.   New York: The Century Co. , 1889.
372 p.
Papers, 1913-1921.   Historical Society of Pennsylvania.
140 items.

PENROSE, Ernest Francis, 1898- . Educator, economist,
geographer.   Born in England, naturalized.   Economic
advisor to Ambassador John G. Winant in London 1941-
46.   Advisor to the United States Delegation at the
United Nations 1946-48.
Agricultural and Mineral Production in Japan.   Tables,
diagrams.   Honolulu: The Institute of Pacific Rela-
tions, 1929.   75 p.
Economic Planning for the Peace.   Princeton: Princeton
University Press, 1953.   384 p.
Population Theories and Their Application, With Special
Reference To Japan.   Stanford: Stanford University
Food Research Institute, 1934.   347 p.
The Revolution in International Relations: A Study in the
Nature and Balance of Power.   London: F. Case,
1965.   290 p.
Industrialization of Japan and Manchuria.   with others.
New York: The Macmillan Co. , 1940.   944 p.
Food Supply and Raw Materials in Japan.   An Index of the
Physical Volume of Production of Foodstuffs, Industrial
Crops, and Minerals 1894-1927.   Chicago: University
of Chicago Press, 1930.   75 p.
(Edited) New Orientations: Essays in International Rela-
tions.   Editors: Ernest Francis Penrose, Peter Lynn,
Edith Penrose.   London: Cass, 1970.   136 p.
Economic Aspects of Medical Services, with Special Re-
ferences to Conditions in California.   with Paul Albert
Dodd.   Washington: Graphic Arts Press, 1939.   499 p.
Maps, tables, illus.
Studies in War Economics.   Montreal: International Labor
Office, 1941.

PHELPS, Edward John, 1822-1900. Minister to Great Britain 1885-89.

Lectures on Medical Jurisprudence. Burlington: The
Free Press Association, 1881. 100 p.

Orations and Essays of Edward John Phelps, Diplomat
and Statesman. Edit. by J. G. McCullough, with a
memoir by John W. Stewart. New York: Harper &
Bros., 1901. 475 p.

PHELPS, Vernon Lovell, 1900- . Teacher in economics
and sales promotion. Economic Officer at the State
Department 1937-52. Foreign Service Officer 1952-
58. Served in Tokyo, Bonn.

The International Economic Position of Argentina. Philadelphia: University of Pennsylvania Press, 1958.
276 p.

PHILLIPS, William, 1878-1968. In Foreign Service almost
continuously 1905-1947. Private secretary to Ambassador Choate in London 1903-05. Served in London,
Peking, State Department, Minister to the Netherlands
and Luxembourg 1920, Under-Secretary of State 1922,
Ambassador to Belgium 1924, Minister to Canada 1927-
29, Under-Secretary of State 1932, Ambassador to Italy
1936-41, Director of The Office of Strategic Services
in London 1942, Personal Representative of the President to Delhi 1942 (rank of Ambassador). Political
Advisor on General Eisenhower's staff in London 1943.
Retired in 1944. Special Assistant to Secretary of
State 1945. Member of Anglo-American Commission
on Palestine 1947. Chairman France-Siamese Commission on Conciliation 1947.

Ventures in Diplomacy. North Beverly, Mass.: Private
printing 1952. 464 p.

Massachusetts Emergency Committee on Unemployment.
William Phillips, Chairman. Boston: Rapid Press,
1932. 128 p.

PIETTE, Onesime L., 1916- . State Department official
1952-55. Foreign Service Officer 1955-67. Served in
New Delhi, Bombay and Portuguese India, State Department.

(Edited) South Asian Varia: Papers Presented at a Graduate Student Symposium, Syracuse University. Co-
edited with Richard P. Cronin. Syracuse, N.Y.:
Syracuse University, 1972. 201 p.

PIKE, Douglas Eugene, 1924- . Newspaper reporter and
editor. Radio network. United Nations in Korea.
Foreign Service Reserve Officer 1958- . United
States Information Agency. Served in Saigon, Hong
Kong, Tokyo, Taipei.
Viet Cong: The Organization and Techniques of the Na-
tional Liberation Front of South Vietnam. Cambridge:
Massachusetts Institute of Technology Press, 1966.
490 p.
War, Peace and the Viet Cong. Cambridge: Massachu-
setts Institute of Technology, 1969. 186 p.
Politics of the Viet Cong. Saigon: South China Morning
Post Publishing Co., 1968. 52 p.

PIKE, Nicholas, 1822-1905. Merchant, naturalist, scientific
research. Introduced English Sparrow into the United
States "to destroy insects." Discovered a sulphur
spray to combat grape fungus. Officer in Union forces
during Civil War. Consul at Lisbon and Oporto 1852-
57. Consul at Port Louis, Mauritius 1866-73.
Subtropical Rambles in the Land of Aphanapterix: Personal Experiences, Adventures and Wanderings in and
around the Island of Mauritius. New York: Harper
Bros., 1873. 509 p.
Fauna and Flora of Mauritius. 1873?

POINSETT, Joel Robert, 1779-1851. Politician. First
American consular and diplomatic representative in
Argentina and Chile, 1811-16. Both colies were then
working toward independence from Spain. Britain, then
at war with the United States, was suspicious of Poinsett and he finally departed for Buenos Aires disguised
as an Englishman on board a British merchant vessel.
The British opposed Poinsett at every turn in his action to encourage the rebels in both colonies, and
Poinsett's efforts eventually failed. He was appointed
the first American Minister to Mexico 1825-29. Here
he again met opposition from the British, who wanted
to keep control of ocean trade, and of the old Spaniards,
monarchists, aristocrats, Europe sympathizers. He
helped organize the York Masonic party in Mexico as
a cover for the liberal Mexicans to oppose the mon-
archistic, Catholic Scottish Rite Masonic party. Official Mexican opposition finally forced his recall to the
United States. He introduced to the United States the
flower, the poinsettia, which was named for him. He
was Secretary of War under President Jackson, 1837-41.

Notes on Mexico Made in Autumn 1822, Accompanied by
an Historical Sketch of the Revolution and Translations
of Official Reports on the Present State of That Country: by a Citizen of the United States. Philadelphia:
H. C. Carey and I. Lea, 1824. 359 p.

POMEROY, Miggs. Wife of Robert L. Pomeroy, 1926- .
Mr. Pomeroy was a Foreign Service Staff Officer,
1956-65, who was with the United States Information
Agency in Benghazi and Mogadiscio.
The Great Saharan Mouse-Hunt. with Catherine Collins.
London: Hutchinson, 1962. 199 p.
The Janus Lovers, A Novel. New York: W. W. Norton
& Co. Inc., 1966. 319 p.
The Rays of July. London: Hutchinson, 1966. 319 p.

POOLE, Dewitt Clinton, 1885-1952. Educator. Office of
Strategic Services. Foreign Service Officer 1910-30.
Served in Berlin, Paris, State Department, Moscow,
Capetown.
Democracy and the Conduct of Foreign Relations under
Modern Democratic Conditions. New Haven: Yale
University Press for the Institute of Politics, 1924.
208 p.
Papers, 1918-1952. In the State Historical Society of
Wisconsin. 12 boxes.

PORTER, Horace, 1837-1921. Union soldier, businessman,
politician, writer, orator. Ambassador to France
1897-1905.
Campaigning with Grant. New York: The Century Co.,
1897. 546 p. Edit. and with notes by Wayne C.
Temple.

PREEG, Ernest H., 1934- . Economist. Foreign Service
Officer 1961- . Served in State Department, London.
Traders and Diplomats. Washington: The Brookings In-
stitution, 1970. 320 p.

PRICE, C. Hoyt, 1918- . Statistical analyst. United Na-
tions Relief and Rehabilitation Administration 1944-45.
Foreign Service Auxiliary Officer 1946-47. Foreign
Service Officer 1947-67. Served in Berlin, Phnom
Penh, Vientiane, Foreign Service Institute, State De-
partment, Bern, Brussels (U.S. Mission to the Euro-
pean Communities).
The Problem of Germany. with Carl E. Schorske.

Introd. by Allen W. Dulles. New York: Council on
Foreign Relations, 1947. 161 p.

PRINGLE, Robert M. , 1936- . Private expert reporter
1960-62. Foreign Service Officer 1967- . Served in
Djakarta.
Rajas and Rebels: The Ibans of Sarawak Under Brooke
Rule, 1841-1942. Ithaca: Cornell University Press,
1970. 416 p. Maps and illustrations.

RADIUS, Walter A. , 1910- . Investment analyst. Institute
of Pacific Relations 1938-42. State Department officer
1942-56. Foreign Service Officer 1956-69. Foreign
Service Inspector 1956. Served in Bonn, London, National Aeronautics and Space Administration.
United States Shipping in Trans-Pacific Trade. 1922-
1938. Stanford: Stanford University Press, 1944.
204 p.

RAINE, Alice. Wife of Foreign Service Officer Philip
Raine. [Q. V.]
Eagle of Guatemala. Justo Rufino Barrios. New York:
Harcourt, Brace Inc. , 1947. 229 p.

RAINE, Philip, 1908- . Foreign Service clerk. State Department official. United States Army. Foreign Service Officer 1931-68. Served in Mexico City, São
Paulo, Rio de Janeiro, Brasilia, San José.
Paraguay. New Brunswick, N. J. : The Scarecrow Press,
1956. 443 p.

RANKIN, Karl Lott, 1898- . Near East Relief. Russia
1925-27. Commerce Department Foreign Service 1927-
39. State Department Foreign Service Officer 1939-
62. Served in Prague, Athens, Tirana, Brussels,
Luxembourg, Belgrade, Manila, State Department,
Cairo, Vienna, Canton, Hong Kong, Macao, Taipei.
Interned in Manila by Japanese January 1942-October
1943. Career Minister 1948. Minister to China
(Taipei) 1950. Ambassador to China (Taipei) 1953, to
Yugoslavia 1957-62.
China Assignment. Seattle: University of Washington
Press, 1964. 343 p.

RAVNDAL, Gabriel Bie, 1865-1946. Born in Norway,
naturalized American. Journalist, politician. Foreign
Service Officer 1898-1930. Served in Beirut, Dawson

City, in Beirut received Red Cross medal for relief of
suffering in massacres in Eastern Turkey in 1909.
Served in Constantinople, Albania, Paris, St. Nazaire,
Nantes, Zurich, Berlin.
The Origin of the Capitulations and of the Consular Insti-
tution. by the American Consul General in Constanti-
nople. Washington: Government Printing Office, 1921.
112 p.
Stories of the East-Vikings. Minneapolis: Augsburg
Publishing House, 1938. 383 p.

RAYNOLDS, David R., 1928- . Publisher, public relations.
Foreign Service Officer 1956- . Served in San Sal-
vador, Paris (NATO), State Department, Port-au-
Prince.
Rapid Development in Small Economies: The Example of
El Salvador. New York: Frederick A. Praeger,
Inc., 1967. 124 p.

REDDING, Jay Saunders, 1906- . Educator, author.
Department of State. Lecturer to India 1952.
An American in India: A Personal Report on the Indian
Dilemma and the Nature of her Conflicts. Indianapolis:
The Bobbs, Merrill Co. Inc., 1954. 277 p.
The Lonesome Road: The Story of the Negro's Part in
in America. Doubleday & Co., Inc., 1958. 355 p.
The Negro. Washington: Potomac Books, 1967. 101 p.
No Day of Triumph. Introd. by Richard Wright. New
York: Harper Bros., 1942. 342 p.
On Being a Negro in America. Indianapolis: The Bobbs,
Merrill Co. Inc., 1951. 156 p.
Stranger and Alone. A novel. New York: Harcourt,
Brace Inc., 1950. 308 p.
They Came in Chains, Americans From Africa. Phila-
delphia: J. B. Lippincott Co., 1950. 320 p.
To Make a Poet Black. Chapel Hill: University of North
Carolina Press, 1939. 142 p.

REID, John Turner, 1908- . Teacher, professor. For-
eign Service Reserve Officer 1942-70. Served in
Quito, Havana, Caracas, State Department inspector
in Germany. Served in Madrid, New Delhi, Buenos
Aires, United States Information Agency.
Modern Spain and Liberalism. Stanford: Stanford Uni-
versity Press, 1937. 236 p.
An Outline History of Spanish American Literature. with
John E. Englekirk, Irving Leonard and John Crow.

New London: Croft Educational Services, 1941. 252 p.
(Edited) An Anthology of Spanish American Literature.
Co-edit. with John E. Englekirk, Irving Leonard and
John Crow. New London: Croft Educational Services,
1947. 772 p.
Trece Ensayos Sobre Literatura Norteamericana. Cara-
cas: Tip. La Nación, 1952. 63 p.
Indian Influence in American Literature and Thought.
New Delhi: Indian Council for Cultural Relations,
1965. 77 p.

REIDY, Joseph W., 1921- . United States Army 1943-57.
Foreign Service Reserve Officer 1957-62. Served in
Rio de Janeiro, Buenos Aires.
Strategy for the Americas. New York: McGraw-Hill
Book Co., 1966. 204 p.

REINSCH, Paul Samuel, 1869-1923. Educator. Professor
at the universities of Wisconsin, Berlin and Leipzig.
Member of American delegations to several Pan Amer-
ican Conferences. Minister to China 1913-18. Died
in Shanghai 1923.
An American Diplomat in China. Garden City: Double-
day Page & Co., 1922. 396 p.
American Legislatures and Legislative Methods. New
York: The Century Co., 1907. 337 p.
Civil Government. Boston: B. H. Sanborn & Co., 1909.
258 p. This volume republished with separate State
supplements, by B. H. Sanborn & Co. in Boston, as
follows:
Ohio Supplement, 1911.
Oklahoma Supplement, 1914.
Mississippi Supplement, 1915.
North Carolina Supplement, 1915.
Washington Supplement, 1915.
Ohio Supplement, 1916.
Pennsylvania and Wisconsin Supplements, 1916.
Montana Supplement, 1917.
Colonial Administration. New York: The Macmillan Co.,
1905. 422 p.
Colonial Government: An Introduction to the Study of
Colonial Institutions. New York: The Macmillan Co.,
English Common Law in the Early American Colonies.
A Thesis Submitted For the Degree of Doctor of Phi-
losophy, University of Wisconsin. 1898. Madison:
University of Wisconsin Bulletin, 64 p.
Intellectual and Political Currents in the Far East.

Boston: Houghton Mifflin Co., 1911. 396 p.
Public International Unions; Their Work and Organization.
A Study in International Administrative Law. Boston:
Published for the World Peace Foundation by Ginn &
Co., 1911. 191 p.
(Edited) Readings on American Federal Government. Boston: Ginn & Co., 1909. 850 p.
Secret Diplomacy, How Far Can It Be Eliminated? New
York: Harcourt, Brace Inc., 1922. 231 p.
World Politics at the End of the Nineteenth Century as
Influenced by the Oriental Situation. New York: The
Macmillan Co., 1900. 366 p.
The Young Citizen's Reader. New York: B. H. Sanborn
& Co., 1909. 258 p.

REISCHAUER, Edwin Oldfather, 1910- . Educator. Fellow
of the Harvard-Yenching Institute (France, Japan,
China) 1933-38, again 1956-61. State Department
1941-61. Ambassador to Japan 1961-68.
Beyond Vietnam: The United States and Asia. New York:
Alfred A. Knopf, Inc., 1967. 242 p.
Ennin's Travels in T'Ang China. New York: The Ronald
Press Co., 1955. 341 p.
Japan, Past and Present. Foreword by Sir George Sansom. New York: Alfred A. Knopf, Inc., 1946.
192 p.
The United States and Japan. Cambridge: Harvard University Press, 1950. 357 p. Maps.
Wanted: an Asian Policy. New York: Alfred A. Knopf,
Inc., 1955. 276 p.
(Translated) Ennin 793 or 4 -864. Diary: The Record
of a Pilgrimage to China in Search of the Law. (from
the Chinese) New York: The Ronald Press Co., 1955.
454 p.
Elementary Japanese for College Students. with Serge
Elisseeff and Takehiko Yoshihashi. Cambridge: Harvard University Press for the Harvard-Yenching Institute, 1944. 3 vols.
A History of East Asian Civilization. with John K. Fairbank. For 2nd vol. add Albert Craig. Boston:
Houghton Mifflin Co., 1960-65. 2 vols.
Translations from Early Japanese Literature. with Joseph
K. Yamagawa. Cambridge: Harvard University Press
for the Harvard-Yenching Institute, 1951. 467 p.
Japan: The Story of a Nation. A totally revised, expanded version of the earlier Japan: Past and Present.
1946, listed above. New York: Alfred A. Knopf,

Inc. , 1970.   345 p.   Includes the Foreword to the
original edition by Sir George B. Sansom.

RHODES, Harold H. , 1908- . Teacher, writer. Foreign
Economic Administration 1942-44; Foreign Service
Auxiliary Officer 1944-47; Foreign Service Officer
1947-62. Served in Madrid, State Department, Rome,
The Hague, Saigon.
No "Four-Letter" Words. Biography of Olaf Taxeraas.
New York: Vantage Press, 1970. 140 p.
Not Realy Anti-, It's For You I Plead. Poems and bal-
lads. Spokane: Postal Instant Press, 1970. 56 p.

RICE, Edward Earl, 1909- . Foreign Service Officer 1935-
68. Chinese language officer. Served Peiping, Canton, Chungking, State Department, Manila, National
War College, Stuttgart, Foreign Service Inspector,
Policy Planning Staff, Deputy Assistant Secretary of
State, Hongkong and Macau. Personal rank of Minister.
MAO'S WAY. Berkeley: University of California Press,
1972. 596 p.

RICHARDSON, Norval, 1877-1940. Businessman and writer.
Foreign Service Officer 1909-24. Served in Havana,
Copenhagen, Rome, Santiago, Lisbon, Tokyo.
My Diplomatic Education. New York: Dodd, Mead &
Co. Inc. , 1923. 337 p.
The Cave Woman. New York: Charles Scribner's Sons,
1922. 268 p.
Dream Boat. Boston: Little, Brown Co. , 1929. 323 p.
Forgotten Lady. Philadelphia: J. B. Lippincott Co. ,
1937. 364 p.
George Thorne. Boston: L. C. Page & Co. , 1911.
333 p.
The Heart of Hope. New York: Dodd, Mead & Co. ,
1905. 361 p.
The Honey Pot: or, In the Garden of Lelita. Boston:
L. C. Page & Co. , 1912. 209 p.
The Lead of Honor. Boston: L. C. Page & Co. , 1910.
341 p.
Living Abroad: The Adventures of an American Family.
Philadelphia: J. B. Lippincott Co. , 1938. 320 p.
Mother of Kings. New York: Charles Scribner's Sons,
1928. 471 p.
Pagan Fire. New York: Charles Scribner's Sons, 1920.
382 p.

Pirate's Face. Boston: Little, Brown Co. , 1928. 307 p.
That Late Unpleasantness. Boston: Small, Maynard &
   Co. , 1924. 314 p.
The World Shut Out. New York: Charles Scribner's
   Sons, 1919. 305 p.

RICHES, Cromwell Adams, 1903- . Educator 1922-41;
   Commerce Department 1942-48; Foreign Service Offi-
   cer 1948-64. Board of Examiners State Department.
   Served in Washington and Beirut. With International
   Cooperation Administration and the Peace Corps.
The Unanimity Rule and the League of Nations. Baltimore:
   The Johns Hopkins University Press, 1933. 224 p.
Majority Rule in International Organization. Baltimore:
   The Johns Hopkins University Press, 1940. 322 p.

RINDEN, Robert Watland, 1914- . Foreign Service Officer
   1938-63. Chinese language officer. Served in Mon-
   treal, Hong Kong, Saigon, Port Elizabeth, Johannes-
   burg, Durban, Pretoria, Ottawa, Peiping, Mukden,
   Shanghai, Chungking, Djakarta, Taipei, State Depart-
   ment, National War College, Conakry. United States
   Information Agency.
Life and Love in the Foreign Service. with Seymour I.
   Nadler. Washington: Foreign Service Journal, 1969.
   60 illus.
The Red Flag Waves: A Guide to the Hung-ch'i p'iao
   Collection. with Roxane Witke. Berkeley: Center for
   Chinese Studies. University of California, 1968.
   160 p.

RIVES, Halle Ermine (Wheeler), 1876-1956. Wife of diplo-
   mat Post Wheeler. [Q. V.] Novelist. Served with her
   husband at Tokyo, Petrograd, Rome, Stockholm, Lon-
   don, Madrid, Rio de Janeiro, Asuncion, Tirana.
As the Heart Panteth. New York: G. W. D. Dillingham,
   1898. 237 p.
The Castaway: Three Great Men Ruined in One Year ...
   A King, A Cad and a Castaway. Illus. by Howard
   Chandler Christy. Indianapolis: The Bobbs-Merrill
   Co. Inc. , 1904. 443 p.
The Complete Book of Etiquette, With Social Forms for
   All Ages and Occasions. Illus. by Gabrielle Rosiere.
   Philadelphia: John C. Winston Co. , 1922. 514 p.
A Furnace of Earth. New York: The Camelot Co. ,
   1900. 224 p.
The Golden Barrier. New York: The Dodd, Mead &

Co. Inc., 1934. 290 p.

Hearts Courageous. Illus. by A. B. Wenzell. Indianapolis: Bowen-Merrill Co., 1902. 407 p.

The John Book. with Gabrielle and Elliot Forbush. New
York: Beechhurst Press, 1947. 304 p.

The Kingdom of Slender Swords. Foreword by Baron
Makino. Illus. by A. B. Wenzell. Indianapolis:
Bobbs-Merrill Co. Inc., 1910. 434 p.

The Magic Man. New York: Dodd, Mead & Co. Inc.,
1927. 323 p.

Satan Sanderson. Illus. by A. B. Wenzell. Indianapolis:
The Bobbs-Merrill Co. Inc., 1907. 399 p.

The Singing Wire, and Other Stories. Clarksville, Tenn.:
W. P. Titus, Printer, 1892. 98 p.

Smoking Flax. London: F. T. Neely, 1897. 232 p.

The Valiants of Virginia. Illus. by Andre Castaigne.
Indianapolis: The Bobbs-Merrill Co. Inc., 1912.
432 p.

Tales From Dickens. Illus. by Reginald B. Birch. Indianapolis: The Bobbs-Merrill Co. Inc., 1905. 473 p.

Dome of Many-Coloured Glass. with her husband, Post
Wheeler. Garden City: Doubleday & Co. Inc., 1955.
878 p.

ROBBINS, Warren M., 1923- . Secondary school teacher.
Foreign Service Staff Officer 1951-63. Served in Bonn,
Stuttgart, Vienna, Department of State, Foreign Service
Institute, United States Information Agency. Founder
and Director of the Frederick Douglass Institute of
Negro Arts and History, Washington, D.C.

African Art in American Collections. New York: Frederick A. Praeger, Publishers, 1966. 237 p.

ROBINSON, Donald Hannibal, 1906- . Foreign Service
Staff Officer 1930-34 and 1949-62. Writer 1935-45
and 1946-49. Served in Vienna, Windsor, Toronto,
Calcutta, State Department, Dusseldorf, Stuttgart,
Coblenz, Port-of-Spain, Vancouver.

The Raj. Boston: Houghton Mifflin Co., 1971. 420 p.

Plays

Title	Where produced	By whom	Year	No pages
Eastward Ho	Greenwich,	James R.	1936	120 p.

Profile	Summer theaters in Dennis, Mass. Saratoga, N. Y. Marblehead, Mass.	Richard Aldrich	1947	124 p.
Potters Notch	Manhattan College	not available	1947	136 p.
Most Likely to Succeed	Clinton, N. J.	Edward Wilson	1948	123 p.

(Also sold to Paramount Pictures, Hollywood, Calif.)

ROBINSON, Edward L., 1921- . United States Information Agency officer 1954-67. Served in Rangoon, Moulmein, Foreign Service Institute, Bonn, Frankfurt, Saigon, Phnom Penh, Bombay.
Sloth and Heathen Folly. New York: The Macmillan Co., 1972.

ROCKHILL, William Woodville, 1854-1914. In the Diplomatic Service or in the State Department most of the time from 1884-1913. Served in Peking, Seoul, Minister and Consul General to Greece, Roumania and Servia 1897-99; Minister to China 1905-09. Ambassador to Russia 1909-11, to Turkey 1911-13. He was Director of the International Bureau of American Republics 1899-1905.
Catalogue of the Tibetan Books in the Library of Congress. Manuscript on linen ledger paper. 1902.
China's Intercourse with Korea From the xvth Century to 1895. London: Lusac & Co., 1905. 60 p.
The Dalai Lamas of Lhasa and Their Relations With the Manchu Emperors of China, 1644-1908. Reprint from Poung-Pao, series 111, Vol. 1. No. 1. Leyden: Oriental Printing Office, late E. J. Brill, 1910. 104 p.
Diary of a Journey Through Mongolia and Tibet in 1891 and 1892. Washington: Smithsonian Institution, 1894.
The Land of the Lamas: Notes of a Journey Through China, Mongolia and Tibet. New York: The Century Co., 1891. 399 p.
(Translation) The Life of Buddha, and the Early History of His Order. Derived from Tibetan Works in The Bkah-Hgyur and Bstan-Hgyur. Followed by Notices on

the Early History of Tibet and Khoten. London: Trubner & Co., 1884. 273 p.

Treaties and Conventions with or Concerning China and Korea, 1894-1904. Together with Various State Papers and Documents Affecting Foreign Interest. Washington: Government Printing Office, 1904. 555 p.

(Edited) Journey to Lhasa and Central Tibet by Sarat Chandra Das, Rai Bahadur. London: J. Murray, 1902. 285 p.

Ma, Shao-Yun. Tibet: A Geographical, Ethnological, and Historical Sketch Derived from Chinese Sources. Maps, plans, etc. Peking: Wen Tien Ko Shuchuang, 1939. 133 p. Title and imprint in Chinese.

ROHDE, Ruth (Bryan) Owen (Mrs.) See Ruth Bryan Owen.

ROLAND, Joseph Morgan, 1915- . State Department and Foreign Service Officer 1939- . Served in Vienna, State Department, Bonn, Berlin, Ankara, Aukland.

National Socialism: Basic Principles, Their Application by the Nazi Party's Foreign Organization, and the Use of Germans Abroad for Nazi Aims. Co-author, with Howard Trivers, Raymond E. Murphy and Francis B. Stevens. Washington: Government Printing Office, State Department Publication #1864. 1943. 510 p.

ROOSEVELT, Anna Eleanor, 1887-1962. Wife of President Franklin Delano Roosevelt. She was the United States Representative to the United Nations General Assembly 1945-61. Author, lecturer.

Autobiography. New York: Harper & Row, 1961. 454 p.

Book of Commonsense Etiquette. New York: The Macmillan Co., 1962. 591 p.

Christmas, A Story. Illus. by Fritz Kredel. New York: Alfred A. Knopf & Co., 1940. 42 p.

Eleanor Roosevelt's Christmas Book, Including Her Own Description of Christmas at Hyde Park and the White House, Together with her Original Story "Christmas," and Her Favorite Selections of Prose and Verse Devoted to the Christmas Season. New York: Dodd, Mead & Co. Inc., 1963. 338 p.

If You Ask Me. New York: D. Appleton-Century, Inc., 1946. 156 p. From the Question and Answer Department of the Ladies' Home Journal.

India and the Awakening East. New York: Harper Bros., 1953. 237 p.

It's Up To the Women. New York: Fredrick A. Stokes

Co., 1933. 262 p.
It Seems to Me. New York: W. W. Norton & Co., Inc.,
1954. 188 p.
Ladies of Courage. with Lorena A. Hickok. New York:
G. P. Putnam's Sons, 1954. 312 p.
The Lady of the White House, an Autobiography. London:
Hutchinson & Co., 1938. 287 p. New York: Harper
& Bros. This is My Story.
The Moral Basis of Democracy. New York: Howell,
Soskin & Co., 1940. 82 p.
My Days. New York: Dodge Publishing Co., 1938.
254 p.
On My Own. New York: Harper & Bros., 1958. 241 p.
Partners: The United Nations and Youth. with Helen
Ferris. Garden City: Doubleday & Co. Inc., 1950.
206 p.
This is America. with Frances Cooke MacGregor. New
York: G. P. Putnam's Sons, 1942. 191 p.
This I Remember. (about Franklin Delano Roosevelt)
New York: Harper & Bros., 1949. 387 p.
This Is My Story. London: Harper & Bros., 1937.
365 p.
This Troubled World. New York: Kinsey & Co., 1938.
47 p.
Tomorrow Is Now. New York: Harper & Row, 1963.
139 p.
A Trip to Washington with Bobby and Betty. New York:
Dodd Publishing Co., 1935. 91 p.
U. N. Today and Tomorrow. with William DeWitt. New
York: Harper & Bros., 1953. 236 p.
When You Grow Up to Vote. Illus. by Manning deV.
Lee. Boston: Houghton Mifflin Co., 1932. 64 p.
You Learn By Living. New York: Harper & Bros.,
1960. 211 p.
Your Teens and Mine. with Helen Ferris. Garden City:
Doubleday & Co. Inc., 1961. 189 p.
Growing Toward Peace. with Regina Tor. New York:
Random House, Inc., 1960. 83 p.

ROOSEVELT, Nicholas, 1893-1965. Editorial writer, au-
thor, foreign correspondent. Attaché at Paris 1914-
16; Minister to Hungary 1930-33. Attaché to the
Peace Commission 1919.
America and England? New York: J. Cape & H. Smith,
1930. 254 p.
Creative Cooking. Introd. by Dione Lucas. N. Y.: Harper
Bros., 1956. 234 p.

A Front Row Seat. Autobiographical. Norman, Okla. :
University of Oklahoma Press, 1953. 304 p.
Good Cooking. New York: Harper & Bros. , 1959.
340 p.
A New Birth of Freedom. New York: Charles Scribner's
Sons, 1938. 274 p.
The Philippines: A Treasure and a Problem. New York:
J. H. Sears & Co. , 1926. 315 p.
The Restless Pacific. New York: Charles Scribner's
Sons, 1928. 219 p. Illus. maps.
Theodore Roosevelt: The Man as I Knew Him. New
York: Dodd, Mead & Co. Inc. , 1967. 205 p.
The Townsend Plan: Taxing for Sixty Days. Introd. by
Lewis W. Douglas. Garden City: Doubleday, Doran
Co. Inc. , 1936. 81 p.
Venezuela's Place in the Sun, A Modernizing and Pioneer-
ing Country. New York: Round Table Press Inc. ,
1940. 87 p.
Wanted: Good Neighbors: The Need for Closer Ties with
Latin America. New York: The National Foreign
Trade Council, Inc. , 1939. 48 p.
Conservation: Now or Never. New York: Dodd, Mead
& Co. Inc. , 1970. 238 p.

ROUDYBUSH, Alexandra (Brown). Wife of Foreign Service
Staff officer Franklin Roudybush. [Q. V.]
A Capital Crime. New York: Doubleday & Co. Inc. ,
1969. 192 p. A Crime Club Book.
Before the Ball Was Over. New York: Doubleday & Co.
Inc. , 1965. 190 p. A Crime Club Book.
Death of a Moral Person. New York: Doubleday & Co.
Inc. , 1967. 215 p. A Crime Club Book.
The House of the Cat. New York: Doubleday & Co.
Inc. , 1972. 191 p. A Crime Club Book.
A Sybaritic Death. New York: Doubleday & Co. Inc. ,
1972. 180 p. A Crime Club Book.
Incident at Darjeeling. New York: Doubleday & Co. Inc. ,
1972. A Crime Club Book.

ROUDYBUSH, Franklin, 1906- . Dean of the Foreign Service School 1931-42. State Department official 1945-
48; Foreign Service Staff officer 1948-57. Served in
Department of State, Strasbourg, Lahore, Dublin,
United States Information Agency.
An Analysis of the Educational Background and Experience
of the United States Foreign Service Officers. Washington: George Washington University Press, 1944.

71 p. Loose leaf, reproduced from typewritten copy
of Master's thesis.
World Diplomatic List. Washington: Government Printing
Office, 1943. 350 p.
Foreign Service Training. A comparative study of foreign
service training in France, Germany, Russia, Brazil,
England, Uruguay, Japan and other countries. Besan-
çon, France: Press Comptoise, 1955. 279 p.
La Situation Actuelle du Capitalism Occidental. (in
French) Paris: Imprimerie St. Ambroise, 1960. 90 p.
XX Century. Paris: Edition SEDEC, 1972. 110 p.
Diplomacy and Art. Paris: Edition SEDEC, 1971. 85 p.
Diplomatic Language. Basle, Switzerland: SATZ, AG.
1972. 90 p.

ROWAN, Carl Thomas, 1925- . News correspondent 1948-
61. Deputy Assistant Secretary of State for public affairs 1961; Ambassador to Finland 1963-65.
Go South Tomorrow. New York: Random House, 1957.
246 p.
The Pitiful and the Proud. New York: Random House,
1956. 432 p.
South of Freedom. New York: Alfred A. Knopf, 1952.
270 p.
Wait Till Next Year: the Life Story of Jackie Robinson.
with Jackie Robinson. New York: Random House,
1960. 339 p.

RUFFIN, John Demosthenes N. , 1869- . Consul at Asun-
cion, Paraguay, 1897-1907.
Anna Wiseman (The Professor's Beautiful Daughter).
London: Kent Garden Printing & Publishing Co. , 1931.
198 p.
The Celebrated Crown Trial. (Over a Thousand Members
on the Jury). London: Sir. I. Pitman & Sons, Ltd. ,
1932. 2 vols.
Forms of Oratorical Expression and Their Delivery: or:
Logic and Eloquence Illustrated. New York: Drucker
Printing Co. Inc. , 1920. 475 p.
The Rhetorlogue: or, Study of the Rhetor or Orator.
Revised and enlarged form of Forms of Oratorical Ex-
pression. New York: E. S. Werner & Co. , 1922.
508 p.
Great Logicians. New York: E. S. Werner & Co. ,
1926. 151 p.
Oratorical Style, Its Art and Science. by Demosthenes
(pseud.). London: Simpkin, Marshall, Hamilton,
Kent & Co. Ltd. , 1923. 99 p.

RUSH, Richard, 1780-1859. Comptroller of the United
    States Treasury, Attorney General, Acting Secretary
    of State, Minister to Great Britain 1817-25, Secretary
    of the Treasury, Minister to France 1847-49.
A Narrative of a Residence at the Court of London from
    1817-1825. Philadelphia: Carey, Lea & Blanchard,
    1833. 460 p.
Washington in Domestic Life. Compiled from letters
    written by Washington to his private secretary in 1790-
    98. Philadelphia: J. B. Lippincott & Co., 1857.
    85 p.
Occasional Productions, Political, Diplomatic and Mis-
    cellaneous. Philadelphia: J. B. Lippincott & Co.,
    1860. 535 p.
American Jurisprudence, Written and Published at Wash-
    ington, being a Few Reflections Suggested on Reading
    "Wheaton on Captures." Washington: 1815. 52 p.
Letter and Accompanying Documents from the Honorable
    Richard Rush to Joseph Gales, Esq. Mayor of the City
    of Washington: Respecting the Loan of a Million and
    a Half Dollars, Negotiated by the Former, in Europe,
    For the Said City and the Towns of Georgetown and
    Alexandria, Under the Authority of an Act of Congress
    of the United States, Passed on the 24th of May, 1828.
    Published by Order of the Corporation of the City of
    Washington. Washington: Printed by P. Force, 1830.
    171 p.
A Letter to Albert Gallatin, on the French Claims to the
    Newfoundland Fisheries. Written October 1, 1822, by
    Richard Rush. Brooklyn Historical Printing Club,
    1890. 40 p. (250 copies printed.)
Remarks on the Loan of a Million and a Half Dollars
    Proposed to Be Raised by the City of Washington and
    the Towns of Georgetown and Alexandria. London:
    (no publisher listed), 1829. 45 p.
Verslag en Bylagen Betrekkelijk de Leeing van 1,500,000
    Dollars Ten Behoeve van de Steden Washington, George-
    town en Alexandria, Krachtens Eene Acte van Het
    Congres der Vereenigte Staten van Noord-Amerika,
    Gepasseerd 24 Mei 1828. Uitgegevan op Last der
    Stedelijke Regering van Washington. I. Verslag.
    Amsterdam: P. den Hengst & Soon, 1830. 80 p.

RUSSELL, Beatrice (Crowley). Wife of H. Earle Russell,
    Jr., 1923-71, Foreign Service Officer 1950-71. He
    served at Addis Ababa, Tunis, Beirut, Jidda, State
    Department, National War College, Rabat.

Living in State. Preface by Robert McClintock. New
    York: David McKay Co. , Inc. , 1959. 272 p.

RUSSELL, Charles Wells, 1856-1927. Legal official of
    various Federal departments 1886-1909. Minister to
    Persia 1909-14.
Iranian Rest and Other Lyrics. Teheran: Pharos, 1912.
    37 p.
Poems. Washington: Press of Gibson Bros. , Inc. ,
    1914. 125 p.
Poems. New York: The Neale Publishing Co. , 1921.
    183 p.
The Secret Place and Other Poems. Washington: Press
    of the Gibson Bros. , Inc. , 1911. 48 p.
(Edited) Mosby's Memoirs. Boston: Little, Brown &
    Co. , 1917. 414 p.

RUSSELL, William. Clerk in Embassy, Berlin, 1937-40.
    Berlin Embassy. New York: E. P. Dutton & Co. , Inc. ,
    1941. 307 p.

SANDERS, Irwin Taylor, 1909- . Professor American
    College in Sofia, Bulgaria, professor in Alabama Col-
    lege and Univ. of Kentucky. Foreign Service Auxiliary
    Officer (Agricultural Attaché) Belgrade 1945-46.
Rainbow in the Rock: The People of Rural Greece.
    Cambridge: Harvard University Press, 1962. 363 p.
Alabama Rural Communities: a Study of Chilton County.
    with Douglas Ensminger. Montevallo, Alabama: Ala-
    bama College in cooperation with Bureau of Agricultural
    Economics, U. S. Department of Agriculture, 1940.
    80 p.
Balkan Village. Lexington: University of Kentucky Press,
    1949. 291 p.
Bridges to Understanding: International Programs of
    American Colleges and Universities. with Jennifer C.
    Ward. Commentary by James A. Perkins. New
    York: McGraw-Hill Book Co. , 1970. 285 p.
(Edited) Collectivization of Agriculture in Eastern Europe.
    by Enno E. Kraebe and others. Lexington: University
    of Kentucky Press, 1958. 214 p.
The Community: An Introduction to a Social System.
    New York: Ronald Press Co. , 1958. 431 p.
Making Good Communities Better: a Handbook for Civic-
    Minded Men and Women. with selected guidepost by
    seventeen authorities. Lexington: University of Ken-
    tucky Press, 1950. 174 p.

(Edited) Societies Around the World, as Interpreted by
Anthropology, Geography and Sociology. Source Book.
Prepared by C. Arnold Anderson and others. Lexing-
ton: University of Kentucky Press, 1948. 2 vols.
New York: Dryden Press, 1956. 811 p.

SANDS, William Franklin, 1874-1946. Advisor to Emperor
of Korea 1900-05. Diplomatic Service 1896-1900,
1905-10, 1916-17. Served in Tokyo, Seoul, Panama,
Guatemala, Mexico City, Minister to Guatemala 1909-
1910, Special Assistant to Embassy Petrograd 1916-
17.
Our Jungle Diplomacy. with Joseph M. Lalley. Chapel
Hill: University of North Carolina Press, 1944.
250 p.
Undiplomatic Memories: The Far East 1896-1904. New
York: Whittlesey House, McGraw-Hill Book Co.,
1930. 238 p.

SANFORD, Henry Shelton, 1823-1891. Lawyer, businessman, diplomat. Attaché Legation St. Petersburg 1847,
Acting Secretary Legation Frankfort 1848, Secretary
Legation Paris 1849-54, Minister Resident Legation
Belgium 1861-69. Associate Delegate at Conference
of Berlin 1884-85. Associate Delegate Brussels in
1890 to sign multi-lateral treaty regarding slave traffic
and traffic in firearms and liquor in Africa.
The Different Systems of Penal Codes in Europe: Also
a Report on the Administrative Changes in France,
Since the Revolution of 1848. Washington: B. Tucker,
Senate printer, 1854. 404 p. This was also published
as Message From the President of the United States,
Communicating, in compliance with a Resolution of the
Senate, A Letter from H. S. Sanford, Late Chargé
d'Affaires at Paris, on the Different Systems of Penal
Codes in Europe, Etc. Etc. Washington: 1854. 390 p.
Papers, 1769-1901. 60 ft. 50,000 items. In the Gen-
eral Sanford Memorial Library, Sanford, Florida.
Microfilmed by the Tennessee State Library and Ar-
chives at Nashville, Tennessee. A register of the
Sanford Papers may be obtained from the Tennessee
State Library.

SANGER, Richard Harlakenden, 1905- . Writer, reporter.
Board of Economic Warfare and Foreign Economic
Administration, Foreign Service Officer, 1941- .
Served in London, Algiers, State Department, Yemen,

Saudi Arabia, Beirut, Amman.
The Arabian Peninsula. Ithaca: Cornell University
Press, 1954. 295 p.
Insurgent Era: New Patterns of Political, Economic and
Social Revolution. Washington: Potomac Books, 1967.
231 p.
Where the Jordan Flows. Washington: Middle East In-
stitute, 1963. 397 p.

SANNEBECK, Norvelle Harrison, 1909- . State Depart-
ment and Foreign Service Officer 1930-42, 1945-54
and 1955-60. Served in State Department, New Delhi,
Karachi, Santiago. Accompanied President Eisenhower
on his Latin American and Far Eastern trips.
Everything You Ever Wanted to Know About Living in
Mexico. Based on replies from questionnaires sent to
over 200 Americans residing in Mexico. Anderson,
South Carolina: Broke House (Grosset & Dunlap, New
York, distributor), 1970. 250 p.

SAWYER, Charles, 1887- . Lawyer. Ambassador to Bel-
gium and Minister to Luxembourg 1944-45.
Concerns of a Conservative Democrat. Foreword by
John Wesley Snyder and Dean Acheson. Notes by
Eugene P. Trani. Carbondale: Southern Illinois Uni-
versity Press, 1968. 399 p.

SAYRE, Francis Bowes, 1885-1972. Lawyer, teacher, public official. Jurisconsultant to Siam 1923-30; Minister
to Siam 1925; Assistant Secretary of State 1933-39;
High Commissioner to the Philippines 1939-42, escaped
from Corregidor by submarine 1942; Ambassador to
the United Nations Trusteeship Council 1949-52.
Experiments in International Administration. New York:
Harper & Bros., 1919. 200 p.
The Advancement of Dependent People: The United Nations and Non-Self-Governing Territories. Documentary
material. New York: Carnegie Endowment for International Peace, Division of Intercourse and Education,
1947. 782 p.
America Must Act. Boston: London World Peace Foundation, 1936. 80 p.
Glad Adventure. New York: The Macmillan Co., 1957.
356 p. [An autobiography.]
The Protection of American Export Trade. Lectures delivered at Westminister College, Fulton, Mo. in 1939.
Chicago: University of Chicago Press, 1940. 93 p.

The Way Foreward: The American Trade Agreements
Program. New York: The Macmillan Co., 1939.
230 p.
(Edited) Siam: Treaties With Foreign Powers, 1920-
1927. Edited by Phya Kalyan Maitri Francis Bowes
Sayre, Jurisconsultant to the Ministry of Foreign Affairs. Published by order of the Royal Siamese Government, H. H. Prince Traidos Prabandh, Minister
for Foreign Affairs. Norwood, Mass.: Plimpton
Press, 1928. 280 p.

SCHOENHOF, Jacob, 1839-1903. Economist. Born in Germany. Came to United States in 1861. Consul at
Tunstall (England) 1885. Confidential Agent of Secretary of State Thomas F. Bayard, and studied industrial
conditions in Great Britain, France and Germany.
The Industrial Situation and the Question of Wages. A
Study in Social Physiology. New York: G. P. Put-
nam's Sons, 1885. 157 p.
Ueber Die Volkswirtschaftlichen Fragen in den Vereinigten
Staaten. Vortrag, Gehalten vor dem Deutschen Ge-
sellif-Wissen-Schaftlichen Vereine von New York, am
16 Mai 1876. New York: E. Steiger & Co., 1882.
54 p.
The Destructive Influence of the Tariff upon Manufacture
and Commerce and the Figures and the Facts Relating
Thereto. New York: G. P. Putnam's Sons, for the
New York Free-Trade Club, 1883. 88 p.
Technical Education in Europe. First Part: Industrial
Education in France. Washington: Government Print-
ing Office, 1888. 136 p.
The Economy of High Wages, an Inquiry into the Cause
of High Wages and Their Effect on Methods and Cost
of Production. Introd. by Thomas F. Bayard. New
York: G. P. Putnam's Sons, 1892. 414 p.
A History of Money and Prices: Being an Inquiry into
Their Relations from the Thirteenth Century to the
Present Time. New York: G. P. Putnam's Sons,
1896. 352 p.

SCHOENRICH, Edwin, 1895- . Teacher 1918-22. Tariff
Commission 1922-24. Foreign Service Officer 1924-
48. Served in Valparaiso, La Paz, Sarnia, Mazatlan,
Santiago (Cuba), Ottawa, Asunción, Washington, Cal-
cutta.
Concise Charted Spanish Grammar, with Exercises and
Vocabularies. New York: N. E. H. Hubbard & Co.,
1942. 252 p.

SCHURMAN, Jacob Gould, 1854-1942. Born in Canada. Naturalized. Educator. President of Cornell University. Minister to Greece and Montenegro 1912-13, to China 1921-25, to Germany 1925-30.

Agnosticism and Religion. New York: Charles Scribner's Sons, 1896. 181 p.

The Balkan Wars, 1912-1913. Princeton: Princeton University Press, 1914. 140 p.

The Ethical Import of Darwinism. New York: Charles Scribner's Sons, 1887. 264 p.

Philippines Affairs: In Retrospect and Outlook. An address. New York: Charles Scribner's Sons, 1902. 109 p.

SCHURZ, Carl, 1829-1906. Born in Germany. Fled Germany for political reasons. Entered the United States in 1852. Union soldier, orator, Senator, Secretary of Interior, Minister to Spain 1861-62.

Schurz Papers, 1841-1906. 23 items and 4 boxes. In the State Historical Society of Wisconsin collections.

Speeches, Correspondence and Political Papers of Carl Schurz. Edit. by Frederic Bancroft. 1913. 6 vols. Republished New York: Negro Universities Press, 1969. 6 vols.

Intimate Letters of Carl Schurz, 1841-1869. Translated and Edited by Joseph Schafer. Madison: State Historical Society of Wisconsin, 1928. 491 p.

Autobiography: An Abridgement in One Volume by Wayne Andrews. Introd. by Allen Nevins. New York: Charles Scribner's Sons, 1961. 331 p.

The Reminiscences of Carl Schurz. New York: The McClure Co., 1907-08. 3 vols.

Eulogy on Charles Sumner. Boston: Lea & Shepard, 1874. 87 p.

Charles Sumner, an Essay. Edit. by Arthur Reed Hogue. Urbana: University of Illinois Press, 1951. 152 p.

Life of Henry Clay. Boston: Houghton Mifflin & Co., 1887. 2 vols.

Abraham Lincoln, an Essay. Boston: Houghton Mifflin & Co., 1891. 117 p.

America and Europe: A Study of International Relations. with David A. Wells and Edward J. Phelps. New York: G. P. Putnam's Sons, 1896. 128 p.

Leberserinnerungen. (Recollections of Life) Berlin: G. Reimer, 1906-12. vols.

Als Amerika Noch Jung War, Leberserinnerungen Aus den Jahren 1852-1869, Herausgegeben von Ernst Ludwig

Werther. (A Young America: Recollections of Life in the years 1852-1869.) Ebenhausen bei Munchen, W. Langewiesche-Brandt, 1941. 135 p.
Lebenserinnerungen, Bearb. von S. v. Radecki. (Recollections of Life) Zurich: Connett & Huber, 1948. 576 p.
Aus den Lebenserinnerunger eines Achtundvierzigers. Neu Erzahlt und Bearb. von S. Nestriepke und R. Ilgner. (Recollections of Life of a Man of 48, Retold new and edited by--) Berlin: Gebr. Weiss, 1948. 234 p.
Vormarz in Deutschland: Erinnerunger, Briefe, Hrag. von Herbert Ponicke. (Before 1848 in Germany. Recollections and letters edit. by) Munchen: Nymphenburger Verlagshandlung, 1948. 170 p.
Flucht in die Enttauschung; aus den Lebenserinnerungen des Deutsch-amerikaners Carl Schurz. Bearb. mit einem Vor- und Nachwort von Franz Fuhmann. 1. Aufl. Berlin: Verlag der Nation, 1952. 303 p. (Escape into Disillusion. Recollections of the German-American Carl Schurz. Edit. with preface and epilogue by Franz Fuhmann.)
Flucht aus dem Spandauer Zuchthaus. Mit Einer Einleitung von Gerhart Eisler. (Escape out of the Prison of Spandau, with Introduction by Herhart Eisler.) Berlin: Das Neue Berlin, 1955. 96 p.
Die Briefe von Carl Schurz an Gottfried Kinkel. Eingeleitet und hrag. von Eberhard Kessel. (The Letters of Carl Schurz to Gottfried Kinkel. Introd. and also published by Eberhard Kessel.) Heidelberg: C. Winter, 1965. 159 p.
Abraham Lincoln, by Carl Schurz. The Gettysburg Speech and Other Papers by Abraham Lincoln. Together with Testimonies by Emerson, Whittier, Holmes, and Lowell, and a Biographical Sketch of Carl Schurz. New York: Houghton Mifflin Co., 1919. 91 p.

SCHURZ, William Lytle, 1886-1962. Trade Commissioner in Paraguay and Bolivia 1919-20; Commercial Attaché in Rio de Janeiro 1920-26; Chief of crude rubber survey in Amazon valley, for U.S. Commerce Department 1923-24; Economic Advisor to Cuba 1926-27; private business 1928-32; National Recovery Administration 1933-35; Social Security Board 1936-41; State Department 1941-46.
American Foreign Affairs: a Guide to International Affairs. New York: E. P. Dutton Co., 1959. 265 p.

Brazil, the Infinite Country. New York: E. P. Dutton
Co., 1961. 346 p.
Latin America, a Descriptive Survey. New York: E. P.
Dutton Co., 1941. 378 p.
Rubber Production in the Amazon Valley. with O. D.
Hargis, C. F. Marbut and C. B. Manifold. Washing-
ton: Government Printing Office, 1925. 365 p.
Maps, tables, diagrams.
The Social Security Act in Operation: a Practical Guide
to the Federal and Federal-State Social Security Pro-
grams. with Birchard E. Wyatt and William H. Wan-
del. Washington: Graphic Arts Press, Inc., 1937.
382 p.
This New World: the Civilization of Latin America. Il-
lus. by Carl Folke Sahlin. New York: E. P. Dutton
Co., 1954. 429 p.
The Manila Galleon. Illus. with maps. New York: E.
P. Dutton Co., 1939. 453 p.

SCHUYLER, Eugene, 1840-1890. Scholar and diplomat.
Consul in Moscow 1867-69, at Revel. Secretary at
St. Petersburg. Secretary and Consul General at
Constantinople 1870-78; Consul at Birmingham 1878;
Consul General at Rome 1879; Minister Resident to
Rumania 1880; Minister Resident and Consul General
to Greece, Rumania and Serbia 1882-84; Minister Resi-
dent to Egypt 1889-90.
American Diplomacy and the Furtherance of Commerce.
New York: Charles Scribner's Sons, 1886. 469 p.
Italian Influences. New York: Charles Scribner's Sons,
1901. 435 p.
Passages from the Life of Peter The Great. London:
Sampson, Low, Marston, Searle & Rivington, 1881.
128 p.
Peter The Great, Emperor of Russia, A Study of Histori-
cal Biography. New York: Charles Scribner's Sons,
1884. 2 vols. Fronts, illus., ports., 1 fold, geneol-
ogy, map.
Selected Essays: with a Memoir by Evelyn Schuyler
Schaeffner. New York: Charles Scribner's Sons,
1901. 364 p. Includes The Minnesota Heir of a Ser-
bian Kingdom.
Turkestan: Notes of a Journey in Russian Turkistan,
Khokand, Bukhara, and Kuldja. New York: Scribner's,
Armstrong, 1876. 2 vols. Ports., plates, etc.
(Translated) The Cossacks. by Tolstoi.
(Translated) Fathers and Sons. by Turgenev, "with the

approval of the author. "
The Schuyler Collection was presented by him to the
Cornell Libraries.

SCIDMORE, George Hawthorne, 1854-1922. Lawyer. Con-
sular clerk and Consular Officer 1876-1922. Served
in Liverpool. Dunfermline. Osaka. Hiogo, Shanghai,
Kanagawa, Fiji Islands, Yokohama, Tokyo, Nagasaki,
Kobe, Seoul.
A Digest of Leading Cases Decided in the United States
Consular Court at Kanagawa, Japan. Relating to Con-
sular Court jurisdiction in Japan. Yokohama: R.
Meiklejohn & Co., Printers, 1882. 34 p.
Outline Lectures on the History, Organization, Jurisdic-
tion, and Practice of the Ministerial and Consular
Courts of the United States of America in Japan.
Tokyo: Igirisu Horitsu Gakko, 1887. 245 p.

SCRUGGS, William Lindsay, 1836-1912. Author, editor.
Minister to Colombia 1872-76, Consul at Chin Kiang
1876, at Canton 1882, Minister to Venezuela 1889-93.
The Venezuelan Question. British Aggressions in Venezuela, or the Monroe Doctrine on Trial; Lord Salisbury's Mistakes: Fallacies of the British "Blue Book"
on the Disputed Boundary. Comprises three papers,
each of which was previously published separately.
Atlanta, Ga. : The Franklin Printing & Publishing Co.,
1896. 91 p. Map.
Case of Venezuela. Brief Concerning the Question of
Boundary Between Venezuela and British Guiana. Sub-
mitted to the tribunal of arbitration constituted in con-
formity with treaty of February 2, 1897. Atlanta,
Ga. : The Franklin Printing and Publishing Co., 1898.
236 p.
The Colombian and Venezuelan Republics, with Notes on
Other Parts of Central and South America. Boston:
Little, Brown & Co., 1900. 350 p. Maps and illus.
Also in 1905. The 1905 edition has an added chapter
on the Panama Canal. 380 p.
Before the Venezuela Boundary Commission. Brief for
Venezuela. First Part: Introduction and Summary.
Note on the Schomburgk Line. Rev. ed. Sept. 1896.
U. S. Commission to investigate and report upon the
true divisional line between Venezuela and British
Guiana. 72 p.

SEBALD, William Joseph, 1901- . United States Navy

1918-30, and 1942-45. Japan language officer. Practiced law in Japan 1933-41. Foreign Service Auxiliary and Foreign Service Officer 1945-62. With Supreme Commander Allied Powers in Tokyo, rank of Ambassador 1950. Ambassador to Burma 1952. Deputy Assistant Secretary of State for Far Eastern Affairs 1954. Career Minister 1956. Ambassador to Australia 1957-62.

With Macarthur in Japan - A Personal History of the Occupation. with Russell Brines. New York: W. W. Norton & Co., 1965. 318 p. Semiautobiographical. Japanese edition under the title Nihon Senryo Gaiko no Shiso.

Japan: Prospects, Options and Opportunities. with C. Nelson Spinks. Washington: American Enterprise Institute for Public Policy Research, 1967. 129 p.

(Translation) The Criminal Code of Japan. Annotated. Kobe: Japan Chronicle Press, 1936. 287 p. With key extracts of relevant digests of decisions rendered by the Supreme Court of Japan.

(Translation) A Selection of Japan's Emergency Legislation. Kobe: Japan Chronicle Press, 1937. 177 p. These regulations were designed to place full control of the national economy into the hands of the Government preparatory to war in China and Pearl Harbor.

(Translation) The Principal Tax Laws of Japan. Kobe: Japan Chronicle Press, 1938. 230 p.

(Translation) The Commercial Code of Japan. United States Army Civil Affairs Handbook. Washington: Government Printing Office, 1945. 140 p. Originally completed the day before Pearl Harbor, but put away during the war and resurrected for the United States Military Government use.

(Translation) The Civil Code of Japan. Kobe, Japan: J. L. Thompson & Co., 1934. 351 p.

SEDGWICK, Theodore, 1811-1859. Author, lawyer. Attaché at Paris 1833-34.

A Treatise on the Measure of Damages, or, an Inquiry into the Principles which Govern the Amount of Pecuniary Compensation Awarded by Courts of Justice. New York: J. S. Voorhies, 1847. 600 p.

A Treatise on the Rules which Govern Interpretation and Application of Statutory and Constitutional Law. New York: J. S. Voorhies, 1857. 712 p. Also with additional notes by John Norton Pomeroy, New York: Baker, Voorhies & Co., 1874.

What Is A Monopoly? or, Some Considerations Upon the
Subject of Corporations and Currency. By a Citizen
of New York. New York: G. P. Scott & Co., 1835.
40 p.

A Memoir of the Life of William Livingston, Member of
Congress in 1774, 1775, 1776; Delegate to the Federal
Convention in 1787, and Governor of the State of New
Jersey from 1776 to 1790. With Extracts from his
Correspondence, and Notices to Various Members of
his Family. New York: J. & J. Harper, 1833. 449 p.

A Statement of Facts in Relation to the Delays and Ar-
rears of Business in the Court of Chancery of the State
of New York, With some Suggestions for a Change in
the Organization. New York: A. S. Gould, printer,
1838. 80 p.

Thoughts On the Proposed Annexation of Texas to the
United States. First published in the New York Evening
Post, under the signature of "Veto." New York:
Printed by D. Fanshaw. 55 p. Also with the address
of Albert Gallatin, delivered at the Tabernacle meeting
held on the 24th of April, 1844.

(Edited) A Collection of the Political Writings of William
Leggett. 1840. 2 vols.

SERVICE, John Stewart, 1909- . Born in China of American parents. Chinese language officer. Foreign Service Officer 1933-52. Served in Yunnanfu, Peiping,
Shanghai, Nanking, Chungking, Kunming, Political Advisor on staff of General Joseph W. Stilwell in the
Burma-India Theater in World War II, also Political
Advisor on staff of the Supreme Commander Allied
Forces, Tokyo. Wellington, Calcutta, New Delhi.
Forced out of the Service in the famous political attack
against the State Department and the Foreign Service
by Senator Joseph R. McCarthy 1951-52. Finally
cleared by a unanimous decision of the Supreme Court
of the United States in 1957.

Amerasia Papers: Some Problems in the History of United
States-China Relations. Berkeley: University of California Press, 1971. 215 p.

SEWARD, George Fredrick, 1840-1910. American Consul at
Shanghai 1861, Consul General 1863-76. Minister to
Peking 1876-80. Special Agent to Korea 1868.

Chinese Immigration in its Social and Economic Aspects.
New York: Charles Scribner's Sons, 1881. 420 p.

The United States Consulates in China. A Letter with

Enclosures of the Consul General in China to the Secretary of State. Washington: Printed for private circulation, 1867. 74 p.

SHALER, William, 1778?-1833. Sea captain, author. Consul and Agent for Commerce and Seamen at Havana
1810-12. Joint Commissioner with Stephen Decatur,
1815-20, to negotiate peace with Algiers. Remained in
Algiers 12 years to 1828. Consul at Havana 1830-33.
Journal of a Voyage Between China and the Northwestern
Coast of America, Made in 1804. Philadelphia: 1808.
175 p. Republished as Journal of a Voyage Between
China and the Northwestern Coast of America, Made in
1804 by William Shaler. Introd. by Lindley Bynum.
Illus. by Ruth Saunders. Claremont, Calif.: Saunders
Studio Press, 1935. 700 copies printed by permission
of the Huntington Library, San Marino, California.
Sketches of Algiers, Political, Historical, and Civil: Containing An Account of the Geography, Population, Government, Revenues, Commerce, Agriculture, Arts,
Civil Institutions, Tribes, Manners, Languages and Recent Political History of That Country. Boston: Cum-
mings, Hilliard & Co., 1826. 310 p.

SHARP, William Graves, 1859-1922. Lawyer, Congressman,
manufacturer. Ambassador to France 1914-19.
The War Memoirs of William Graves Sharp, American
Ambassador to France, 1914-1919. Edit. with a bio-
graphical introd. and notes by Warrington Dawson, and
with a preface by Marshall Joffre. London: Constable
& Co., 1931. 431 p.
Le Secours Americain en France (American Aid in France.)
(Addresses at the presentation to the people of the
United States of a collection of drawings by French
artists and autographs of French authors.) Paris: F.
Alcan, 1915. 59 p.

SHAW, Samuel, 1754-1794. First American Consul in Can-
ton, China.
The Journals of Major Samuel Shaw, the First American
Consul at Canton. With a Life of the Author by Josiah
Quincy. Boston: Wm. Crosby and H. P. Nichols,
1847. 360 p.

SHEPARD, Charles Otis, 1840-1928. First American consul
in Yedo (Tokyo) 1868-74.
Tales from McClures' Magazine. Being true stories of

camp and battlefield, war stories, one of which is In a
Bowery Regiment.   New York: Doubleday & McClure
Co. , 1898.   193 p.

SHERRILL, Charles Hitchcock, Jr. , 1867-1936.   Lawyer,
author, Minister to Argentina 1909-11, Ambassador to
Turkey 1932-33.
The Descendants of Samuel Sherrill, of Easthampton, Long
   Island, New York. by Charles H. Sherrill, Jr.   New
   York: 1894. 132 p.
The Sherrill Genealogy: The Descendents of Samuel Sher-
   rill of Easthampton, Long Island, New York.   Revised
   edition, compiled and edit. by Louis Effingham de
   Forest, New Haven: Printed by Tuttle, Morehouse &
   Taylor Co. , 1932. 281 p.
A Year's Embassy to Mustafa Kemal.   New York: Charles
   Scribner's Sons, 1934. 277 p.
Bismark and Mussolini.   Boston: Houghton Mifflin & Co. ,
   1931. 304 p.
French Memories of Eighteenth-Century America.   New
   York: Charles Scribner's Sons, 1915. 335 p.
Have We A Far Eastern Policy?   Introd. by the Honorable
   David Jayne Hill, L. L. D.   New York: Charles Scrib-
   ner's Sons, 1920. 309 p.
Kemal - Roosevelt - Mussolini.   Bologna: N. Zanichelli,
   1936. 307 p.
Modernizing the Monroe Doctrine.   Introd. by Nicholas
   Murray Butler.   Boston: Houghton Mifflin Co. , 1916.
   202 p.
Prime Ministers and Presidents.   New York: George H.
   Doran Co. , 1922. 314 p.
Stained Glass Tours in France.   New York: J. Lane Co. ,
   1908. 298 p.
Stained Glass Tours in Germany, Austria and the Rhine
   Lands.   New York: Dodd, Mead & Co. , 1927. 304 p.
A Stained Glass Tour in Italy.   New York: The John
   Lane Co. , 1913. 174 p.
Stained Glass Tours in Spain and Flanders.   New York:
   Dodd, Mead & Co. , 1924. 245 p.
Mosaics in Italy, Palestine, Syria, Turkey and Greece.
   London: John Lane Co. , 1933. 304 p.
My Story Book.   Brattleboro, Vermont: Privately printed,
   1937. 159 p.

SHILLOCK, John Christopher, Jr. , 1906-   .   Foreign Service
   Officer 1929-1962.   Served in Buenos Aires, La Paz,
   Santiago, Lisbon, Tangier, Lima, Ottawa, State

Department, Asunción, Geneva, Panama.
The Post-War Movements to Reduce Naval Armaments.
New York: Carnegie Endowment for International
Peace. Division of Intercourse and Education, 1928.
92 p.

SHORT, Dorothy. Wife of V. Roxor Short, 1906- . He is
a Foreign Service Reserve Officer with the Administration for International Development since 1958. He
served in Kabul, Bangkok, Washington.
Camel Land Cookery. National Cash Register Press at
Beirut: 1964. 160 unnumbered pages. offset. Printed
for the Women's Club of Kabul for the benefit of Afghan
girls college education. Illus. by the author.

SHORT, William, 1759-1849. Aid to Thomas Jefferson in
Paris. Sent to The Hague to arrange a commercial
treaty. Secretary of Legation at Paris, Chargé d'Affaires 1789. Minister to The Hague 1792. Joint Commissioner, with William Carmichael, to Madrid 1793-
95.
Short Papers, 1783-1847. 292 items. In College of William and Mary, the Earl Gregg Swem Library, Williamsburg, Va.
Correspondence, 1787-1838. About 250 items. In the
American Philosophical Society Library. Philadelphia.

SHRIVER, Robert Sargent, Jr., 1915- . Lawyer, business
executive. Director of the Peace Corps 1961-65, Director of the Office of Economic Cooperation and Development 1964-68, Ambassador to France 1968-69.
Point of the Lance. New York: Harper & Row, 1964.
240 p.

SIKES, William Wirt, 1836-1883. Journalist, author. Con-
sul at Cardiff 1876-83, where he died.
A Book for the Winter Evening Fireside. (stories and
poems) Watertown, N.Y.: Ingalls & Haddock, 1858.
96 p.
Collected British Goblins, Welch Folklore, Fairy Mythol-
ogy, Legends, Traditions. Illus. by T. H. Thomas.
Boston: R. J. Osgood & Co., 1881. 412 p.
One Poor Girl. Philadelphia: J. B. Lippincott & Co.,
1869. 255 p.
Rambles and Studies in Old South Wales. London: S.
Low, Marston, Searle and Rivington, 1881. 304 p.
Studies of Assassination. London: S. Low, Marston,
Searle and Rivington, 1881. 192 p.

SIMPSON, Howard Russell, 1925- . Freelance writer,
news correspondent. United States Information Agency
and Foreign Officer 1953- . Served in Saigon, Lagos,
Marseilles, Paris, Naval War College, Washington,
Canberra.
To a Silent Valley. New York: Alfred A. Knopf, Inc.,
    1961. 248 p.
Assignment for a Mercenary. New York: Harper & Row,
    1965. 210 p.
The Three Day Alliance. New York: Doubleday & Co.
    Inc., 1971. 180 p.

SIMPSON, Robert Smith, 1906- . Authority on labor. For-
eign Service Officer 1943-62. Served in Washington,
Brussels, Athens, Mexico City, Bombay, Lourenço
Marques, Labor Department.
Anatomy of the State Department. Boston: Houghton
    Mifflin Co., 1967. 285 p.
War and Post-War Social Security. with Wilbur J. Cohen
    and others. Washington: American Council on Public
Affairs, 1942. 89 p.
(Edited) Resources and Needs of American Diplomacy.
    Vol. 380 of American Academy of Political and Social
Sciences. Philadelphia: 1968. 250 p.
(Edited) Instruction in Diplomacy: The Liberal Arts Ap-
    proach. Monograph 13 in a series sponsored by The
American Academy of Political and Social Science.
Philadelphia: 1972. 342 p. Includes a bibliography
on United States diplomacy.

SKINNER, Robert Peet, 1866-1960. Newspaper publisher.
Foreign Service Officer 1897-1936. Consul at Mar-
seilles 1897; Commissioner and Plenipotentiary to
Ethiopia to establish relations and to negotiate treaty
1903; Consul General at Hamburg 1908; Special detail
to Liberia to adjust claims of creditors of Liberia to
Great Britain, France, Germany and the Netherlands
1912; Consul General at Berlin 1913, London 1914,
Paris 1924. Minister to Greece 1926, to Estonia,
Latvia and Lithuania 1931, Ambassador to Turkey 1933-
36.
Abyssinia of Today: An Account of the First Mission Sent
    by the American Government to the Court of the King
of Kings, 1903-1904. New York: Longmans Green &
Co., 1906. 227 p.

SMITH, Earl E. T., 1903- . Financier, investment broker.

Ambassador to Cuba 1957-59.
The Fourth Floor. An account of the Castro Communist
Revolution. New York: Random House, 1962. 242 p.

SMITH, Leland Leslie, 1885- . Businessman and musician.
Assistant Military Attaché in Rumania 1918-20. Foreign Service Officer 1921-1933. Served in Saigon,
Tunis, Prague, Nice. He and his wife, Gilbert, are
accomplished musicians. He composed approximately
twenty pieces for the piano, several of which were
publicly performed, none published.
Waveland. An opera, performed three times at the Seamen's Institute in Portland, Oregon, in 1913, and at
the World Woodman's Union in Salem, Oregon, the
same year.

SMITH, Mary Jane (Sainte-Marie), 1930- . Mrs. Smith is
the wife of Foreign Service Officer Norris P. Smith.
She is a graduate nurse, free-lance writer and editor.
She served on the staff of the United States Operations
Mission in Laos 1960-63. She accompanied her hus-
band on his assignments to Laos, Taiwan, Vietnam,
Thailand, Tokyo. Mr. Smith is a writer, a Foreign
Service Officer since 1958, assigned to the United
States Information Agency, and has Japanese and Chi-
nese language training.
Beyond Bangkok. A Guide to Travel in Thailand. Bang-
kok: American University Alumni Center, 1969.
160 p. Maps and photographs.

SMITH, Walter Bedell, 1895-1961. Lieutenant-General United
States Army. From private to Chief of Staff, European
Theater. Ambassador to Russia 1946-49. Director of
the Central Intelligence Administration 1950-53. Under-
Secretary of State 1953-54.
My Three Years in Moscow. Philadelphia: J. B. Lippin-
cott & Co., 1950. 346 p.
Eisenhower's Six Great Decisions: Europe 1944-1945.
New York: Longmans Green & Co., 1956. 237 p.

SMITH, Walter Evans, 1874-1953. Missionary in China 1920-
21. Vice Consul in Nanking 1921-25.
Manual of Probate Procedure in American Consular Courts
in China. with John Ker Davis [Q.V.]. Washington:
Government Printing Office, 1923. 32 p.

SMITH, William L. G., 1814-1878. Consul in Shanghai

1858-61?
Fifty Years of Public Life. The Life and Times of Lewis
Cass. New York: Derby & Jackson, 1856. 781 p.
Life At the South: or, 'Uncle Tom's Cabin' as It Is. Be-
ing Narratives, Scenes, and Incidents in the Real 'Life
of the Lowly.' Buffalo: G. H. Derby & Co., 1898.
519 p.
Observations On China and the Chinese. New York:
Carleton, Publisher, (late Budd & Carleton), 1863.
216 p.

SMITH, William Loughton, 1758-1812. Congressman, politi-
cal pamphleteer. Minister to Portugal 1797-1801.
The Politiks and Views of a Certain Party Displayed.
(An attack on Thomas Jefferson.) No publisher given.
1792. 36 p.
The Pretensions of Thomas Jefferson to the Presidency
Examined. Anonymous, but thought to be Smith. Pub-
lished in the "Gazette of the United States," Vol. 1.
October-November 1796. Vol. 2 Philadelphia: "The
Federalist" 1796. Republished from the "Gazette of
United States" by Mathew Carey. 2 vols. in 1.
Comparative View of the Constitutions of the Several States
with Each Other, and With that of the United States.
Washington: Thompson and Homans, 1832. 135 p.
The Numbers of Phocian. Also appeared as American
Arguments for British Rights. London: 1806.
Charlestown, South Carolina: Reprinted for J. Butter-
worth, 1806. 74 p.
A Candid Examination of the Objections to the Treaty of
Amity, Commerce, and Navigation Between the United
States and Great Britain, as Stated in the Report of the
Committee Appointed by the Citizens of the United
States in Charleston, S. C. Printed in New York.
Reprinted for James Rivington, 156 Pine Street, 1795.
43 p.
Journal of William Loughton Smith, 1790-1791. Edit. by
Albert Matthews. Cambridge: Harvard University
Press, 1911. 88 p.

SMYTHE, David Mynders, 1915- . Foreign Service Officer
1938-41. Served in Le Havre, Paris, Bilbao.
American Vice Consul. Boston: The Christopher Publish-
ing House, 1942. 207 p.
Careers in Personnel Work. with Evelyn Steele, Director
Vocational Guidance Research. Intro. by Forrest H.
Kirkpatrick. New York: E. P. Dutton & Co. Inc.,

1946. 253 p.
Golden Venus. Garden City: Doubleday & Co. Inc., 1960.
331 p.
Madame de Pompadour: Mistress of France. New York:
Wilfred Funk Inc., 1953. 370 p.

SMYTHE, Hugh H., 1913- . Teacher, research various
colleges and universities 1937-53; Brooklyn College
1953-65; member of U.S. delegations to UN 1962-65;
Ambassador to Syria 1965, to Malta 1967-69.
Educating the Culturally Disadvantaged Child. with Lester
D. Crow and Walter I. Murray. New York: David
McKay, 1966. 306 p.
The New Nigerian Elite. with Mabel N. Smythe. Stan-
ford: Stanford University Press, 1960. 196 p.

SORENSON, Thomas C., 1926- . Radio announcer, news-
paper reporter and editor, teacher. Foreign Service
Staff, and Reserve Officer, 1951-66. Deputy Director
United States Information Agency. Served in Beirut,
Cairo, Washington.
The World War: The Story of American Propaganda.
New York: Harper & Row, 1968. 337 p.

SOWELL, Benjamin Luther, 1907- . Born in Argentina of
American parents. Teacher, newspaper reporter,
Foreign Service Officer 1941-66. Served in Montevideo,
St. Stephen, Port-of-Spain, Quito, State Department,
Caracas, São Paulo, Lima.
Por Sendas de Gloria y Humildad. Vida de Sidney Mc-
Farland Sowell. Buenos Aires: Junta Bautista de Pub-
licaciones, 1969. 148 p. English edition. Pioneer
Parson. Nashville: Baptist Historical Commission,
1970. 148 p.

SPAULDING, Ernest Wilder, 1899- . Teacher, historical
writer. State Department and Foreign Service Reserve
Officer 1930-56. Chief of Division of Research and
Publications, United States Information Agency. Served
in Washington, Vienna, Bonn.
Ambassadors Ordinary and Extraordinary. Washington:
Public Affairs Press, 1961. 302 p.
His Excellency George Clinton: Critic of the Constitution.
New York: The Macmillan Co., 1938. 325 p.
New York in the Critical Period, 1783-1789. New York:
Columbia University Press, 1932. 334 p.
The Quiet Invaders. The Story of the Austrian Impact

Upon America. Fore. by Josef Stummvoll. Vienna: Osterreichischer, Bundesverlag, 1968. 324 p.

SPEER, William S., 1822-1904. Editor of Shelbyville, Tenn. "Expositor," a supporter of Lincoln. Consul at Zanzibar, Jan. -Nov. 1862.
The Law of Success. Nashville, Tenn. : Southern Methodist Publishing House, 1885. 288 p.
Sketches of Prominent Tennesseans. Containing Biographies and Records of Many of the Families who have Attained Prominence in Tennessee. Compiled and ed. by Hon. W. S. Speer. Nashville: A. B. Tavel, 1888. 579 p.
The Encyclopaedia of the New West. Containing Fully Authenticated Information of the Agricultural, Mercantile, Commercial, Manufacturing, Mining, and Grazing Industries, and Representing the Character, Development, Resources, and Present Condition of Arkansas, Colorado, New Mexico and Indian Territory. Also Biographical Sketches of their Representative Men and Women. William S. Speer, Managing Editor. Hon. John Henry Brown, Revising Editor. Marshall, Texas: The Biographical Publishing Co., 1881. 1014 p.

SPINKS, Charles Nelson, 1906- . Teacher, researcher, writer, editor English language weekly in Tokyo 1938-41. English professor Tokyo University of Commerce 1936-41. Director of research analysis SCAP (Office of Supreme Commander of Allied Powers) Tokyo 1946-48. Foreign Service Officer 1948-66. Served in Tokyo, Bangkok, Djakarta, Canberra, Department of State. United States Information Agency. Director of Office of Research-Analysis for Far East 1961, in State Department.
Manpower, Food and Civilian Supplies in Japan, 1939-45. United States Strategic Bombing Survey. Washington: Government Printing Office, 1946. 250 p.
Siam and the Pottery Trade of Asia. Bangkok: Journal of the Siam Society, 1956. 51 p. 17 plates, 3 maps.
Thai Pottery in Indonesia. Bangkok: The Siam Society, 1958. 35 p. 50 plates, maps and drawings.
Japan: Prospects, Options and Opportunities. with William J. Sebald. Washington: American Enterprise Institute, 1967. 129 p.
The Ceramic Wares of Siam. Bangkok: The Siam Society, 1965. 196 p. 52 plates, maps and drawings.

SQUIER, Ephraim George, 1821-1888. Editor, archeologist.

Chargé d'Affaires to Central America 1849-53; United
States Commissioner to Peru 1863-65; Honduran Consul
General in New York 1869.

Aboriginal Monuments of the State of New York.   Washington: Smithsonian Institution, 1850.   188 p.

Antiquities of the State of New York, with a Supplement on
the Antiquities of the West. Buffalo: G. H. Derby,
1851. 343 p.

Ancient Monuments of the Mississippi Valley: Comprising
the Results of Extensive Surveys and Explorations. with
E. H. Davis. Washington: Smithsonian Institution,
1848. 304 p.

Honduras: Descriptive, Historical and Statistical. Issued
by permission of the author and under authority of
Carlos Gutierrez. London: Trubner & Co. , 1870.
278 p.

Honduras: Interoceanic Railway. Preliminary Report.
New York: Tubbs, Nasmith & Teall, printers, 1854.
63 p.

Waikna: or Adventures on the Mosquito Shore. by Samuel
A. Bard, (pseud.). New York: Harper & Bros. , 1855.
366 p.

Nicaragua: Its People, Scenery, Monuments, and the
Proposed Interoceanic Canal. New York: D. Appleton
& Co. , 1852. 2 vols.

The States of Central America. New York: Harper &
Bros. , 1858. 782 p.

Die Staaten von Central Amerika Includondere Honduras,
San Salvador und Die Moskitokuste. Leipzig: G. Senf,
1865. 275 p.

Peru: Incidents of Travel and Exploration in the Land of
the Incas. New York: Harper & Bros. , 1877. 599 p.

Tropical Fibres: Their Production and Economic Attrac-
tion. New York: Charles Scribner's Sons, 1861.
64 p.

The Ephraim George Squier Manuscripts in the Library of
Congress. New York: Bibliographical Society of
America, 1959. 326 p.

(Edited) Frank Leslie's Pictorial History of the American
Civil War. New York: F. Leslie, 1861-62. 2 vols.

Honduras: Descripcion Historica, Geografica y Estadistica
de Esta Republica de la America Central. Tegucigalpa:
Tipografia Nacional, 1908. 446 p.

Question Anglo-Americaine: Documents Officials Echangés
entre les Etats-Unis et l'Angleterre au Sujet de l'Amerique Centrale et du Traité Clayton-Bulwer. Paris:
Stassin et Xavier, 1856. 225 p.

The Serpent Symbol, and the Worship of the Reciprocal
Principles of Nature in America. New York: G. P.
Putnam's Sons, 1851. 254 p.
Notes on Central America: Particularly the States of
Honduras, and San Salvador. New York: Harper &
Bros., 1855. 397 p.
Monograph of Authors Who Have Written on the Languages
of Central America, and Collected Vocabularies or Com-
posed Works in the Native Dialects of That Country.
London: Trubner & Co., 1861. 70 p.
Collection of Rare and Original Documents Concerning the
Discovery and Conquest of America. Chiefly from the
Spanish Archives. Albany: J. Munsell, 1860. 129 p.
Compendio de la Historia Politica de Centro-America.
Escrito en Ingles. Paris: Impr. de Gratiot, 1856.
114 p.

SQUIRE, Paul Chapin, 1890-1966. Business 1911-19. For-
eign Service Officer 1919-49. Served in St. Nazaire,
Nantes, Dunkirk, Lille, Windsor, Kingston (Jamaica),
Newcastle-on-Tyne, Nice, Monaco, Venice, Buenos
Aires, Dublin, Geneva.
Fit To Print? New York: Vantage Press, Inc., 1965.
172 p.

STABLER, Jordan Herbert, 1885-1938. Foreign Service Officer 1909-1927. Chief of the Division of Latin American Affairs 1918. Served in Quito, Guatemala, Stockholm, Washington, Santo Domingo, London.
The Jargon of Master François Villon. (text in English
and French) Boston: Houghton Mifflin Co., 1918.
42 p. 385 copies printed.
(Compiled and translated) Fragments from an XVIII Century Diary: The Travels and Adventures of Don Francisco de Miranda. Preface by R. B. Cunninghame
Graham, Caracas: Tipografía La Naçion, 1931. 196 p.
Illus.

STALLO, John Bernard, 1823-1900. Lawyer, teacher, sci-
entist. Minister to Italy 1885-89.
General Principles of the Philosophy of Nature. Boston:
W. Crosby & H. P. Nichols, 1848. 520 p.
The Concepts and Theories of Modern Physics. In Apple-
ton's International Scientific Series. Vol. XXXVIII.
New York: D. Appleton & Co., 1882. 313 p.
Die Begriffe und Theorien der Modernen Physik. Leipzig:
J. A. Barth, 1911. 328 p.

STANDLEY, William Harrison, 1872-1963. United States
Navy 1891-1937. Member U.S. delegation General
Disarmament Conference, London, 1934. Ambassador
to Russia 1942-44.
Admiral Ambassador to Russia. with Arthur A. Ageton.
Chicago: H. Regency Co., 1955. 533 p.

STANTON, Edwin Forward, 1901-1968. Foreign Service Officer 1921-53. Chinese language officer. Served in
Peking, Mukden, Kalgan, Tientsin, Tsinan, Hangkow,
Nanking, Shanghai, State Department, Career Minister
1946. Minister to Siam 1946. Ambassador to Siam
1947-53. (Siam became Thailand in 1949.)
Brief Authority: Excursions of a Common Man in an Un-
common World. N.Y.: Harper Bros., 1956. 290 p.

STEEL, Ronald Leslie, 1931- . Foreign Service Officer
1957-58. Served in Foreign Service Institute and
Nicosia.
Federal Aid to Education. New York: H. W. Wilson
Co., 1961. 207 p.
United States Foreign Trade Policy. New York: H. W.
Wilson Co., 1962. 200 p.
The End of Alliance: America and the Future of Europe.
New York: Viking Press, 1964. 148 p.
Italy. New York: H. W. Silson Co., 1963. 182 p.
New Light on Juvenile Delinquency. New York: H. W.
Wilson Co., 1967. 221 p.
North Africa. New York: H. W. Wilson Co., 1967.
224 p.
Pax Americana. New York: Viking Press, 1967. 371 p.
Tropical Africa Today. with George H. T. Kimble. St.
Louis: Webster Division, McGraw-Hill Book Co.,
1966. 138 p.

STEINHARDT, Lawrence Adolph, 1892-1950. Lawyer. Min-
ister to Sweden 1933, Ambassador to Peru 1937, to the
Soviet Union 1939, to Turkey 1942, to Czechoslovakia
1944-46.
Papers, 1929-1950. Manuscript Division. Library of
Congress.

STEPHENS, John Lloyd, 1805-1852. Archeologist, writer.
Special Agent for the United States in Central America--
appointed by President Van Buren in 1839.
Incidents of Travel in Central America, Chiapas and
Yucatan. New York: Harper & Bros., 1841. 2 vols.

Incidents of Travel in Egypt, Arabia Petraea, and the
Holy Land. By an American. (pseud.) New York:
Harper & Bros., 1838. 2 vols.
Incidents of Travel in Greece, Turkey, Russia and Poland.
New York: Harper & Bros., 1838. 2 vols.
Incidents of Travel in Yucatan. New York: Harper &
Bros., 1843. 2 vols.
Yucatan, Its People, Customs, "Vast Ruins," Etc. (In
Spanish) Campeche, Yucatan: under direction of J.
Castillo Peraza, 1848-50. 2 vols. Norman, Oklahoma:
engravings by Catherwood. Edit. and with introd. by
Victor Wolfgang von Hagen. Oklahoma University
Press, 1962. 2 vols.

STEVENS, Francis Bowden, 1905- . Foreign Service Officer 1931-58. Served in Prague, Warsaw, Paris, Riga,
Pretoria, Moscow, State Department, National War College, Berlin, Frankfort, Tehran.
National Socialism: Basic Principles, Their Application
by the Nazi Party's Foreign Organization, and the Use
of Germans Abroad for Nazi Aims. Co-author, with
Howard Trivers, Raymond E. Murphy and Joseph Morgan Roland. Washington: Government Printing Office,
Department of State Publication #1864. 1943. 510 p.

STEVENS, John Leavitt, 1820-1895. Journalist, editor.
Minister to Paraguay and Uruguay 1870-74, to Sweden
and Norway 1877-83, to Hawaii 1889-93.
History of Gustavus Adolphus. New York: G. P. Putnam
& Sons, 1884. 427 p.
Picturesque Hawaii. Republished as Riches and Marvels
of Hawaii. Philadelphia: Edgewood Publishing Co.,
1900. 354 p.

STEVENSON, Adlai Ewing, 1900-1965. Lawyer, politician,
Government official. Chief of Economic Mission to
Italy 1943; on War Department Mission to Europe 1944;
Chief of United States Delegation to Preparatory Com-
mission United Nations, London 1945. Governor of
Illinois 1949-53; Democratic candidate for President
1952 and 1956. Ambassador to the United Nations
1961-65.
Adlai Stevenson Sampler, 1945-65. Selected by Alden
Whitman. New York: Harper & Row, 1965. 45 p.
Call to Greatness. New York: Harper Bros., 1954.
110 p. (Godkin lectures.)
An Ethic for Survival: Adlai Stevenson Speaks on

International Affairs, 1936-65. Edit. with introd. and
comment by Michael H. Prosser, assisted by Laurence
H. Sherlick. New York: William Morrow & Co. Inc.,
1969. 571 p.
Friends and Enemies: What I Learned in Russia. A
journey, summer of 1958. New York: Harper Bros.,
1959. 102 p.
Looking Outward: Years of Crisis at the United Nations.
(Speeches and papers.) Edit. with commentary by
Robert L. and Selma Schiffer. Preface by J. F. Ken-
nedy. New York: Harper & Row, 1963. 295 p.
Major Campaign Speeches 1952. Introd. by author. New
York: Random House, 1953. 320 p.
Man of Honor, Man of Peace: The Life and Words of
Adlai Stevenson. by the editors of Country Beautiful.
Editorial direction of Michael P. Dineen. Edit. by
Robert L. Polley. New York: G. P. Putnam's Sons,
1965. 98 p.
The New America. Edit. by Seymour E. Harris, John
Bartlow Martin and Arthur Schlesinger, Jr. New
York: Harper Bros., 1957. 285 p.
Putting First Things First, a Democratic View. New
York: Random House, 1960. 115 p.
Speeches. Foreword by John Steinbeck and a brief biog-
raphy of Adlai Stevenson by Debs Meyers and Ralph
Martin. New York: Random House, 1952. 128 p.
The Stevenson Wit and Wisdom. Edit. by Paul Steiner.
New York: Pyramid Publications, 1965. 126 p.
The Stevenson Wit. Compiled and edit. by Bill Adler.
New York: Doubleday & Co. Inc., 1966. 95 p.
United Nations, Guardian of Peace. Washington: Govern-
ment Printing Office (State Department publication),
1961. 45 p.
What I Think. New York: Harper Bros., 1956. 240 p.
The Wit and Wisdom of Adlai Stevenson. Compiled by
Edward Hanna, Henry Hicks and Ted Coppel. New
York: Hawthorn Books, 1965. 96 p.
The Papers of Adlai Stevenson. Vol. I: beginnings of
education. 1900-1941. Edit. by Walter Johnson and
Carol Evans. Boston: Little Brown & Co., 1972.
586 p.

STILLMAN, William James, 1828-1901. Consul in Rome
1861, in Candia 1865.
The Amateurs' Photographic Guide Book, Being a Complete
Resumé of the Most Useful Dry and Wet Collodion Processes Especially for the Use of Amateurs. London:

M. P. Trench, 1874. 92 p.
The Autobiography of a Journalist, William James Stillman.
Boston: Houghton Mifflin Co., 1901. 2 vols.
Billy and Hans, My Squirrel Friends: A True History.
First published in Century Magazine Feb. 1897. Port-
land, Maine: T. B. Masher, 1914. 47 p. 950 copies.
In Warner's Library of the World's Best Literature.
The Cretan Insurrection of 1866-67-68. New York: H.
Holt, 1874. 203 p.
Francesco Crispi, Insurgent, Exile, Revolutionist and
Statesman. Boston: Houghton Mifflin Co., 1899.
287 p.
The Old Rome and the New, and Other Studies. Boston:
Houghton Mifflin Co., 1898. 296 p.
On the Track of Ulysses, an Excursion in Quest of the
So-Called Venus de Milo, Two Studies in Archeology
During a Cruise Among the Greek Islands. Boston:
Houghton Mifflin Riverside Press, 1888. 106 p.
The Union of Italy, 1815-1895. Cambridge, England:
Cambridge University Press, 1898. 412 p.
(Edited) Venus and Apollo in Painting and Sculpture. Lon-
don: Bliss, Sands & Co., 1897. 170 p. 555 copies.
Ovid in Exile. [a poem] New York: Libre Scriptorum,
1893.
Poetic Localities of Cambridge. Boston: J. R. Osgood
& Co., 1876. 41 p.

STIMSON, Fredrick Jesup, 1855-1943. (Pseud. J. S. Dale.)
Lawyer, professor, government official, writer. Am-
bassador to Argentina 1914-21.
The American Constitution as It Protects Private Rights.
New York: Charles Scribner's Sons, 1923. 239 p.
The American Constitution: the National Powers, the
Rights of the States, the Liberties of the People.
Lowell Institute lectures, delivered at Boston, October
and November 1907. New York: Charles Scribner's
Sons, 1908. 259 p.
American Statute Law: an Analytical and Compared Digest.
Boston: C. C. Soule, 1886. 2 vols. (2nd vol. has
imprint of Boston Book Co., 1892.)
A Concise Law Dictionary of Words, Phrases, and Maxims,
with an Explanatory List of Abbreviations Used in Law
Books. Reviewed and edit. by Harvey Courtlandt Voor-
hees. Boston: Little, Brown & Co., 1911. 346 p.
The Crime of Henry Vane: A Study with a Moral. J. S.
Dale (pseud.). New York: Charles Scribner's Sons,
1884. 206 p.

Glossary of Technical Terms, Phrases, and Maxims of
the Common Law.   Boston: Little,   Brown & Co. ,
1881.   305 p.
Guerndale, an Old Story.   J. S. Dale (pseud.).   New
York: Charles Scribner's Sons, 1882.   444 p.
Handbook to the Labor Law of the United States.   New
York: Charles Scribner's Sons, 1896.   385 p.
In Cure of Her Soul.   New York: D. Appleton & Co. ,
1906.   612 p.
In Three Zones.   by J. S. Dale (pseud.).   New York:
Charles Scribner's Sons, 1893.   204 p.
Jethro Bacon of Sandwich: The Weaker Sex.   New York:
Charles Scribner's Sons, 1902.   222 p.
King Moanett: a Story of Old Virginia and the Massachu-
setts Bay.   Illus. by Henry Sandham.   Boston: Lam-
son, Wolffe & Co. , 1896.   327 p.
The King's Men: a Tale of Tomorrow.   with Robert
Grant, John Davis O'Reilly, J. S. Dale (pseud.), and
John T. Wheelwright.   New York: Charles Scribner's
Sons, 1884.   270 p.
The Law of the Federal and State Constitutions of the
United States, With an Historical Study of Their Prin-
ciples, a Chronological Table of English Social Legis-
lation and a Comparative Digest of the Constitutions of
Forty Six States.   Boston: The Boston Book Co. ,
1908.   386 p.
The Light of Provence, a Dramatic Poem by J. S. Dale.
(pseud.) New York: G. P. Putnam's Sons, 1917.
115 p.
Mrs. Knollys, and Other Stories.   New York: Charles
Scribner's Sons, 1897.   207 p.
My Story: Being the Memoirs of Benedict Arnold: Late
Major General in the Continental Army and Brigadier
General in that of His Britannic Majesty.   Stimson and
Dale (pseud.).   New York: Charles Scribner's Sons,
1917.   622 p.
My United States.   An autobiography, dealing especially
with the author's diplomatic experience in Argentina
during the World War.   New York: Charles Scribner's
Sons, 1931.   478 p.
Pirate Gold.   Stimson & Dale (pseud.).   Boston: Houghton
Mifflin, 1896.   209 p.
Popular Law-Making: A Study of the Origin, History and
Present Tendencies of Law-Making by Statute.   New
York: Charles Scribner's Sons, 1910.   390 p.
The Residuary Legatee: or, the Posthumous Jest of the
Late John Austin.   New York: Charles Scribner's

Sons, 1888. 142 p.
The Sentimental Calendar, Being Twelve Funny Stories.
by J. S. Dale (pseud.). New York: Charles Scribner's
Sons, 1886. 280 p.
The Western Way: the Accomplishment and Future of
Modern Democracy. New York: Charles Scribner's
Sons, 1929. 391 p.

STIMSON, Henry Lewis, 1867-1950. Secretary of War 1911-
13. Lawyer. Special Representative to Nicaragua 1927.
Governor General of the Philippines 1927-29. Secre-
tary of State 1929-33. Secretary War 1940-45.
American Foreign Policy in Nicaragua. New York:
Charles Scribner's Sons, 1927. 129 p. In Spanish,
Washington: Government Printing Office, 1928. 66 p.
Democracy and Nationalism in Europe. Princeton, N.J.:
Princeton University Press, 1934. 88 p.
The Far Eastern Crisis: Recollections and Observations.
New York: Harper Bros., published for the Council on
Foreign Relations, 1936. 293 p.
My Vacations. New York? 1949. 180 p. (Rare Book
Collection of Library of Congress.) Illus. ports.
On Active Service in Peace and War. with McGeorge
Bundy. New York: Harper Bros., 1948. 698 p.

STOVALL, Pleasant Alexander, 1857-1935. Editor, politi-
cian. Minister to Switzerland 1913-20.
Robert Toombs, Statesman, Speaker, Sage. New York:
Cassell Publishing Co., 1892. 396 p.
Switzerland and the World War. (posthumous) Savannah:
Mason Inc., 1939. 253 p.

STOWELL, Ellery Cory, 1875- . International law author-
ity. Professor. Secretary of the 2nd Peace Confer-
ence at The Hague 1907. Secretary to same at Pan-
ama. Secretary to American Delegation of the Naval
Conference, London 1908-09. Writer.
Consular Cases and Opinions. From the Decisions of the
English and American Courts, and the Opinions of the
Attorneys General. Washington: John Burne & Co.,
1909. 811 p.
The Diplomacy of the War of 1914. The Beginnings of the
War. Boston: Houghton Mifflin Co., 1915. 728 p.
Intervention in International Law. Washington: J. Byrne
Co., 1921. 558 p.
International Law: a Restatement of Principles in Con-
formity with Actual Practice. New York: H. Holt Co.,

1931. 829 p.
International Cases: Arbitration and Incidents Illustrative
  of International Law as Practiced by Independent States.
  with Henry F. Munro. Boston: Houghton Mifflin Co.,
  1916. 2 vols.
Le Consul; fonctions, immunités, organisation, exequatur;
  essai d'exposé systématique. Paris: A. Pedone,
  1909. 353 p.

STRAUS, Oscar Solomon, 1850-1926. Born in Bavaria.
  Came to the United States in 1854. Attorney, mer-
  chant, Secretary of Commerce. Minister to Turkey
  1887-89 and 1898-1900. Member Permanent Court of
  Arbitration at The Hague 1902, 1908, 1912, 1920.
  Ambassador to Turkey 1909-10.
The American Spirit. New York: The Century Co. (partly
  reprinted from various periodicals), 1913. 379 p.
The Origin of Republican Form of Government in the
  United States of America. New York: G. P. Putnam's
  Sons, 1885. 149 p.
Roger Williams, The Pioneer of Religious Liberty. New
  York: The Century Co., 1894. 257 p. New York:
  with interpretation by R. E. E. Harkness, and an ad-
  dress by Chief Justice Charles Evans Hughes. D. Ap-
  pleton-Century, for the Oscar S. Straus Memorial As-
  sociation, 1936. 257 p.
Under Four Administrations: from Cleveland to Taft.
  Recollections with illus. Boston: Houghton Mifflin
  Co., The Riverside Press, 1922. 456 p.

STRAUSZ-HUPE, Robert, 1903- . Born in Vienna, came
  to the United States in 1923, naturalized in 1938. Educator, author, expert in investment banking. Ambassador to Ceylon and Maldives 1970-71; to Belgium
  1972- .
Axis America: Hitler Plans Our Future. New York:
  G. P. Putnam's Sons, 1941. 274 p.
The Balance of Tomorrow: A Reappraisal of Basic Trends
  in World Politics. Ph. D. thesis. Philadelphia: University of Pennsylvania Press, 1945. 302 p. Published
  also as The Balance of Power: Power and Foreign
  Policy in the United States. New York: G. P. Putnam's Sons, 1945. 302 p.
The Estrangement of Western Man. London: Gollancz,
  1953. 312 p.
Geopolitics: the Struggle for Space and Power. New
  York: G. P. Putnam's Sons, 1942. 274 p.

In My Time. New York: W. W. Norton, 1965. 284 p.
Power and Community. New York: Frederick A. Praeg-
er, Inc., 1956. 134 p.
Protracted Conflict. New York: Harper & Bros., 1959.
203 p.
The Zone of Indifference. New York: G. P. Putnam's
Sons, 1952. 312 p.
International Relations in the Age of Conflict Between De-
mocracy and Dictatorship. with Stephen T. Possony.
Maps and charts by Harold K. Faye. New York: Mc-
Graw-Hill Book Co., 1950. 947 p.
Building the Atlantic World. with James E. Daugherty,
William R. Kintner, Stefan T. Possony and others.
New York: Harper & Row, 1963. 400 p.
A Forward Strategy for America. with William Kintner,
Stefan T. Possony, Alvin J. Cottrell and others. New
York: Harper & Row, 1961. 451 p.
(Edited) with Alvin J. Cottrell and James E. Daughterty.
American-Asian Tensions. New York: ˙ Frederick A.
Praeger, Inc., 1956. 239 p.
(Edited) with Harry Hazard. The Idea of Colonialism.
New York: Frederick A. Praeger Inc., 1958. 496 p.

STROBEL, Edward Henry, 1855-1908. Lawyer, professor.
Secretary at Madrid 1885-90. Third Assistant Secre-
tary of State 1893-94. Minister to Ecuador 1894, to
Chile 1894-97. Arbitrator between France and Chile.
Counsel for Chile before United States-Chilean Claims
Commission at Washington 1899. General advisor to
the Government of Siam (rank of Minister) 1903-09.
Mr. Blaine and His Foreign Policy: An Examination of
His Most Important Dispatches While Secretary of State.
Boston: A. W. Hall, 1884. 69 p.
Resumption of Specie Payments in Chile. Washington:
Government Printing Office, 1896. 50 p.
The Spanish Revolution, 1868-75. Boston: Small, May-
nard & Co., 1898. 293 p.

STUART, Graham H., 1887- . Professor of political sci-
ence. Advisor to the Department of State 1942-43.
Minister to Tangier 1946.
American Diplomatic and Consular Practice. New York:
D. Appleton-Century Co., Inc., 1936. 560 p. 2nd
edit. 1952.
Conception Américaine des Relations Internationales: Dip-
lomatie Americaine. with John B. Whitten. Paris:
Publications de la Conciliation Internationale, 1935.

272 p.

Cuba and Its International Relations. New York: The Institute of International Education, 1923. 46 p.

The Department of State: a History of Its Organization,
Procedure, and Personnel. Drawings by Gloria E.
Anderson. New York: The Macmillan Co., 1949.
517 p.

French Foreign Policy from Fashoda to Serajevo. (1898-
1914). New York: The Century Co., 1921. 392 p.

The Governmental System of Peru. Washington: Carnegie
Institute of Washington, 1925. 156 p.

The International City of Tangier. California: Stanford
University Press, 1955. 270 p. 2nd edit. 1st edit.
1931. 323 p.

Latin America and the United States. 5th edit. New
York: Appleton-Century-Crofts Co. c1955. 496 p.
1st edit. 1922.

La Politique Etrangére des Etats Unis et l'Amerique Nationale. Paris: Conciliation Internationale, 1930.
162 p.

The Tacna-Arica Dispute. Boston: World Peace Foundation, 1927. 136 p.

STUART, John Leighton, 1876-1956. Born in China of American parents. Educated in the United States. Missionary in China from 1905. President of Yenching University, Peking, 1919-1946. American Ambassador to
China 1946-53.

Fifty Years in China: The Memoirs of John Leighton Stu-
art, Missionary and Ambassador. Prefatory Note by
General George Catlett Marshall. New York: Random
House, 1946. 347 p.

Essentials of New Testament Greek. (in Chinese) 1916.

Greek-Chinese-English Dictionary of the New Testament.
Shanghai: Presbyterian Mission Press, 1918. 238 p.

Commentary on the Apocalypse. (in Chinese) 1922.

SWIFT, John Franklin, 1829-1891. Lawyer, writer. Minister to Japan 1889-91.

Going to Jericho. New York: A. Roman & Co., 1868.
447 p.

Robert Greathouse. New York: Carleton, 1870. 573 p.

TAYLOR, Bayard, 1825-1878. Traveler, writer, poet,
translator, correspondent. Secretary of Legation at
St. Petersburg during American Civil War. Minister
to Berlin 1878.

Bayard Taylor's Works. New York: G. P. Putnam's
Sons, 1863-1903. 15 vols.
Selections from "Eldorado," "Views Afoot," "At Home and
Abroad," etc. and Poems. New York: Street & Smith,
1902. 202 p.
Beauty and the Beast: a Story of Old Russia and Tales of
Home. New York: G. P. Putnam's Sons, 1872. 340 p.
Boys of Other Countries: Stories for American Boys.
New York: G. P. Putnam's Sons, 1876. 164 p.
By-Ways of Europe. New York: G. P. Putnam's Sons,
1869. 470 p.
Central Asia: Travels in Cashmere, Little Tibet and
Central Asia. New York: Scribner, Armstrong Co.,
Colorado: A Summer Trip. New York: G. P. Putnam's
Sons, 1867. 185 p.
Critical Essays and Literary Notes. New York: G. P.
Putnam's Sons, 1880. 382 p. (Sequel to "Studies in
German Literature.")
Cyclopedia of Modern Travel: a Record of Adventure,
Exploration and Discovery for the Past Fifty Years:
Comprising Narratives of the Most Distinguished Tra-
velers Since the Beginning of This Century. Prepared
and arranged by Bayard Taylor. Cincinnati: Moore,
Wilstach, Keys Co., 1856. 956 p.
The Dramatic Works of Bayard Taylor: with Notes by
Marie Hansen-Taylor. Boston: Houghton Mifflin Co.,
1902. 345 p. (Original edition 1880.)
The Echo Club. and Other Literary Diversions. Boston:
1876. New York: Prologue by Richard Henry Stod-
dard. 1895. 196 p.
Eldorado, or, Adventure in the Path of Empire: Compris-
ing a Voyage to California, via Panama: Life in San
Francisco and Monterey: Pictures of the Gold Region,
and Experiences of Mexican Travel. New York: G. P.
Putnam's Sons, 1850. 2 vols.
Egypt and Iceland in the Year 1874. New York: G. P.
Putnam's Sons, 1874. 282 p.
Germany. Rev. and edit. by Sidney B. Fay. Philadel-
phia: J. D. Morris Co., 1907. 489 p.
Handbook of Literature and the Fine Arts. Compiled and
arranged with George Ripley. New York: G. P. Put-
nam's Sons, 1852. 647 p.
Hanna Thurston: A Story of American Life. London: S.
Low & Son, 1863. 464 p.
Home Ballads. Boston: Houghton Mifflin Co., 1882.
61 p.
Home Pastorals. Ballads and Lyrics. Boston: J. R.

Osgood Co., 1875. 214 p.
Japan in Our Day. Compiled and arranged by Bayard
  Taylor. New York: Charles Scribner's Sons, 1872.
  280 p.
John Godfrey's Fortunes, Related by Himself, a Story of
  American Life. New York: G. P. Putnam's Sons,
  Hurd and Houghton, 1864. 511 p.
Joseph and His Friend: a Story of. Philadelphia: G. P.
  Putnam's Sons, 1870. 361 p.
A Journey to Central Africa: or, Life and Landscapes
  from Egypt to the Negro Kingdoms of the White Nile.
  New York: G. P. Putnam's Sons, 1852. 522 p.
The Lake Regions of Central Africa. Negro University
  Press, 1969. 397 p. (Originally published in 1881
  Scribner's, N.Y.)
The Lands of the Saracen: or, Pictures of Palestine,
  Asia Minor, Sicily and Spain. London: S. Low &
  Co., 1856. 451 p.
Lars: A Pastoral of Norway. Boston: Houghton Mifflin
  Co., 1873. 84 p.
Life and Letters of Bayard Taylor. Edit. by Marie Han-
  sen-Taylor and Horace E. Scudder. Boston: Houghton
  Mifflin Co., 1884. 2 vols.
Melodies of Verse. Boston: Houghton Mifflin Co., 1884.
  56 p.
The National Ode. Boston: W. F. Gill & Co., 1876.
  74 p.
Northern Travel: Summer and Winter Pictures of Sweden,
  Denmark and Lapland. New York: G. P. Putnam's
  Sons, 1858. 436 p.
The Picture of St. John. Boston: Ticknor & Fields,
  1866. 220 p. (in verse)
The Poems of Bayard Taylor. Boston: Ticknor & Fields,
  1865. 419 p.
Poems of the Orient. Boston: Ticknor & Fields, 1856.
  203 p.
The Prophet: A Tragedy. Boston: T. R. Osgood Co.,
  1874. 300 p.
Prose Writings of Bayard Taylor. New York: G. P.
  Putnam's Sons, 1868. 2 vols.
A School History of Germany: From the Earliest Period
  to the Establishment of the German Empire in 1871.
  Illus. and maps. New York: D. Appleton & Co.,
  1874. 608 p.
A Sheaf of Poems. Translated by Bayard Taylor and
  Liliam Bayard Taylor Kiliana. Boston: R. G. Badger,
  1911. 134 p.

The Story of Kannett.   New York: G. P. Putnam's Sons,
    1894.   418 p.
Studies in German Literature.   Introd. by George H. Bak-
    er. New York: G. P. Putnam's Sons, 1879.   418 p.
Travels in Arabia.   New York: Scribner, Armstrong &
    Co., 1872.   325 p.
Travels in Greece and Russia, with an Excursion to Crete.
    New York: G. P. Putnam's Sons, 1859.   426 p.
Travels in South Africa.   New York: Scribner, Arm-
    strong & Co., 1872.   336 p.
The Unpublished Letters of Bayard Taylor in the Hunting-
    ton Library.   Edit. with introd. by John Richie Schultz.
    San Marino, Calif.: 1937.   231 p.
Pedestrian Tour in Europe.   Views A-Foot: or, Europe
    Seen With Knapsack and Staff.   Preface by N. P. Wil-
    lis. New York: G. P. Putnam's Sons, 1848.   404 p.
A Visit to India, China and Japan in the Year 1853.   New
    York: G. P. Putnam's Sons, 1855.   539 p.
Ximena: or, the Battle of Sierra Morena, and Other Po-
    ems. Philadelphia: H. Hooker, 1844.   86 p.
At Home and Abroad: A Sketch-book of Life, Scenery and
    Men. New York: G. P. Putnam's Sons, 1860.   500 p.
The Masque of the Gods.   Boston: James R. Osgood &
    Co., 1872.   47 p.
Prince Denkalion.   See The Dramatic Works of Bayard
    Taylor.   Boston: Houghton, Mifflin & Co., 1878.
    345 p.

TAYLOR, Carl, 1937- . Foreign Service Officer 1962- .
    Served in Djakarta, State Department, Medan, Manda-
    lay.
Getting to Know Indonesia.   New York: Coward McCann,
    Inc., 1961.   64 p.
Getting to Know Burma.   New York: Coward McCann,
    Inc., 1962.   64 p.

TAYLOR, Hannis, 1851-1922.   Lawyer, scholar, writer.
    Minister to Spain 1893-97.
The Origin and Growth of the English Constitution.   Bos-
    ton: Houghton Mifflin Co., 1889-98.   2 vols.
The Science of Jurisprudence.   New York: The Macmil-
    lan Co., 1908.   676 p.
The Origin and Growth of the American Constitution.
    Boston: Houghton Mifflin Co., 1911.   676 p.
To the Congress of the United States: A Memorial in
    Behalf of the Architect of our Federal Constitution,
    Pelatiah Webster.   Washington: Government Printing

Office, 1908. 53 p.
A Treatise on International Public Law. Chicago: Callag-
han & Co., 1901. 912 p.
Jurisdiction and Procedure of the Supreme Court. Rochester: The Lawyers' Co-operative Publishing Co., 1905.
1007 p.
Cicero - A Commentary on the Roman Constitution. Chicago: A. C. McClurg & Co., 1916. 615 p.

TAYLOR, Henry Junior, 1902- . Economist, Newspaper
columnist and foreign correspondent, writer. Radio
commentator. Ambassador to Switzerland 1957-61.
An Ambassador Speaks His Mind. Garden City: Doubleday & Co., Inc., 1957. 282 p.
The Big Man. New York: Random House, 1964. 311 p.
Men and Moments. New York: Random House, 1966.
208 p.
Men and Power. New York: Dodd, Mead & Co. Inc.,
1946. 257 p.
Menn Og Makt. (Norwegian) Oslo: Bergendahl, 1947.
268 p.
Men in Motion. Garden City: Doubleday, Doran & Co.,
1943. 306 p.
Time Runs Out. Garden City: Doubleday, Doran & Co.,
1942. 333 p.
Why Hitler's Economy Fooled the World. (An explanation
of capital and the German economy.) Boston: The
Christopher Publishing House, 1941. 45 p.

TAYLOR, James Wickes, 1819-1893. Lawyer, journalist.
Consul at Winnipeg 1870-93.
The Victim of Intrigue. Cincinnati: Robinson & Jones,
1847. 120 p.
History of the State of Ohio. (up to 1857) Cincinnati:
H. W. Derby & Co., 1854. 557 p.
Northwest British America and Its Relation to the State of
Minnesota. St. Paul: Newson, Moore, Foster & Co.,
1860. 53 p.
Report on the Mineral Resources of the United States.
Washington: Government Printing Office, 1867. 360 p.
A Manual of the Ohio School System. Cincinnati: H. W.
Derby & Co., 1857. 413 p.

TAYLOR, Maxwell Davenport, 1901- . Career Army offi-
cer. Japanese language officer. Lieut. General.
Army Chief of Staff. Chairman Joint Chiefs of Staff.
Ambassador to Vietnam July 1964-September 1965.

The Uncertain Trumpet. New York: Harper Bros., 1960.
203 p.
Responsibility and Response. (lectures at Lehigh Univer-
sity) New York: Harper & Row, 1967. 84 p.
Swords and Plowshares. New York: W. W. Norton &
Co. Inc., 1972. 434 p.

TAYLOR, Myron Charles, 1874-1959. Industrialist. Lawyer.
Personal Representative of President Franklin Roosevelt
and of President Harry Truman to Pope Pius XII 1939-
50.
Wartime Correspondence between President Roosevelt and
Pope Pius XII. Introd. and notes by Myron C. Taylor,
Personal Representative of the President of the United
States of America to His Holiness Pope Pius XII. New
York: The Macmillan Co., 1947. 127 p.

TENNEY, Charles Daniel, 1857-1930. Principal of Anglo-
Chinese School in Tientsin 1886-95; President of Im-
perial Chinese University in Tientsin 1895-1900; Direc-
tor of Chinese Government students in the United States
and England 1906-08. Vice Consul and Interpreter at
Tientsin 1894-96; Chinese Secretary of Legation in
Peking 1908; Member of Joint International Opium Commission at Shanghai 1909; Consul at Nanking 1912;
Chinese Secretary, then Secretary of Legation and Counselor in Peking 1914-22. Decorated by the Chinese
Government in 1895 and 1921.
Geography of Asia. New York: The Macmillan Co.,
1906. 76 p.
English Lessons. Shanghai: Presbyterian Mission Press,
1890. 128 p.

TEWKSBURY, Howard Hobson, 1895- . Commerce Depart-
ment and Foreign Service Officer 1921-51. Served in
Havana, Buenos Aires, Guatemala, San Salvador,
Tegucigalpa, Department of State, Career Minister,
Ambassador to Paraguay 1950-51.
The Automotive Market in Argentina. Washington: Gov-
ernment Printing Office, 1929. 106 p.
The Automotive Market in Brazil. Washington: Govern-
ment Printing Office, 1930. 129 p.
The Automotive Market in Chile. (includes Market in
Paraguay) Washington: Government Printing Office,
1930. 52 p.
Motor Roads in Brazil. Washington: Government Print-
ing Office, 1931. 129 p.

THAYER, Alexander Wheelock, 1817-1897. (See "Thayer
  Centenary" by Kenneth Linlithgow in January 1966,
  Foreign Service Journal.) After graduating from Harvard in 1843, Thayer went to Austria for the purpose
  of translating the biography of Ludwig von Beethoven
  by a German author. Finding the biography inadequate
  he decided to stay in Austria and write his own biography of Beethoven. After struggling along with earn-
  ings from feature articles for American Newspapers
  and from donations from friends he finally was appointed
  assistant to the American Minister to Austria in 1862,
  and then, in November 1864, he was appointed American Consul in Trieste where he served until his death.
  Though Thayer had not completed the Beethoven biography, his friend, Herman Dieters, carried on for ten
  years until his death. It was finally finished by Hugo
  Riemann. This was published in German. It was not
  published in English until 1921. The newest and best
  edition of Thayer's work is by Professor Elliot Forbes,
  in English. Thayer wrote other books, as listed be-
  low, while working on his Beethoven.
Chronologisches Verzeichniss der Werke Ludwig von
  Beethoven's von Alexander W. Thayer. Berlin:
  Schneider, 1865. 208 p.
The Hebrews and the Red Sea. Andover, Mass.: W. F.
  Draper, 1883. 140 p.
The Hebrews in Egypt and Their Exodus. Peoria, Ill.:
  E. S. Wilcox, 1897. 315 p. (300 copies)
Life of Beethoven. Revised and edit. by Elliot Forbes.
  Princeton: Princeton University Press, 1964. 2 vols.
  (1136 p.) Some of original text deleted because recent
  knowledge proved it to be inaccurate. First publication
  of his works since Beethoven's death. Three editors--
  H. Deiters, H. Rismann and H. Krehbiel in addition to
  Forbes.
Ludwig von Beethoven's Leban: Alexander Wheelock Thay-
  er nach dem Original Manuscript Deutsch Bearb. Ber-
  lin: F. Schneider, 1866-79. 3 vols. Berlin: W.
  Weber, 1901-11. 5 vols., and Nach dem Original
  Manskript Deutsch Bearbeitet von Hermann Deiters.
  Leipzig: Breitkopf & Hartel, 1917. 5 vols.
The Life of Ludwig von Beethoven. Edit., rev. and
  amended from the original English manuscript and the
  German editions of Hermann Deiters and Hugo Riemann,
  concluded, and all the documents newly translated by
  Henry Edward Krehbiel. New York: The Beethoven
  Association, 1921. 3 vols. The first English edition

of Thayer.
(Edited) Signor Masoni and Other Papers of the Late I.
Brown. Berlin: F. Schneider, 1862. 282 p.
Ein Kritischer Beitrag zur Beethoven-Literatur, Vorgele-
sen im "Schillerverein" zu Triest. von Alexander W.
Thayer. Berlin: W. Weber, 1877. 50 p.

THAYER, Charles Wheeler, 1910-1969. Foreign Service
Officer 1933-53. Served in Moscow, Hamburg, Kabul,
London, Office of Strategic Services in Austria, Voice
of America, Bonn, Munich, Seoul, Belgrade.
Bears in the Caviar. Philadelphia: J. B. Lippincott
Co., 1951. 303 p.
Checkpoint. [Fiction] New York: Harper & Row, 1964.
303 p.
Diplomat. Foreword by Sir Harold Nicolson. New York:
Harper Bros., 1959. 299 p.
Guerilla. Foreword by Sir Fitzroy MacLean. Harper &
Row, 1963. 195 p.
Hands Across the Caviar. Philadelphia: J. B. Lippin-
cott Co., 1952. 251 p.
Moscow Interlude. [Fiction] New York: Harper Bros.,
1962. 338 p.
Muzzy. New York: Harper & Row, 1966. 196 p.
Natasha. London: M. Joseph, 1962. 270 p.
Russia. with the editors of LIFE, TIME, INC. New
York: Life World Library, 1960. 152 p.
The Unquiet Germans. New York: Harper Bros., 1957.
275 p.

THOMAS, William Widgery, Jr., 1839-1927. Lawyer, politician, diplomat. Diplomatic courier 1862. Vice-Con-
sul-General Constantinople; Acting Consul General
Galatz, Moldavia; Consul Gothenburg; Minister to Sweden and Norway 1883-85; 1889-94; 1897-1905.
Sweden and the Swedes. Chicago: Rand McNally & Co.,
1892. 749 p.
(Translated) The Last Athenian. by Viktor Rydberg.
Philadelphia: T. B. Peterson & Bro., 1869. 555 p.

THOMPSON, Edward H., 1860-1935. Consul at Merida
1885-94, at Pregreso 1897-1900.
Children of the Cave. Illus. by Abby May Thompson.
Boston: Marshall Jones Co., 1929. 250 p.
The High Priest's Grave, Chichén Itzá, Yucatan. Chicago:
Field Museum of Natural History. Anthropological
Series, vol. 27, No. 1 of April 1938. Publication

No. 412.
People of the Serpent: Life and Adventure Among the
Mayas. Boston: Houghton Mifflin Co., 1932. 301 p.
Ruins of Xkichmook, Yucatan. Chicago: Field Columbian
Museum, Anthropological Section. Vol. 2, No. 3.
1898. 229 p.

THOMPSON, Waddy, 1798-1868. Congressman, lawyer,
Army general. Minister to Mexico 1842-44.
Recollections of Mexico. New York: Wiley & Putnam,
1846. 304 p. In microfilm, Ann Arbor, Mich.

THORP, Willard Long, 1899- . Economist, professor of
economics. Deputy Assistant Secretary of State on
Economic Affairs 1945-46. Assistant Secretary of
State 1946-52. American Representative on United Na-
tions Economic and Social Council 1947-50.
Aspects of International Petroleum Policy. Substance of
a statement made before the special subcommittee on
petroleum of the House Committee on Interstate and
Foreign Commerce on Apr. 5, 1950. Washington:
Office of Public Affairs, Department of State, 1950.
645 p.
Business Annals: United States, England, France, Ger-
many, Austria, Russia, Sweden, Netherlands, Italy,
Argentina, Brazil, Canada, South Africa, Australia,
India, Japan, China. with Hildegarde E. Thorp. New
York: National Bureau of Economic Research, Inc.,
1926. 380 p.
Cyprus: Suggestions for a Development Programme.
Prepared for the Government of the Republic of Cyprus.
New York: United Nations, 1961. 113 p.
Economic Institutions. New York: The Macmillan Co.,
1928. 306 p.
The Integration of Industrial Operation: a Statistical and
Descriptive Analysis of the Development and Growth of
Industrial Establishments and of the Size, Scope and
Structure of Combinations of Industrial Establishments
Operated from Central Offices. Washington: Govern-
ment Printing Office, 1924. 272 p.
The New Inflation. with Richard E. Quandt. New York:
McGraw-Hill Co., 1959. 233 p.
The Reality of Foreign Aid. New York: published for the
Council on Foreign Relations, by Frederick Praeger
Publishers, 1971. 370 p.
The Structure of Industry. with Walter F. Crowder and
associates. Washington: Government Printing Office,

1941. 759 p.

The Potash Industry: a Report Submitted to the Department of Justice by the Department of Commerce. May 1, 1940. with Ernest A. Tupper. Washington: 95 p.

Trade, Aid, or What? A Report Based Upon a Conference on International Economic Policy at the Merrill Center for Economics. Summer, 1953. Baltimore: Johns Hopkins Press, 1954. 224 p.

(Edit.) Economic Problems in a Changing World. by Edward Berman, O. W. Blackett, and others. New York: Farrar & Rinehart, Inc., 1939. 820 p.

THURBER, James Grover, 1894-1961. Humorist, short-story writer, play-wright, essayist, cartoonist. Code clerk in American Embassy in Paris 1918-1920.

Alarms and Diversions. New York: Harper Bros., 1957. 367 p.

Credos and Curios. New York: Harper & Row, 1962. 180 p.

The Beast in Me and Other Animals. A New Collection of Pieces and Drawings About Human Beings and Less Alarming Creatures. New York: Harcourt, Brace & Co., 1948. 340 p.

Le Derniére Fleur: Parabole en Images. Traduite par Albert Camus. Paris: Gallimar, 1952. unpaged.

Fables for Our Time and Famous Poems Illustrated. New York: Harper Bros., 1954? 124 p. c1940.

Further Fables for Our Time. Illus. by author. New York: Simon & Schuster, 1956. 174 p.

Is Sex Necessary? or, Why You Feel the Way You Do. with E. B. White, with a new introduction by E. B. White. New York: Harper Bros., 1950. 190 p.

Lanterns and Lances. New York: Harper Bros., 1961. 215 p.

The Last Flower: a Parable in Pictures. New York: Harper Bros., 1962. c1939. unpaged.

Let Your Mind Alone: And Other More or Less Inspirational Pieces. Drawings by author. New York: Harper Bros., 1937. 245 p.

The Middle-Aged Man on the Flying Trapeze. A Collection of Short Pieces. Drawings by author. Garden City, N.Y.: Blue Ribbon Books, 1946. 226 p.

Des Hommes, Des Femmes et Des Chiens. Adapté de l'Américain par Alex Grall. Paris: Dencel, 1967. 199 p.

Thurber's Men, Women and Dogs, a Book of Drawings. Preface by Dorothy Parker. New York: Bantam Books,

1946. 241 p.

Many Moons. Illus. by Louis Slobodkin. New York:
Harcourt, Brace & Co. , 1943. 47 p.

The Owl in the Attic and Other Perplexities. Drawings
by author. New York: Harper Bros. , 1931. 151 p.

The Seal in the Bedroom & Other Perplexities. Introd.
by Dorothy Parker. New York: Harper Bros. , 1932.
148 p. With an Author's Memoir. 1950. 1 vol.
Chiefly illus.

The Wonderful O. Illus. by Marc Simont. New York:
Simon & Schuster, 1957. 72 p.

The 13 Clocks. Illus. by Marc Simont. New York:
Simon & Schuster, 1950. 124 p.

The Thurber Album: a New Collection of Pieces About
People. New York: Simon & Schuster, 1952. 346 p.

Thurber & Company. Introd. by Helen Thurber. New
York: Harper & Row, 1966. 208 p.

The Thurber Carnaval. Written and illus. by James
Thurber. New York: Modern Library, 1957. c1945.
369 p.

Thurber Country: a New Collection of Pieces About Males
and Females, Mainly of Our Own Species. New York:
Simon & Schuster, 1953. 276 p.

Thurber's Dogs: a Collection of the Master's Dogs.
Written and Drawn, Real and Imaginary, Living and
Long Ago. New York: Simon & Schuster, 1955.
294 p.

Vintage Thurber: a Collection in Two Volumes of the
Best Writings and Drawings of James Thurber. Introd.
by Helen Thurber. London: H. Hamilton, 1963. 2
vols.

The Years with Ross. Drawings by author. Boston:
Little, Brown & Co. , 1959. 310 p.

The Male Animal. (play) with Elliott Nugent. New York:
Cort Theater Jan. 9, 1940.

My Life and Hard Times. New York: 1933.

My World and Welcome To It. Collection of essays between 1938-42. Includes the Secret Life of Walter
Mitty. New York: 1942.

The Great Quillow. New York: 1944.

The White Deer. New York: 1945.

TIMS, Richard Wonser, 1912- . Private expert, instructor, political analyst. Office of Strategic Services
1942-45; State Department 1945-55; Foreign Service Officer 1955-68. Served in Washington, Prague, Budapest.

Germanizing Prussian Poland: The H. K. T. Society and the Struggle for the Eastern Marches in the German Empire, 1894-1919. New York: Columbia University Studies in History, Economics and Public Law. No. 487. 1941. 312 p.

TIPTON, John Bruce, 1935- . Foreign Service Officer 1958- . Served in Mexico City, La Paz, Guatemala, State Department.
Participation of the United States in the International Labor Organization. Champagne: University of Illinois, Institute of Labor and Industrial Relations, 1959. 150 p.

TODD, Charles Stewart, 1791-1871. Lawyer, soldier, editor. Diplomatic Agent in Columbia 1820-23.
Sketches of the Civil and Military Services of William Henry Harrison. with Benjamin Drake. Cincinnati: U. P. James, 1840. 165 p.

TOTTEN, Ralph J., 1877-1949. Foreign Service Officer 1908-37. Served in Puerto Plata, Maricaibo, Trieste, Montevideo, Inspector, State Department, Barcelona, Ethiopia, Cape Town, Minister to South Africa 1930-37.
Rhymes and Things. Boston: B. Humphries, Inc., 1938. 58 p.

TOWER, Charlemagne, 1848-1923. Lawyer, businessman, writer. Minister to Austria-Hungary 1897-99; Ambassador to Russia 1899-1902, to Germany 1902-08.
The Marquis de Lafayette in the American Revolution. New York: Da Capo Press, 1895. 2 vols.
Essays Political and Historical. Philadelphia: J. B. Lippincott Co., 1914. 306 p.

TOWNSEND, Francis Edward, 1912- . Cultural affairs expert. Foreign Affairs officer 1951-72. Served in Recife, Ciudad Trujillo, Washington, Lima, Bogotá.
(Edited) Quisqueva. The poetry of Santo Domingo. Mexico, D. F.: Editores Unidos, 1947. 104 p. Bogotá: United States Information Service, 1964. 63 p. Bilingual.

TRAUTMAN, Kathleen. Wife of Foreign Service Reserve Officer Robert G. Trautman, 1931- . He served as writer-editor in United States Information Agency, 1965-68. In Kabul, Afghanistan for about a year.
Spies Behind the Pillars, Bandits at the Pass. New York:

David McKay Company, Inc., 1972. 244 p. [Autobiographical.]

TRESCOTT, William Henry, 1822-1898. Historian, Assistant
Secretary of State 1860-61. One of three commissioners, with James B. Angell and John F. Swift, to China
in 1880 to arrange for a modification of the Burlingame
Treaty regarding Chinese immigration. Sent to Chile
in 1881 to warn Chile against excessive demands on
Bolivia and Peru after the War of the Pacific. In 1861
he acted as intermediary between the Confederate Government and the British and French Consuls in Charleston regarding privateering.
Diplomacy of the Revolution: an Historical Study. New
York: D. Appleton & Co., 1852. 169 p.
The Diplomatic History of the Administrations of Washington and Adams. Boston: Little, Brown & Co., 1857.
283 p.
Memorial of the Life of J. Johnston Pettigrew. Charleston, S.C.: J. Russell, 1870. 65 p.

TRESIDER, Argus J., 1907- . Teacher, Foreign Service
Reserve and United States Information Agency officer
1949-69. Served in Colombo, Ankara, Pretoria, Stockholm.
Ceylon, an Introduction to the Resplendent Land. Princeton, N.J.: D. Van Nostrand Co. Inc., 1960. 237 p.

TRIPP, Bartlett, 1842-1911. Jurist. Minister to Austria-
Hungary 1893-97. Chairman of American-British-
German Commission on Samoa, 1899. As a result,
the United States got control of Pago Pago when the
islands were partitioned.
My Trip to Samoa. Cedar Rapids, Iowa: The Torch
Press, 1911. 182 p.

TRIST, Nicholas Philip, 1800-1874. Lawyer, friend of
President Jackson. Clerk in State Department 1829-
33. Consul in Havana 1833-41. Chief Clerk in State
Department 1845-47. Special Agent to negotiate peace,
in Mexico City 1847-48.
Trist Papers. In Library of Congress. 44 vols.

TRIVERS, Howard, 1909- . State Department and Foreign
Service Officer 1941-69. Served in Washington, National War College, Copenhagen, Berlin, Merit Service
Award (1961), Board of Examiners, Zurich, Vaduz

(Lichtenstein).
Three Crises in American Foreign Affairs and a Continuing Revolution. Carbondale, Ill. : Southern Illinois University Press, 1972. 224 p.
National Socialism: Basic Principles, Their Application by the Nazi Party's Foreign Organization, and the Use of Germans Abroad for Nazi Aims. Co-author with Raymond E. Murphy, Francis B. Stevens and Joseph Morgan Roland. Washington: Government Printing Office, Department of State Publication #1864. 1943. 510 p.

TSUKAHIRA, Toshio George, 1915- . History professor, Japanese language expert. Foreign Service Officer 1953- . Served in State Department, Tokyo, Fukuoka, Bangkok.
The Postwar Evolution of Communist Strategy in Japan. Cambridge: Center for International Studies, Massachusetts Institute of Technology, 1954. 188 p.
Feudal Control in Tokugawa Japan: The Sankin Kotai System. Harvard East Asian Monographs No. 20. Cambridge: Harvard University Press, 1966. 228 p.

TUCKER, Harriet Elizabeth, 1828-1889. Wife of John Morgan Francis, 1823-97, who was Minister to Greece 1871-74, Chargé d'Affaires and then Minister Resident in Lisbon 1882-84, Minister to Austria 1884-85.
Land and Sea: Incidents of Travel. Troy, N.Y. : Nims & Knight, 1891. 198 p.
Across the Meridians and Fragmentary Letters. New York: The DeVinne Press, 1887. 300 p.

TUDOR, William, 1779-1830. Businessman, politician, writer, editor. Consul at Lima 1823. Chargé d'Affaires at Rio de Janeiro 1827-30, where he died.
Letters on the Eastern States. New York: Kirk & Mercein, 1820. 356 p.
Miscellanies. Boston: Wells & Lilly, 1821. 156 p.
The Life of James Otis, of Massachusetts. Boston: Wells & Lilly, 1823. 508 p.
Gebel Teir. Boston: Carter & Hendee, 1829. 158 p.

TURKEL, Harry Raymond, 1906-1970. Foreign Service Staff officer 1929-42; U.S. Army 1942-45; Foreign Service Officer 1945-61. Served in State Department, London, Havana, Mexico City, Paris, Ottawa, Lima, Athens, Bonn. Ambassador to the Inter-American

Economic Council of the Organization of American
States. Research Associate with Johns Hopkins School
of Advanced International Studies.
International Peace Observations. A History and Forecast. with David W. Wainhouse, Bernard G. Bechhoeffer, Benjamin Gerig and John C. Dreier. Baltimore: Johns Hopkins University Press, in Cooperation
with the Washington Center of Foreign Policy Research
School of Advanced International Studies, 1966. 663 p.

TYLER, William Royall, 1910- . Born in France of Amer-
ican parents. Banking, radio broadcasting. Office of
War Information 1943-45. Foreign Service Officer
1945-70. Served in Paris, State Department, Bonn.
Assistant Secretary of State 1962-65. Ambassador to
the Netherlands 1965-70.
Dijon and the Valois Dukes of Burgundy. Norman, Okla. :
University of Oklahoma Press, 1971. 176 p. (Part of
the "Centers of Civilization" series.)
(Translated from the Dutch) A Moment of Silence. by
Pierre Janssen. New York: Atheneum Publishers,
1970. 58 p. Photos by Hans Samsam.

UNDERWOOD, Francis Henry, 1825-1894. Lawyer, writer.
One of the founders of the ATLANTIC MONTHLY in
1857. Consul at Glasgow 1886-89. (Succeeded Bret
Harte.) Consul at Leith 1893.
Cloud Pictures. (short stories) Published by Francis H.
Underwood. Boston: Lee & Shepard, 1872. 166 p.
Lord of Himself. Boston: Lee & Shepard, 1874. 512 p.
Man Proposes. Boston: Lee & Shepard, 1885. 344 p.
Doctor Gray's Quest. Boston: Lee & Shepard, 1895.
406 p.
Quabbin, the Story of a Small Town. Boston: Lee &
Shepard, 1893. 375 p.
The Builders of American Literature. Boston: Lee &
Shepard, 1893. 302 p.

VAN BUREN, Martin, 1782-1862. Lawyer, politician, Sena-
tor, Secretary of State 1829-31, Minister to Great
Britain 1831-32 (on recess appointment that failed of
confirmation by the Senate in 1832). Vice President
1833-37, President 1837-41.
Van Buren Manuscripts. In the Library of Congress.
Prepared by Elizabeth Howard West. Washington:
Government Printing Office, 1910. 757 p.
Inquiry into the Origin and Course of Political Parties in

the United States. (posthumous) Edit. by his sons.
New York: Hurd & Houghton, 1867. 436 p.
The Autobiography of Martin Van Buren. Edit. by J. C.
Fitzpatrick. Annual Report of the American Historical
Association for the year 1918. Vol. II. Washington:
Government Printing Office, 1920. 808 p.
Opinions of Martin Van Buren, Vice President of the
United States, Upon the Powers and Duties of Con-
gress, in Reference to the Abolition of Slavery Either
in the Slave-Holding States or the District of Columbia.
Washington: Blair & Rives, Printers, 1836. 32 p.

VANDENBERG, Arthur Hendrick, 1884-1951. Lawyer, editor, Senator. Delegate to United Nations Organiza-
tion, San Francisco, 1945; Delegate to first and second
General Assemblies of the United Nations, New York,
1946; Council of Foreign Ministers and Peace Confer-
ence in Paris; Advisor to Secretary Byrnes at Big
Four Foreign Ministers Meeting in Paris.
The Greatest American, Alexander Hamilton: An Histori-
cal Analysis of His Life and Works Together with a
Symposium of Opinions by Distinguished Americans.
New York: G. P. Putnam's Sons, 1921. 353 p.
If Hamilton Were Here Today: American Fundamentals
Applied to Modern Problems. New York: G. P. Put-
nam's Sons, 1923. 366 p.
The Private Papers of Senator Vandenberg. Edit. by
Arthur H. Vandenberg, Jr. with the collaboration of
Joe Alex Morris. Boston: Houghton Mifflin Co.,
1952. 599 p.
The Trail of Tradition. New York: G. P. Putnam's
Sons, 1926. 405 p.

VAN DYCK, Edward Abbott, 1841-1939. Consular clerk in
Cairo 1873-82. Taught in the schools of Cairo and
translated ancient ethics.
History of the Arabs and Their Literature Before and
After the Rise of Islam Within the Limits of Their
Peninsula and Beyond It. An outline for the use of the
pupils of the Khediviah school, compiled from Arab
and European sources. Laibach, Austria: I. V.
Kleimayre and F. Bomberg, 1894. 222 p. In Arabic
1897. 677 p.
(Translated from the original Italian) Real Property,
Mortgage and Wakf. According to Ottoman Law. by
D. Catteshi. London: Wyman & Sons, 1884. 96 p.

VAN DYKE, Henry, 1852-1933.   Clergyman, poet, author,
  lecturer, editor.   Minister to the Netherlands and
  Luxembourg, 1913-17.
The Works of Henry Van Dyke.   Avalon edition.   New
  York: Charles Scribner's Sons, 1920-21.   15 vols.
The Americanism of Washington.   New York: Harper
  Bros., 1906.   71 p.
The Broken Soldier and the Maid of France.   Illus. by
  Frank E. Schoonover.   New York: Harper & Bros.,
  1919.   65 p.
The Builders - An Ode.   New York: Charles Scribner's
  Sons, 1897.   87 p.
Camp Fires and Guide Posts.   New York: Charles Scrib-
  ner's Sons, 1921.   319 p.
The Childhood of Jesus Christ.   Illus. from paintings of
  great masters.   New York: Fredrick A. Stokes Co.,
  1905.   121 p.
Chosen Poems.   New York: Charles Scribner's Sons,
  1927.   355 p.
The Christ Child in Art.   A Study of Interpretation.   New
  York: Harper & Bros., 1894.   236 p.
(Edited) A Creelful of Fishing Stories.   A Pastime Book.
  Illus. by Robert Ball.   New York: Charles Scribner's
  Sons, 1932.   419 p.
Days Off and Other Digressions.   New York: Charles
  Scribner's Sons, 1907.   322 p.
Essays in Application.   New York: Charles Scribner's
  Sons, 1905.   282 p.
Fighting for Peace.   New York: Charles Scribner's Sons,
  1917.   247 p.
The First Christmas Tree.   Illus. by Howard Pyle.   New
  York: Charles Scribner's Sons, 1897.   76 p.
The Golden Key.   Stories of Deliverance.   New York:
  Charles Scribner's Sons, 1926.   347 p.
The Gospel for a World of Sin.   A Companion Volume to
  "The Gospel for an Age of Doubt."   New York: The
  Macmillan Co., 1899.   192 p.
The Gospel for an Age of Doubt.   (Originally written as
  Lyman Beecher Foundation lectures to divinity students
  at Yale.) New York: The Macmillan Co., 1896.
  457 p.
Great Short Works.   Introd. by Ella DeMers.   New York:
  Harper & Row, 1966.   209 p.
Half Told Tales.   New York: Charles Scribner's Sons,
  1925.   150 p.
Henry Jackson Van Dyke.   Signed by Henry Van Dyke and
  Paul Van Dyke.   New York: A. D. F. Randolph &

Co., 1892. 168 p.
An Introduction to the Poems of Tennyson. Boston: Ginn
   & Co., 1903. 93 p.
Light my Candle. A book of Reflections by Henry Van
   Dyke and Tertius Van Dyke. New York: Fleming H.
   Revell Co., 1926. 322 p.
(Edited) Little Masterpieces of English Poetry by British
   and American Authors. Edit. by Henry Van Dyke,
   assisted by Hardin Craig. New York: Doubleday Page
   & Co., 1905. 6 vols.
Little Rivers. A Book of Essays in Profitable Idleness.
   New York: Charles Scribner's Sons, 1895. 291 p.
The Man Behind the Book. New York: Charles Scrib-
   ner's Sons, 1929. 357 p.
The Poems of Henry Van Dyke. Now First Collected and
   Revised, with Many Heretofore Unpublished. New
   York: Charles Scribner's Sons, 1911. 467 p.
The Poetry of Tennyson, First Baron. 1809-1892. New
   York: Charles Scribner's Sons, 1889. 296 p.
Six Days of the Week. New York: Charles Scribner's
   Sons, 1924. 355 p.
The Spirit of America. (lectures in English, 1908-09)
   Paris: The Hyde Foundation, University of Paris,
   1887. 259 p.
The Story of the Psalms. New York: Charles Scribner's
   Sons, 1887. 259 p.
The Travel Diary of an Angler. New York: Derrydale
   Press, 1929. 143 p.
The White Bees and Other Poems. New York: Charles
   Scribner's Sons, 1909. 105 p.
The Story of the Other Wise Man. New York: Harper
   Bros., 1892. 82 p.
The Unknown Quantity: a Book of Romance and Some
   Half-told Tales. New York: Charles Scribner's Sons,
   1912. 370 p.
The Valley of Vision: a Book of Romance, and some
   Half-told Tales. New York: Charles Scribner's Sons,
   1919. 306 p.
The Van Dyke Book, Selected from the Writings of Henry
   Van Dyke. Edit. by Edwin Mims, with biographical
   sketch by Brooke Van Dyke. New York: Charles
   Scribner's Sons, 1905. 187 p.
(Edited) Scenes in Fiction. Boston: Hall & Locke, 1902.
   376 p.
Straight Sermons to Young Men and Other Human Beings.
   New York: Charles Scribner's Sons, 1893. 233 p.
Sermons to Young Men: a New and Enlarged Edition of

"Straight Sermons." New York: Charles Scribner's
Sons, 1898. 253 p.
The House of Rimmon: a Drama in Four Acts. New
York: C. Scribner's Sons, 1908. 121 p.
Fisherman's Luck and Some Other Uncertain Things.
New York: Charles Scribner's Sons, 1899. 247 p.

VAN DYNE, Frederick, 1861-1915. Entered State Depart-
ment as clerk in Law Bureau 1891-1900; Assistant
Solicitor 1900-1907; Consul Kingston, Jamaica 1907-
10; Assistant Solicitor 1910-13; Consul Lyons 1913-15.
Citizenship of the United States. Rochester, N. Y.:
The Lawyer's Cooperative Publishing Co., 1904.
385 p.
Our Foreign Service: The ABC of American Diplomacy.
Rochester, N.Y.: The Lawyer's Cooperative Publish-
ing Co., 1909. 316 p.
A Treatise on the Law of Naturalization of the United
States. Washington: F. Van Dyne, 1907. 528 p.

VAUX, Richard, 1816-1895. Lawyer, public official, penolo-
gist, Congressman. Secretary of Legation, London
1837-38.
Short Talks on Crime - Cause and Convict Punishment.
Philadelphia: (no publisher given), 1882. 135 p.
Brief Sketch of the Origin and History of the State Peni-
tentiary for the Eastern District of Pennsylvania, at
Philadelphia. Philadelphia: McLaughlin Brothers,
printer, 1872. 143 p.
Reports of Some of the Criminal Cases on Primary Hear-
ing. Philadelphia: T. & J. W. Johnson, 1846. 236 p.
The Prevention and Punishment of Crime. Philadelphia:
Allen, Lane & Scott's Printing House, 1885. 59 p.
Some Remarks on Crime-Cause. 2nd edit. Philadelphia:
McLaughlin Brothers Book and Job Printing Establish-
ment, 1879. 80 p.

VIGNAUD, Henry, 1830-1922. New Orleans journalist, historian, Confederate officer, Member of Confederate
Mission in Paris 1862-66; Secretary of Roumanian Mission in Paris 1869; translator for United States Government in Paris for Alabama Claims Mission 1872;
2nd Secretary of American Legation in Paris 1875; 1st
Secretary 1885-1909; Honorary Counselor 1909 till his
death in 1922. Received French Government decorations.
Americ Vespuce, L'Attribution de Son Nom au Nouveau

Monde. (extracts from the Journal of the American Society of Paris.) Paris: Au Siege de la Societé, 1912. pp. 239-299.

A Critical Study of the Various Dates Assigned to the Birth of Christopher Columbus: the Real Date, 1451, with a Bibliography of the Question. London: H. Stevens, Sons, and Stiles, 1903. 121 p.

Etudes Critiques sur la Vie de Colomb Avant ses Descouvertes; les Origines de sa Famille; les Deux Colomb. ses Prétendus Parents; la Vraie Date de sa Naissance; les Etudes et les Premieres Campagnes Qu'il Aurait Faites, son Arrivée en Portugal et le Combat Naval de 1476; son Voyage au Nord; son Etablissement en Portugal; son Mariage; sa Famille Portugaise. Paris: H. Welter, 1905. 543 p.

Henry Harisse: Etude Biographique et Morale, Avec la Bibliographie Critique de ses Ecrits. Paris: C. Chadenat, 1912. 83 p.

Histoire Critique de la Grande Enterprise de Christophe Colomb. Comment Il Aurait Conçu et Formé son Projet, sa Presentation à Differents Cours, son Acceptation Finale, sa Mise a Execution, son Veritable Caractére. Paris: H. Welter, 1911. 2 vols.

La Lettre et la Carte de Toscanilli sur la Route des Indes par L'Ouest Adressées en 1474 au Portugais Fernam Martins et Transmises plus tard á Christophe Colomb: Etude Critique sur L'Authenticité et la Valeur de ses Documents et sur les Sources des Idées Cosmographiques de Colomb, Suivie des Divers Textes de la Lettre de 1474 avec Traductions, Annotations et Fac-Similé. Paris: E. Leroux, 1901. 319 p.

Le Vrai Christophe Colomb et la Légende. La Date Exacte de la Naissance du Grand Genois. Sa Famille, les Indications qu'il Avait. Toscanelli, Prétendu Initiateur de la Découverte de L'Amérique. L'Object Veritable de L'Entreprise de 1492. Paris: Picard, 1921. 230 p.

VILLARD, Henry Serrano, 1900- . Foreign Service Officer 1928-62. Served in Teheran, Department of State, Rio de Janeiro, Caracas, Liberia, Union of South Africa, Policy Planning Staff, Oslo, Minister to Lybia 1952-54, United Nations (N.Y.) 1954, National War College 1955, Career Minister 1958, United Nations (Geneva) 1958, Ambassador to Mali, Senegal and Mauritania 1960-62.

Affairs at State: A Career Diplomat's Candid Appraisal

of the United States Foreign Service. Introd. by James
Reston. New York: Thomas Y. Crowell Co., 1965.
254 p.
Contact: The Story of the Early Birds. Man's First
Decade of Flight from Kitty Hawk to World War I.
New York: Thomas Y. Crowell Co., 1968. 263 p.
Lybia. The New Arab Kingdom of North Africa. Ithaca:
Cornell University Press, 1956. 169 p.
The Great Road Races 1894-1914. London: Arthur Bark-
er, Ltd., 1972. 249 p. Illus. index.

VINCENT, John Carter, 1900-1972. Foreign Service Officer
1924-53. Chinese language officer. Served in Chang-
sha, Hankow, Swatow, Peking, Tsinan, Mukden, Dairen,
Geneva, Shanghai, Chungking, Chief of Division of Far
Eastern Affairs, Minister to Switzerland 1947-51. Dip-
lomatic Agent to Tangier (rank of Minister) 1951-53.
Career Minister.
The Extra-territorial System in China: Final Phase.
Cambridge, Mass.: East Asia Research Center, Har-
vard University Press, 1970. 119 p.
America's Future in the Pacific. Brunswick, N.J.:
Rutgers University Press, 1947. 179 p. [with others]

VOPICKA, Charles Joseph, 1857-1935. Business, brewing,
politics. Minister to Rumania, Serbia and Bulgaria
1913-20.
Secrets of the Balkans and Seven Years of a Diplomatist's
Life in the Storm Center of Europe. Chicago: Rand
McNally & Co., 1921. 330 p.

WABEKE, Bertus Harry, 1914- . Born in South Africa.
Naturalized in 1922. Teacher, writer. Library of
Congress. Navy. Foreign Service Officer 1951-69.
Served in Washington, Stuttgart, Ankara.
Dutch Emigration to North America: 1624-1860. New
York: Netherlands Information Bureau, 1944. 160 p.
A Guide to Dutch Bibliographies. Washington: Library
of Congress, 1951. 193 p.

WADSWORTH, James Jeremiah, 1905- . New York State
legislator, business executive, official in various Federal Government agencies. Deputy Representative of
the United States to the United Nations and to the Security Council, with rank of Ambassador, 1953-60.
The Glass House: the United Nations in Action. New
York: Frederick A. Praeger, Inc., 1966. 224 p.

The Price of Peace. New York: Frederick A. Praeger,
Inc., 1962. 127 p.

WAINHOUSE, David W., 1900- . Born in Vilan, Lithuania.
Naturalized citizen. International lawyer. Assistant
United States Attorney 1934-41. Lecturer at New York
University. Foreign Service Officer 1946-62. Served
in Washington, Paris, Vienna.
A History of American Foreign Policy. with John Holla-
day Latané. New York: The Odyssey Press, 1940.
1026 p.
Remnants of Empire: The United Nations and the End of
Colonialism. For the Council on Foreign Relations.
New York: Harper & Row, 1964. 153 p.
Arms Control Agreements: Designs for Verification and
Organization. with others. Baltimore: Johns Hopkins
University Press, 1968. 179 p.
International Peace Observations, A History and Forecast.
with Bernard G. Bechhoeffer, Benjamin Gerig, John
C. Dreier and Harry R. Turkel. Baltimore: Johns
Hopkins University Press, in cooperation with the
Washington Center of Foreign Policy Research School
of Advanced International Studies, 1966. 663 p.

WALKIN, Jacob, 1917- . Private expert and lecturer political science. State Department staff 1952-55. Foreign Service Officer 1955-70. Served in Belgrade,
Hongkong, Djakarta, Surabaya, Washington.
The Rise of Democracy in Pre-Revolutionary Russia: Political and Social Institutions Under the Last Three
Czars. New York: Frederick A. Praeger Inc., 1962.
320 p.

WALLACE, Hugh Campbell, 1863-1931. Financier, politician.
Ambassador to France 1919-21. Collected and gave to
the Embassy in Paris a valuable library on Franco-
American relations.
The Speeches of the Honorable Hugh Campbell Wallace -
1919-1921. Paris: Plon Nourrit et Cie., 1921. 195 p.

WALLACE, Lewis (Lew), 1827-1905. Major General in Union Forces in Civil War. Governor of New Mexico
Territory. Writer, politician. Unsuccessfully applied
for consular and diplomatic appointments to Santarem
(Brazil) and Bolivia. Refused later appointments to
Brazil, Holland, Bolivia and Paraguay. Became Minister to Turkey 1881-85.

Ben Hur. A Tale of the Christ. New York: Harper
Bros., 1880. 560 p. Louisville, Ky.: The American
Printing House for the Blind, 1887. 4 vols.
Ben Hur. A Tale of Christ. The Garfield edition. Illus.
by William Martin Johnson. New York: Harper Bros.,
1892. 2 vols.
The Boyhood of Christ. New York: Harper Bros., 1889.
101 p.
Comodus. An Historical Play. Crawfordville, Ind.:
1876. 65 p.
The Fair God: or, The Last of the 'Tzins, a Tale of the
Conquest of Mexico. 31st edit. Boston: Houghton
Mifflin Co., 1887. 586 p. 38th edit. London: F.
Warne Co., 1887. 411 p.
Lew Wallace: An Autobiography. New York: Harper
Bros., 1906. 2 vols. Plates, portraits, facsimiles.
Life of General Ben Harrison, by General Lew Wallace,
Also Life of Honorable Levi P. Morton, by George
Aldred Townsend. Philadelphia: Hubbard Press, 1888.
578 p.
The Prince of India: or, Why Constantinople Fell. New
York: Harper Bros., 1893. 2 vols.
The Wooing of Malkatoon. Commodus. Illus. by deMond
& Waguelin. New York: Harper Bros., 1893. 167 p.

WALLACE, Susan Arnold (Elston), 1830-1907. Wife of Lew
Wallace, Minister to Turkey. [Q.V.]
Along the Bosphorus, and Other Sketches. Chicago:
Rand McNally & Co., 1898. 383 p.
The City of Kings: What the Child Jesus Saw and Heard.
Indianapolis: Bobbs-Merrill Co. Inc., 1903. 97 p.
The Land of the Pueblos. New York: J. B. Alden,
1888. 285 p.
The Repose in Egypt: A Medley. (and Along the Bos-
phorus.) New York: J. B. Alden, 1888.
The Storied Sea. Boston: J. R. Osgood & Co., 1883.
233 p.

WALSH, Robert, 1784-1859. Lawyer, journalist, biographer, publisher. Settled permanently in Paris in 1837
and served as Consul General in Paris, 1844-51. After his death his papers were accidentally destroyed.
An Appeal from the Judgements of Great Britain Respecting the United States of America. Part First, Containing an Historical Outline of their Merits and Wrongs
as Colonies; and Strictures Upon the Calumnies of the
British Writers. by Robert Walsh, Jr. Philadelphia:

Published by Mitchell Ames, and White. William
Brown, printer. 1819. 512 p.
Correspondence Respecting Russia Between Robert Goodloe
Harper, Esq. and Robert Walsh, jun. Together with
the Speech of Mr. Harper, Commemorative of the
Russian Victories. Delivered at Georgetown, Colum-
bia, June 5th, 1813. And an Essay on the Future
State of Europe. Philadelphia: Printed by W. Fry,
1813. 140 p.
Didactics: Social, Literary, and Political. Philadelphia:
Carey, Lea & Blanchard, 1836. 2 vols.
Free Remarks on the Spirit of the Federal Constitution,
the Practice of the Federal Government, and the Obli-
gations of the Union, respecting the Exclusion of
Slavery from the Territories and New States. by a
Philadelphian. Philadelphia: A. Finley, 1819. 116 p.
An Inquiry into the Past and Present Relations of France
and the United States of America. London: Printed
for J. Hatchard, 1811. 87 p.
A Letter on the Genius and Dispositions of the French
Government, Including a View of the Taxation of the
French Empire. Addressed to a Friend, by an Amer-
ican Recently Returned from Europe. Philadelphia:
Hopkins and Earle, 1810. 253 p.

WANAMAKER, Allison Temple, 1918-1968. Foreign Service
Officer 1941-68. Served in Barcelona, Bilbao, Lisbon,
Ciudad Trujillo, Cebu, Manila, State Department, Tel
Aviv, Nassau, Cordoba, San José.
American Foreign Policy Today. New York: Bantam
Books, Inc., 1964. 250 p.

WARDEN, David Baille, 1772-1845. Author, book collector.
Born in Ireland. An Irish patriot, arrested and offered choice of prison or emigration, 1799. Went to
United States, naturalized in 1804. To Paris as private secretary to the American Minister, General John
Armstrong, in 1804. Consul pro-tempore in Paris
1808-10. Appointed Consul 1810-14. Removed from
office in 1814 for having without authority assumed title
of Consul General. Remained in France the remainder
of his life, promoting American interests.
Bibliotheca American Being a Choice Collection of Books
Relating to North and South America and the West Indies, including Voyages to the Southern Hemisphere,
maps, engravings and medals. Paris: Printed by Fain
& Thunot, 1840. 124 p. This is the second library

of Americana collected by Warden. 1979 volumes, ex-
clusive of maps, prints, etc. Acquired by the New
York State Library in 1845. The first collection was
bought for Harvard University in 1823.

Bibliotheca Americana - Septentrionalis: Being a Choice
Collection of Books in Various Languages, Relating to
the History, Climate, Produce, Population, Agricul-
ture, Commerce, Arts, Sciences, etc. of North Amer-
ica from its First Discovery, to Its Present Existing
Government, With All the Important Official Documents
Published ... by the Authority of Congress. Same in
French. Paris: L'Imprimerie de Nouzou, 1820.
147 p. 1200 volumes and some maps purchased by
Samuel A. Eliot (for $5,000) and presented to Harvard
University in 1823.

A Chorographical and Statistical Description of the District
of Columbia, Seat of the General Government of the
United States. Paris: printed by Smith, 1816. 212 p.

Chronologie Historique de l'Amerique. Paris: A. Dupont
et Roret, 1826-1844. 10 vols. Vols. 4-7 published
by A. J. Denain. Vols. 8-10, chez l'editeur.

Chronologie Historique de l'Amerique Espagnole. Paris:
1826-1837. 8 vols.

Chronologie Historique des Etats-Unis d'Amerique. Paris:
1842-1844. 2 vols.

On the Origin, Nature, Progress and Influence of Consular Establishments. Paris: Printed and sold by
Smith, 1813. 331 p.

A Statistical, Political and Historical Account of the
United States of North America from the Period of
Their First Colonization to the Present Day. Edinburgh: Printed for A. Constable & Co., 1819. 3
vols. This evoked a 48 page letter by William James
defending the British Navy "against the misrepresenta-
tion of a work recently published in Edinburgh entitled
'A Statistical Account of the United States of North
America.'" London: Printed for M. Richardson,
1819.

WARNE, William Elmo, 1905- . Newspaper editor. Department of the Interior 1935-51. Technical Cooperation Administration, Tehran 1951-55.

Mission for Peace: Point Four in Iran. New York:
The Bobbs-Merrill Co., Inc., 1956. 320 p.

California Commands Her Water Destiny. A series of 8
articles prepared for publication in California newspapers. Sacramento: Department of Water Resources,

1966. 1 vol.
The State Water Project Is Unifying California. Sacramento: State of California, The Resources Agency,
Department of Water Resources, 1966. 1 vol. A
series of twelve articles for publication in California
newspapers. Various pagings.

WARNE, W. Robert, 1937- . Foreign Service Reserve Officer 1962-64. Foreign Service Officer 1964- .
Served in Saigon, State Department, Buenos Aires.
Without Guns: American Civilians in Rural Vietnam.
with William A. Nighswonger, Earle J. Young and
George K. Tanham. New York: Frederick A. Praeger, Inc., 1966. 320 p.

WASHBURN, Charles Ames, 1822-1889. Minister Resident
to Paraguay 1863-68.
From Poverty to Competence. Graduated Taxation.
Philadelphia: J. B. Lippincott Co., 1887. 163 p.
Gomery of Montgomery: A Family History, by the Au-
thor of "Philip Thaxter." New York: Carleton Co.,
1865. 2 vols.
The History of Paraguay, with Notes of Personal Observa-
tions, and Reminiscences of Diplomacy Under Difficul-
ties. Boston: Lee, Shepherd & Dillingham, 1871.
2 vols.
Political Evolution: or, From Poverty to Competence.
Philadelphia: J. B. Lippincott Co., 1885. 301 p.
Une Question du Doit des Gens. Paris: Imprimerie de
Dubuisson et Cie., 1868. 96 p.
Philip Thaxter: a Novel. New York: Rudd & Carleton,
1861. 350 p.

WASHBURNE, Elihu Benjamin, 1816-1887. Lawyer, politician, Congressman. Secretary of State only 12 days in
1869, under President Grant. Minister to Paris 1869-
77. Only official foreign representative to remain in
Paris during the Siege of Paris 1870-71 and the days
of the Commune. Historian and writer.
America's Aid to Germany in 1870-71. An abstract from
the Official correspondence of E. B. Washburne, Ambassador to Paris. The English text with a German
translation, prefaced by Adolph Hepner. St. Louis:
1905. 463 p.
Recollections of a Minister to France, 1869-77. New
York: Charles Scribner's Sons, 1887. 2 vols.
Edward Coles, Second Governor of Illinois, and the Slavery

Struggle of 1823-24. Prepared for the Chicago Histor-
ical Society. Chicago: Jansen, McClurg & Co., 1882.
253 p.
United States Embassy, France. Franco-German war and
insurrection of the Commune. Correspondence of E.
B. Washburne, Minister Plenipotentiary of the United
States to France. Washington: Government Printing
Office, 1878. 222 p.
Washburne Papers. 101 vols. Library of Congress.
(Edited) The Edwards Papers: Being a Portion of the
Collection of the Letters, Papers, and Manuscripts of
Ninian Edwards. Chicago: Fergus Printing Co., 1884.
633 p.

WASHINGTON, Samuel Walter, 1901- . Foreign Service
Officer 1926-51. Instructor in economics at Carnegie
School of Technology. Served in Buenos Aires, Rio de
Janeiro, Tokyo, Bogota, Istanbul, Ankara, Riga, Stock-
holm, San José, Mexico City, Madrid, Washington.
A Study of the Causes of the Hostility Toward the United
States in Latin America: Argentina. Washington:
Department of State External Research Staff, 1957.
115 p.
A Study of the Causes of Hostility Toward the United
States in Latin America: Brazil. Washington: De-
partment of State External Research Papers, 1956.
51 p.

WAYNICK, Capus Miller, 1889- . Business executive,
editor and publisher, politician. Ambassador to
Nicaragua 1950-51, to Colombia 1951-53.
North Carolina and the Negro. with John C. Brooks and
Elsie W. Pitts. Raleigh, North Carolina: Mayor's
Cooperative Committee, 1964. 309 p.

WEBB, James Watson, 1802-1884. Journalist. Chargé
d'Affaires in Austria 1850, not confirmed. He resigned
from the Army in 1827 as First Lieutenant. He was
given the title of "General" as a courtesy when he was
appointed Chargé d'Affaires to Austria. Congress did
not confirm his appointment to Austria because of
animosity toward that country. Minister to Brazil
1861-69.
Reminiscences of Gen'l Samuel B. Webb of the Revolutionary Army. by his son, J. Watson Webb. New
York: Globe Stationery and Printing Co., 1882.
402 p. A collection of some of the letters and

correspondence of General Webb and of Silas Deane;
published exclusively for family circulation. Biographical sketch of General Webb by J. A. Stevens. A
roster of the men enlisted during 1777 into the 9th,
afterward the 3rd Connecticut regiment commanded by
Samuel B. Webb. Names and rank of officers in the
3rd Connecticut, June 1782. Geneology of the Webb
family.
General J. Watson Webb, late U. S. Envoy Extraordinary
to Brazil, vs Hamilton Fish and E. R. Hoar. New
York? 1875. 64 p. Pamphlet written by Gen. J. W.
Webb in relation to action brought by the United States
against Webb to recover difference in settlement of
private claim against Brazil, in which a less sum than
amount received was paid over to the United States.

WEDDELL, Alexander Welbourne, 1876-1948. Foreign Service Officer 1908-42. Served in Copenhagen, Zanzibar,
Catania, Athens, Cairo, Calcutta, Mexico City, Am-
bassador to Argentina 1933-39, to Spain 1939-42.
Introduction to Argentina. New York: Greystone Press,
1939. 301 p.
United States Delegation to the Pan American Commercial
Conference, Held at Buenos Aires, May 26-June 19,
1935. Washington: Government Printing Office, 1936.
164 p.
A Memorial Volume of Virginia Historical Portraiture.
Richmond, Va. : The William Byrd Press, Inc. , 1930.
556 p.
Richmond, Virginia, In Old Prints 1737-1887. Richmond:
Johnson Publishing Co. , 1932. 254 p.

WEEKES, Richard Van Allen, 1924- . Foreign Service
Staff Officer Karachi, 1951-53.
Pakistan, Birth and Growth of a Muslim Nation. Prince-
ton, N. J. : D. Van Nostrand Co. Inc. , 1964. 278 p.

WEHLE, Louis Brandeis, 1880- . Lawyer. Government
official. Head of Foreign Economic Administration
mission to the Netherlands, 1944-45.
Hidden Threads of History. Wilson Through Roosevelt.
Introd. by Allan Nevins. New York: The Macmillan
Co. , 1953. 300 p.

WEIL, Thomas Eliot, 1906- . Teacher. Foreign Service
Officer 1935-65. Served in Marseilles, Canton, Nanking, Shanghai, Chungking, Wellington, New Delhi,

Kabul, State Department, National War College, Nepal,
Seoul, Foreign Service Institute, Foreign Service In-
spector, London.
(Co-author with Jan Knippers Black, Kenneth W.
Martindale, David S. McMorris, Frederick P. Munson
and Kathryn E. Parachina of the following books.)
Area Handbook for Colombia. Washington: Department of
the Army Pamphlet 550-26, 1970. 595 p. Includes
bibliography.
Area Handbook for Brazil. Washington: Government
Printing Office, 1971. 645 p. Includes bibliography.
Area Handbook for Venezuela. Washington: Government
Printing Office, 1971. 525 p. Includes bibliography.
Area Handbook for Paraguay. Washington: Government
Printing Office. 516 p. Includes bibliography.
Area Handbook for Uruguay. Washington: Government
Printing Office, 1971. 439 p. Includes bibliography.
Area Handbook for Panama. Washington: Government
Printing Office, 1972. Includes bibliography.
(Note: similar handbooks on Peru and Ecuador are in
process.)

WEINER, Herbert E., 1921- . Foreign Service Officer
1947- . Served in London, Sydney, Labor Department Washington, Ottawa, Naval War College, Lisbon,
Department of State.
British Labor and Public Ownership. Introd. by Michael
Ross. Washington: Public Affairs Press, 1960.
111 p.

WEINTRAUB, Sidney, 1922- . Newspaper editor. Foreign
Service Officer 1948- . Served Tananarive, Mexico
City, State Department, Tokyo, Bangkok, Santiago.
Superior Award 1964.
Mexican Slay Ride. London: Robert Hale, Ltd., 1962.
188 p. New York: Abelard Schuman, 1962. 188 p.
The Siamese Coup Affair. London: T. V. Boardman &
Co. Ltd., 1963. 174 p.
Trade Preferences for the Less Developed Countries. An
Analysis of United States Policy. New York: Frederick
A. Praeger, Inc., 1966. 231 p. In Spanish, Prefer-
encias Para Los Paises en Desarrollo. Buenos Aires:
Editorial Trequel, S.A., 1969. 232 p.

WELLS, Henry Bartlett, 1908- . Foreign Service Officer
1931-68. Served in Mexico City, Montevideo, Managua, Reykjavik, Havana, Helsinki, Bucharest, State

Department, Athens.   Translates from twenty-one
languages into English, mostly technical, diverse sub-
jects.
(Translation from the Russian) A Night at the Airport.   by
Mark Aldanov.   New York: Charles Scribner's Sons,
1949. 224 p.
(Translation from the Russian) The Escape.   by Mark
Aldanov.   New York: Charles Scribner's Sons, 1950.
389 p.
(Translation from the Russian) The Restless Heart.   by
Sergei Maksimov.   New York: Charles Scribner's
Sons, 1950. 349 p.
(Translation from the Finnish) The Winter War.   by Vaino
Tanner.   Stanford, Calif. : Stanford University Press,
1957. 274 p.

WELLES, Sumner, 1892-1961.   Foreign Service Officer 1915-
43.   Served in Tokyo, Buenos Aires, State Department,
Minister to Dominican Republic 1922-25, Assistant
Secretary of State 1933, Ambassador to Cuba 1933,
Under Secretary of State 1937, Presidential Mission to
European Heads of State 1940, Chairman of Inter-de-
partmental Committee on Co-operation with the Amer-
ican Republics 1940-43.
(Edited) An Intelligent American's Guide to Peace.   New
York: The Dryden Press, 1945. 370 p.
Naboth's Vineyard: The Dominican Republic, 1844-1924.
New York: Payson & Clarke, Ltd. , 1928. 2 vols.
Seven Major Decisions.   London: H. Hamilton, 1951.
224 p.
We Need Not Fail.   Boston: Houghton Mifflin Co. , 1948.
143 p.
The Time for Decision.   New York: Harper & Bros. ,
1944. 431 p.
Where Are We Heading?   New York: Harper & Bros. ,
1946. 397 p.
The World of the Four Freedoms.   Foreword by Nicholas
Murray Butler.   New York: Columbia University
Press, 1943. 121 p.
Beeld der Wereld Een Historisch, Aard-Dryjeskundig en
Volkendig, Etc.   Amsterdam: C. Hafkamp, 1948.
377 p.

WHEATON, Henry, 1785-1848.   Jurist, authority on international law, author, Chargé d'Affaires in Denmark 1827-
35.   Berlin 1835.   Minister to Prussia 1837-46.
Digest of the Law of Maritime Captures and Prizes.   New

York: R. M'Dermut & D. D. Arden. Forbes & Co.,
1815. 380 p.
Digest of the Decisions of the Supreme Court of the United
States. New York: R. Donaldson, 1821. 527 p.
Some Account of the Life, Writings and Speeches of Wil-
liam Pinkney. New York: E. Bliss & E. White,
1826. 616 p.
History of the Northmen. London: J. Murray, 1831.
367 p.
Histoire des Progrés du Droit des Gens en Europe, De-
puis la Paix de Westphalie Jusqu'au Congres de Vi-
enne, Avec un Precis Historique du Droit des Gens
Européenes Avant la Paix de Westphalie. Leipzig:
F. A. Brockhaus, 1841. 462 p. In New York this
was published as History of the Law of Nations in
Europe and America From the Earliest Times To the
Treaty of Washington. 1842.
Enquiry into the Validity of the British Claim to a Right
of Visitation and Search of American Vessels Suspected
to be Engaged in the African Slave Trade. Philadel-
phia: Lea & Blanchard, 1842. 151 p.
The Progress and Prospects of Germany: A Discourse
Before the Phi Beta Kappa Society of Brown University
at Providence, R. I. Boston: C. C. Little & J.
Brown, 1847. 54 p.
Report of the Copyright Case of Wheaton V. Peters. New
York: Printed by J. Van Norden, 1834. 176 p.
Elements of International Law. Philadelphia: Carey,
Lea & Blanchard, 1836. 375 p.
Cases Argued and Decided in the Supreme Court of the
United States, 1790. Henry Wheaton, reporter. Ro-
chester, N. Y.: The Lawyers Cooperative Publishing
Co., 1901. 1 vol.
(Edited) Abridgement of the Law of Nisi Prius. by Wil-
liam Selwyn. Philadelphia: R. H. Small, 1823. 2
vols.

WHEELER, John Hill, 1806-1882. Lawyer, historian. Minister to Nicaragua 1854-56. Involved himself in the
William Walker revolution and was recalled.
Historical Sketches of North Carolina. Philadelphia: Lippincott, Grambo & Co., 1851. 2 vols. Republished
as Historical Sketches of North Carolina From 1584 to
1851. Compiled from Original Records, Official Documents, and Traditional Statements, with Biographical
Sketches of Her Distinguished Statesmen, Jurists,
Lawyers, Soldiers, Divines, Etc. Baltimore: Regional

Publishing Co., 1964. 2 vols. in 1.

Reminiscences and Memoirs of North Carolina and Eminent North Carolinians. (originally issued in 4 parts,
arranged by counties.) Columbus, Ohio: Columbus
Printing Works, 1884. 478 p.

The Mecklinberg Declaration of Independence. Washington: 1875. 80 p.

The Legislative Manual and Political Register of the State
of North Carolina for the Year 1874. Raleigh, N.C.:
Josiah Turner, Jr., State and Binder, 1874. 388 p.
2 errata p.

Indexes of Documents Relative to North Carolina During
the Colonial Existence of Said State. Raleigh, N.C.:
T. Loring, Printer - Office of "The Independent, "
1843. 120 p.

WHEELER, Post, 1869-1957. Editor, author, newspaper
correspondent, teacher. First career diplomat after
the passage of the Act of 1906, and served until 1934.
Served in Tokyo, Petrograd, Rome, Stockholm, London, Madrid, Rio de Janeiro. Minister to Paraguay
1929, to Albania 1933-34.

Albanian Wonder Tales. Illus. by Maud & Miska Peter-
sham. Garden City, N.Y.: Doubleday, Doran & Co.,
1936. 282 p.

Dome of Many-Coloured Glass. with Halle Ermine Rives
[Mrs. Post Wheeler]. Autobiographical. Garden City,
N.Y.: Doubleday & Co. Inc., 1955. 878 p.

Dragon in the Dust. Hollywood: The Marcel Rodd Co.,
1946. 253 p.

The Golden Legend of Ethiopia: The Love Story of Maqe-
da, Virgin Queen of Axum and Sheba and Solomon the
Great King. New York: Appleton-Century Co., 1936.
185 p.

Hathoo of the Elephants. New York: the Viking Press
Inc., 1943.

Hawaiian Wonder Tales. Illus. by Jack Mathew. New
York: Beechhurst, 1953. 232 p.

India Against the Storm. New York: Books Inc. Distributed by E. P. Dutton & Co. Inc., 1944. 350 p.

Love in a Mist. (poems) New York: Camelot Co., 1901.
216 p.

Russian Wonder Tales: With a Foreword on the Russian
Skazki. with 12 famous Bilibin illustrations in color.
New York: Century Co., 1912. 323 p.

(Edited and translated) The Sacred Scriptures of the Japanese. Translations of the Kojiki and the Nihongi and

a number of lesser tales. New York: H. Schuman,
1952. 562 p.
(Edited and translated) Tales from the Japanese Storytell-
ers as Collected in the Do-Dan-Zo. by Post Wheeler.
Selected and edited by Harold G. Henderson. Rutland,
Vt. : C. E. Tuttle Co. , 1964-65. 139 p.
The Writer: A Concise, Complete and Practical Textbook
of Rhetoric, Etc. with George L. Raymond. New
York: G. P. Putnam's Sons, 1911. 203 p.

WHITE, Andrew Dickson, 1832-1918. University president,
historian. Minister to Russia 1892-94. Ambassador
to Germany 1897-1901.
Autobiography of Andrew Dickson White. New York:
Century, 1905. 2 vols.
A history of the Warfare of Science with Theology in
Christendom. New York: D. Appleton Co. , 1896. 2
vols.
Fiat Money in France: How It Came, What It Bought and
How It Ended. New York: D. Appleton Co. , 1896.
85 p.
Seven Great Statesmen in the Warfare of Humanity with
Unreason. New York: Century Co. , 1910. 552 p.
The Warfare of Science. New York: D. Appleton Co. ,
1876. 151 p.

WHITLOCK, Brand, 1869-1934. Lawyer, journalist, writer,
politician. Minister to Belgium 1913-1921.
Abraham Lincoln. Boston: Small, Maynard Co. , 1909.
205 p.
Belgium: A Personal Narrative. New York: D. Appleton
Co. , 1919. 2 vols.
Belgium Under the German Occupation. A Personal Nar-
rative. London: W. Heinemann, 1919. 2 vols.
Big Matt. New York: D. Appleton Co. , 1928. 283 p.
The Fall Guy. Indianapolis: The Bobbs-Merrill Co. Inc. ,
1912. 382 p.
Forty Years of It. New York: D. Appleton Co. , 1914.
373 p.
Un Americain D'Aujourd'hui: Scenes de la Vie Publique
et Privée. Trans. by Mme. Henry Carton de Wiart.
Paris: Berger-Levrault, 1917. 350 p.
The Gold Brick. Indianapolis: The Bobbs-Merrill Co.
Inc. , 1910. 342 p.
The Happy Averages. Indianapolis: The Bobbs-Merrill
Co. Inc. , 1904. 347 p.
Her Infinite Variety. Illus. by Howard Chandler Christy.

Decorations by Ralph Fletcher Seymour. Indianapolis:
The Bobbs-Merrill Co. Inc. , 1904. 167 p.
J. Hardin & Son. New York: D. Appleton Co. , 1923.
451 p.
La Fayette. New York: D. Appleton Co. Inc. , 1929.
2 vols.
The Letters and the Journal of Brand Whitlock. Selected
and edited with a biographical introd. by Allen Nevins.
Intro. by Newton D. Baker. New York: Appleton-
Century Co. , 1936. 2 vols.
The Little Green Shutter. New York: D. Appleton Co. ,
1931. 157 p.
Narcissus: A Belgian Legend of Van Dyck. New York:
D. Appleton Co. , 1931. 121 p.
The Stranger on the Island. New York: D. Appleton Co. ,
1933. 267 p.
The 13th District: A Story of a Candidate. Indianapolis:
Bobbs-Merrill Co. Inc. , 1902. 490 p.
Papers, 1893-1934. Catalogue in Main Bldg. of Library
of Congress. 65 ft. circa 40,000 items.
Transplanted. New York: Appleton, 1927. 244 p.
The Turn of the Balance. Illus. by J. Hambidge. Indi-
anapolis: Bobbs Merrill Co. , 1907. 622 p.
Uprooted. New York: Appleton, 1926. 333 p.

WHITNEY, Thomas Porter, 1917- . Social scientist. Attaché Moscow 1945-48.
Has Russia Changed? New York: Foreign Policy Associ-
ation--World Affairs Center, 1960. 95 p.
(Edited and translated) The New Writing in Russia. In-
trod. by Thomas P. Whitney. Ann Arbor: University
of Michigan Press, 1964. 412 p.
Russia In My Life. New York: Reynal & Co. Inc. , 1962.
307 p.
(Edited) The Communist Blueprint for the Future, The
Complete Texts of all Four Communist Manifestoes:
1848-1961. Introd. by Thomas Porter Whitney. New
York: E. P. Dutton & Co. Inc. , 1962. 240 p.
(Edited) Kruschev Speaks: Selected Speeches, Articles
and Press Conferences, 1949-1961. Commentary by
Thomas Porter Whitney. Ann Arbor: University of
Michigan Press, 1963. 406 p.

WIEDENMAYER, Joseph Emil, 1905- . Business executive.
Foreign Service Officer 1944-65. Served in Montevideo, Madrid, Rome, Milan, State Department, Melbourne, Curitiba, International Cooperation Administration

Palermo.   Since leaving the Service Mr. Wiedenmayer
has been with the Alexander Graham Bell Association
for the Deaf, Inc. in Washington, D. C.
What? Listen Please.   Specific Suggestions to Improve
    Understanding Between Hard of Hearing Persons and
    Their Friends.   Washington, D. C.   Privately printed
    by Joseph Wiedenmayer, P. O. Box 4083.   Chevy
    Chase, Maryland 20015.   1968.   10 p.
Look or Listen.   Suggestions for Blind People Who are
    Also Hard of Hearing.   Being reproduced in Braille
    and recordings by the Library of Congress, Division of
    the Blind.   Copies in imprint also planned through
    H. E. W. later on.

WIKOFF, Henry, 1813-1884.   Author, adventurer.   Attaché
    in London 1836.   Although an American the British ap-
    pointed him a British Foreign Office Agent in France
    in 1850.   He became involved in an erratic courtship
    of an American heiress whom he tried to kidnap in
    Genoa.   She got the British Consul to have him jailed.
    He was released fifteen months later.   This furnished
    material for two of his books.   He died in England.
Napoleon Louis Bonaparte, First President of France.
    New York: G. P. Putnam's Sons, 1849.   155 p.
My Courtship and Its Consequences.   New York: J. C.
    Derby, 1855.   438 p.
The Adventures of a Roving Diplomatist.   New York: W.
    P. Petridge & Co. , 1857.   299 p.
Secession and Its Causes, in a Letter to Viscount Palmer-
    ston.   New York: Rose and Tousey, 1861.   84 p.
Memoir of Ginevra Guerrabella.   New York: T. J. Cro-
    wan, 1863.   63 p.
The Reminiscences of an Idler.   New York: Fords,
    Howard & Hulbert, 1880.   596 p.
A New Yorker in the Foreign Office, and His Adventures
    in Paris.   London: Tribner & Co. , 1858.   299 p.
The Four Civilizations of the World.   Philadelphia: J. B.
    Lippincott Co. , 1874.   416 p.
Trial of Wikoff, Vannoud, and Cavallari for a Conspiracy
    to Effect a Forced Marriage Between Miss Gamble and
    One of the Accused.   London: W. Shoberl, 1852.
    64 p.

WILDMAN, Edwin, 1867-1932.   Vice and Deputy Consul Gen-
    eral at Hong Kong 1898-99.
Aguinaldo: A Narrative of Filipino Ambitions.   Boston:
    Lothrop Publishing Co. , 1901.   374 p.

The Builders of America.   Lives of Great Americans
From the Monroe Doctrine to the Civil War.   Boston:
L. C. Page, 1925.   314 p.
Famous Leaders of Character in America From the Latter
Half of the Ninteenth Century: the Life Stories of Boys
Who Have Impressed Their Personalities on the Life
and History of the United States.   Boston: L. C. Page
& Co. , 1922.   344 p.
The Founders of America in the Days of the Revolution:
the Lives and Deeds of the Great Patriots Who Gave
This Nation Its Independence.   Boston: L. C. Page &
Co. , 1924.   326 p.
Reconstructing America: Our Next Big Job, the Latest
Word on the Vital Subject of the Hour.   Boston: L. C.
Page Co. , 1919.   422 p.
Writing to Sell: A Textbook of Literary Craftsmanship.
New York: Wildman Magazine and News Service, 1914.
111 p.
Famous Leaders of Industry: The Life Stories of the
Boys Who Have Succeeded.   Boston: The Page Co. ,
1920.   6 vols.

WILEY, Irena Monique (Baruch), d. 1972.   Wife of Foreign
Service Officer John Cooper Wiley.   Mrs. Wiley was
born in Poland.   She married Mr. Wiley in 1934.   Mr.
Wiley (1893-1967) was born in Bordeaux where his
father was American Consul.   Mr. Wiley was a Foreign Service Officer 1915-54.   He served in Paris,
The Hague, Santiago, Buenos Aires, Caracas, Copenhagen, Madrid, Lima, Berlin, Warsaw, State Department, Vienna, Minister to Latvia and Estonia 1938-40,
Ambassador to Colombia 1944, to Portugal 1947, to
Panama 1951-54.
Around the Globe in Twenty Years.   Illus. with drawings
by the author.   New York: David McKay Co. Inc. ,
1962.   249 p.

WILLIAMS, Edward Thomas, 1854-1944.   Missionary in
China, translator at the Kiangnan Arsenal at Shanghai.
Interpreter at Consulate in Shanghai 1896; Vice-Consul-
General Shanghai 1897-98.   Chinese Secretary at Lega-
tion in Peking 1901; Consul-General Tientsin 1908; As-
sistant Chief Div. Far Eastern Affairs, Department of
State 1909; Sec. Legation Peking 1911; Chinese Secre-
tary Peking 1911; Chief Div. Far Eastern Affairs,
State Department 1913-18.
China Yesterday and Today.   New York: Thomas Y.

Crowell Co., 1923.   613 p.
Recent Chinese Legislation Relating to Commercial, Railway and Mining Enterprises, with Regulations for Registration of Trade Marks and for Registration of Com-
panies.   Shanghai: Shanghai Mercury Ltd., 1904.
146 p.
A Short History of China.   New York: Harper Bros.,
1928.   170 p.

WILLIAMS, G. Mennen, 1911- .   Government official, politician, Governor of Michigan 1949-60.   Assistant Secretary of State for African Affairs 1961-66.   Ambassador to Philippines, 1968-69.
Africa for the Africans.   Grand Rapids: Eerdmans, 1970.
218 p.

WILLIAMS, James, 1796-1869.   Journalist.   Minister to
Turkey 1858-60.   Confederate propagandist and Minis-
ter-at-Large 1860-66.   In London he edited the Con-
federate organ "the Index," and wrote articles for The
Times and the Standard.
Letters on Slavery From the Old World.   Nashville: 1861.
Enlarged and republished in London as The South Vin-
dicated.   Chicago: Afro-American Press, 1969.
444 p.
The Rise and Fall of the Model Republic.   London: R.
Bentley, 1863.   424 p.

WILLIAMS, John Brown, 1810-1860.   Foreign trader from
Salem, Mass.   Appointed Consul at Bay of Islands,
New Zealand 1842-55.   Consulate moved to Auckland
1855, where he served until his death of dysentery in
1860.   Appointed concurrently Consular Agent at
Lanthala, Fiji, 1842-60.   He combined trading with
consular duties.
The New Zealand Journal, 1842-1844, of John B. Williams
of Salem, Massachusetts.   Edited with an account of
his life by Robert W. Kenny.   Salem: Peabody Museum
of Salem and Brown University Press, 1956.   120 p.

WILLIAMS, Samuel Wells, 1812-1884.   Missionary.   Chinese
scholar.   Chinese Interpreter American Legation Peking
1859.   Diplomatic Secretary Peking 1870.   See "Life
and Letters of Samuel Wells Williams, LLD. Missionary, Diplomatist, Sinologue." by his son, Fredrick
Wells Williams.   New York: G. P. Putnam's Sons,
1889.   490 p.

A Syllabic Dictionary of the Chinese Language: Arranged
    According to the "Wu Fang Yuen Yin" with Pronuncia-
    tion as Heard in Peking, Canton, Amoy and Shanghai.
    Shanghai: American Presbyterian Press, 1874.
    1,252 p.   An index to the above, arranged according
    to Sir Thomas Wade's system of orthography, by
    James Acheson.   Hong Kong: Kelly & Walsh, 1879.
    124 p.
Easy Lessons in Chinese: or, Progressive Exercises to
    Facilitate the Study of That Language, Especially
    Adapted to the Canton Dialect.   Macao: Printed at the
    Office of the Chinese Repository, 1842.   287 p.
Ying Hwa Yun-Fu Lih-Kiai.   An English and Chinese vo-
    cabulary in the Court Dialect.   Macao: Printed at the
    Office of the Chinese Repository, 1844.   440 p.
Ying, Wa, Fan Wan 'Tsut. 'Iu.   A tonic dictionary of the
    Chinese language in the Canton dialect.   Canton:
    Printed at the Office of the Chinese Repository, 1856.
    571 p.
The Middle Kingdom: A Survey of the Geography, Gov-
    ernment, Literature, Social Life, Arts, and History of
    the Chinese Empire and Its Inhabitants.   New York:
    Wiley & Putnam, 1848.   2 vols.
A History of China: Being the Historical Chapters from
    "The Middle Kingdom" by the late Samuel Wells Wil-
    liams.   Concluding chapter by Fredrick Wells Williams.
    New York: Charles Scribner's Sons, 1897.   472 p.
Chinese Immigration.   Paper read before the Social Sci-
    ence Association at Saratoga, Sept. 10, 1879.   New
    York: Charles Scribner's Sons, 1879.   48 p.
A Journal of the Perry Expedition to Japan (1853-1854).
    by Samuel Wells Williams and edit. by his son, Freder-
    ick Wells Williams.   Yokohama: Kelly & Walsh Ltd. ,
    1910.   259 p.
A Chinese Commercial Guide, Consisting of a Collection
    of Details and Regulations Respecting Foreign Trade
    with China, Sailing Directions, Tables, Etc.   Original
    edition written and published by John R. Morrison.
    5th edition entirely by Williams.   Hongkong: A.
    Shortrede & Co. , 1863.   266 p.
(Edited) The Chinese Repository.   Vols. 1-20.   May 1832-
    Dec. 1857.   Canton: Printed for the Proprietors.
Errors Chains: How Forged and Broken.   A Comparative
    History of the National, Social and Religious Errors
    that Mankind Has Fallen Into and Practised From the
    Creation Down to the Present Time.   with Frank S.
    Dobbins and Prof. Isaac Hall.   New York: Standard

Publishing House, 1884. 785 p.
Story of the World's Worship, Etc. Etc. Etc. with Frank
  S. Dobbins and Prof. Isaac Hall. Chicago: The Do-
  minion Company, 1901. 785 p.
A Chinese Chrestomathy in the Canton Dialect. with Elijah
  Coleman Bridgeman. 1841. ?p.

WILLIAMSON, John Gustavus Adolphus, 1793-1840. Businessman, politician, Southern slave-owner Scotch Presbyterian. Secured appointment as first American diplomat (Chargé d'Affaires) to Venezuela 1835-40, as a
  "situation . . . that should be a permanent and honorable
  one to which there might be attached a salary and
  perquisites, or salary alone sufficient for a genteel
  living. "
Caracas Diary, 1835-40. The Journal of John G. A.
  Williamson. First Diplomatic Representative of the
  United States to Venezuela. Edit. by Jane Lucas de
  Grummond. Baton Rouge, La.: Camelia Publishing
  Co., 1954. 444 p.

WILLOUGHBY, Amea (Brewin), 1909-70. Wife of Woodbury
  Willoughby, who was a State Department official 1937-
  49 and a Foreign Service Officer 1949-62. He served
  in Washington, Manila, Tokyo, Ottawa and Vienna.
I Was On Corregidor. New York: Harper & Bros.,
  1943. 249 p.

WILSON, Evan Morris, 1910- . Foreign Service Officer
  1937-67. Served in Guadalajara, Cairo, Alexandria,
  Mexico City, State Department, Tehran, National War
  College, Calcutta, Katmandu, London, International Co-
  operation Administration, Foreign Service Inspector,
  Beirut, Jerusalem.
Jerusalem, Key To Peace. New York: Middle East In-
  stitute, 1970. 176 p.

WILSON, Francis Mairs Huntington. See HUNTINGTON-
  WILSON.

WILSON, Henry Lane, 1857-1932. Newspaper editor, lawyer,
  banker. Minister to Chile 1897-1905, to Belgium 1905-
  09, Ambassador to Mexico 1909-13.
Diplomatic Episodes in Mexico, Belgium and Chile. New
  York: Doubleday, Page & Co., 1927. 399 p.

WILSON, Hugh Robert, 1885-1946. Foreign Service Officer

1911-40. Served in Lisbon, Guatemala, Buenos Aires, Berlin, Berne, Vienna, State Department, Tokyo, Mexico City, Board of Examiners, Minister to Switzerland 1927, Assistant Secretary of State 1937, Ambassador to Germany 1938, to the Dominican Republic 1940.
A Career Diplomat, The Third Chapter, The Third Reich. Edited by Hugh R. Wilson, Jr. New York: Vantage Press, 1961. 112 p. (Letters and diary excerpts.)
Diplomat Between Wars. New York: Longmans, Green, 1941. 344 p. (Continuation of "Education Of A Diplomat.")
Disarmament and the Cold War in the Thirties. New York: Vantage Press, 1963. 87 p.
The Education of a Diplomat. Introd. by Claude G. Bowers. New York: Longmans, Green, 1938. 224 p.
For Want of a Nail: The Failure of the League of Nations in Ethiopia. New York: Vantage Press, 1959. 96 p.

WILSON, Thomas W., Jr., 1912- . Newspaper reporter, foreign correspondent, educator, public relations. Office of Economic Co-operation Administration. Foreign Service Reserve Officer 1949-68. Served in London, State Department, Paris, Brussels.
The Great Weapons Heresy. (the J. Robert Oppenheimer story) Boston: Houghton Mifflin Co., 1970. 275 p.

WINANT, John Gilbert, 1889-1947. Politician, government official. Governor of New Hampshire 1925 and 1931-34. Ambassador to Great Britain 1941-45.
Economic and Social Council of the United Nations. Report to the Secretary of State. July 15, 1946. Washington: Government Printing Office, 1946. 74 p. Another report to October 15, 1946. Washington: Government Printing Office, 1946. 69 p.
Letter From Grosvener Square: An Account of Stewardship. Decorations by John O'Hara Cosgrove II. Boston: Houghton Mifflin Co., 1947. 278 p.

WINFIELD, Gerald Freeman, 1908- . Ecologist. Teacher in China 1933-48. Foreign Service Staff Officer, Economic Cooperation Administration 1951- . Served in Rangoon, Washington. Superior Honor Award 1970.
China, the Land and the People. Issued in cooperation with the American Institute of Pacific Relations. New York: William Sloane Associates, 1948. 437 p.

WINFIELD, Louise. Wife of Gerald Freeman Winfield.

[Q. V.]
Living Overseas. Foreward by Harlan Cleveland. Washington: Public Affairs Press, 1962. 237 p. (Advice
to American families going abroad to live, especially
for the Agency for International Development.)

WOLF, Charles, Jr. , 1924- . Foreign Service Auxiliary
Officer 1945-47; General Services officer 1949-53.
Served in Batavia and State Department.
Capital Formation and Foreign Investment in Underde-
veloped Areas: An Analysis of Research Needs and
Program Possibilities Prepared from a Study Supported
by the Ford Foundation. with Sidney C. Sufrin. Syra-
cuse: Syracuse University Press, 1955. 134 p.
Economic Development and Mutual Security: Some Prob-
lems of United States Foreign Assistance Programs in
Southeast Asia. Santa Monica: Rand Corporation,
1956. 76 p.
The Indonesian Story: The Birth, Growth and Structure of
the Indonesian Republic. Issued under the auspices of
the American Institute of Pacific Relations. New York:
John Day & Co. , 1948. 201 p.
United States Policy and the Third World: Problems and
Analysis. Boston: Little, Brown & Co. , 1967. 204 p.
Foreign Aid: Theory and Practice in Southern Asia.
Princeton: Princeton University Press, 1960. 442 p.

WOOD, Eric Fisher, 1889- . Architect, engineer. At-
taché to Ambassador Herrick, Paris, 1914.
The Note-Book of an Attaché: Seven Months in the War
Zone. New York: Century, 1915. ?p.

WOOD, John Rhoden, 1894-1938. School teacher. Foreign
Service Staff and Reserve Officer 1919-62. Consul
General 1961-62. Served 39 years in Paris, and 3
years in the Department of State during World War II.
Merit Service Award 1956.
Diplomatic Ceremonial and Protocol: Principles, Proce-
dures and Practices. Co-author with Jean Serres,
former French ambassador and one-time Director of
the French Foreign Office. London: Macmillan &
Co. , 1970. 400 p. New York: Columbia University
Press, 1970. 384 p.

WOODWORTH, Lewis A. and Bernadine H. Mr. Woodworth
(1891-) was a Foreign Service Staff officer 1947-63.
Mr. and Mrs. Woodworth served in San Salvador,

Rome, Athens, New Delhi, São Paulo and Tijuana.
The Four Corners - Memories and Recipes. Recipes of
Iceland, Australia, Finland, Argentina, etc. etc.
Chula Vista, Calif.: Privately printed, 1964. 116 p.

WYNNE, George G., 1925- . Born in Austria. Naturalized
1944. Private expert reporter. Voice of America and
United States Information Service officer 1951- .
Served in State Department, Munich, Frankfurt, Seoul,
Rome, Saigon, Geneva.
Early Americans in Rome. Rome: Rome Daily American
Publishing Co., 1966. 156 p. (in English and Italian)
Frankfurt Through the Centuries. Frankfurt: Verlag
Waldemar Kramer, 1968. 200 p.
The Imperial Chamber. Frankfurt: Verlag Waldemar
Kramer, 1958. 64 p. An account of the history of
the banquet hall where the newly-elected Holy Roman
Emperors presided over their first official ceremony.

WYTHE, George, 1893- . Economist, public official with
the Department of Commerce and the State Department
1920-32. Served in Constantinople, Mexico City, Com-
mercial Attaché-at-Large in Europe. Lecturer at
George Washington University. Director of the Amer-
ican Republics Division of the Commerce Department.
Member of various delegations to Inter-American con-
ferences.
Brazil's Foreign Economic Policy. Thesis for Ph. D.
Washington: George Washington University, 1938.
234 p.
Industry in Latin America. New York: Columbia Univer-
sity Press, 1945. 371 p.
An Outline of Latin American Development. New York:
Barnes & Noble, 1947. 266 p.
History of the 90th Division United States Army. Pub-
lished by the 90th Division Association, 1920. 251 p.
Brazil: An Expanding Economy. with Royce A. Wight
and Harold Midkiff. New York: Twentieth Century
Fund, 1949. 412 p.
The United States and Inter-American Relations. Gaines-
ville: University of Florida Press, 1964. 251 p.
The Inter-Allied Games. Paris: Publications Periodiques,
1919. 494 p.

YATES, Matthew Tyson, 1819-1888. Missionary in China
1847-88. Interpreter to American Consulate and Vice
Consul in Shanghai 1869-76.

Ancestral Worship and Fung Shuy. Shanghai: American
Presbyterian Mission Press, 1878. 48 p.
The Story of Yates, the Missionary, as Told in His Let-
ters and Reminiscences. Originally published in the
Biblical Recorder in Raleigh, N.C. 1880-1881, entitled
"Reminiscences of a Long Missionary Life." Edit. by
C. E. Taylor. Nashville: The Sunday School Board
of the Southern Baptist Convention, 1898. 304 p.

YOST, Bartley Francis, 1877-1963. Teacher, Government
employee, publisher. Foreign Service Officer 1908-
1938. Served in Almeria, Barcelona, Paris, Genoa,
State Department, Santa Rosalia, Guaymas, Torreon,
Sault St. Marie, Nogales, Cologne.
Memoirs Of A Consul. New York: Vantage Press, 1955.
186 p.

YOST, Charles Woodruff, 1907- . Journalist. Foreign
Service Officer 1930-1971. Served in Alexandria,
Warsaw, State Department, Political Advisor to Com-
manding General India-Burma Theater, Bangkok, Vienna, United Nations, Athens, Ambassador to Laos 1954-
1956, Minister-Counselor in Paris 1956, Ambassador
to Syria 1957, Career Minister 1958, Ambassador to
Morocco 1958, Career Ambassador 1964, Deputy Re-
presentative to United Nations with rank of Ambassador
1965-66, Ambassador to United Nations Security Coun-
cil 1969-71.
The Age of Triumph and Frustration: Modern Dialogues.
New York: Robert Speller & Sons. Illus. by Shane
Miller. 1964. 244 p.
The Insecurity of Nations: International Relations in the
Twentieth Century. New York: New York Council on
Foreign Relations by Frederick A. Praeger, Inc.,
1968. 276 p.
The Conduct and Misconduct of Foreign Affairs. New
York: Random House, 1973.

YOUNG, Arthur Nichols, 1890- . Economist, educator,
advisor to Mexican Government 1918, United States
Trade Commissioner to Spain 1919, State Department
1919-20, Financial advisor to Honduras 1920-21, State
Department 1921-28, Advisor to Chinese Government
1929-46, Point Four Director in Saudi Arabia 1951-58.
China and the Helping Hand, 1937-1945. Cambridge:
Harvard University Press, 1963. 502 p. Map.
China's Economic and Financial Reconstruction. New

York: Committee on International Economic Policy,
1947.   81 p.

China's Wartime Finance and Inflation, 1937-1945. Cambridge: Harvard University Press, 1965. 421 p.

Finances of the Federal District of Mexico. Mexico City:
M. B. Brown Co., 1918. 71 p.

The Single Tax Movement in the United States. (thesis)
Princeton: Princeton University Press, 1916. 340 p.

Oil Pollution of Navigable Waters. Report to Secretary
of State by the Interdepartmental Committee. March
13, 1926. Washington: Government Printing Office,
1926. 119 p.

Report on Financial Reform in Honduras, 1920-21. Tegucigalpa: Central Bank of Honduras, 1957. 66 p. Also in Spanish.

Spanish Finance and Trade. Washington: Government
Printing Office, 1920. 199 p.

Report on the Establishment of the Saudi Arabian Monetary
Agency. Jidda: Ministry of Finance, 1952. In Arabic
and English. 57 p.

China's Nation-Building Effort, 1927-37. The Financial
and Economic Record. Stanford: Hoover Institution
Press, 1971. 553 p.

YOUNG, Earl J., 1919- . Budget expert. Foreign Service
Reserve Officer 1963- . Served in Saigon, Vientiane,
Agency for International Development.

War Without Guns: American Civilians in Rural Vietnam.
with William A. Nighswonger, Robert Warne and George
K. Tanham. New York: Frederick A. Praeger, Inc.,
1966. 320 p.

YOUNG, John Russell, 1841-1899. Minister to China 1882-
85.

Around the World With General Grant: A Narrative of the
Visit of General U. S. Grant, Ex-President of the
United States, to Various Countries in Europe, Asia,
and Africa 1877, 1878, 1879. To which are added
certain conversations with General Grant on questions
connected with American politics and history. New
York: American News Co., 1879. 2 vols.

(Edited) Memorial History of the City of Philadelphia from
its First Settlement to the Year 1895. New York:
History Co., 1895-98. 2 vols.

Men and Memories: Personal Reminiscences, by John
Russell Young. Edit. by his wife, May D. Young.
New York: Fort Neely, 1901. 2 vols.

YOUNG, Nellie May (Bailey).   Wife of Arthur Nichols Young
     [Q. V.].
An Oregon Idyll: A Tale of an Early Transcontinental
     Journey, and of Pioneer Life in Oregon in 1883-1884.
     Glendale, Calif. :   The Arthur H. Clark Co. , 1961.
     111 p.
William Stewart Young, Builder of California Institutions.
     A biography of the father of Arthur N. Young.   Glen-
     dale, Calif. :   The Arthur H. Clark Co. , 1967.   196 p.